THE WORLD BANK
ANNUAL REPORT 1991

The World Bank
Washington, D.C. 20433

Photo Credits

Cover: Dacho Buranabunpot
Page 86: Yosef Hadar/World Bank
Page 101: Herb Floyd
Page 111: UNDP
Page 119: Edwin G. Huffman/World Bank
Page 127: Amy Zuckerman/UNDP
Page 135: Jaime Martin/World Bank

Cover:
An Aka girl washing her hands after coming back with her family from working in the fields near Chiang Rai in northern Thailand. It is an Aka tradition that girls work in the fields. In the old days, opium was the main cash crop; more recently, with assistance provided by both the Thai royal family and the Bank, farmers have switched to corn, vegetables, and flowers.

Cover design by Joyce C. Petruzzelli

ISSN 0252–2942
ISBN 0–8213–1830–6

The World Bank, the IFC, and MIGA

"The World Bank," as used in this *Annual Report,* refers to the International Bank for Reconstruction and Development (IBRD) and its affiliate, the International Development Association (IDA). The IBRD has two other affiliates, the International Finance Corporation (IFC) and the Multilateral Investment Guarantee Agency (MIGA). The Bank, the IFC, and MIGA are sometimes referred to as the "World Bank Group."

The common objective of these institutions is to help raise standards of living in developing countries by channeling financial resources to them from developed countries.

The IBRD, established in 1945, is owned by the governments of 155 countries. The IBRD, whose capital is subscribed by its member countries, finances its lending operations primarily from its own borrowings in the world capital markets. A substantial contribution to the IBRD's resources also comes from its retained earnings and the flow of repayments on its loans. IBRD loans generally have a grace period of five years and are repayable over fifteen to twenty years. They are directed toward developing countries at more-advanced stages of economic and social growth. The interest rate the IBRD charges on its loans is calculated in accordance with a guideline related to its cost of borrowing.

The IBRD's charter spells out certain basic rules that govern its operations. It must lend only for productive purposes and must stimulate economic growth in the developing countries in which it lends. It must pay due regard to the prospects of repayment. Each loan is made to a government or must be guaranteed by the government concerned. The use of loans cannot be restricted to purchases in any particular member country. And the IBRD's decisions to lend must be based on economic considerations alone.

The International Development Association was established in 1960 to provide assistance for the same purposes as the IBRD, but primarily in the poorer developing countries and on terms that would bear less heavily on their balance of payments than would IBRD loans.

IDA's assistance, therefore, is concentrated on the very poor countries—those with an annual per capita gross national product of $580 or less (in 1989 dollars). More than forty countries are eligible under this criterion.

Membership in IDA is open to all members of the IBRD, and 139 of them have joined to date. The funds used by IDA, called credits to distinguish them from IBRD loans, come mostly in the form of subscriptions, general replenishments from IDA's more industrialized and developed members, and transfers from the net earnings of the IBRD. The terms of IDA credits, which are made only to governments, are ten-year grace periods, thirty-five- or forty-year maturities, and no interest.

The IFC was established in 1956. Its function is to assist the economic development of less-developed countries by promoting growth in the private sector of their economies and helping to mobilize domestic and foreign capital for this purpose. Membership in the IBRD is a prerequisite for membership in the IFC, which totals 141 countries. Legally and financially, the IFC and the IBRD are separate entities. The IFC has its own operating and legal staff, but draws upon the Bank for administrative and other services.

MIGA, established in 1988, has a specialized mandate: to encourage equity investment and other direct investment flows to developing countries through the mitigation of noncommercial investment barriers. To carry out this mandate, MIGA offers investors guarantees against noncommercial risks; advises developing member governments on the design and implementation of policies, programs, and procedures related to foreign investments; and sponsors a dialogue between the international business community and host governments on investment issues. By June 30, 1991, the convention establishing MIGA had been signed by 101 countries, of which seventy-six had also ratified.

While the World Bank has traditionally financed all kinds of capital infrastructure, such as roads and railways, telecommunications, and port and power facilities, the centerpiece of its development strategy emphasizes investments that can directly affect the well-being of the masses of poor people of developing countries by making them more productive and by integrating them as active partners in the development process.

The Bank's efforts to reduce poverty cut across sectoral lines and include investments to improve education, ensure environmental sustainability, expand economic opportunities for women, strengthen population-planning, health, and nutrition services, and develop the private sector. The Bank's support of economic restructuring in many of its borrowing member countries is based on the knowledge that the precondition for restoring economic growth—the cornerstone of successful development and poverty reduction—is structural adjustment.

Contents

Boxes

Text Figures

Letter of Transmittal

The details of events covering the period July 1, 1990, to June 30, 1991, are found in this *Annual Report*, which has been prepared by the executive directors of both the International Bank for Reconstruction and Development (IBRD) and the International Development Association (IDA) in accordance with the by-laws of the two organizations. Barber B. Conable, president of the IBRD and IDA and chairman of the boards of executive directors, has submitted this *Report,* together with accompanying administrative budgets and audited financial statements, to the boards of governors.

The directors express their appreciation to the staff members of the Bank for their dedication to the institution's ideals. They note that the continued professionalism of the staff made it possible for the Bank to respond to the exceptional challenges posed by the Gulf crisis and the needs of Eastern European members with both flexibility and imagination.

The directors also take note of the volunteer work that many staff members of the Bank have undertaken to help the less fortunate in the Washington, D.C., metropolitan area—in particular, of the work of staff to help the homeless. Staff volunteer assistance was recognized by the Coalition for the Homeless when it gave the Bank its annual "Part of the Solution Award" in July 1991.

The annual reports of the International Finance Corporation, the Multilateral Investment Guarantee Agency, and the International Centre for Settlement of Investment Disputes are published separately.

Executive Directors	**Alternates**
Ibrahim A. Al-Assaf	Ahmed M. Al-Ghannam
Fawzi Hamad Al-Sultan	Mohamed W. Hosny
J. S. Baijal	M. A. Syed
Mohamed Benhocine	Salem Mohamed Omeish
Rosario Bonavoglia	Fernando S. Carneiro
Félix Alberto Camarasa	Nicolás Flaño
E. Patrick Coady	Mark T. Cox, IV
John H. Cosgrove	A. John Wilson
Jacques de Groote	Walter Rill
Fritz Fischer	Harald Rehm
Eveline Herfkens	Boris Skapin
Jean-Pierre Landau	Philippe de Fontaine Vive
J. Ayo Langley	O. K. Matambo
Jean-Pierre Le Bouder	Ali Bourhane
Ernest Leung	Paulo C. Ximenes-Ferreira
Einar Magnussen	Jorunn Maehlum
Moisés Naim	Gabriel Castellanos
David Peretz	Robert Graham-Harrison
Frank Potter	Clarence Ellis
Masaki Shiratori	Kiyoshi Kodera
Vibul Aunsnunta	Aung Pe
Wang Liansheng	Jin Liqun

August 20, 1991

Overview of World Bank Activities in Fiscal 1991

More than a billion people—about one third of the total population in developing countries—live in poverty. Despite progress, as measured by aggregate per capita consumption and improvements (in some countries) in social indicators, poverty increased in many countries during the 1980s.

In fiscal 1991, a comprehensive, long-term strategy to address the protracted challenge of poverty reduction was adopted by the Bank. The strategy, which was designed to make sure that the poor gain from growth and that they contribute to growth, will ensure that all assistance programs undertaken by the Bank are clearly geared to the reduction of poverty.

Fiscal 1991 was also a year that challenged the Bank in other, extraordinary ways. The Bank had to respond promptly to the post-August 1990 events in the Gulf that threatened the development prospects of numerous countries throughout the world. It also had to meet the increasing need for advice and capital of the countries of Eastern and Central Europe that are making the transition from command-driven economies to those that are market-oriented.

At the same time, longer-standing challenges—concerning, among other things, the development of sub-Saharan African countries; the checking of environmental degradation at the national, regional, and global levels; the alleviation of the debt burden faced by many countries; and efforts to encourage private-sector development—continued to dominate the Bank's diverse agenda.

Poverty reduction remains the centerpiece of the Bank's work. The strategy to reduce poverty that was adopted during the year integrates fully into the Bank's operations a two-part approach for reducing poverty. The first part encourages broadly based economic growth through productive use of the poor's most abundant asset—their labor. The second part requires investment in social services—especially basic education and health, family planning, and nutrition—to improve living conditions and increase the capacity of the poor to respond to income-earning opportunities arising from economic growth.

Some people—the old and the infirm, for example—will not be able to respond to these new opportunities. And others, although benefiting, will still not have enough income to pay for basic necessities or will be vulnerable to such income-reducing shocks as drought or loss of the family breadwinner. To help these groups, a system of transfers and safety nets is needed as a complement to the basic two-part approach.

Lending for social services—so essential to the poverty-reduction strategy—continued to increase dramatically during the year. Fiscal 1990 marked the first year in which lending for education topped the $1 billion mark. In fiscal 1991, Bank commitments for twenty-six education projects further increased to $2,252 million. Lending for population, health, and nutrition (PHN), which averaged $205 million a year during the five years before the president of the Bank pledged to double PHN lending (fiscal 1983–87), amounted to $1,568 million for twenty-eight projects in fiscal 1991.

The outbreak of the crisis in the Gulf created major uncertainties for Bank programs in terms of oil prices, the potential for a diversion of financial resources, and the eventual requirements of postwar reconstruction. Nevertheless, the Bank's response to the crisis was rapid: A program of additional assistance ($1 billion from the IBRD and 314 million in special drawing rights, or SDRs, from IDA in fiscal 1991) to many of the Bank's current borrowers that were most affected by the crisis as a result of losses of workers' remittances, losses of revenue from services, and increases in oil prices was put into place during the year.

The Bank also responded to the increased needs of new member countries, especially in Eastern and Central Europe. In fiscal 1991, lending to the reforming European countries increased by $1,098 million over the previous year's total, to $2,937 million. The Bank now has an active program of lending and economic and sector work in all the Eastern and Central European countries with the exception of Albania. Albania applied for membership in both the Bank (see box on the following page) and the International Monetary Fund in January

Becoming a Global Institution

The Bank's founders envisioned a global institution, the membership of which would eventually comprise all nations. Shortly after the Bretton Woods meetings, however, it became apparent that the spirit of international cooperation had been supplanted by an ideological split extending to the structure of economic systems. The Soviet Union, although it sent delegates to Bretton Woods, did not become a founding member of the Bank. The countries within its sphere of influence that were original members of the Bank soon withdrew.

Of the forty-five founding members in 1947, thirty-two were European or Latin American. They were joined during the subsequent decade by many Asian countries, and in 1967, following an influx of newly independent African nations, membership stood at 106. Today, 155 countries are members of the Bank, and only five countries with populations in excess of 3 million are currently nonmembers: Albania, Cuba (a former member that withdrew in 1960), the Democratic People's Republic of Korea, the Soviet Union, and Switzerland. Of these, Albania and Switzerland are currently seeking membership.

The events of the past year have brought the Bank much closer to its founders' vision of a global economy and membership, as the countries of Central and Eastern Europe and other planned economies have quickly developed political mandates for transition to market economies. These countries, having found themselves in serious need of financial and technical assistance to make the transition a successful one, have turned to the Bank for that assistance.

However, the persistence of regional conflicts gives renewed meaning to the Bank's original mission of postwar reconstruction and development. The challenge will be to meet the demands, which are increasing in number as well as complexity, made of the institution by its now nearly global membership.

1991, and an initial fact-finding mission was undertaken.

Continuity of assistance to the adjusting, low-income countries in sub-Saharan Africa was guaranteed through the launching of the second phase of the special program of assistance (SPA II). For the second phase of the program, which covers the three-calendar-year period 1991–93, eighteen donors pledged $7.4 billion in cofinancing and coordinated financing to support adjustment programs in these countries. Commitments by IDA during the same period are expected to reach almost $3 billion.

In February 1991, the African capacity-building initiative (ACBI) was established. Co-sponsored by the Bank, the United Nations Development Programme (UNDP), and the African Development Bank, the ACBI has as its goal the building up of local capacity for economic analysis and management.

The Bank's involvement with the range of activities that can benefit women and unlock their potential to contribute to the development process continued to expand. About 40 percent of the Bank's projects during the year included specific recommendations for action to integrate women into the development process. In fiscal years 1988, 1989, and 1990, the comparable percentages were 11, 22, and 30, respectively. Operational activities that enhance the well-being of women are designed not only to help reduce the incidence of poverty, but also to help increase national economic growth because women contribute substantially to national output. Moreover, such programs particularly help to slow population growth and thus ease pressures on the environment.

Environmental concerns are now routinely scrutinized and addressed in Bank activities. In addition to fourteen projects that had primarily environmental objectives, almost 40 percent of projects approved in fiscal 1991 had significant environmental components (excluding projects whose environmental costs or benefits amount to less than 10 percent of total costs or benefits). During the year, an 800-page manual was completed that codifies all the Bank's environmental policies and guidelines into one source. All relevant sectors and all types of projects with potential for major environmental effects are addressed, with emphasis on large infrastructure projects.

In November 1990, the Global Environment Facility (GEF), to be run jointly by the Bank, the UNDP, and the United Nations Environment Programme, was established. The three-year pilot program, which will start with commitments of about $1.5 billion, has as its goal the provision of resources to help finance programs and projects in developing countries in four areas: protection of the ozone layer, of biodiversity, and of international waters, and the limitation of emissions of greenhouse gases. Projects will be designed so as to ensure that there is a clear distinction between GEF and regular development programs and projects. At the end of the fiscal year, twenty-one countries (including eight developing

Operational and Financial Overview, Fiscal 1987–91
(millions of US dollars unless otherwise noted)

Item	1987	1988	1989	1990	1991
IBRD					
Commitments[a]	14,188	14,762	16,433	15,180	16,392
Gross disbursements[a]	11,383	11,636	11,310	13,859	11,431
Net disbursements[a]	5,656	3,428	1,921	5,717	2,090
Borrowing, medium- to long-term	8,779	10,537	8,744	11,481	10,883
Net income	1,113	1,004	1,094	1,046	1,200
Subscribed capital	85,231	91,436	115,668	125,262	139,120
Statutory lending limit	89,870	100,474	125,429	137,046	152,327
Loans outstanding	75,792	81,791	77,942	89,052	90,638
Key ratios					
Loans outstanding as a percentage of lending limit	84	81	62	65	59
Interest coverage ratio	1.18	1.15	1.17	1.17	1.17
Liquidity ratio (percent)	50	50	52	47	51
Reserves-to-loans ratio	8.7	9.3	10.2	10.8	11.2
IDA					
Commitments	3,486	4,459	4,934	5,522	6,293
Gross disbursements	3,088	3,397	3,597	3,845	4,549
Net disbursements	2,940	3,241	3,404	3,628	4,274

a. Excludes loans to the IFC.

countries) had contributed a total of about $871 million to the GEF's core fund.

Fiscal 1991 also saw the Bank continue to provide support for the program of debt and debt-service reduction. A $65 million stand-alone loan was approved for Uruguay to reimburse that country for (a) a portion of the costs of the cash buyback of its debt and (b) a portion of the costs of the purchase of the interest collateral associated with par bonds that had been converted from Uruguay's stock of debt. Venezuela was provided with $150 million in interest support, which will be utilized to purchase part of the collateral for the par bonds it issued. The interest-support funds, together with related measures, will help the country implement its agreement, involving debt and debt-service reduction, with its commercial-bank creditors. The Debt Reduction Facility for IDA-only Countries was utilized for the first time during the year when grants of $10 million each were extended to Niger and Mozambique. The grant to Niger, together with contributions from France and Switzerland, virtually eliminated all of Niger's commercial-bank debt. The grant to Mozambique, together with contributions of up to $12.87 million from France, the Netherlands, Sweden, and Switzerland, would be sufficient to permit the purchase of all of that country's eligible debt.

The strengthening of the Bank's efforts to encourage private-sector development (PSD) continued. During fiscal 1991, the responsibilities and role of each member of the World Bank Group in the implementation of the private-sector development action plan that had been adopted in 1989 were more clearly delineated; improved procedures for cooperation among the Bank, the International Finance Corporation (IFC), and the Multilateral Guarantee Agency (MIGA) were initiated; a program of country-specific private-sector assessments, which will form a basis for the Bank's strategy and work program for private-sector development, was begun; and selected divisions throughout the Bank were restructured, expanded, and staffed to assume additional responsibility for supporting PSD.

Total commitments by the World Bank during fiscal 1991 amounted to $22,685.5 million: $16,392.2 million from the IBRD and $6,293.3 million from IDA (see table above). Despite the disruption of operational work caused by the Gulf crisis, commitments by the IBRD represented an increase of $1,212.5 million over fiscal 1990. Commitments from IDA were $771.3 million above fiscal 1990's record amount of $5.5 billion.

World Bank assistance to the poorest countries—those with a per capita GNP of $580 or less—totaled $9,355 million: $4,025 million from the IBRD and $5,329 million from IDA (see figure on the following page).

Adjustment lending totaled $5,886.4 million, or 26 percent of total commitments. Of that

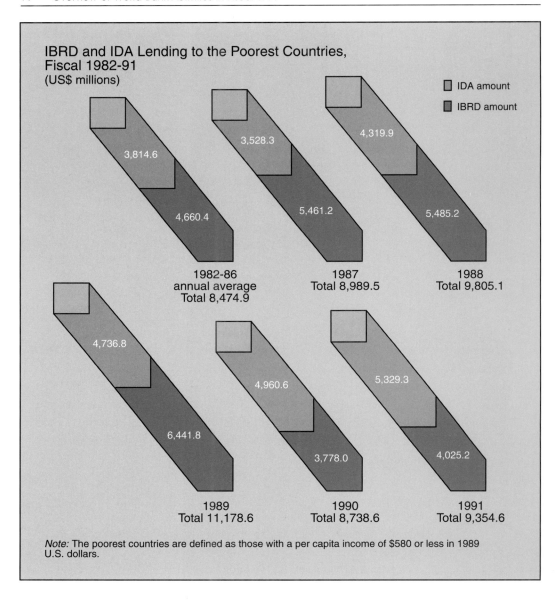

IBRD and IDA Lending to the Poorest Countries,
Fiscal 1982-91
(US$ millions)

☐ IDA amount
■ IBRD amount

3,814.6
4,660.4
1982-86
annual average
Total 8,474.9

3,528.3
5,461.2
1987
Total 8,989.5

4,319.9
5,485.2
1988
Total 9,805.1

4,736.8
6,441.8
1989
Total 11,178.6

4,960.6
3,778.0
1990
Total 8,738.6

5,329.3
4,025.2
1991
Total 9,354.6

Note: The poorest countries are defined as those with a per capita income of $580 or less in 1989 U.S. dollars.

amount, $215 million was accounted for by debt and debt-service reduction assistance to Uruguay and Venezuela. The $5,671.4 million in structural-adjustment and sector-adjustment assistance represented an increase of $1,703 million over fiscal 1990's total (see table on the following page). Most of the increase was the result of increased adjustment lending to countries in Eastern and Central Europe.

Net disbursements from the IBRD to member countries declined to $2.1 billion, down 63 percent from the previous year's total of $5.7 billion. The drop in net disbursements is the direct result of reduced gross disbursements

caused, in part, by a decline during the year in Bank support for debt and debt-service reduction operations. In addition, a large percentage of the volume of adjustment lending was committed in the last month of the fiscal year; disbursements on those operations will take place early in fiscal 1992. IDA's net disbursements were up $646 million, to $4.3 billion.

The IBRD borrowed the equivalent of $10.9 billion in the world's financial markets. Net income was $1,200 million.

On July 13, 1990, the Republic of Yemen became a member of the IBRD and IDA following the merger of the Yemen Arab Republic

World Bank Adjustment Operations, Fiscal 1991
(millions of US dollars)

Country	Project	World Bank financing IBRD	IDA	Total
Sector-adjustment loans				
Algeria	Enterprise and financial-sector restructuring	350.0	—	350.0
Argentina	Public-enterprise reform adjustment	300.0	—	300.0
Bangladesh	Financial-sector adjustment (supplement)	—	3.5	3.5
Bolivia	Financial-sector adjustment III (supplement)	—	14.5	14.5
Colombia	Public-sector reform	304.0	—	304.0
Comoros	Macroeconomic reform and capacity building	—	8.0	8.0
Indonesia	Private-sector development II	250.0	—	250.0
Jamaica	Trade and financial-sector adjustment II	30.0	—	30.0
Kenya	Agricultural-sector adjustment II	—	75.0	75.0
Kenya	Export development	—	100.0	100.0
Kenya	Financial-sector adjustment	—	67.3	67.3
Madagascar	Public-sector adjustment (supplement)	—	1.7	1.7
Malawi	Industry and trade adjustment (supplement)	—	7.2	7.2
Mauritania	Public-enterprise sector adjustment (supplement)	—	4.0	4.0
Mexico	Agricultural-sector adjustment II	400.0	—	400.0
Mexico	Export-sector loan	300.0	—	300.0
Morocco	Financial-sector development	235.0	—	235.0
Pakistan	Energy-sector loan II (supplement)	28.0	—	28.0
Philippines	Environment and natural-resources management	158.0	66.0	224.0
Poland	Restructuring and privatization	280.0	—	280.0
Poland	Financial-institutions development	200.0	—	200.0
Sri Lanka	Public manufacturing-enterprises adjustment	—	120.0	120.0
Tanzania	Agricultural adjustment (supplement)	—	16.1	16.1
Togo	Population/health adjustment	—	14.2	14.2
Uganda	Agricultural-sector adjustment	—	100.0	100.0
Total		2,835.0	597.5	3,432.5
Structural-adjustment loans				
Benin	Structural adjustment II	—	55.0	55.0
Burkina Faso	Structural adjustment I	—	80.0	80.0
Czechoslovakia	Structural adjustment I	450.0	—	450.0
Egypt	Structural adjustment I	300.0	—	300.0
El Salvador	Structural adjustment I	75.0	—	75.0
Ghana	Structural adjustment II (supplement)	—	8.3	8.3
Ghana	Private-investment promotion	—	120.0	120.0
Guyana	Structural adjustment II (supplement)	—	18.0	18.0
Guyana	Structural adjustment II (supplement)	—	4.3	4.3
Honduras	Structural adjustment I (supplement)	—	20.0	20.0
Honduras	Structural adjustment II	90.0	—	90.0
Hungary	Structural adjustment II	250.0	—	250.0
Mali	Structural adjustment I	—	70.0	70.0
Poland	Structural adjustment I	300.0	—	300.0
Rwanda	Structural adjustment I	—	90.0	90.0
Senegal	Structural adjustment IV (supplement)	—	7.1	7.1
Sri Lanka	Economic restructuring (supplement)	—	7.0	7.0
Togo	Structural adjustment IV	—	55.0	55.0
Uganda	Economic recovery program II (supplement)	—	2.0	2.0
Zambia	Economic recovery program	—	210.0	210.0
Zambia	Economic recovery program (supplement)	—	27.2	27.2
Total		1,465.0	773.9	2,238.9
Grand total		4,300.0	1,371.4	5,671.4

— Zero.

NOTE: Table does not include $150 million in interest support to Venezuela and $65 million to Uruguay for debt and debt-service reduction support.

and the People's Democratic Republic of Yemen. Czechoslovakia rejoined the IBRD and became a member of IDA on September 20, 1990. Bulgaria and Namibia became members of the IBRD on September 25, 1990. Mongolia joined the IBRD and IDA on February 14, 1991. This brings total membership of the IBRD to 155 and of IDA to 139.

At the end of the fiscal year, action was pending on membership in the IBRD and IDA for Albania and Switzerland, and in IDA for Portugal.

Section One
The Executive Board

Under the Articles of Agreement of the Bank, all the powers of the Bank are vested in a board of governors consisting of one governor from each member country. With the exception of certain powers specifically reserved to them by the Articles of Agreement, the governors of the Bank have delegated their authority to a board of executive directors that performs its duties on a full-time basis at the Bank's headquarters. This board consists of twenty-two executive directors, each of whom selects an alternate. As provided for in the Articles of Agreement, five of the executive directors are appointed by the five members having the largest number of shares of capital stock, while the rest are elected by the governors representing the other member countries.

The president of the Bank is the chairman of the executive directors. Formal votes by the executive directors are rare since, in practice, most decisions of the board are reached by consensus. The executive directors are responsible for the conduct of the general operations of the Bank, which includes deciding on Bank policy within the framework of the Articles of Agreement and approving all loan and credit proposals. The president is the chief of the operating staff of the Bank and conducts, under the direction of the executive directors, the ordinary business of the Bank.

The executive directors are also responsible for presenting to the board of governors at its annual meetings an audit of accounts, an administrative budget, the *Annual Report* on the operations and policies of the World Bank, and any other matters that, in their judgment, require submission to the board of governors. Matters may be submitted to the governors at the annual meetings or at any time during the year.

The executive board exercises its authority, under the Articles of Agreement, in three general areas: (a) through its annual oversight of the financial and operating programs, and administrative budgets, it determines the allocation of financial and staff resources for the coming year; (b) through its review and approval of policy proposals, either annually (for example, on the allocation of net income, staff compensation, the environment) or periodically (for example, on the Bank's capital requirements, financial policies, lending terms, sectoral priorities), it determines the direction of Bank policies; and (c) through its review of evaluations of completed Bank projects and the Bank's experience in individual sectors and with particular policies, and through its consideration of proposals for future evaluation activities, the board ensures that the Bank and its member countries can benefit from the lessons of experience.

In fulfilling their responsibility to oversee the IBRD and IDA financial and operating programs, the executive directors approved, at the start of the fiscal year, a flexible borrowing program for fiscal 1991 of $11 billion to $12 billion equivalent, which was carried out according to agreed broad parameters. Halfway through the fiscal year, the board reviewed the status of the 1991 fiscal year financial and operating programs and administrative budgets and discussed fiscal 1992 budget priorities and policy directions. The board also considered the distribution of fiscal 1991 annual allocations from IDA reflows and approved supplemental credits to a number of countries. As a committee of the whole, the executive directors discussed the medium-term (fiscal 1992–94) budget-planning framework. Before the end of the fiscal year, the board set indicative IBRD lending for fiscal 1992 at between $17 billion and $19 billion, with an indicative IDA lending program of 4.8 billion in special drawing rights (SDRs).

Financial Policy Actions

An important financial policy issue that concerned the board during the course of fiscal 1991 was the disposition of net income. The executive directors met several times during the year to discuss this issue, beginning with a seminar on the uses of net income. In a subsequent board session, the executive directors discussed the medium-term outlook and policy on annual allocation of net income and established a policy framework to guide the annual allocation of Bank net income. This policy framework provides that:

• the first claim against net income will be an allocation to the general reserve sufficient to achieve the reserve target at the end of the following year;

• if the net income exceeds the amount needed for allocation to the general reserve, consideration in the use of available income will first be given to increasing the general reserve to allow for a waiver in the following year of up to twenty-five basis points on the interest rate charged to borrowers who have serviced all their loans in a timely fashion;

• the executive directors will recommend to the board of governors that available income not required to implement a twenty-five basis-point waiver of interest charges be transferred to surplus, with its use to be decided subsequently;

• currencies held in surplus may be converted, as in the general reserve, to maintain alignment with currencies on loan; and

• if the balance in surplus reaches 1.5 percent of callable guarantees and disbursed outstanding loans net of loan-loss provisions, the executive directors will decide whether to recommend further additions to surplus to the board of governors.

The board agreed that the guidelines provided in the policy framework were intended to be used with flexibility, especially in extraordinary circumstances such as those that arose from the Gulf crisis.

Later in the year, the board considered the allocation of fiscal 1990 net income that had been retained as surplus from a year earlier. This income, amounting to $296 million equivalent at the end of fiscal 1990, had been exempted from the newly established framework on net income. The board agreed to recommend to the governors that the equivalent of up to SDR200 million be given as a grant to IDA and that any balance of the surplus be transferred to the Global Environment Trust Fund.

The board was also involved in issues concerning the Bank's practices with respect to countries in arrears. It approved the recommendations contained in a report by the board's Joint Audit Committee and approved additional workout programs in countries with protracted arrears. The board also reviewed the Bank's capital adequacy and a modification of the Bank's general conditions with respect to the Bank's lending limit and approved modifications to IBRD repayment terms for middle-income borrowers applicable to new loans committed between July 1, 1991 and June 30, 1994 and agreed that future calculations of the statutory lending limit should include a safety margin of 20 percent. The board also authorized a global U.S.-dollar bond issue and associated anticipatory and deferred rate-setting arrangements.

Late in the fiscal year, the board agreed to revisions in the Bank's loan-loss provisioning policy and set Bank provisions, inclusive of a long-standing special reserve, at 2.5 percent of its total portfolio of outstanding loans and guarantees.

Under the revised policy, the annual review of provisions will be based on an assessment of collectibility risk of the total portfolio, including a specific assessment for loans in nonaccrual status. Only the latter assessment was made under the previous policy. The extension of the provisioning policy required an increase in provisions to $1,990 million, compared with $1,250 million in fiscal 1990.

In addition to considering these specific financial policies, the executive directors followed closely the status of the Bank's borrowing program through monthly briefings on markets and quarterly reviews of funding-operations reports.

Operations Evaluation; Project Implementation and Supervision

To fulfill its responsibility to review project evaluations and proposals for future evaluation activities, the board continued to give particular attention to the Operations Evaluation Department (OED). The OED, under the direction of the director-general, is linked administratively to the Bank's president, but is directly responsible to the executive directors. The board considered the OED report on its work program and staff budget for fiscal 1991, the current status of the department's work, and the report on operations evaluation. The executive board also discussed the OED's annual review of evaluation results and agreed that the review should be published for distribution outside the Bank.

In addition, the board considered the sixteenth annual report on project implementation and supervision, which summarized the status of ongoing operations in fiscal 1990. The report, an annual product of the Bank's operations complex, highlighted assessments of the Bank's initiatives in the areas of poverty alleviation, the environment, and women in development.

Operational Policy Actions

In fiscal 1991, the board dealt with several issues fundamental to the Bank's operational priorities and strategies. Following on their work in fiscal 1990 on the Bank's operational guidelines and procedures concerning debt strategy, the executive directors considered the Bank's negative-pledge policy with respect to debt and debt-service reduction operations (DDSR) and approved clarifications and affirmations of the Bank's policy on waivers to the negative clause, including continuing the policy of granting waivers in connection with Bank-financed DDSR operations.[1] The board also reviewed the Bank's progress under the program to support DDSR, with the executive directors generally agreeing that the program was working according to its objectives and that while no changes in the guidelines were necessary at that stage, continued flexibility in implementation would be needed in future cases.[2]

In preparation for the meetings of the Development Committee, the board considered a report on the implementation of the debt strategy and its impact on the development prospects of severely indebted countries. The Development Committee subsequently reaffirmed its support for the strengthened debt strategy and the progress achieved so far and encouraged the Bank and the International Monetary Fund (IMF) to continue to provide support, with the necessary flexibility under the established guidelines, for debt and debt-service reduction packages negotiated between debtors and commercial banks.

With regard to debt operations in individual countries, the board kept abreast of the status of debt negotiations in Uruguay and approved negative-pledge waivers for Uruguay and Venezuela.

The board also reaffirmed the importance of poverty alleviation as an integrating theme in all Bank assistance. The board considered the Bank's assistance strategies to reduce poverty and agreed that the Bank should integrate the two-part poverty-reduction strategy set out in *World Development Report 1990* into its country-assistance programs to support and complement countries' own approaches for reducing poverty.[3]

In the area of private-sector development, the board took note of a report on Bank Group efforts in strengthening private-sector development.[4]

The board reviewed the results of the Bank's pilot program of expanded cofinancing, which is intended to support borrowers' access to private capital markets within the context of the Bank's overall country-assistance strategies and risk-management constraints. The executive directors approved the continuation of the program and agreed to review it again within twelve to eighteen months.[5] As a committee of the whole, the executive directors discussed the Bank Group's approach to finan-

cial-intermediary lending, its impact on the financial sector, and the respective roles of the IBRD and the International Finance Corporation in lending to financial intermediaries.[6]

The board also carefully followed the developments in the international economic and political environment and their effect on member countries. The board kept abreast of (a) the impact of the Gulf crisis on member countries through timely updates on the Bank's response to the Gulf crisis, (b) the effect of the Gulf crisis on the Bank's portfolio risk, and (c) the effect of oil-price increases; the Bank's assistance strategy for countries affected by the Gulf crisis was also reviewed.[7]

The board received a number of briefings on a study prepared by the Bank, in conjunction with other international agencies, at the request of the July 1990 Houston economic summit, on the economy of the Soviet Union.[8] The board also discussed in a seminar the issues of the transformation towards a market economy of the Eastern and Central European countries, including the progress made to date and future prospects.

The role of the environment in the Bank's operations remained an important issue for the board. Directors discussed the first annual report on the Bank and the environment covering fiscal year 1990 and endorsed its publication and submission to the Development Committee as background material for its fall meetings. In addition, the board held two seminars to discuss the Bank's approach to the forestry sector. The board also approved resolutions that enabled the Bank to accept contributions from participating countries to the Global Environment Facility and to implement programs for protecting the global environment. The facility, which began as a proposal at the 1989 annual meetings, will address protection of the ozone layer, reduction of emissions of greenhouse gases, protection against degradation of international water resources, and protection of biodiversity. With total financing available of about $1.5 billion, the facility became operational in mid 1991.[9]

The board also reviewed in regular board sessions, committees of the whole, seminars, and briefings a number of sector reports covering Bank policies and ''best practice.'' These

[1] For details, see page 66.
[2] For details, see page 64.
[3] For details, see page 47.
[4] For details, see page 67.
[5] For details, see page 79.
[6] For details, see page 69.
[7] For details, see page 40.
[8] For details, see page 43.
[9] For details, see page 61.

Table 1-1. **Aid Coordination Group Meetings Chaired by the World Bank in Fiscal 1991**
(consortia, consultative groups, and aid groups)

Date	Country	Location
1990		
October 23	Nepal aid group	Paris
October 25	Sri Lanka aid group	Paris
November 6–8	Bolivia consultative group	Paris
November 19–20	Kenya consultative group	Paris
December 3–4	Nicaragua consultative group	Paris
December 5	Honduras consultative group	Paris
December 10–12	Mozambique consultative group	Paris
1991		
February 25–26	Philippines consultative group	Hong Kong
March 18–19	Zambia consultative group	Paris
March 21–22	Uganda consultative group	Paris
May 2–3	Pakistan consortium	Paris
May 10	Caribbean Group for Cooperation in Economic Development	Mérida (Mexico)
May 14–15	Ghana consultative group	Paris
May 15–16	El Salvador consultative group	Paris
May 16–17	Nicaragua consultative group	Paris
May 29–30	Bangladesh aid group	Paris
May 30–31	Papua New Guinea consultative group	Singapore
June 24–26	Tanzania consultative group	Paris

included vocational training in developing countries,[10] urban policy and economic development,[11] lessons of tax reform, the extent of the relevance of issues of governance in borrowing members under the Articles of Agreement, and a colloquium on policy directions. The board also reviewed a number of the major products of the Bank's policy, research, and external affairs complex, including the annual report on the Bank's research program, the work program of the Economic Development Institute, a report on global economic prospects, and the outline and final draft of *World Development Report 1991.*

Recognizing the importance of the international economic environment for development prospects, the board also discussed reports on the developing countries and the short-term outlook for the global economy, held a briefing on the *World Debt Tables,* and attended a two-day colloquium on global savings.

The board also followed the development strategies of many member countries. This included discussions of economic and development issues in each of the Bank's four regions and country-strategy reviews of twenty-eight countries that receive IDA funds in accordance with guidelines established by the executive directors in fiscal year 1990 in response to a recommendation in the report sent to governors in fiscal 1990 on the IDA-9 replenishment.

The board also discussed the policy-framework papers of sixteen countries that were jointly prepared by Bank and IMF staffs and the countries concerned. The board heard briefings on the outcome of the Bank's consultative-group and aid-group meetings (see Table 1–1), the progress of the onchocerciasis-control program, and the meetings of the Consultative Group on International Agricultural Research.

The board monitored the progress of the Bank's lending program through quarterly briefings from the senior vice president, operations, and through discussions of the flow of Bank operations to the board. In addition, the board held biannual discussions of its own work program, as recommended by the executive directors' Steering Committee, covering fiscal year 1991.

Administration

The board continued to be active in terms of setting major policies for the Bank's administration. In connection with personnel policies, the executive directors held informal meetings and seminars on staff benefits in preparation for their formal board review of benefits pol-

---

[10] For details, see page 56.
[11] For details, see page 53.

icy. They approved a revised benefit plan for staff that included changes in the medical-insurance plan and changes in financial assistance and dependency allowances for staff. They reviewed the situation with regard to interim measures that they had approved in fiscal 1990 to protect non-U.S. Bank staff from the effect of a 1988 change in U.S. estate-taxes law. In the wake of the Gulf crisis, the board was also briefed on the issue of security of Bank staff on mission in the Middle East. Through the work of its Committee on Personnel Policy Issues, the board received a progress report on the Bank's human-resources strategy. In the light of the Bank's revised compensation system, the board reviewed the compensation for executive directors' assistants and, as it does each year, considered a review of staff compensation and approved an annual salary adjustment.

The executive directors considered the nomination of Lewis T. Preston as president of the IBRD, IDA, the IFC, and MIGA and unanimously selected him to be the institution's eighth president. He will succeed Barber B. Conable on September 1, 1991. On the occasion of the selection of Mr. Preston, the executive directors expressed their deep appreciation to Mr. Conable for his leadership of the World Bank Group.

In the area of collaboration with the IMF, the board discussed a progress report on Bank-IMF collaboration and emphasized the need for, and importance of, continued close collaboration between the two institutions to serve member countries effectively.[12] The board also reviewed the desirability of establishing a joint Bank/IMF Committee on Administrative Matters. The board members decided against establishing such a committee, but agreed that informal consultations would be sought between the personnel committees of the institutions' two boards to improve collaboration.

After authorizing in fiscal 1989 a plan for the rehabilitation of the Bank's main complex, the board continued to follow closely the progress of the program, including the approval of a special capital-budget supplement in fiscal 1991.

Development Committee

The executive directors were actively involved with the Development Committee, assisting committee members in preparing for their meetings, considering the draft provisional agenda, and discussing the president's reports and background papers that were used as the basis for the ministers' discussions. In addition, several months prior to each meeting, the executive directors met as a committee of the whole to discuss the preliminary agenda and the outlines for the background papers in order to ensure that the main issues and concerns of Development Committee members were reflected in the documentation.

In preparing for the Development Committee's biannual meetings the board discussed a broad range of background papers that touched on many of the most important issues for the Bank such as poverty alleviation, debt and debt-service reduction, private-sector development, the effect of industrialized countries' policies on development, and women in development.

The executive directors' Steering Committee reviewed the communiqués released by the Development Committee following its biannual meetings and made suggestions to ensure that the board's work program was responsive to the directions set out by the Development Committee.

Committees of the Executive Board

The Joint Audit Committee. Established in 1970, the Joint Audit Committee represents shareholders in overseeing the soundness of the Bank's financial practices and the adequacy of the work of the operations evaluation and internal audit units. The committee provides a channel through which the internal and external auditors can communicate with the executive directors.

In pursuing its responsibilities during fiscal 1991, the committee nominated a firm of private, independent, internationally established accountants to conduct the annual audits of the Bank. The committee reviewed the scope of the independent accountants' examination and their annual audited financial statements. In addition, through regular meetings with the Bank's senior financial officers, the committee helped to provide assurance to the executive board that the financial affairs of the Bank were properly conducted. In this regard, the committee reviewed and endorsed recommendations pertaining to the fiscal 1991 implementation of the IBRD's policy for loan-loss provisioning. The committee also reviewed the situation of countries in arrears and endorsed measures for additional support for workout programs in countries with protracted arrears, which would be implemented on a case-by-case basis.

As part of its oversight function, the committee undertook its annual review of the work programs of the Operations Evaluation and Internal Auditing Departments. Through two

---

[12] For details, see page 99.

subcommittees, it examined specific audit reports to determine whether the departments had performed their functions adequately and efficiently. In addition, the committee reviewed numerous papers by the Operations Evaluation Department as part of an ongoing effort to identify problems or policy issues for consideration by the executive directors.

The committee consists of eight executive directors who are appointed by the board after each regular election for a term of two years. E. Patrick Coady has served as chairman of the committee since December 1990.

Committee on Personnel Policy Issues. The committee, which was established in 1980, is charged with keeping under continuing review, and, where appropriate, advising the executive directors on, staff compensation and other significant personnel-policy issues, and maintaining close liaison with the executive directors of the IMF on these issues, bearing in mind the need for general parallelism between the two institutions.

The major topics addressed by the committee during the past year were the Bank's human-resources strategy, changes in benefits policy, and the 1991 review of staff compensation.

Following extensive review of the 1989 update of the Bank's human-resources strategy, the committee, in a report to the board, stated that a number of areas merited attention. They were managerial development, recruitment, use of consultants, staff-diversification objectives, centralized and decentralized functions, staff planning and technical expertise, and staff morale. The committee's work program includes a follow-up to these items, as well as a consideration of management's responses to the 1990 Staff Attitude Survey.

During the year, the committee reviewed management proposals for changes in benefits policy. As a result, management refined its proposals and recommended changes in the Bank's medical-insurance plan, in financial assistance, and in dependency allowances; the changes were subsequently approved by the board. The benefits study also outlined a flexible benefits program that the management of the Bank is considering. If approved by the board, the program is expected to be ready in time to be implemented at the start of fiscal 1993.

The committee considered the 1991 review of staff compensation, which was the third compensation review based on the 1989 revised compensation system.

The committee consists of eight executive directors. Jonas H. Haralz has served as chairman of the committee since November 1990.

Ad Hoc Committee on Criteria for Allocation of Shares of Bank Capital. The Ad Hoc Committee on Criteria for Allocation of Shares of Bank Capital was established by the executive directors in August 1989. Under its terms of reference, the committee reviews criteria applied in the past for special share allocation, considers options for new criteria, and makes recommendations on the criteria that would be applicable to all member countries. In this context, the committee also reviews the issue of the voting power of small member countries on the basis of the final report of the Ad Hoc Committee on Voting Power of Smaller Members. In approaching this mandate, the committee is called upon to take into account the timing of the decision on the ninth general review of quotas by the IMF and, in any case, to report periodically to the executive directors on its work programs and progress.

The committee's activities were summarized in a progress report that was endorsed by the executive directors in October 1990. The report noted that, initially, the committee considered the central question of whether the present share-allocation system, which is based on parallelism with actual IMF quotas, should be modified. After reviewing various considerations underlying parallelism, the committee supported the retention of parallelism with IMF quotas for reasons that have justified its use in the past.

The committee's subsequent work concentrated on addressing issues relating to criteria for share adjustments. The committee discussed relevant background material on the subject, several technical notes on the issue, as well as a possible approach for adjusting share allocations. Because of a divergence of views among committee members, the committee was unable to reach a consensus on the form that a new set of share-allocation criteria might take.

In terms of special share allocations to particular subgroups of countries, most committee members supported the use of some mechanism to safeguard the voting power of smaller members. On the question of which smaller members should be eligible for special consideration, the committee preferred a restrictive definition. With respect to countries that had forgone shares in the past, many committee members saw no need for any additional special adjustment and urged that adjustments based on an agreed formula be used to restore their shares to some extent.

Referring to the Bank's strong capital position, many committee members did not feel that there was a pressing need for a selective capital increase to follow the IMF ninth general review of quotas. Given the absence of agreement on criteria for share allocations, the committee concluded that it would be desirable to defer further work on share-allocation criteria until a selective capital increase was imminent. The committee also noted that, should a consensus be reached on ad hoc share allocations before a selective capital increase, the executive directors could consider the appropriate procedure at that time.

The committee is composed of seventeen executive directors and is chaired by Masaki Shiratori.

Committee on Cost Effectiveness and Budget Practices. The committee was established in 1986 to examine aspects of the Bank's business processes, administrative policies, standards, and budget practices that significantly affect the cost-effectiveness of its operations.

During the past year, the committee completed and forwarded to the board its "Report on Budget Process," which accompanied the report of the Budget-Process Task Force. The report on the budget process was the result of collaborative reviews by the committee and a task force on the Bank's process for planning and budgeting. The committee supported the Budget-Process Task Force's main recommendations, the aims of which were to strengthen and simplify procedures for setting priorities, increase transparency, strengthen accountability, heighten cost consciousness, and increase efficiency and promote simplicity in planning, budgeting, and monitoring.

Supplementing the task force's recommendations, the committee recommended that an informal colloquium of executive directors and senior Bank managers be held annually to discuss the Bank's priorities, and that each year's retrospective review of the previous year's budget be discussed by the committee rather than by the full board. The committee also asked that budget figures and tables be presented, where feasible, in both real and nominal values, following examples that were used in the fiscal 1991 budget document.

In September 1990, the board approved the recommendations contained in both the committee and task-force reports. At the same time, the board considered a report on the progress and future role of the committee and, as recommended therein, confirmed the committee as a standing board committee and expanded its mandate to include examination of the retrospective review. The committee's terms of reference remain unchanged.

The committee subsequently considered the fiscal 1990 retrospective review and, in accordance with the fiscal 1991 work program, undertook to examine the Bank's special-grants program and externally funded programs (trust funds and reimbursable programs). Its work

program also includes review of technical assistance and efficiency indicators.

The committee is composed of eight executive directors. J. S. Baijal has served as chairman of the committee since November 1990.

Committee on Directors' Administrative Matters. The committee was established in 1968. It considers, makes recommendations, and reports its findings to the executive directors for their decision on administrative matters relating to executive directors, alternates, advisers, and their staffs.

The committee's terms of reference charge it with responsibility for assisting executive directors in the formulation and implementation of new administrative policies and changes in existing policies. Matters taken up during the year included executive directors' travel-subsistence expenses, directors' travel to member countries outside their constituencies, staffing of executive directors' offices, travel of executive directors' assistants, the status of the Bank's main-complex rehabilitation, and compensation for executive directors' assistants within the revised compensation system.

The committee coordinates many of its recommendations with a similar committee established by the executive directors of the IMF. In this regard, the committee had a joint meeting with the Committee on Executive Board Administrative Matters of the IMF to review compensation for executive directors' assistants within the revised compensation system.

In its recommendations, the committee tries to maintain a balance between the organizational and administrative objectives of the institution and the unique circumstances faced by the directors in discharging their dual responsibilities.

The committee meets as frequently as necessary, normally about once a month. The membership consists of six executive directors. Félix Alberto Camarasa has served as its chairman since November 1990.

Ad Hoc Committee on Board Procedures. The ad hoc committee was established in February 1991 to review the functioning and procedures of the executive board and to report to the board on ways to conduct the board's work more efficiently. Included in the committee's work program are reviews of board procedures as they relate to policy discussions and policy implementation, discussions of Bank country-assistance policy, consideration of the external environment, lending operations and board reports, and board discussions in general. The committee was scheduled to complete its work by July 1991.

The committee is composed of six executive directors and is chaired by Jonas H. Haralz.

The Executive Directors' Steering Committee. The Executive Directors' Steering Committee, an informal advisory body of executive directors composed of the dean and the codean of the board and the chairmen of the other standing board committees, meets monthly to consult on, and review with the Bank's vice president and secretary, the executive directors' work program. The committee also provides a consultative framework on various board issues. In addition, the committee reviews the Development Committee's communiqués to ensure that the implications for the executive directors' work program are fully considered.

The meetings of the committees of the executive board are open to participation by all executive directors.

Section Two
The Economic Scene: A Global Perspective

In many respects, 1990 was a year of set-backs for the global economy. The longest postwar run of economic expansion in the industrialized countries appears to have ended in 1990–91, as the economies of the major industrial countries slowed and as North America and the United Kingdom slipped into recession. The growth in the volume of world trade, which had already slowed to 7.5 percent in 1989 from 9 percent in 1988, continued its downward trend and was only 5 percent in 1990. Moreover, the easing of oil prices, which characterized much of the past decade, was abruptly interrupted by the Gulf crisis that followed Iraq's invasion of Kuwait.

Other noteworthy events during the year included the inconclusive state of the Uruguay Round of the multilateral trade negotiations under the auspices of the General Agreement on Tariffs and Trade and instability in West Asia in the aftermath of the Gulf war.

The past year also left its mark in other ways. There were some promising developments, as well, such as the unity of resolve to achieve a stable international political order, as evidenced by the concerted response to the Gulf crisis of countries in different economic circumstances; the quickening and deepening of economic reform in all the countries of Eastern and Central Europe, including Albania, which has applied for membership in the Bank; continued high levels of growth in the developing countries of Asia; solid indications that the process of economic reform is beginning to pay dividends in the low-income countries of sub-Saharan Africa; the completion of the process of German unification, which culminated in orderly elections in the newly integrated nation; and indications that, despite the Gulf crisis, the superpowers are likely to continue to reduce their military expenditures.

Major Industrial Countries

Over most of the past decade, the seven major industrial countries (G-7) had expanded in a more or less synchronized fashion.[1] Because the concerted expansion had led to an increase in the demand for both labor and credit, inflation and interest rates drifted upward over the latter half of the 1980s. The synchrony of the G-7 business cycles may have been disrupted, however: The preliminary data for 1990 suggest that the cycles of the G-7 countries diverged in 1990 (Table 2-1).

The performance of the United Kingdom, Canada, and the United States, as measured by the growth of real gross domestic product (GDP), slackened in 1990, with all three countries growing by less than 1 percent in real terms (as opposed to between 1.9 percent and 3 percent in 1989). The economies of the United Kingdom and Canada were clearly in recession during the second half of the year, and, toward the end of 1990, the United States also appeared to have entered a recession. France and Italy grew moderately in 1990, with business indicators recording a moderate deceleration of growth in both countries. Germany and Japan, however, were centers of growth and sources of import demand: Germany grew by more than 4 percent, and growth in Japan was more than 5 percent.

The unification of Germany, the Gulf war, and contrasting monetary policies may explain some of these differences. A common theme, however, underlies the performance of all the G-7 countries: the persistence of relatively high real interest rates (Figures 2-1 and 2-2). The normal cyclical upswing in the demand for credit was reinforced by the fiscal deficit of the United States and by a sharp shift into deficit in Germany as a result of unification. In many G-7 countries, monetary policy offset an actual or expected acceleration of inflation and limited the growth of credit.

In Canada and the United States, higher real interest rates increased the burden of servicing the debt that had accumulated during the period of economic expansion, cutting into profit margins and hence investment. Growth in the supply of credit in the United States was

---

[1] The G-7 countries are Canada, France, Germany, Italy, Japan, the United Kingdom, and the United States.

Table 2-1. **G-7 Countries: Output, Inflation, Investment, and Unemployment, 1980–90**
(average annual percentage change; unemployment rates in percent)

G-7 country	1980–90[a]	1989	1990[b]	1980–90[a]	1989	1990[b]
	Real GNP or GDP[c]			GNP or GDP deflator[c]		
Canada	3.4	3.0	0.9	4.5	4.8	3.1
France	2.3	3.9	2.8	6.0	3.1	2.7
Germany[d]	2.1	3.8	4.5	2.7	2.6	3.4
Italy	2.4	3.0	2.0	9.8	6.0	7.5
Japan	4.2	4.7	5.6	1.5	2.0	1.8
United Kingdom	3.0	1.9	0.6	5.8	6.8	6.1
United States	3.1	2.5	0.9	3.9	4.1	4.1
Aggregate weighted average[e]	3.2	3.3	2.6	4.0	3.7	3.7
	Gross fixed investment			Unemployment rate		
Canada	4.4	4.5	−2.4	9.2	7.5	8.1
France	2.4	7.5	4.0	9.1	9.4	9.0
Germany[d]	1.9	7.2	8.8	5.6	5.6	5.1
Italy	2.2	4.5	3.0	10.4	12.1	11.0
Japan	5.6	8.9	10.8	2.5	2.3	2.1
United Kingdom	5.4	4.0	−1.9	9.3	6.2	5.5
United States	3.9	1.6	−0.1	7.1	5.3	5.5
Aggregate weighted average[e]	4.0	4.8	3.6	6.7	5.7	5.6

a. Data are least-square estimates of the period averages.
b. Preliminary.
c. Gross national product (GNP) for Germany, Japan, and the United States; GDP for others.
d. The part of Germany corresponding to the country's western *länder*.
e. Aggregates are weighted on the basis of 1987 values of GNP or GDP expressed in 1980 U.S. dollars.
SOURCE: Organisation for Economic Co-operation and Development (OECD).

probably slowed by the contraction of savings and loan banks and the loan-quality and capital-adequacy problems of commercial banks.

In Germany, heavy government borrowing and restrictive monetary policy helped to drive rates upward. High rates did not suppress an acceleration of growth in the western *länder*. In contrast, the eastern *länder* began a difficult adjustment (Box 2-1). In Japan, monetary policy was used to slow price inflation and the inflation of certain asset markets. Nevertheless, Japan had the highest growth rate of the G-7 countries and performed better than it did during most of the 1980s. Growth was sustained by a continued shift toward domestic demand and a vigorous expansion of investment.

Growth in Japan and Germany at a rate faster than in the United States helped narrow long-standing current-account imbalances (Table 2-2). The trend was reinforced by the shift toward domestic demand in Japan and by the unification of Germany. Moreover, a 6.5 percent depreciation during calendar 1990 in the effective exchange rate of the dollar, along with past depreciation, improved the competitiveness of U.S. goods and services and thus contributed to the narrowing of the imbalances.

Although the Gulf crisis was not the primary explanation for economic developments in the G-7 countries in 1990, the surge of oil prices that followed the invasion of Kuwait may have contributed to the slowdown of investment in most of the G-7 countries by reducing profit margins. It may also have reduced consumption through its effects on real income and consumer confidence.

Low-income, Middle-income Countries

Growth in the low-income and middle-income countries (LMICs), of 2.3 percent in 1990, was considerably lower than the already low rates that have characterized recent years (see Table 2-3). The disappointing nature of economic performance in the LMICs in 1990 might be underscored by noting that it was the lowest growth rate since 1982; to find a period when developing countries grew at a pace slower than the industrialized countries, one has to go as far back as 1966 and 1967, years in which both China and India contracted. The fall in income was accompanied by a sharp reduction in consumption and investment in Eastern and Central Europe; a very low rate of investment in Latin America, especially Brazil; a fall in per capita consumption in sub-

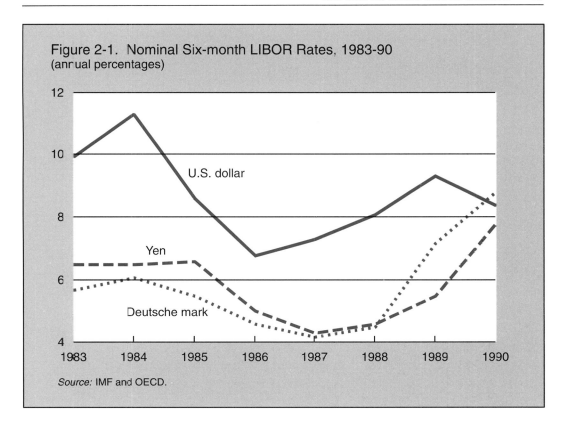

Figure 2-1. Nominal Six-month LIBOR Rates, 1983-90
(annual percentages)

Source: IMF and OECD.

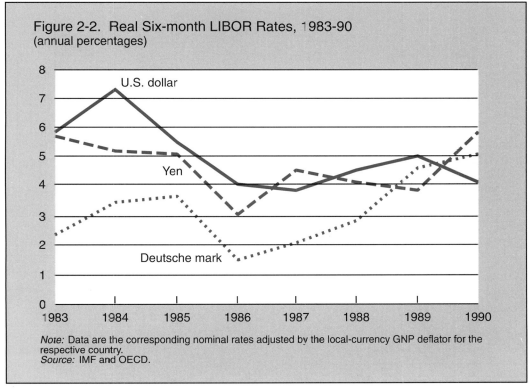

Figure 2-2. Real Six-month LIBOR Rates, 1983-90
(annual percentages)

Note: Data are the corresponding nominal rates adjusted by the local-currency GNP deflator for the respective country.
Source: IMF and OECD.

Box 2-1. The Unification of Germany

Unification brought an expansionary fiscal policy that stimulated growth in the western *länder* of Germany. In 1990, transfers to the east shifted the federal government fiscal balance into a deficit of about DM45 billion. The transfers were mostly subsidies to the eastern social-security system and local governments. Most of these funds apparently came back to the western *länder* in the form of demand for consumer goods. Another wave of immigration from the eastern *länder* and from outside of Germany also reinforced growth in the west.

The nominal income of the eastern *länder* contracted by about 20 percent in 1990. There were many reasons for the contraction: For example, the difficulty of establishing property rights, an excess of deutsche mark–denominated debt, and liability for past damage from pollution probably discouraged foreign investment. But the most important reason was a lack of international competitiveness.

The freeing of prices pressured each enterprise to lower its price to world levels. Wages were also freed; nominal wages in the east rose under the influence of national wage accords and because of the emigration of skilled labor. Labor productivity, however, remained relatively low, partly because of widespread overemployment.

So, falling output prices and rising wage costs squeezed profit margins. Moreover, technical and quality problems prevented some German firms in the east from finding customers in the market economies, while the breakup of the Council for Mutual Economic Assistance and the slump in Eastern Europe limited trade with traditional partners. The resulting loss of profits shut down some enterprises and increased unemployment in the east.

Table 2-2. **Current-account Balances of the G-7 Countries, 1983–90**

G-7 country	1983	1984	1985	1986	1987	1988	1989	1990[a]
Billions of U.S. dollars								
Canada	2.5	2.1	−1.5	−7.3	−6.9	−8.3	−14.1	−13.7
France	−4.8	−1.2	−0.3	1.8	−5.0	−4.4	−4.6	−7.8
Germany[b]	5.3	9.8	16.4	39.5	45.9	50.5	57.2	47.9
Italy	1.7	−2.3	−3.6	2.4	−1.1	−5.8	−10.6	−14.4
Japan	20.8	35.0	49.2	85.8	87.0	79.6	57.2	35.8
United Kingdom	5.7	2.4	3.5	−0.1	−7.1	−27.6	−32.6	−22.7
United States	−40.1	−99.0	−122.3	−145.4	−162.3	−128.9	−110.0	−99.3
Total G-7	−8.9	−53.1	−58.6	−23.2	−49.5	−44.7	−57.5	−74.3
Percentage of GDP								
Canada	0.8	0.6	−0.4	−2.0	−1.7	−1.7	−2.6	−2.4
France	−0.9	−0.2	−0.1	0.2	−0.6	−0.5	−0.5	−0.6
Germany[b]	0.8	1.6	2.6	4.4	4.1	4.2	4.8	3.2
Italy	0.4	−0.6	−0.9	0.4	−0.1	−0.7	−1.2	−1.3
Japan	1.7	2.8	3.6	4.3	3.6	2.7	2.0	1.2
United Kingdom	1.2	0.6	0.7	0.0	−1.0	−3.3	−3.9	−2.4
United States	−1.2	−2.6	−3.0	−3.4	−3.6	−2.6	−2.1	−1.8
G-7 average	0.0	−0.3	−0.3	−0.1	−0.5	−0.4	−0.4	−0.6

NOTE: Details may not add to totals because of rounding.
a. Preliminary.
b. The part of Germany corresponding to the country's western *länder*.
SOURCE: OECD.

Saharan Africa from the level of the previous year; and a deliberate slowing of economic activity by China. All regions were affected, in varying degrees, by the Gulf crisis (see Box 2-2).

The regional breakdown of economic performance of the LMICs mostly follows the pattern of the aggregate picture; all geographic regions, excluding East Asia, showed a lower growth rate in 1990 than in the previous year. At mid year, it appeared that sub-Saharan Africa was going to register an increasing growth rate for the third year in a row. But the unanticipated surge in oil prices in the second

Box 2-2. The Effect of the Gulf Crisis on the Developing Countries

The Gulf crisis had a profound and continuing economic and financial effect on the global economy. In particular, many developing countries suffered significant losses. The brunt of the losses was borne by the "front-line" states—Egypt, Jordan, and Turkey. A number of other countries, heavily dependent on workers' remittances, as well as on trade with Iraq and Kuwait, were also immediately affected. In addition, many countries dependent on imported oil for their energy needs, especially in Eastern and Central Europe and in sub-Saharan Africa, were seriously affected.

The first-wave impact of the crisis on the world economy was that of an oil-price shock. After Iraq's invasion of Kuwait in August and the subsequent United Nations' embargo of oil exports from Kuwait and Iraq, oil prices rose sharply, from around $18 a barrel in July to as high as nearly $40 a barrel. Although oil prices declined from this peak towards the end of the year (as other oil-producing nations stepped up production), they continued to fluctuate as a result of uncertainty in the oil markets regarding the outcome of the crisis. By the end of hostilities, oil prices had declined to around $20 a barrel.

The three front-line states, which had extensive economic ties to Kuwait and Iraq, faced the largest losses as a result of the effects of the Gulf events. These included losses of workers' remittances (for Egypt and Jordan), losses in tourism revenues, losses in revenues for transportation services (Suez canal and air-transport fees for Egypt, trucking revenues for Jordan, oil-pipeline fees for Turkey), and the loss of Kuwaiti and Iraqi markets for exports. In addition, forgone debt service due by Iraq primarily affected Turkey and, to a smaller extent, Jordan, which had extended trade credits to Iraq. While Egypt stood to gain somewhat from higher oil prices, Jordan and Turkey faced higher import bills.

For most of the other countries that were immediately affected by the Gulf crisis, sharp drops in workers' remittances represented a significant setback, as did increased outlays for imported oil. For Morocco, losses in tourism revenues were substantial. The Asian countries in this group (including Pakistan) paid more for refined petroleum as a result of lost refinery capacity in the Gulf countries.

Many Eastern and Central European countries faced special hardship because, since the beginning of 1990, they could no longer pay for oil imported from the Soviet Union with nonconvertible currency. Furthermore, because some of these countries were importing oil from Kuwait and Iraq under special trade arrangements that could no longer be honored, they had to make new arrangements. Most of the countries in sub-Saharan Africa faced a worsening of their external-payments position as a result of higher oil prices and slower growth of world trade; in addition, Sudan was adversely affected by losses in workers' remittances. Other countries whose external-balance position worsened appreciably included the Dominican Republic, Guyana, Haiti, Honduras, Jamaica, Nicaragua, Papua New Guinea, and Uruguay.

Some of the disruptions leading to the exceptional losses have persisted beyond the end of the Gulf war, thus offsetting any terms-of-trade improvement resulting from a decline in oil prices. In addition, the financial cost of reconstruction in Kuwait, and to an even greater extent in Iraq, will be large, and the resulting demand for long-term investment funds will exacerbate the capital shortage in the international financial markets.

On a positive note, the international community acted promptly to assist countries adversely affected by the crisis. For example, the World Bank made available additional financial assistance to these countries: $1 billion by the IBRD and SDR314 million by IDA in fiscal year 1991. A key role in mobilizing resources for countries most directly affected by the Gulf crisis was played by the Gulf Crisis Financial Coordination Group, whose membership included most of the countries of the Organisation for Economic Co-operation and Development, the Republic of Korea, Kuwait, Qatar, Saudi Arabia, the United Arab Emirates, and the Commission of the European Communities. The Bank and the International Monetary Fund provided technical advice and analytical support to the group.

half of the year adversely affected the growth of the majority of African countries that are oil importers. Nigeria, however, appears to have been a major beneficiary during 1990 of improvement in the terms of trade. The current preliminary estimate for growth in sub-Saharan Africa over the entire year is 1.1 percent. In per capita terms, this translates into a negative growth rate of 2.1 percent. The investment and saving rates were also very low (15.8 percent

and 12.8 percent of GDP, respectively, in 1990; see Table 2-4). Thus, the prospects for raising and sustaining a growth rate of 5 percent or higher through the 1990s, as envisioned in the World Bank's long-term perspective study for sub-Saharan Africa, appear to be daunting.[2]

_____

[2] See World Bank, *Sub-Saharan Africa: From Crisis to Sustainable Growth—A Long-Term Perspective Study* (Washington, D.C., 1989).

Table 2-3. **Low- and Middle-income Economies: Growth of GDP and GDP Per Capita, 1981–90**
(average annual percentage change unless otherwise noted)

Region or income group	GDP					1989 GDP (US$ billions)
	1981–86	1987	1988	1989	1990[a]	
Low- and middle-income economies	3.9	3.6	4.2	3.2	2.3	3,560.3
By regional group						
Sub-Saharan Africa[b]	1.8	0.3	2.6	3.0	1.1	164.6
East Asia[c]	8.0	8.9	9.3	5.6	6.2	821.0
South Asia[d]	5.2	4.3	8.1	4.9	4.4	353.3
Europe, Middle East, and North Africa[e]	3.7	0.6	2.1	2.0	0.4	1,201.2
Latin America and the Caribbean[f]	1.5	3.1	0.6	1.4	−0.7	943.6
By income group						
Low-income economies[g]	6.4	6.1	7.8	4.5	4.3	930.8
Middle-income economies[h]	3.0	2.5	2.6	2.5	1.3	2,652.1
Severely indebted, middle-income economies[i]	1.9	2.9	1.3	1.3	−1.6	1,071.1

a. Preliminary.

b. Excludes South Africa.

c. China, Fiji, Indonesia, Democratic Kampuchea, Kiribati, Republic of Korea, Lao People's Democratic Republic, Macao, Malaysia, Mongolia, Papua New Guinea, the Philippines, Solomon Islands, Thailand, Tonga, Vanuatu, Viet Nam, and Western Samoa.

d. Bangladesh, Bhutan, India, Maldives, Myanmar, Nepal, Pakistan, and Sri Lanka.

e. Afghanistan, Algeria, Bulgaria, Czechoslovakia, Egypt, Greece, Hungary, Islamic Republic of Iran, Iraq, Jordan, Lebanon,

However, the currently active countries covered by the special program of assistance (SPA) for Africa, which have been implementing reforms, showed positive growth of per capita income for a second straight year, demonstrating that commitment to adjustment can foster growth, even in difficult times.[3]

In 1990, Asian LMICs grew slightly faster than they did in 1989. China sought to cool down its economy by contracting the demand for investment, but slower-than-average growth in China was offset by the vigorous gains achieved in Indonesia, Malaysia, and Thailand. This pattern is likely to continue in the short run. India's economy grew at a steady rate in 1990, and, while it is likely to continue to do so in the short run (provided weather conditions remain favorable), the sharp curtailment of imports brought about by a shortage of foreign exchange will have a negative influence. India's financial difficulties go beyond the temporary effects of the Gulf crisis, encompassing as they do heightened indebtedness, slim reserves, and a growing public deficit. Furthermore, the fluidity of the current political situation makes it difficult to introduce needed fiscal reform. A number of countries in the region, including Bangladesh, Pakistan, the Philippines, and Sri Lanka, had weak economic growth in 1990. These coun-

tries, among others, were adversely affected by the events in the Gulf and suffered higher import bills, reduced exports, losses of workers' remittances, and the costs of resettling returning workers. Domestic political problems, as well as natural disasters (in the Philippines), were also a contributing factor.

The growth rate was nearly zero for the countries in the Europe, Middle East, and North Africa region. In per capita terms, growth was negative (−1.3). The regional aggregate is the result of disparate sets of processes and events, however.

A number of the Middle Eastern countries in the region were directly affected by the Gulf crisis. In addition to the effects mentioned earlier, these countries also suffered from the loss of tourism revenues and oil-passage fees. For Egypt and Turkey, while the Gulf events caused economic activity in 1990 to worsen, the prospects for improved performance in the near future are promising: Egypt is receiving substantial debt relief and has initiated an ambitious program of structural reform; Turkey is likely to receive considerable compensation and to have improved access to commercial-bank lending. Jordan, which along

---

[3] For details, see page 44.

1989 population (millions)	GDP per capita					Region or income group
	1981–86	1987	1988	1989	1990[a]	
4,053.2	1.8	1.4	2.0	1.0	0.2	Low- and middle-income economies
						By regional group
480.4	−1.3	−2.8	−0.6	−0.2	−2.1	Sub-Saharan Africa[b]
1,552.4	6.4	7.1	7.4	3.8	4.3	East Asia[c]
1,130.8	2.8	2.0	5.7	2.6	2.1	South Asia[d]
433.2	1.6	−1.4	0.1	0.1	−1.3	Europe, Middle East, and North Africa[e]
421.4	−0.6	1.0	−1.4	−0.6	−2.6	Latin America and the Caribbean[f]
						By income group
2,948.4	4.3	3.9	5.5	2.3	2.1	Low-income economies[g]
1,104.9	0.8	0.4	0.6	0.5	−0.6	Middle-income economies[h]
554.3	−0.3	0.8	−0.7	−0.6	−3.4	Severely indebted, middle-income economies[i]

Libya, Malta, Morocco, Oman, Poland, Portugal, Romania, Syrian Arab Republic, Tunisia, Turkey, Republic of Yemen, and Yugoslavia.

f. All American and Caribbean economies south of the United States, except Cuba.

g. Economies with a GNP per capita of $580 or less in 1989.

h. Economies with a GNP per capita of more than $580 but less than $6,000 in 1989.

i. Argentina, Bolivia, Brazil, Chile, the Congo, Costa Rica, Côte d'Ivoire, Ecuador, Egypt, Honduras, Hungary, Mexico, Morocco, Nicaragua, Peru, the Philippines, Poland, Senegal, Uruguay, and Venezuela.

with Egypt and Turkey sustained some of the heaviest losses, is also receiving some assistance, but is likely to need a great deal more.

The Maghreb countries continued to do well in 1990. The increase in oil prices enabled Algeria to improve its financial situation; despite adverse effects on the economies of Morocco and Tunisia caused by the Gulf crisis through higher oil prices, as well as losses of tourism income and workers' remittances, both countries performed well during the year. In addition, Morocco was able to reschedule its debt.

The European countries in the region—Czechoslovakia, Hungary, and especially Bulgaria, Poland, Romania, and Yugoslavia—experienced negative growth rates because of several factors, both domestic and external. The domestic factors come primarily from the disruptions characteristic of the transitional, but possibly long-drawn-out, phase these economies are going through as they attempt to restructure their current economic system toward one that is more market-based. The external factors, apart from the repercussions of the Gulf crisis, include the decline in regional trade, the movement toward increased convertible-currency trade, and the shortfall in the production and export of oil in the Soviet Union.

Hungary, Poland, and Yugoslavia have embarked on wide-ranging stabilization programs, Poland opting for "shock treatment," with an attendant sharp fall in GDP. Poland has received a significant amount of debt relief from bilateral donors and is expected to face improved prospects in the near future. In Yugoslavia, any significant economic recovery awaits the resolution of political difficulties. In all the countries in this group, the importance of effective legal and financial institutions as a prerequisite for a successful transition to a market economy is becoming apparent.

The GDP growth rate was also stagnant in the Latin America and the Caribbean region, with a sharply negative performance in per capita terms. Moreover, it was the only region in 1990 to have a positive resource balance. The economic situation in Argentina, Brazil, and Peru continued to be precarious, with Brazil and Peru having a particularly dismal year owing to a severe terms-of-trade shock. Their experience underscores the importance of reducing the debt overhang before political support for a sustainable structural-reform program is further eroded. While Chile's growth rate (1.8 percent) showed a sharp decline from its 1989 high (about 10 percent), the outlook is for sustained growth at respectable rates of 4 percent to 5 percent a year. Mexico's growth

Table 2-4. **Low- and Middle-income Economies: Gross Domestic Investment and Gross Domestic Savings as a Percentage of GDP, 1981–90**

Region or income group	1981	1982	1983	1984	1985	1986	1987	1988	1989	1990[a]
Low- and middle-income economies										
Investment	27.0	24.5	23.5	22.6	24.2	24.8	24.7	26.1	27.8	25.3
Savings	24.4	23.2	23.7	23.6	24.9	24.7	25.8	27.1	28.4	25.2
By geographical region										
Sub-Saharan Africa										
Investment	20.6	17.5	14.1	10.8	12.1	15.1	15.7	15.5	15.2	15.8
Savings	14.3	10.5	9.6	10.6	12.2	11.0	12.3	11.1	12.0	12.8
East Asia										
Investment	29.5	29.0	29.7	29.7	35.5	33.7	33.5	36.3	38.9	40.1
Savings	28.8	28.6	29.0	30.2	34.0	34.1	36.2	38.4	39.4	41.1
South Asia										
Investment	24.1	22.6	21.5	21.2	23.6	22.7	21.6	22.2	22.2	21.4
Savings	19.2	17.6	17.4	17.2	18.8	18.8	18.1	18.1	18.4	17.8
Europe, Middle East, and North Africa										
Investment	30.6	26.3	27.7	25.6	25.5	27.8	25.1	26.4	29.4	24.0
Savings	27.3	26.1	27.0	24.9	25.4	26.8	25.5	27.6	29.2	n.a.
Latin America and the Caribbean										
Investment	24.3	21.8	17.4	16.8	17.6	17.7	20.5	21.0	21.4	18.7
Savings	22.7	21.7	21.5	22.0	22.3	19.9	23.1	23.6	24.6	20.8
By income group										
Low income										
Investment	25.6	24.3	23.7	23.5	28.9	28.7	28.7	30.8	32.0	31.1
Savings	23.4	21.8	21.8	22.4	25.6	25.2	26.9	28.2	29.8	30.6
Middle income										
Investment	27.6	24.5	23.5	22.0	22.0	23.1	23.0	24.2	26.2	23.3
Savings	24.9	23.8	24.6	24.1	24.5	24.4	25.3	26.6	27.7	23.3

n.a. Not available.
a. Preliminary.

performance of 3.4 percent, attributable in part to favorable oil prices, was particularly encouraging. Strong oil prices might also facilitate financing for Venezuela.

The group of twenty severely indebted middle-income countries (SIMICs)[4] also experienced negative income growth in 1990, primarily as a result of the sharp decline in Brazil and, especially, in Poland. In many countries in this category, slowing inflation has been a priority objective for some time, and the very low (sometimes negative) growth rates reflect the short-term deflationary effect of adjustment policies. Rising interest rates and domestic financial and political difficulties have also contributed to the prolonged adjustment process.

Debt, Investment, and Financial Flows

Preliminary data indicate that, in 1990, aggregate long-term net resource flows—made up of net flows of long-term lending, foreign direct investment, and official grants—to developing countries continued their recovery from the low point reached in 1987 (see Table 2-5). The increase in 1990 was mainly the result of growth in net official lending, with a substantial proportion being absorbed in purchasing collateral in Brady-initiative debt and debt-service reduction operations rather than in financing increased imports. Foreign direct investment (FDI) continued at the higher level reached in 1988. During the five-year period 1986–90, FDI increased greatly over the preceding five years: FDI to the twenty largest recipients grew from $40.5 billion in 1981–85 to $65.5 billion in the five years ending in 1990. Net private lending continued to be de-

---

4 The SIMICs are listed in footnote i of Table 2-3.

Table 2-5. **Long-term Financial Flows to Low- and Middle-income Economies, 1981–90**
(billions of US dollars)

Item	1981	1982	1983	1984	1985	1986	1987	1988	1989	1990[a]
Long-term aggregate net										
resource flows	99.9	88.4	68.2	61.9	56.6	51.2	46 1	60.9	63.3	71.0
Official development finance	33.7	33.8	31.6	34.0	31.8	33.6	32 2	36.2	36.6	46.9
Official grants	11.4	10.4	9.9	11.4	13.2	14.0	14 9	18.0	18.6	19.5
Net official lending	22.3	23.4	21.7	22.6	18.6	19.6	17.3	18.3	18.0	27.4
Bilateral	12.9	11.9	10.6	10.3	6.4	6.3	4.9	6.8	6.1	10.4
Multilateral	9.4	11.5	11.0	12.4	12.2	13.3	12.4	11.5	11.9	16.9
Net private loans	53.3	43.6	28.1	19.6	14.3	8.1	0.7	5.5	4.3	2.3
Commercial banks	44.0	30.9	19.8	14.6	4.7	2.4	−1.1	0.7	3.0	n.a.
Bonds	1.3	4.8	1.0	0.3	5.0	1.3	0.2	2.2	0.3	n.a.
Others	8.0	7.8	7.4	4.7	4.5	4.4	1.6	2.6	1.0	n.a.
Foreign direct investment	12.9	11.1	8.5	8.4	10.5	9.5	13.2	19.1	22.4[b]	21.8
Long-term aggregate net										
transfers[c]	45.7	27.4	10.5	−0.9	−7.4	−10.0	−16.8	−9.5	−1.0	9.3

n.a. Not available.
a. Preliminary.
b. Estimate.
c. Long-term aggregate net resource flows minus interest payments and reinvested and remitted profits.
SOURCE: Loans: World Bank Debtor Reporting System; foreign direct investment: IMF; grants: OECD.

pressed.[5] Thus, the shift in the composition of net flows that took place in 1987—away from commercial-bank lending and toward official grants, net official loans, and foreign direct investment—persisted in 1990.

Aggregate net (long-term) transfers—aggregate net resource flows minus the cost of servicing the stock of external capital, including interest on debt and reinvested and remitted profits—turned positive in 1990 after having been negative since 1984; the magnitude is still well below the level of the early 1980s, however. The decline in aggregate net transfers since the early 1980s has been chiefly the result of the decline in private lending as highlighted by the substantial negative transfers on account of long-term debt in this period (see Table 2-6). The increase in aggregate net transfers in 1990 was caused mainly by an increase in net lending from official sources, much of which, as noted earlier, was used to purchase collateral.

As for the debt situation, the debt indicators showed a modest improvement in 1990. The factors responsible for the improvement include major debt-relief operations such as the implementation of the Brady initiative for private debt, forgiveness of official development assistance (ODA) debt, easier terms on Paris Club reschedulings of official debt, continuation of other programs of debt and debt-service

reduction, and, notwithstanding the impact of adverse terms of trade on some severely indebted, middle-income countries (Côte d'Ivoire and the Philippines, for example), the strong export performance of many of the severely indebted, middle-income countries (Costa Rica and Mexico, for example).

The nominal value of the debt of the developing countries increased by about 6 percent in U.S. dollar terms in 1990. Two factors, in particular, were responsible: an increase in net lending flows and a significant appreciation in the dollar value of the nondollar debt stock. Also, the strong export performance of many SIMICs contributed to an improvement in the debt-to-exports ratio. While nondollar interest rates rose sharply in 1990, dollar interest rates declined. This factor, along with the continued implementation of the Brady initiative and improved terms on Paris Club reschedulings, resulted in a lower ratio of debt service to exports.

---

[5] Toward the end of 1990, an important development in voluntary commercial lending to highly indebted sovereign borrowers in Latin America did take place. Following reentry into the international capital markets by Mexican and Venezuelan corporate borrowers, Chile obtained a $20 million loan from a Dutch bank at a rate one percentage point above LIBOR, the first totally voluntary unsecured sovereign bank loan to the region since late 1982.

Table 2-6. **Low- and Middle-income Economies: Long-term Debt and Debt Service, Selected Years, 1985–90**
(billions of US dollars and percent)

Item	All low- and middle-income economies[a]			Severely indebted, middle-income economies			Sub-Saharan Africa		
	1985	1989	1990[b]	1985	1989	1990[b]	1985	1989	1990[b]
Debt outstanding	767.8	958.8	1,015.1	419.3	467.8	474.3	76.1	124.6	139.1
Official (%)	38.3	47.4	51.3	27.9	38.2	43.7	60.1	70.1	72.2
Private (%)	61.7	52.6	48.7	72.1	61.8	56.3	39.9	29.9	27.8
Debt as % of GNP	37.4	34.9	36.4	56.2	45.4	47.6	42.6	83.3	96.8
Debt service	105.2	115.3	119.6	49.5	45.2	43.1	9.1	6.7	9.4
Interest payments	53.4	51.9	52.3	32.4	25.3	21.8	3.4	3.3	4.7
Official (%)	21.1	32.1	38.3	13.7	26.1	31.4	34.1	52.1	65.7
Private (%)	78.9	67.9	61.7	86.3	73.9	68.6	65.9	47.9	34.3
Principal repayments	51.9	63.4	67.4	17.1	19.9	21.3	5.7	3.4	4.7
Official (%)	24.5	33.9	35.7	24.2	34.7	32.5	25.2	45.5	52.7
Private (%)	75.5	66.1	64.3	75.8	65.3	67.5	74.8	54.5	47.3
Debt-service ratio[c]	24.0	18.8	17.9	31.4	0.0	20.7	23.1	16.9	20.6
Average interest rate on new commitments (%)	7.7	6.7	n.a.	8.7	7.4	n.a.	5.9	3.9	n.a.
Official (%)	6.3	5.6	n.a.	7.6	6.6	n.a.	4.1	3.3	n.a.
Private (%)	8.9	8.5	n.a.	9.5	9.0	n.a.	9.6	8.6	n.a.
Disbursements	84.7	85.7	97.1	29.6	22.5	33.6	8.3	9.0	10.1
Official (%)	36.9	46.1	52.9	38.0	51.1	58.7	53.1	66.6	79.9
Private (%)	63.1	53.9	47.1	62.0	48.9	41.3	46.9	33.4	20.1
Net resource flows on long-term lending[d]	32.9	22.3	29.8	12.5	2.6	12.3	2.6	5.6	5.3
Net transfers on long-term lending[e]	−20.5	−29.6	−22.5	−19.9	−22.7	−9.5	−0.9	2.3	0.7

n.a. Not available.

a. Covers 110 countries in the World Bank Debtor Reporting System.

b. Preliminary.

c. Debt service as a percentage of exports of goods and services.

d. Disbursements minus (actual) principal repayments on long-term lending.

e. Net resource flows minus (actual) interest payments on long-term debt.

Brady-initiative operations have been concluded, in chronological order, in Mexico, the Philippines, Costa Rica, Venezuela, and, in 1991, Uruguay. Morocco has a conditional agreement with its Bank Advisory Committee, and other operations within the framework of the initiative are under discussion. The initiative calls for a negotiation between the given country and its creditor banks, utilizing a market-based menu of options so that a balance can be reached between the specific needs of the country (cash-flow relief, debt-service relief, and reduction of debt overhang, for instance) and the diverse interests of its creditor banks.

Several new financial instruments evolved in the course of 1990—for example, collateralized par bonds with low fixed-interest rates, bonds with low initial interest rates that rise over time, and recapture clauses linking debt service to objective indicators. As a result of the four operations completed in 1990, the face value of commercial-bank debt has been reduced by $11.5 billion: In net terms, the principal of most commercial-bank debt has been effectively offset in Mexico and has been reduced by 62 percent, 8 percent, and 54 percent, respectively, in Costa Rica, the Philippines, and Venezuela. Some of the new instruments have reduced interest rates and have converted floating-rate debts to fixed-rate ones. The collateralization of principal and the buyback were financed through multilateral and bilateral (principally Japan) disbursements on loans of $6.4 billion, as well as through use of the countries' reserves. In addition, new funds, amounting to $3.5 billion, have been provided by commercial banks (to Mexico and Venezuela, in particular).

The results have been very positive for Mexico, in terms of both growth and improved financial condition, through return of flight capital, increased foreign direct investment, and access to external capital, albeit at higher spreads. It should also be noted that Mexico has benefited from increased oil prices, as well as from its strong adjustment program. In the case of the other countries, the impact of the Brady-initiative operations is not yet clear.

For many of the middle-income countries, the burden of official debt is also significant. Traditionally, reschedulings of official debt have been handled in the Paris Club and bilaterally. In September 1990, the Paris Club agreed to provide longer maturities and grace periods on reschedulings and to provide for the possibility of debt swaps. Through January 1991, four lower-middle-income countries (the Congo, El Salvador, Honduras, and Morocco) and one low-income country (Nigeria) had benefited from the new terms. In addition, understandings that reduced the net present value of future debt-service payments by 50 percent were agreed to with Poland and Egypt. Bilaterally, official creditors have contributed to debt relief for countries implementing strong adjustment through provision of new finance, reduction of concessional debt stock, reduction of interest rates, and debt forgiveness. The main beneficiaries in 1990 were Egypt, some of the smaller Latin American countries, and some East African countries.

Low-income, severely indebted countries are concentrated in sub-Saharan Africa. Almost 70 percent of their $116 billion external debt is owed to official, mainly bilateral, creditors. During 1990, almost four dozen of these countries received relief in the form of debt forgiveness totaling an estimated $4 billion (Senegal and Madagascar had about $600 million in debts forgiven, while some $500 million of Zaire's debt was forgiven). The Paris Club rescheduled about $2.3 billion of seven countries' official bilateral debt under Toronto terms[6] with concessional options, and multilateral institutions provided support through ve-

hicles such as the World Bank's SPA for debt-distressed African countries and the International Monetary Fund's structural-adjustment facility (SAF) and enhanced structural-adjustment facility (ESAF).

For some of these countries, this external support is likely to help restore healthier growth and ease balance-of-payments pressures, although the effects for the oil importers are likely to be delayed. For other countries, a deeper concessionality in debt-relief measures is needed. In this regard, one proposal (the so-called Trinidad terms), made by the U.K. Chancellor of the Exchequer at the time, John Major, and another by the Netherlands Minister of Development Cooperation, Jan P. Pronk, would represent significant advances.[7] For example, the Trinidad terms would increase the grant element from about 20 percent under the current Toronto terms to 67 percent.

The limited access of developing countries to external resources continues to be a vexing problem. Although net flows of resources to developing countries have recently increased, they have been absorbed by interest payments, by profit remittances, and, more recently, by purchases of collateral, by debt buybacks, and by debt-equity swaps, leaving little to finance additional imports. In fact, in a reversal of the trend prior to the 1980s, developing countries as a group have been running a surplus in trade in goods and nonfactor services with the high-income industrial countries.

Primary-commodity Market Conditions

As growth slowed markedly in the industrial countries, the World Bank's nominal-dollar price index of nonoil primary commodities declined 6.4 percent in 1990, following a 2 percent fall in 1989 (Table 2-7). The price decline in 1990 was more pervasive than in 1989, and all the major groups (beverages, cereals, fats and oils, and metals) but energy were affected. Because the U.S. dollar depreciated against the other major currencies in 1990, the decline in the primary-commodity price index was much higher in real terms (using the unit-value index of exports of manufactured goods from the G-5 countries—France, Germany, Japan, the United Kingdom, and the United States—to the developing countries, or the MUV index for short, as the deflator) and in terms of special drawing rights (SDRs) than the nominal drop. The constant-dollar index, after deflation by the MUV index, fell 11.9 percent.

---

[6] See page 66 for details of Toronto terms.

[7] See footnote 7 on page 46 for details of Trinidad terms.

Table 2-7. Commodity Prices, 1983–90
(average annual percentage change)

Commodity price	1983–88	1988	1989	1990
In current-dollar terms				
Food and beverages	−0.2	18.3	−5.9	−7.6
Nonfood agriculture	−2.2	1.6	−0.1	−0.2
Metals and minerals	5.6	38.5	3.5	−6.9
Total nonoil	1.8	20.5	−2.0	−6.4
Petroleum	−13.5	−21.0	19.8	30.2
In real terms[a]				
Total nonoil	−4.4	12.1	−1.5	−11.9
Petroleum	−18.8	−26.3	20.3	22.2
In special drawing rights				
Total nonoil	−2.9	15.7	3.3	−11.2
Petroleum	−17.6	−24.1	26.3	23.6

NOTE: Weights in the commodity-price indexes are commodity exports of all developing countries.

a. Deflated by unit-value index of manufactures exports from the G-5 countries (France, Germany, Japan, the United Kingdom, and the United States) to the developing countries.

Coffee prices declined 17.4 percent in 1990 in current-dollar terms, the first full year after the collapse of the International Coffee Agreement's export-quota system. Large increases in coffee exports, some from accumulated stocks, contributed to the price decline. Cocoa and tea prices continued to be depressed, despite dry weather in West Africa for cocoa and supply disruptions in India and Bangladesh for tea. Among cereal crops, the drop in wheat prices was the steepest (22.4 percent), as world wheat production in both wheat-importing and wheat-exporting countries increased sharply. The prices of rice and coarse grains fell, though to a smaller extent, for the same reasons. World sugar production also increased sharply in 1990, by 4.3 percent, pulling prices rapidly downward in the second half of the year. Prices of most fats and oils generally declined because of higher production in the 1989–90 season, although prices of groundnut and soybean oil rose somewhat.

Among the industrial raw-material commodities, cotton prices increased because of poor production in the Southern Hemisphere and relatively strong demand. Natural-rubber prices declined only moderately despite slackened demand from the automobile industry, as Malaysian production was adversely affected by bad weather, and higher petroleum prices increased the cost of synthetic rubber. The prices of most metals and minerals weakened substantially, clearly signaling the end of the price boom of the preceding three years. The main causes were the slowdown in the growth of industrial production in the industrialized countries, from 3.7 percent in 1989 to 1.8

percent, and relatively smooth mine production.

Crude oil prices declined during the first half of 1990 (the result of higher output from member states of the Organization of the Petroleum Exporting Countries, or OPEC), and then rose sharply in the wake of Iraq's invasion of Kuwait. Although about 4 million barrels a day of Iraqi and Kuwaiti crude oil vanished from the market, this volume was quickly offset by increased production by other countries; nevertheless, prices increased and remained volatile at high levels mainly because of concerns about disruptions to supplies in the event of war. The backdrop of sluggish demand for petroleum products did not seem to have had an effect in this situation. Petroleum prices remained the only exception to the otherwise downward trend of all commodity prices.

Trends in World Trade

In 1990, the volume of world merchandise trade increased by 5 percent, a deceleration from the 7.5 percent expansion in world trade in 1989 (see Table 2-8). The value in U.S. dollars of world merchandise trade, inflated by the weakening of the dollar against European currencies, expanded by 13 percent to a record level of $3,470 billion. The value of trade in commercial services also expanded significantly, by 12 percent, to $770 billion. Preliminary figures indicate that, as of December 1990, for most countries, the effect of the Gulf crisis on merchandise trade was minimal; it did substantially affect the trade in commercial services, particularly air transport, however. Several countries were adversely affected by a

Table 2-8. **Selected Trade-performance Indicators, 1965–90**
(average annual percentage change)

Country group and indicator	1965–89	1980–89	1989	1990ᵃ
Low- and middle-income countries				
Import volume	5.4	2.4	9.5	5.9
Export volume	5.2	6.5	5.2	6.7
Terms of trade	0.5	−2.1	3.2	−0.2
Sub-Saharan Africa				
Import volume	3.3	−5.2	2.8	4.3
Export volume	2.1	−0.3	8.7	5.9
Terms of trade	0.2	−4.8	1.7	0.6
Asia				
Import volume	7.7	7.7	14.3	6.3
Export volume	8.4	9.7	6.0	10.4
Terms of trade	−0.2	−0.6	3.2	−1.0
Europe, Middle East, and North Africa				
Import volume	4.8	1.9	6.2	4.6
Export volume	4.9	5.5	3.4	6.2
Terms of trade	0.1	−1.5	−0.3	0.5
Latin America and the Caribbean				
Import volume	3.9	−1.5	6.1	7.2
Export volume	3.4	5.4	4.5	0.5
Terms of trade	1.7	−3.2	8.4	1.1
Memorandum item				
World trade	4.8	4.3	7.5	5.0

NOTE: Terms of trade are calculated as the ratio of export price to import price.
a. Estimate.

decline in their merchandise exports (India, Jordan, Romania, Turkey, and Yugoslavia), loss of service income (Djibouti and Egypt), or the loss of remittances from workers in Kuwait and Iraq (Bangladesh, Egypt, India, Pakistan, the Philippines, and Sri Lanka). Exports from Central and Eastern Europe and the Soviet Union decreased sharply, by 13 percent, as the disruptions and adjustments taking place in these economies took their toll.

The volume of exports of the developing countries grew faster than that of the industrial countries in 1990. Among the developing countries, export growth was particularly strong for the group of leading Asian exporters of manufactures. Among the industrial countries, export volume grew most rapidly in North America. The worldwide slowdown in the growth of export volume affected all commodity categories; still, the growth of manufactures continued to outpace other categories. The deceleration in the growth of exports can be attributed mainly to the lower rate of growth of imports by North America (caused by sluggish demand and a weaker dollar), Japan, Western Europe, Central and Eastern Europe, and the Soviet Union.

Increases in the value of exports were dominated by above-average growth in Western Europe (up 19.5 percent), in the OPEC countries (up 25.5 percent), and China (up 18 percent). The expansion of trade by value in Western Europe, which accounts for 47 percent of world exports, was mainly caused by a weaker dollar, while increases in the value of OPEC exports, accounting for 5 percent of world exports, resulted from the rise in crude-oil prices. In the developing regions, export growth was above average in Africa and Asia, but below the world average in Latin America (mainly the result of a contraction in Brazil's exports). Trends in commodity prices were the driving force behind many developing countries' growth of exports.

The most important of the institutional developments related to international trade concerned the Uruguay Round of the multilateral trade negotiations under the General Agreement on Tariffs and Trade (GATT).

The negotiations seek further trade liberalization through reductions in tariffs and non-tariff barriers. They are also attempting to reinforce trading discipline; to extend the coverage of international rules to sectors, such as agriculture and textiles and clothing, previously excluded from normal GATT rules, and to new areas such as services, to trade-related investment measures, and to intellectual property; and to strengthen the institutional basis of the GATT. The result of these endeavors will shape the trading system for many years to come.

The interests at stake for developing countries are considerable. A recent report, prepared by the staffs of the Bank and the IMF, documents the effects that numerous agricultural and industrial policies—including domestic subsidy and price-support programs, as well as tariffs, quotas, and other nontariff barriers to trade—have on developing countries. Although it is difficult to put a precise number on these effects, several studies have concluded that the annual costs in forgone income to the developing countries amount to about twice the annual interest they pay on their public external debt and are about twice the annual volume of the official development assistance they receive from the industrial countries —although the benefits may differ substantially from one country to another.

At the meeting of the Trade Negotiations Committee in Brussels during the week of December 3, 1990, ministers failed to reach agreement on the conclusion of the negotiations. Several outstanding issues remained, the most prominent of which is liberalization in the agricultural sector. Following the suspension of negotiations in December 1990, the director-general of the GATT conducted a series of informal discussions to reengage the negotiations. As a result of those discussions, participants agreed to conduct negotiations on agriculture to achieve specific binding commitments in each of three areas: domestic support, market access, and export subsidies. With this breakthrough, the Trade Negotiations Committee met in February 1991 and resumed the negotiations.

The impasse on agriculture has slowed progress and prevented the conclusion of agreements in the other areas covered in the negotiations. The resolution of many of these outstanding issues would appear to hinge on substantive progress being made on agriculture. Furthermore, the developing countries—which have participated more actively in these multilateral trade negotiations than ever before—are reluctant to make concessions in several areas until there is tangible progress on issues of importance to them, including textiles. Although the broad outlines of a consensus had emerged toward the end of 1990 on plans to phase out the Multi-Fibre Arrangement's regime of textile trade restric-

tions, no final resolution will be possible before other important matters are settled. In July 1991, however, the Commission of the European Communities approved a proposal— which must still be acted on by the members of the European Community (EC)—that would revamp the EC's agricultural program by reducing production and cutting subsidies to farmers. The proposal represented the most fundamental reshaping of the EC's common agricultural policy since its inception thirty years ago. With so many central issues to be resolved, the negotiations may well continue through 1992, although many countries have expressed a desire to complete them by the end of 1991.

The Environment

Environmental issues continued to receive a great deal of attention as countries grappled with the question of the sustainability of economic growth. While most would agree that sustainability is a desirable objective, there is as yet no consensus as to how to evaluate the long-run viability of alternative development strategies.

The momentum for addressing environmental problems has been accelerated by the forthcoming United Nations Conference on Environment and Development, to be held in Brazil in 1992. National governments and international organizations have begun preparatory work on environmental priorities and policy proposals that will contribute to an Earth Charter and an environmental agenda for the twenty-first century. Preparatory committee meetings are being held to commission research and review and organize material for the upcoming conference. The World Bank is devoting *World Development Report 1992* to the theme of environment and development.

The issue of global warming continued to be debated in international fora. There is some evidence that the burning of fossil fuels, deforestation, some agricultural practices, and other human activities will raise global temperatures through a "greenhouse effect." There remains considerable uncertainty, however, about the magnitude and consequences of such an effect. Moreover, the question of burden sharing is critical, since past accumulations of greenhouse gases have come largely from the industrial countries, while future growth in emissions is likely to come increasingly from the developing countries.

The first meeting to establish a framework for an international treaty to address global warming was held in Chantilly, Virginia, in February 1991. Although there is still uncertainty about global warming, there was a consensus on the need for further research and for increases in energy efficiency to reduce carbon emissions. The European Community, as well as a few national governments, has committed itself to stabilizing its carbon-dioxide emissions by the year 2000 and reducing them thereafter.

The Global Environment Facility (GEF), to be jointly implemented by the World Bank, the United Nations Development Programme, and the United Nations Environment Programme, was launched in 1990. The GEF is a three-year pilot program to provide concessional financing for projects that help developing members address global environmental issues. For example, developing countries that incur incremental costs for complying with the targets for reductions in chlorofluorocarbons, agreed to under the Montreal Protocol, could receive reimbursements from the facility. GEF funds are intended for projects in the areas of greenhouse gases, ozone-layer depletion, international waters, and biodiversity. The total financing available, $1.5 billion, will be provided by a number of donors in tranches over a three-year period.[8] As of June 30, 1991, twenty-one countries, including eight developing countries, had contributed funds to the facility. It is expected that results of GEF activities will be incorporated into the ongoing lending programs of the World Bank and the regional development banks.

An agreement governing exploitation of the Antarctic was drafted in Madrid in April 1991. The members of the thirty-year-old Antarctic Treaty have agreed not to mine the Antarctic for fifty years. This agreement was an important example of how countries can forge treaties that serve the global commons, even where there are conflicting national claims.

---

[8] For details, see page 61.

Section Three
The World Bank—Fiscal Year 1991

The Gulf Crisis and the Bank's Response

The Gulf crisis, which affected a large number of developing member countries of the Bank, both inside and outside the Middle East region, triggered a swift reaction by the Bank to help those members whose near-term prospects were put in jeopardy.

By mid September 1990, staff analysis of the effects of the crisis indicated that many developing countries would be seriously affected, at least in the near term, primarily as a result of higher oil prices (these are the MSA, or most seriously affected, countries). In addition, some ten or so countries (the MII, or most immediately impacted, countries) were immediately affected by losses in revenue from tourism, workers' remittances, trade and related services, and Iraqi debt service, as well as by substantial reflows of workers who would need to be resettled.[1]

The Bank gave immediate priority in its dialogue with its borrowing member countries to designing and implementing appropriate policy responses that recognized the uncertainties ahead. Initial results were encouraging. Several oil-exporting developing countries (Indonesia, Mexico, Nigeria, and Venezuela, for example) acted on the assumption that the extra oil revenue would be temporary and thus did not increase the volume of their domestic spending; many oil-importing developing countries prudently treated the oil-price increase as permanent and adjusted domestic petroleum prices.

The Bank prepared an operational response that, because of the volatility of the situation, had to be both phased and gradual, and, at the same time, intensified its policy dialogue. Its actions focused on the most immediate problems faced by its member countries, while it built up capacity to respond effectively to the needs of its member countries. For fiscal 1991, therefore, the emphasis was on actions that could be taken to help countries deal with the specific effects of the crisis that were either most severe in magnitude or that came on top of already fragile adjustment programs or financing situations.

The Bank's response included:
- preparation, where needed, of emergency-assistance operations to help countries resettle and integrate returning workers and improve infrastructure and social services;
- plans to increase cost-sharing limits to enable the Bank to finance a higher proportion of costs of ongoing and new projects;
- where feasible and appropriate, plans to accelerate disbursements, advance lending operations, supplement ongoing operations, and increase lending for structural and sectoral adjustment;
- provision of policy advice, based on a careful case-by-case review, on how countries could further adjust their economies to cope with the crisis and sustain their poverty-reduction efforts; and
- use of existing mechanisms, such as consultative groups and the special program of assistance for Africa, to help mobilize and coordinate support for the affected countries as required.

The Gulf assistance program led to an increase in IBRD lending of $1 billion in fiscal 1991 and an increase in IDA lending of SDR314 million over the previously planned IDA commitments.

Funds needed for the additional IDA lending were covered by the use of existing mechanisms (carryover of funds, totaling SDR190 million, from the eighth replenishment of IDA, or IDA-8, that had not been committed in fiscal year 1990 and reprogramming of resources available under the ninth replenishment, or IDA-9, totaling SDR80 million) and additional commitments, totaling SDR130 million, against IDA reflows.

In addition, SDR200 million was transferred to IDA from the Bank's fiscal 1990 net income, and Kuwait agreed in principle to increase its IDA-9 contribution to $50 million. IDA was thus provided with sufficient additional commitment au-

---

[1] Originally, the MII countries were Bangladesh, Egypt, India, Jordan, Morocco, Pakistan, the Philippines, Sri Lanka, Sudan, and Turkey. The Republic of Yemen was subsequently treated, de facto, as an MII country.

thority to meet virtually the whole of its operational program in those developing countries that were affected by the crisis.

The board also agreed to raise to a limit of 35 percent—from the previously agreed 30 percent—the share of IDA quick-disbursing lending during fiscal year 1991. The objective was not to have a higher level of adjustment lending in each of the three years covered by IDA-9. Rather, it was to avoid deciding now that increases in fiscal 1991 must be offset by decreases in the next two years in order to stay within the agreed 30 percent limit for the IDA-9 period, regardless of the circumstances.

During fiscal year 1991, additional IDA lending, totaling SDR314 million, was approved by the executive board; lending totaling about SDR310 million is expected to be presented to the board early in fiscal 1992. Of the total IDA program planned in fiscal 1991 in response to the Gulf crisis, some SDR475 million, or about 76 percent, is assisting MII countries such as Bangladesh, India, Pakistan, the Philippines, and Sri Lanka. Emergency operations in Egypt and Yemen were approved that aimed at setting up infrastructure, social services, and employment-creation programs for repatriated workers. The rest of the program (about SDR150 million) is being directed at several African and a few Central American low-income MSA countries.

On the IBRD side, additional lending of $1 billion during fiscal 1991 was committed. A substantial part of the program was in the form of additions to adjustment operations in Eastern and Central Europe. Another major element consisted of investment operations in MII countries in the Europe, Middle East, and North Africa region, including a small emergency operation in Jordan. That operation financed part of the foreign-exchange and local costs of that country's overall emergency-response program, whose total cost is estimated to be $235 million.

On the basis of specific agreements reached with several of the Bank's borrowers, additional disbursements from the IBRD and IDA through changes in cost-sharing limits are estimated at $500 million in fiscal 1991.

Although serious losses were sustained by a number of oil-importing countries of sub-Saharan Africa and Latin America, the negative effects of the crisis on the MSA countries were more limited in scope and duration than originally feared. As a result of a number of factors, notably the increase in oil supplies by Saudi Arabia to make up for lost production elsewhere, stability was restored to the oil markets, and the probability of sustained high oil prices was much reduced. In addition, quick action by MSA countries in raising domestic energy prices and introducing revenue-enhancing measures helped to limit the fiscal impact of the oil shock. Many uncertainties nevertheless remain over the pace of recovery, especially in Eastern and Central Europe, where increased petroleum prices have added to the financial burden of countries already experiencing serious terms-of-trade and trade-volume losses because of the breakdown of the arrangements among the members of the Council for Mutual Economic Assistance, as well as difficulties caused by their transition to market economies.

The MII countries, particularly the "frontline" states of Egypt, Jordan, and Turkey, were most seriously affected by the crisis, notwithstanding emergency financial assistance to them from the international community. Significant losses were also incurred by a number of countries heavily dependent on migrants' remittances and/or trade (Bangladesh, India, Lebanon, Morocco, Pakistan, the Philippines, Sri Lanka, and Yemen, for instance). The adverse effect on tourism was also great in countries such as Egypt, Morocco, and Turkey.

Overall, however, the negative effects of the Gulf crisis are expected to be somewhat less than was originally thought likely late in 1990—despite the fact that the negatives for many of the Bank's developing member countries are still substantial. The basic elements of the Bank's original operational response, however, remain valid, and the Bank intends to press forward with the bulk of the Gulf crisis-related lending operations and other support that was originally laid out.

The Bank is also ready to play an active role in helping to design and administer programs of reconstruction and development, in supplying technical assistance and additional financing, and in working with other multilateral institutions to develop appropriate mechanisms for coordinating financial resources. Together with the International Monetary Fund (IMF), the Bank has been in close consultation with the members of the Gulf Crisis Financial Coordination Group[2] to explore ways in which it might be of assistance. The objective is to mobilize assistance for emergency rehabilitation and economic reconstruction of the countries affected by the Gulf war and to respond to the longer-term development needs of the

---

[2] Consists of most of the members of the Organisation for Economic Co-operation and Development, as well as the Commission of the European Communities, the Republic of Korea, Kuwait, Qatar, Saudi Arabia, and the United Arab Emirates.

countries in the Middle East.[3] In this regard, the Bank welcomes the opportunity to resume activities in Lebanon, which has been devastated by fifteen years of civil war, and whose difficulties were compounded by the effects of the Gulf crisis.

The Bank's response to the crisis in the Gulf was the subject of several discussions with the executive directors during the year. Beyond endorsing specific recommendations on easing limitations on provision of quick-disbursing IDA finance and on advancement of drawdowns from the IBRD, wide support was given to the Bank's general two-phased approach—one that combined immediate action to support the most seriously affected countries with careful monitoring of developments over the near term.

At its April 1991 meeting in Washington, D.C., the Development Committee welcomed the prompt response and ongoing efforts of the Bank, as well as the IMF, to assist those countries seriously affected by the Middle East crisis. The committee also urged the two institutions to continue to analyze the financial requirements of all the developing countries directly affected by the crisis. The Bank and the IMF were called upon to assist in the mobilization of resources in support of the affected countries.

Members of the committee stressed that financial assistance to these countries should seek to facilitate, rather than substitute for, the sustained implementation of sound economic policies and adjustment programs. The committee underscored the importance of an appropriate and effective coordination arrangement to deal with reconstruction, as well as with the adjustment and longer-term developmental needs of the countries of the region.

Eastern and Central Europe

In contrast to the euphoria that existed in Eastern and Central Europe (ECE) a year ago, developments during the second half of 1990 and early 1991 have led to a sobering realization of the difficulties of transition and the short-term cost of reform. These difficulties have been greatly magnified by large, and to an extent unforeseen, external shocks.

Most countries have opted for rapid economic transformation towards a market economy and have experienced difficulties as production declined and unemployment rose. (See Box 3-1 for details of a study that analyzed reform efforts in the Soviet Union.) This has been particularly marked in Poland. In addition, these countries have been hit by a number of exogenous shocks—including the breakdown in trade arrangements of the Council for Mutual Economic Assistance (CMEA), the in-

crease in the international price of oil following Iraq's invasion of Kuwait, and the changed position of the East German market.

The breakdown in CMEA trade arrangements occurred in two stages. In the first stage, it was decided that prices for goods traded would be set equal to world market prices, and payment would be made in convertible currency starting January 1, 1991. This decision caused a substantial deterioration in the terms of trade of the Eastern and Central European countries vis-à-vis the Soviet Union, as they had previously benefited from low-priced energy imports from the Soviet Union.

In the second stage, the political situation in the Soviet Union led to a disruption of centrally negotiated bilateral trade arrangements. With bilateral arrangements decentralized to the enterprise level, substantial uncertainty emerged regarding both the competitive advantage of many traditional exports of the Eastern and Central European countries and the ability of Soviet enterprises to secure convertible currency for payment.

With respect to imports, the disruption of crude-oil production in the Soviet Union and the diversion of some crude exports to markets outside Eastern and Central Europe caused a physical supply problem, as well as a price shock, as countries of this subregion had to turn to alternative sources of supply.

The further but temporary increase in the price of crude oil, the result of the events in the Middle East, was a heavy blow to the energy-intensive ECE countries. The energy-price rises in the second half of 1990 resulted in an estimated $1.5 billion increase in the import bill of the six major ECE countries. Moreover, several countries have lost export markets, workers' remittances, and/or construction contracts in the Gulf region. Iraqi debt to these countries (excluding Yugoslavia) totaled $4.5 billion in 1990. These countries' imports from Iraq in 1989 exceeded their exports to it by some 70 percent, and ECE countries expected repayment through expanded crude-oil imports, which would have offset some of the costs of the CMEA dissolution.

German economic and monetary union, following the unification, also had an adverse effect on these countries. The former German Democratic Republic was the most important

---

[3] In addition, the members of the Gulf Cooperation Council (Bahrain, Kuwait, Oman, Qatar, Saudi Arabia, and the United Arab Emirates) are establishing a program to support development in the Arab countries. This program will put special emphasis on the promotion of trade and private-sector activities, as well as on economic reform.

Box 3-1. The Economy of the Soviet Union

During fiscal 1991, the Bank undertook its first substantial analytical work on the economy of the Soviet Union. In July 1990, the leaders of the seven major industrial countries (G-7), after consulting with the Soviet authorities, asked the World Bank, the International Monetary Fund, the Organisation for Economic Co-operation and Development, and the European Bank for Reconstruction and Development to carry out a joint study of the Soviet economy. The purposes of the study were to recommend to the Soviet authorities ways in which they might accomplish their goal of establishing a market-oriented economy and to recommend to the industrial nations the criteria under which assistance could effectively support such economic reforms.

A report, *The Economy of the USSR—Summary and Recommendations,* was submitted to the G-7 countries and to the Soviet government in December 1990.[1] The full report, in three-volumes, became available in March.[2] Both reports were made available to the public.

Bank participants in the joint-study missions found the Soviet economy in serious disarray, and the situation deteriorated further during the course of the study.

Dissatisfied with the results of central planning and administrative management of the country, the Soviet authorities initiated a series of economic-reform measures in 1985. These initial *perestroika,* or restructuring, measures were significantly expanded after 1987, when major systemic changes began to be introduced. Although the reforms effectively dismantled the old system, the basic elements needed for a market economy were not established, and measures to maintain adequate macroeconomic control during the transition process had not been adopted.

The recent situation—one of increasing economic disruption, with growing shortages and declines in output—has been caused, in large measure, by the breakdown in the system for supplying inputs needed in the production process. Although it now seems impossible for the government to revert to the earlier system of administrative management—at least without completely abandoning both *perestroika* and *glasnost*—it is also proving exceedingly difficult for it to establish a market-oriented economy.

To overcome the current problems and establish a market-oriented economy, both improved macroeconomic management and a number of major and systemic reforms are needed. The interrelationships among the many elements in a workable reform program mean that many difficult issues must be tackled at the same time.

The joint study recommends a significant and broadly based liberalization of prices; while prices would surely rise, supply networks could be reestablished by letting goods be allocated and prices determined by market forces. Price liberalization would have to take place in an environ-ment of increased domestic and external competition, and be supported by a clarification of property rights, the encouragement of private ownership, and the commercialization of larger state enterprises. The development of the private sector could be fostered by the sale of small-scale enterprises and encouragement of new private-sector activities. The commercialization of large state-owned enterprises would provide budget discipline and would be a step toward both more efficient management and privatization. The establishment of a commercial banking system is yet another essential change that is required. Since voluntary contracts would replace administrative directives, the legal framework and judicial system necessary for a market economy would also have to be put in place.

These reform efforts would need to be buttressed by tighter financial policies and a realistic exchange-rate policy so as to contain inflationary pressures and prevent major external imbalances. As the introduction of reforms would substantially affect both employment and the cost of living, the program would have to include an incomes policy and provision of an effective social safety net (including the creation of an adequate system of unemployment compensation). The report of the joint study recommends, as a way of cushioning the impact of the reforms on the poorer segments of society, some continuation of subsidies; however, the report cautions that subsidies should apply only to a limited quantity of food for each household.

The report indicated that technical assistance from industrialized countries could play an important role in supporting the Soviet reform effort. Food aid and selected project assistance (in particular, in the environment, energy, and infrastructure sectors) could also play an important role. Balance-of-payments support, perhaps including assistance through a stabilization fund, would be appropriate only when the Soviet government had adopted a major and comprehensive economic-reform program. The report concluded that, "without such a reform, additional financial resources would be of little or no lasting value. With it, assistance could provide important support, during a time of a difficult transition, to integrate the economy of the USSR into the world economy, with benefits for all partners."

---

[1] International Monetary Fund, World Bank, Organisation for Economic Co-operation and Development, and European Bank for Reconstruction and Development, *The Economy of the USSR—Summary and Recommendations* (Washington, D.C.: World Bank, 1990).
[2] International Monetary Fund, World Bank, Organisation for Economic Co-operation and Development, and European Bank for Reconstruction and Development, *A Study of the Soviet Economy* (Paris: Organisation for Economic Co-operation and Development, 1991).

supplier of high-technology engineering products and chemicals within the CMEA and was an important customer for consumer goods from the Eastern and Central European countries, as well. In the short run—until a greater range of ECE exports becomes more competitive—German unification means the likely loss of the eastern part of Germany as a major market for such goods.

In addition to these economic shocks, the spread of democratic processes in Eastern and Central Europe has inevitably resulted in more complex decisionmaking. Delays in the design of reform programs and in policy initiatives have occurred in Hungary as a result of strikes; in Poland, as a result of presidential elections; in Czechoslovakia, because of differing views on the priorities for reform; and in Bulgaria, where the political opposition held out for a coalition government to implement an agreed agenda of reform. (The greatest disruption of all has occurred in the southern European country of Yugoslavia, where declarations of sovereignty by the two northern republics have been challenged by the most populous and militarily strong republic, Serbia, which favors a continuation of the federal state.)

Political and economic reforms continued throughout the subregion, however, and, in the past year, Romania and Albania have made important and sustained efforts to improve their political and economic systems.

The Bank and the International Monetary Fund (IMF) initiated programs with the Romanian government during the course of the fiscal year, and, on January 30, 1991, the group of twenty-four industrialized nations agreed to bring Romania into the economic-aid program set up more than a year earlier to help emerging democracies in Eastern Europe. Albania applied for membership in both the Bank and the IMF in January 1991, and an initial fact-finding mission was undertaken.

The Bank now has an active program of lending and economic and sector work in all the Eastern and Central European countries with the exception of Albania. The economic and sector work attempted has taken the form of comprehensive introductory reports on the Bank's two new borrowers, Bulgaria and Czechoslovakia.

In the other countries, analysis has emphasized the industrial sector, the environment, and the social safety net and human resources. Economic dialogue has been strengthened by close collaboration between the Bank and the IMF, with regular joint participation in missions and exchanges of views on financial and technical-assistance programs. In an effort to ensure consistency in the main components of

their reform programs, the governments of Poland and Hungary prepared brief medium-term policy documents with the joint support of Bank and IMF staff. Effective coordination of assistance plans with the Commission of the European Communities, the Organisation for Economic Co-operation and Development, the European Investment Bank, and the European Bank for Reconstruction and Development was developed.

The Bank's lending strategy for Eastern and Central Europe aims at supporting structural and institutional measures critical for the success of reform programs through structural-adjustment loans, as well as through technical-assistance loans that provide external expertise in priority areas and support needed institutional development. The amount of Bank commitments to the ECE countries during the year expanded rapidly, reaching $2.9 billion, an increase of $1,098 million over the previous year. Some $809 million was disbursed during the course of the year.

The Special Program of Assistance for Sub-Saharan Africa

The second phase of the special program of assistance (SPA II) was officially launched in late October 1990, when eighteen donors pledged $7.4 billion in cofinancing and coordinated financing to support adjustment programs in the low-income, highly indebted countries of sub-Saharan Africa.[4]

The cofinancing pledges are one of five components that comprise the resources within the SPA framework. The others are adjustment lending under the ninth replenishment of IDA; supplemental IDA adjustment credits from a share of the investment income of, and repayments to, IDA; resources from the International Monetary Fund's structural-adjustment facilities (both the regular facility, the SAF, and the enhanced facility, the ESAF); and debt relief, including forgiveness of concessional loans and rescheduling of non-concessional debt on softer terms.

The strong donor support for the second phase of the SPA stems from the evidence amassed during the SPA's first phase, covering calendar years 1988–90, that domestic policy reform, coupled with adequate financial assistance from bilateral donors and international agencies, substantially improves economic

---

[4] Pledges were made by Belgium, Canada, Denmark, Finland, France, Germany, Italy, Japan, Kuwait, the Netherlands, Norway, Spain, Sweden, Switzerland, the United Kingdom, the United States, the African Development Fund, and the Commission of the European Communities.

Table 3-1. **Sub-Saharan Africa's GDP Growth, 1980–90**

Indicator and country group	Unweighted averages			Weighted averages		
	1980–84	1985–87	1988–90	1980–84	1985–87	1988–90
Average annual growth rates (percentage change)						
SPA core countries	1.0	3.2	4.0	1.1	3.6	4.3
Non-SPA countries[a,b]	3.3	3.2	2.2	1.5	2.5	1.5
Other IDA-only[a]	2.4	2.9	1.4	2.4	2.7	0.5
IBRD borrowers[b]	4.3	3.4	3.0	1.0	2.4	2.1
All sub-Saharan Africa[a,b]	2.2	3.2	3.1	1.4	2.9	2.4
Non-SPA countries less Nigeria[a,b]	3.6	3.2	2.0	3.6	2.7	0.1
Non-African developing countries	..	..	..	3.1	5.0	3.4
Diversity of growth rates (number of countries)						
SPA core countries	20	20	20			
Over 6 percent	0	3	2			
3+ to 6 percent	5	7	12			
0 to 3 percent	9	8	6			
Negative	6	2	0			
Non-SPA countries[a,b]	20	20	20			
Over 6 percent	4	3	2			
3+ to 6 percent	4	5	6			
0 to 3 percent	9	9	8			
Negative	3	3	4			

.. Not applicable.

a. Includes Somalia, Zaire, and Zambia. (Zambia is now an SPA core country.) Excludes Comoros, Djibouti, and Equatorial Guinea because of incomplete data.

b. Excludes Angola and Swaziland because of incomplete data.

performance. The following figures illustrate the SPA performance dividend:

• growth in gross domestic product (GDP) of 4 percent on average during the past three years, up from 1 percent in 1980–84, and almost double the recent growth rate in other African countries (see Table 3-1);

• growth in export volumes at a pace 50 percent above GDP growth (see Table 3-2); and

• growth in the volume of investment at a pace three to four times faster than GDP.

This strong economic performance contrasts sharply with that registered by African countries outside the SPA.[5]

During the first phase of the SPA (SPA I), eligible countries received total adjustment support amounting to $17.5 billion (of which almost $7.5 billion was in the form of gross disbursements of adjustment assistance from SPA donors, IDA, and the IMF and about $10 billion in the form of debt relief on official debt from all creditors, over half of which was rescheduling of nonconcessional debt by Paris Club creditors on the softer terms of the Toronto menu of options). As of December 31, 1990, 81 percent of commitments by SPA donors had been disbursed during the first phase of the SPA—some $4.3 billion. These funds

were provided as cofinancing or coordinated financing of IDA adjustment operations, for which IDA also disbursed $1.8 billion.

Gross disbursements from the IMF under its regular and enhanced structural-adjustment facilities (established in 1986 and 1987, respectively) totaled $1.5 billion during the 1988–90 period. This amount was roughly equivalent to about a tenth of total gross aid flows under the SPA.

During SPA I, Paris Club creditors officially rescheduled over $5.6 billion owed by seventeen SPA countries, almost all on Toronto terms. SPA donors also reported canceling debts on official development assistance (ODA) in the amount of about $5.5 billion during the period 1988–90.

Funds for the SPA's second phase are to be committed over three calendar years, 1991–93. If realized, the October 1990 pledges would represent an increase of between 15 percent and 20 percent (in real terms) over the pledges delivered during the first phase of the SPA. Together with the SPA I cofinancing and coordinated financing already pledged, disburse-

[5] For more details, see page 110.

Table 3-2. Sub-Saharan Africa: Selected Performance Indicators, 1980–90
(average annual percentage change, unless otherwise specified)

Indicator and country group	1980–84	1985–87	1988–90
Gross domestic investment (GDI)			
SPA core countries	−6.3	12.5	8.5
Non-SPA countries	1.9	1.2	3.5
Export volume			
SPA core countries	−0.6	3.0	5.7
Non-SPA countries	1.3	2.0	2.4
Import volume			
SPA core countries	−1.3	2.6	4.1
Non-SPA countries	2.0	−0.5	3.0
Consumption per capita			
SPA core countries	−0.7	−0.8	−0.1
Non-SPA countries	0.7	−0.7	−0.6
GDI/GDP ratio (percent)			
SPA core countries	18.4	16.7	19.3
Non-SPA countries	23.9	21.2	19.6
GDS/GDP ratio (percent)			
SPA core countries	2.9	4.0	4.9
Non-SPA countries	8.9	9.3	8.8
Terms-of-trade index (1987 = 1.000)			
SPA core countries	1.055	1.064	0.939
Non-SPA countries	1.208	1.058	1.024

Note: Non-SPA countries include Somalia, Zaire, and Zambia, and exclude Angola, Comoros, Djibouti, Equatorial Guinea, and Swaziland because of incomplete data. (Zambia is now an SPA core country.) GDS = gross domestic saving.

ments of cofinancing and coordinated financing to support eligible SPA countries during the 1991–93 period could total more than $7 billion, nearly double the disbursements achieved during SPA I.

Planned IDA commitments during 1991–93 to the twenty-one SPA countries[6] could add $2.9 billion to the total, while estimates are that resources provided by the International Monetary Fund could range between $1 billion and $2 billion.

In addition to pledges of SPA funds, SPA creditors are likely to provide substantial debt relief by continued cancellation of ODA debt and reschedulings of official, bilateral nonconcessional debt-service obligations on Toronto terms. However, the current rescheduling on Toronto terms in the aggregate provides a grant element of only 20 percent and remains less concessional than new aid. In addition, the debt-service payments by these low-income countries, even after rescheduling on Toronto terms, will continue to absorb a significant amount of resources that could otherwise be used for investments and imports, leading to improved growth and development. (Debt-service payments by active SPA countries, after debt relief on current terms, are expected to amount to about 25 percent of export earnings during 1991–93.) The most far-reaching proposal for Paris Club creditors to increase debt relief is that

of the United Kingdom called the Trinidad terms.[7] Paris Club creditors are currently attempting to reach a consensus on steps that might be taken to realize the objectives of the Trinidad terms without jeopardizing future aid flows.

The external financing provided from all sources through the SPA II framework should be sufficient to cover the financing gaps of the currently active countries, as well as the three additional countries declared eligible in June 1991. The task, then, is to commit, manage, and disburse the resources of SPA II in a way that facilitates their efficient use.

It is estimated that as much as 85 percent of SPA assistance will likely be broadly untied.

---

[6] These are Benin, Burundi, Central African Republic, Chad, The Gambia, Ghana, Guinea, Guinea-Bissau, Kenya, Madagascar, Malawi, Mali, Mauritania, Mozambique, Niger, São Tomé and Principe, Senegal, Tanzania, Togo, Uganda, and Zambia. Somalia and Zaire became ineligible in 1990 because of weakened reform efforts. On June 30, 1991, three additional countries—Burkina Faso, Comoros, and Rwanda—were declared eligible.

[7] These call for a cancellation of two thirds of the stock of eligible debt and a rescheduling of the remainder over twenty-five years with five years of grace. Interest due during the first five years after rescheduling could be capitalized, providing further cash-flow relief; later payments could be graduated and related to the debtor country's ability to pay.

Substantial progress was made during SPA I in harmonizing and simplifying procurement and disbursement procedures, thus putting SPA II in a stronger position to deliver adjustment support where and when it is required.

Evaluation missions, made up of staff from several donor aid agencies and the Bank, visited six SPA countries over the the course of the first phase of the SPA and made several recommendations to improve further the quality of SPA adjustment support. They include:

• the phasing out by all SPA recipients by the end of 1993 of their import and exchange controls and, to help reinforce these market-oriented reforms, the elimination by SPA donors of their tight administrative control over their individual import programs;

• fully untying by SPA donors of their import-support programs;

• expansion by recipient governments of preshipment inspection to cover virtually all imports, and, as appropriate, extension of pre-shipment inspection to include assessment of custom duties to be paid;

• regular consultations within each recipient country on the use and management of donors' import programs, to be supported by periodic joint evaluations in SPA countries; and

• provision of specific technical-assistance programs to SPA recipients to strengthen public procurement, banking practices, customs administration, and foreign-exchange operations.

The special program of assistance has shown that development efforts can be made more effective through joint action. Indeed, there has been a strong demand from donors to broaden the range of SPA activities. Although SPA resources remain focused in support of adjustment, SPA meetings are also becoming fora for discussions of broader issues associated with adjustment such as the linkage between adjustment support and poverty alleviation and the quality of recipient countries' public-expenditure programs. In this connection, SPA donors have endorsed guidelines for improving the management of counterpart funds to support on-budget public-expenditure programs and to reduce earmarking of such funds, as the recipient country's public-expenditure planning and budget implementation improve.

Strategies to Reduce Poverty

"The objective of a sizable reduction in the incidence of poverty is the highest priority for the international development community."
Development Committee communiqué,
September 24, 1990

"Poverty reduction is an integrating theme for the many facets of the World Bank's work,

and it is the raison d'être for our operational emphases."
Barber Conable, Address to the Board
of Governors of the World Bank Group,
September 25, 1990

The eradication of poverty remains the World Bank's top priority. World Bank experience helped set the stage for the publication in fiscal 1991 of a major study on poverty, *World Development Report 1990,* and, subsequently, for the adoption of assistance strategies to reduce poverty.

In fiscal 1987, a special task force, composed of senior staff of the Bank, was established to review the Bank's poverty work and propose new activities.

This task force defined a program of action for the Bank that was designed to help achieve the objective of eliminating the worst forms of poverty in developing member countries by the year 2000. The program was based on the belief that, although economic growth, over the long term, was the major factor in the reduction of mass poverty, growth alone was not sufficient for the alleviation of absolute poverty at the desired speed. Growth policies, therefore, had to be supplemented by clearly defined poverty-reduction efforts.

By fiscal 1989, food security had become a part of poverty-reducing initiatives, efforts were stepped up to help borrowers ensure that the poor were protected during periods of adjustment, and involvement by nongovernmental organizations in Bank-supported undertakings expanded.

In fiscal 1990, each region in the Bank developed a set of activities (a "core program") aimed at directly reducing poverty, and steps to monitor their implementation were taken.

For maximum effectiveness in reducing poverty, *World Development Report 1990* recommends that developing countries adopt a two-part strategy. The first part of the approach requires the encouragement of broadly based economic growth. Policies that make productive use of the poor's most abundant asset—labor—are consistent with rapid growth and reduced poverty. The second part requires the provision of social services—especially primary education, basic health care, family planning, and nutrition—to improve living conditions and increase the capacity of the poor to respond to whatever income-earning opportunities arise from economic growth.

To implement the first part of the strategy, *World Development Report 1990* argues that countries must put in place incentive structures that make the best use of their available resources, including those of the poor. By maintaining competitive exchange rates and avoiding excessive protection in manufacturing, countries such as Indonesia and Thailand have encouraged agriculture—the most labor-intensive sector in an economy—and achieved a fast-growing and relatively labor-intensive form of manufacturing.

This is not enough, however. Public-expenditure programs to support the activities in which the poor are engaged are also required. Equally important are measures to ensure that the delivery of services, such as roads, irrigation, and agricultural extension, is not biased against the poor.

Even if economic growth generates income-earning opportunities for the poor, many will be unable to take full advantage of them because of ill health, lack of skills, illiteracy, or malnutrition. Ensuring access for the poor to basic social services, therefore, is doubly essential: It alleviates the immediate consequences of poverty and it attacks one of the key causes of poverty.

This two-part approach ensures that the poor gain from growth and that they contribute to growth. But some, the old and the infirm, will not be able to respond to new opportunities. And others, although benefiting, will still not be able to afford the basic necessities or will be vulnerable to such income-reducing shocks as a drought or the loss of the family breadwinner. To help these groups, *World Development Report 1990* calls for the establishment of a system of targeted transfers and safety nets as a essential component of the basic approach.

Building on the findings in *World Development Report 1990*, policies were adopted in fiscal 1991 for fully integrating into Bank operations the two-part approach for reducing poverty. The key ingredients are:

• analysis that assesses the consistency of each country's policies, programs, and institutions with the reduction of poverty; and

• recommendations for country policy and design of the Bank's program of assistance to support and complement country efforts to reduce poverty.

The two are linked. Analysis of the appropriateness of public policy, especially the effectiveness of economic management in securing broadly based growth and the adequacy of basic social services, will shape both the Bank's policy dialogue and its program of assistance. Bank assistance strategies will reflect and be consistent with an analysis of the factors determining poverty.

Analyzing country policy. Bank staff are already equipped to analyze the policies required to achieve growth. The link between growth and poverty, however, is not automatic, and the pattern of growth has an important bearing on changes in the incidence of poverty. The main modification to existing practice, therefore, will be periodic review and analysis of the links between growth and poverty.

Two recent country economic memoranda—for India and Malawi—illustrate the required analysis well. Both begin with a traditional analysis of recent economic events and a macroeconomic assessment. They then investigate trends in poverty and the characteristics of the poor. The latter involve location, demographic characteristics, sources of income, patterns of expenditure, access to social services, and so forth. The "poverty profiles" of the two countries that emerge provide the key input for subsequent analysis of the interaction between macroeconomic and sectoral policies on the one hand and the incidence of poverty on the other.

From this starting point, the analysis will try to identify the factors underlying the observed outcomes and draw the implications for policy. The main steps are, first, to juxtapose the analysis of overall economic policy and the poverty profile, and second, to trace the links between the two.

World Development Report 1990 confirmed the critical importance of effective adjustment to the long-run reduction of poverty and demonstrated that, in general, adjustment programs move economies in a direction consistent with the two-part approach. But efforts to restructure and stabilize an economy can have short-run costs. Although some of these costs may be unavoidable, analysis of likely consequences can improve design of adjustment programs and provide a firmer basis for judging the need for compensatory programs.

Whether the concern is with long-run growth or short-run economic management, reviews of public-expenditure programs are critical to an overall assessment of efforts to reduce poverty. Again, the Bank already has considerable experience in this area. Few country reviews, however, have examined the distribution of expenditures between the poor and the nonpoor. Detailed analysis by income group will not be possible in most countries, but analysis by location and type of service will be feasible in all cases.

The adequacy of social services is the second element that needs to be considered in assessing the consistency of a country's policies with the objective of reducing poverty. Here, too, the Bank is developing considerable expertise in analyzing the provision of social services, especially the link between public provision of services and measures of health and educational attainment. Such analysis has been done for many countries and will be extended.

To be effective, country analysis of the kind described must be reviewed regularly. Periodic assessment of each country's policies and their effect on the poor provides the foundation for the Bank's policy dialogue and the design of its assistance strategies. Through careful analysis, the Bank is better placed to suggest appropriate policies to governments and to design programs of assistance that most effectively support government efforts.

Designing assistance strategies. The objective of this second step is to ensure that the volume and composition of Bank assistance support and complement the efforts of individual countries to reduce poverty.

Because Bank assistance strategies depend on circumstances in each country, they must be country specific. Moreover, many factors—political, institutional, and economic—influence their design. Nevertheless, a few general principles do exist. For example:

• The Bank's volume of lending will be linked to, among other things, a country's efforts to reduce poverty. If a country's policies, programs, and institutions are broadly consistent with the two-part strategy, a prima facie case for substantial Bank support can be made, for existing evidence indicates that external assistance is most effective in such countries. The reverse is also true, and intermediate cases would warrant intermediate levels of assistance.[8]

• The composition of Bank lending will support efforts to reduce poverty. If the incomes of the poor are increasing rapidly but their access to social services is stagnating, the Bank will work with the government to redress the imbalance by emphasizing the provision of social services. And, within sectors, Bank lending can be used to influence the pattern of public investment and expenditures by emphasizing programs most likely to benefit the poor.

Developing an information base. The analysis of poverty in several countries has revealed the importance of good data. The analyst, whether from the country concerned or the Bank, will and must continue to do as much as possible with existing sources; ultimately, however, the quality of the analysis depends on the quality of the underlying data. According to *World Development Report 1990,* fewer than two dozen countries in the developing world have national household surveys—important sources of information—of reasonable reliability. Both the living standards measurement study (LSMS) and the social dimensions of adjustment (SDA) project are helping countries to conduct such surveys, and these efforts

will continue. In the meantime, simpler approaches may be more cost effective. Several variables that indicate changes in the well-being of the poor are relatively easy to collect. The choice of variables will depend on country-specific needs and administrative capacities, but, in line with the two-part strategy, the variables should reflect the incomes of the poor (income indicators) and their access to social services (social indicators).

Implementing the strategy. Implementation of the Bank's strategies to reduce poverty starts with carrying out the necessary analysis. The first round of periodic assessments, for all intents and purposes, will be completed for all countries within three years. By that time, therefore, all Bank assistance strategies will reflect and be consistent with an analysis of the key factors determining poverty. Country assessments will be made widely available to facilitate coordination of poverty-reduction efforts within the international donor community—through consultative-group meetings and through the Development Assistance Committee of the Organisation for Economic Co-operation and Development.

Follow-up work is continuing on two fronts: a handbook on best practices in poverty reduction for the use of operational staff and an operational directive (OD) summarizing the Bank's guidelines on operational issues.

The objective of the handbook will be to provide Bank staff with ready access to relevant examples of successful approaches to poverty reduction. The handbook will focus on problems that arise in designing and executing projects that reach the poor and on examples of innovative and effective solutions to those problems.

The OD, scheduled to be finalized in fiscal 1992, will summarize, among other things, the poverty-relevant results of a review, currently under way, of the methodology for the economic analysis of projects. It will also incorporate the findings of task forces on local-cost financing in Bank-supported programs and projects. This is relevant because local costs tend to form a larger share of project costs in social-sector and poverty-related projects.

In its discussion of the Bank's strategies to assist countries in reducing poverty, the executive board reaffirmed the Bank's commitment to poverty reduction as the integrating theme for all of its activities.

---

[8] *World Development Report 1990* also stresses that the seriousness of a country's own commitment to sustainable development policies geared to poverty reduction is basic to the proposed strategy to reduce poverty.

During the discussion, several important points were endorsed.

• It was confirmed that the Bank should, in its own assistance strategies, support the two-part poverty-reduction strategy set out in *World Development Report 1990.*

• There was broad agreement that the Bank should integrate this poverty strategy into its country assistance.

• There was agreement that the transparency and consistency with which the Bank applies this strategy should be increased.

• On the relationship of the strategy to lending, borrowers' efforts to reduce poverty will be a key criterion in determining the volume of lending and will also be reflected in the composition of lending.

• Concern was widespread about the paucity of good data on poverty. It was agreed that the Bank should be prepared to help organize appropriate financial support and technical assistance, in cooperation with other donors and agencies of the United Nations, for implementation of proposals to improve data related to poverty.

• The board expressed great interest in the steps the Bank is taking in pursuit of this approach. It endorsed the Bank's intention to support these steps through the preparation of a handbook of best practices and an operational directive.

It was also agreed that a progress report on the implementation of the Bank's poverty-reduction strategies would be prepared for board consideration late in 1992.

The Development Committee, in its April 1991 meeting, also welcomed the conclusions of *World Development Report 1990,* as well as the Bank's intention to implement a plan of action designed to translate those conclusions into its operational practices and budgetary priorities. Members requested that a progress report on the action plan be made available to them in a year's time.

*   *   *

In fiscal 1991, commitments, totaling $1,885.8 million, were made for twenty-two projects whose primary objective is to reduce poverty (see Table 3-3). Another ninety-five projects, involving $7.9 billion in commitments, contained poverty-reduction components.

A recent internal study of poverty projects supported by the Bank over the five-year period fiscal 1985–89 shows that a large percentage of targeted poverty lending (more than 90 percent) was in five sectors—agriculture and rural development; population, health, and nutrition; education; urban development; and water supply and sewerage. Among these sectors, the concentration of targeted poverty lending was overwhelmingly in population, health, and nutrition.

The study also found that the largest absolute amount of targeted poverty lending was in Asia, followed by Latin America and the Caribbean; Europe, Middle East, and North Africa; and Africa. Comparing each region's share of targeted poverty lending with the region's share of total Bank lending, a somewhat different picture emerges. In both Asia and Africa, the share of targeted poverty lending in total lending to the region was similar to the Bankwide average of targeted poverty lending. By contrast, the Latin America and the Caribbean region's share of targeted poverty lending in total lending to the region was roughly twice the Bankwide average.

At the local level, targeted poverty projects are characterized by relatively greater participation by nongovernmental organizations (NGOs) or the beneficiaries themselves (who may or may not be organized in formal groups). In the five-year period under study, one third of targeted poverty projects included NGO or beneficiary involvement, as opposed to 10 percent of total Bank projects. This reflects experience that has shown that projects aimed at meeting the needs of specific groups are more effective and sustainable when beneficiaries are involved and actively cooperate to make the projects work.

The data on Bank lending for projects whose primary objective is to reduce poverty considerably understate the true impact of the Bank's lending on poverty, since they take no account of the indirect effects of other lending. These effects, although difficult to monitor, are often more important than targeted programs.

An increasingly poverty-conscious approach is evident across the range of Bank lending. For example:

• Operational activities in the area of human-resource development aim at efficient and effective delivery of services, with emphasis on vulnerable groups such as women and children, and diverse regional topics: population growth (Africa), female employment and social safety nets (Europe, Middle East, and North Africa), and improved targeting of service-delivery systems and reallocation of public funds (Latin America and the Caribbean).

• Lending for environment and forestry features an emphasis on the linkages among environment, energy, and poverty (particularly in Africa).

• Adjustment operations continue to be a mechanism by which the Bank can support policy reforms that encourage economic growth and poverty reduction, while protecting priority public expenditures.

Table 3-3. Lending Operations Whose Primary Objective Is to Reduce Poverty, Fiscal 1990–91
(millions of US dollars)

Region and country	Project	IBRD	IDA
Africa			
Burkina Faso	Public works and employment project (FY91)	—	20.0
Cameroon	Social dimensions of adjustment project (FY90)	21.5	—
Central African Republic	Social dimensions of adjustment and development project (FY91)	—	6.5
Chad	Social development action project (FY90)	—	13.4
Malawi	Agricultural sector adjustment project (FY90)	—	70.0
Niger	Public works and employment project (FY91)	—	20.0
São Tomé and Principe	Second multi-sector rehabilitation project (FY91)	—	6.0
Senegal	Agricultural services project (FY90)	—	17.1
Senegal	Public works and employment project (FY90)	—	20.0
Tanzania	Agricultural adjustment program (FY90)	—	200.0
Tanzania	Agricultural adjustment credit (FY91)	—	16.1
Uganda	Alleviation of poverty and the social costs of adjustment project (FY90)	—	28.0
Zaire	Pilot extension project (FY90)	—	5.9
Zambia	Social recovery project (FY91)	—	20.0
Asia			
Bangladesh	National minor irrigation development project (FY91)	—	54.0
China	Hebei agricultural development project (FY90)	—	150.0
China	Henan agricultural development project (FY91)	—	110.0
China	Irrigated agriculture intensification project (FY91)	147.1	187.9
China	Mid-Yangtze agricultural development project (FY91)	—	64.0
India	Seventh population project (FY90)	10.0	86.7
India	Punjab irrigation and drainage project (FY90)	15.0	150.0
India	Second Tamil Nadu nutrition project (FY90)	—	95.8
India	Integrated watershed development (plains) project (FY90)	7.0	55.0
India	Integrated watershed development (hills) project (FY90)	13.0	75.0
India	Integrated child development services project (FY91)	10.0	96.0
Indonesia	Provincial irrigated agricultural development project (FY91)	125.0	—
Indonesia	Yogyakarta upland area development project (FY91)	15.5	—
Lao People's Democratic Republic	Upland agricultural development project (FY90)	—	20.2
Malaysia	Rubber Industry Smallholders Development Authority project (FY90)	71.0	—
Philippines	Small coconut farms development project (FY90)	121.8	—
Philippines	Second municipal development project (FY90)	40.0	—
Philippines	Second communal irrigation development project (FY91)	46.2	—
Philippines	Rural finance project (FY91)	150.0	—
Sri Lanka	Poverty alleviation project (FY91)	—	57.5
Europe, Middle East, and North Africa			
Egypt	Social fund project (FY91)	—	140.0
Pakistan	Sindh primary education development program (FY90)	—	112.5
Pakistan	Rural water supply and sanitation project (FY91)	—	136.7
Turkey	National education development project (FY90)	90.2	—
Yemen	Health sector development project (FY90)	—	15.0
Latin America and the Caribbean			
Bolivia	Agricultural technology development project (FY91)	—	21.0
Colombia	Small-scale irrigation project (FY90)	78.2	—
Colombia	Rural development investment program (FY91)	75.0	—
Haiti	Economic and social fund (FY91)	—	11.3
Mexico	Second low-income housing project (FY90)	350.0	—
Mexico	Decentralization and regional development project (FY91)	350.0	—
Subtotal		1,736.5	2,081.6
Total IBRD and IDA			3,818.1

— Zero.

• In the area of private-sector development and public-sector management, several initiatives are aimed at enhancing income-earning opportunities for the poor—chiefly through elimination of rigidities that drive smaller businesses to the informal sector and through the development of well-functioning financial systems. In regions where industrial restructuring might involve significant social costs (Eastern Europe, for example), the Bank is helping to ensure that social safety nets will be in place to mitigate those costs.

• Within basic infrastructure, a significant effort is under way to address issues of management of urban productivity, including the productivity of the urban informal sector (see Box 3-2). The provision of social and productive infrastructure and the support of social safety nets for the urban poor continue to be emphasized.

Human-resource Development

Investments in human capital are increasingly recognized as being of central importance to sustainable development. Education, population, health, nutrition, and women-in-development concerns are becoming an integral part of virtually all aspects of development and Bank activities.

The realization that sustainable development cannot occur without investments being made in people is growing in the developing world and in the international aid community. It is translated into political commitment at the highest level and has been reflected, over the past thirteen years, in several worldwide health and education initiatives.

The Alma Ata Conference on Primary Health Care (1978) affirmed that health promotion has to be an integral part of the overall developmental and political process and aimed at attainment by all, by the year 2000, of a level of health that would enable individuals to lead socially and economically productive lives. As a follow-up, a broadly based group of international agencies and health professionals launched the Task Force for Child Survival. The goal was to immunize all the children of the world and to promote other effective health measures, ranging from oral rehydration to family planning.

The Safe Motherhood Initiative, begun at a conference in Nairobi in 1987, integrated health care for the mother with that of the child and promoted the role of women, who bear a disproportionate burden of poverty. By improving the health, nutrition, and education of women, and by providing family-planning information and services, the participants sought to reduce the half million deaths from causes related to pregnancy each year in the developing world.

As the alleviation of poverty requires not only primary health care to safeguard physical well-being but also the development of cognitive and productive skills through education and training, the launching of the World Conference on Education for All, in Jomtien, Thailand, in March 1990 was a logical and complementary step. This conference, attended by 1,500 participants, including delegates from 155 governments, reaffirmed not only that education was a "fundamental right for all people" but also that it could "help ensure a safer, healthier, more prosperous, and environmentally sound world." The conference called for universal access to basic education by the year 2000.

These international initiatives for human development were articulated at the highest political level at the World Summit for Children, held in New York in September 1990. Attended by sixty-five heads of state, the summit reiterated all previous concerns for human development. By setting the survival, protection, and development of children as the focal point of international commitment, the summit magnified the importance of education, nutrition, health, family planning, and empowerment of women and girls in building the foundation for the future.

Education. At the Jomtien conference, the president of the Bank pledged to increase education lending by the Bank over the following three years to more than $1.5 billion a year (see Box 3-3). Fiscal 1990 marked the first year in which Bank lending for education projects topped the $1 billion mark. In that year, twenty-one projects, involving Bank assistance of $1,487 million, were approved.

In fiscal 1991, Bank commitments for education projects further increased to $2,252 million for twenty-six projects. Most of the education projects were aimed either at improving the effectiveness of basic education or at upgrading the quality of training in the vocations or sciences at the secondary and tertiary levels.

For example, the Bank is supporting the Philippine government's goal of expanding access to quality education and training with a $200 million loan for an elementary education project. The project seeks to increase the levels of participation and achievement in elementary education and to reduce drop-out rates. The government is also emphasizing full implementation of free secondary education and the provision of functional literacy and livelihood skills through nonformal alternatives. Equity improvement in the educational system, with consequent long-term implications for poverty

Box 3-2. A Shift in Urban Policy

Since the early 1970s, government efforts, particularly those supported by donors, have addressed urban-growth and urban-poverty issues through low-cost investment projects in shelter, water supply, sanitation, and urban transport. Sites-and-services and slum-upgrading projects were intended to demonstrate replicable approaches that could provide benefits to the poor while recovering costs and reducing the financial burden on the public sector.

While many of these projects were reasonably successful in meeting their physical objectives, attention necessarily had to be devoted to physical implementation rather than to sustaining policy change and strengthening institutions. As a result, neither national and local-government policies nor the broader issues of managing the urban economy were greatly affected.

Building on an intensive analysis of the fiscal, financial, and real sector linkages between urban economic activities and macroeconomic performance, the Bank has developed a policy framework and strategy that redefines the urban challenge in developing countries. The framework and strategy has four main elements:

Improving urban productivity. The importance of urban economic activities in national production requires that urban productivity increase. Improved macroeconomic management, along with the easing of key constraints, is essential.

Alleviating urban poverty. Alleviation of urban poverty, caused by the short-term effects of macroeconomic adjustment and longer-term structural problems, requires an appropriate strategy to stimulate the demand for labor while ensuring, through provision of adequate social services and infrastructure, that the poor can take advantage of the opportunities provided. It also requires a safety net for the most vulnerable.

Protecting the urban environment. Because the problems associated with urban environmental degradation are poorly understood in developing countries, a major research effort is needed to identify effective approaches to their solution. Improvements to the information base and understanding of the dynamics of environmental deterioration in urban areas are needed. Needed, too, are city-specific urban environmental strategies and programs of curative action. Incentives to prevent further environmental deterioration are required.

Increasing understanding of urban issues. The need is great for research on urban issues. Priority areas for research include the linkages between the urban economy and macroeconomic aggregates, the internal efficiencies of cities and urban productivity, the urban poor and the informal sector, the financing of urban investments, the role of government in the urban-development process, and the urban environment.

How might this new urban-policy framework affect World Bank activities?

Lending for urban development, based on projects in the pipeline, is expected to increase by 45 percent during the period fiscal 1991–93. The issue, therefore, is how to ensure that the impact of Bank lending will increase with the projected expansion in lending.

Current and future Bank operations in support of urban development are being designed to include three principal elements.

Policy reform, which would improve urban productivity, is one element.

A second is institutional development, which would strengthen (a) the financial and technical capacities of municipal institutions, including reinforcement of the local capacity for operations and maintenance of citywide infrastructure and services; (b) national institutions involved in the financing of housing and infrastructure; and (c) national, regional, and municipal institutions involved in the management of the urban environment, including the formulation, monitoring, and enforcement of environmental policies and standards.

The third is investments in citywide—rather than neighborhood—infrastructure, including rehabilitation where needed, housing and land development through financial intermediaries that mobilize private savings and private-sector involvement, curative environmental improvements, slum upgrading, provision of social services, urban-transport facilities, and citywide networks of services such as markets.

Bank research into urban-development problems is scheduled to increase, as well. But, because the range of priority research areas extends beyond the current capacity of the Bank and because urban research capacity in developing countries is weak, the Bank, the Ford Foundation, and other international organizations are currently assessing the state of urban research in developing countries to determine whether substantial additional funding is needed.

*   *   *

Recognizing the need to improve urban productivity, alleviate urban poverty, and manage the urban environment, the executive directors generally endorsed the modifications in Bank thinking on urban-development issues. They devoted particular attention to the importance of policy reform and institutional development. In this context, stress was laid on the need to identify and define the respective roles of local and central governments in light of growing decentralization, especially with respect to financial concerns; to achieve the right balance of support for appropriate development of larger and smaller cities and different regions; to discourage regulation that hinders optimal urban development while fostering that which is in line with basic social welfare; and to encourage private-sector participation in providing urban services whenever feasible and desirable.

Box 3-3. Commitments by the President of the World Bank

During his term as president of the World Bank, Barber B. Conable made three public commitments that were both explicit and quantifiable, and which could be related to specific operational programs. These commitments concerned three types of lending: education; population, health, and nutrition; and forestry.

Education. In a speech at the World Conference on Education for All in Jomtien, Thailand (March 1990), Mr. Conable promised that the Bank would double its education lending over the next three years to an annual figure of more than $1.5 billion. In connection with the World Summit for Children (September 1990), Mr. Conable promised that lending for primary education would increase substantially in the future, to become the largest single element in the Bank's education program.

Lending for education has grown from $964 million in fiscal 1989 to $1.5 billion in fiscal 1990 and $2.3 billion in fiscal 1991. At the same time, lending for primary education accounted for 31 percent of education lending in fiscal 1989, 24 percent in fiscal 1990, and 36 percent in fiscal 1991. It is expected to reach nearly 50 percent in fiscal 1992.

Population, health, and nutrition. In a speech to the International Planned Parenthood Federation in Ottawa (November 1989), Mr. Conable pledged to renew the Bank's commitment to issues of population growth and substantially increase Bank lending for the delivery of effective family-planning services. He promised that the Bank would be increasing its lending to the sector to $800 million for the next three years, compared with an average of $500 million during the previous three years.

Population, health, and nutrition lending in fiscal 1990 totaled $933 million and increased to $1.6 billion in fiscal 1991.

Forestry. In a speech at an environmental conference in Tokyo in September 1989, the president of the Bank announced that the Bank would triple lending to forestry in the next few years and that there would be more direct involvement of World Bank staff in the Tropical Forestry Action Plan (TFAP).

World Bank lending for forestry rose from $90 million in fiscal 1989 to $536 million in fiscal 1990. Lending in fiscal 1991 was substantially lower, however, as the Bank completed work on a forest-policy paper. The Bank is now collaborating with other agencies in an effort to make the TFAP a more effective instrument for addressing the problems surrounding the use and conservation of tropical forests. A series of recommendations has been proposed for approval by the heads of the four agencies most directly involved. If these recommendations are adopted, the Bank will be significantly more involved in the revamped program.

---

alleviation, is being pursued by targeting investment expenditures towards the more disadvantaged areas. In addition, a system for assessing student achievement will be developed to provide the basis for improved sector-wide monitoring and evaluation.

The project's design pays close attention to the conclusions of a fiscal 1990 study on primary education—that improvements are essential in three areas: enhancement of the learning environment, the preparation and motivation of teachers, and strengthened institutional capacity of the education system.

Projects that seek to improve the quality of basic education were also approved for Brazil, Burkina Faso, the Dominican Republic, Haiti, Morocco, Mozambique, Nigeria, Rwanda, and Zaire.

While it is important for countries to extend access to basic education to all, it is equally important for them to provide opportunities for the acquisition of intermediate and advanced knowledge and skills. Countries must pursue the two strategies concurrently in order to advance development of their own economies and to be able to utilize new technologies to participate fully in the global economic network.

Creating a technological basis for development requires, for most countries, an emphasis on technology transfer. The effectiveness of technology transfer will be largely dependent on the national capacity to receive, adapt, and apply new technologies. Developing such a capacity requires investing in the education and training of scientific and technical personnel, establishing national science and research and development centers, and attracting foreign investments that will transfer technology.

In Brazil, the Bank is helping to finance the Support Program for Scientific and Technological Development (PADCT) through a $150 million loan approved in fiscal 1991. The PADCT provides support, through competitive grants for basic research and graduate training in chemistry and chemical engineering, biotechnology, the geosciences, and mineral technology. These areas were chosen because of their perceived importance for future economic development and the relative inadequacy of their human-resource base.

Other projects approved during the year that aim at enhancing vocational or scientific skills included those for Algeria, China, India, Indonesia, Korea, Mexico, Togo, and Trinidad and Tobago.

To enhance its capacity to provide both advice and assistance of high quality, the Bank has embarked on two related work programs. The first deals with higher education and advanced training, while the second focuses on science and technology. Both programs will study strategies for improving the effectiveness and efficiency of higher education in order to address the crisis many countries face in this subsector and to promote the development of the human-resource base required to adapt new technologies and participate in the global economy.

In developing an adequate training capacity, it is crucial to ensure that the outputs respond as closely as possible to labor-market demands. Following the recently completed work on vocational and technical education (see Box 3-4), the Bank launched a study on employment and labor markets. In particular, the study is identifying how government policies impede or support the competitive operation of labor markets and how they affect incentives for public and private investments in human-resource development.

As a follow-up to the call by the World Conference on Education for All to improve and implement systems for assessing learning achievement, the Bank embarked on a work program during the year to develop effective educational-assessment systems in developing countries. It is anticipated that, at the end of the three-year program, a handbook of "how to do it" tools for sector assessment based on student achievement will be published. The handbook will enable countries wishing to use achievement testing as a means for planning future growth and investments to gain a reasonable appraisal of the requirements for doing so.

In recent years, the focus of Bank lending for education has become much more sectoral and policy-oriented. To ensure that the quality of its assistance remains high, the Bank has developed a multifaceted staff-development program for its education-sector staff. The program includes training activities ranging from half-day in-house seminars to disseminate "best practices" in project design to longer seminars aimed at the development of technical skills.

The most extensive program of the latter type was carried out over the two-year period June 1989–91. Each year, two two-week workshops were organized in cooperation with the School of Education at Stanford University in the United States. Four workshops in all were held; each was attended by about twenty-five participants, which means that about 100 Bank staff benefited from the eight weeks of training. The main objective of these workshops was to bring Bank staff up to date with the latest research on issues normally addressed through the Bank's education lending.

Women in development. In fiscal 1991, further progress was made in integrating women-in-development (WID) activities into Bank operations. About 40 percent of Bank operations approved in fiscal 1991 included specific recommendations for action to integrate women into the development process. In fiscal years 1988, 1989, and 1990, the comparable percentages were 11, 22, and 30, respectively.

A detailed review of all economic and sector reports written during the year shows that 62 percent contained substantive discussions or recommendations on WID issues as compared with 41 percent in fiscal 1990 and 25 percent in fiscal 1989. Of all fiscal 1991 country macroeconomic reports, 72 percent treated WID as an important topic, compared with only 50 percent in fiscal 1990.

The Bank's main emphasis in its WID activities is to improve women's economic productivity as a way to address poverty, economic inefficiency, and other developmental problems. To improve women's economic productivity, the Bank is focusing on five areas: education, reproductive health care, agricultural services, credit and other support for women entrepreneurs, and labor-force participation. As circumstances warrant, the Bank is also taking a look at the productivity of women in forestry, water supply, and other sectors, as well as related legal issues.

Sector trends reflect the Bank's WID priorities: All projects in the population, health, and nutrition sector, as well as most of those in the small-scale enterprises sector, addressed women's concerns in fiscal 1991. More than half of all agriculture and rural-development projects addressed women's concerns, and structural-adjustment operations, more often than not, did the same. About a third of all education projects approved concerned gender issues.

As operational activity increases, Bank staff are asking for more guidelines on effective approaches for assisting women. Sector-specific guidelines on "what works," with examples of good practice, were issued for agricultural extension and primary and secondary education during the year (see Box 3-5), and work is under way on guidelines for other sectors, in conjunction with expanded research on ways to improve opportunities for women.

Box 3-4. Policies for Vocational and Technical Education and Training

In many cases, developing-country governments can best increase the technical and vocational skills of their nation's work force by improving the quality of education at the primary and secondary levels.

This was one of the three principal conclusions of a policy study on enhancing productivity skills through vocational and technical education. The study was the second building block in a comprehensive program of policy analysis and research designed to guide national investment decisions and Bank support for education and training.[1]

The heightened relevance of general education to increased productivity in skilled occupations, the study argues, has been caused by technological change, which has expanded the cognitive and theoretical knowledge required to master needed skills. Workers, therefore, must have the foundation of basic competence to make their future training effective. Competencies gained through academic secondary education of good quality affect not only immediate productivity but also the ability to learn new skills over the course of a career.

The study reports that "diversified" education programs—in which a part of the academic program is replaced with a few vocational courses—are not the answer. The limited training delivered in these programs produces equally limited skills, does little to change student aspirations for higher education and white-collar employment, and takes the place of more preparation in the basic competencies.

The policy study's second principal conclusion is that governments should seek to expand private-sector training through the creation of a favorable policy environment. The existence of such an environment demands that distortions in incentives—high minimum wages, guaranteed public employment, and narrow skill differentials in publicly administered wage systems, for example—be reduced. And, if, for political or social reasons, it proves impossible to change such policies, then adoption of "compensatory" measures may be the second-best answer. Examples of compensatory measures include exempting apprentices from the minimum-wage scale or providing partial public subsidies to employers and workers to compensate for artificially high training costs.

Governments can also act positively (rather than stop doing things) to enhance the policy environment. Employer training can be encouraged, for instance, by providing employers with information on external training opportunities,

furnishing technical assistance in the training of trainers, developing enterprise-training policies and plans, and reimbursing firms for the costs of training.[2]

Finally, the policy paper points out the need to improve the effectiveness and efficiency of public training.

In many cases, the record of public training has not been satisfactory, often because the system had been expanded to address objectives other than compensating for weak private training such as using pre-employment training to reduce youth unemployment, to create a reserve of skilled workers to attract new capital investment, or to divert youth from aspirations for higher education.

In the absence of sustained growth in wage employment, such policies have led to too many trained workers and too few jobs. Scarce public resources have been wasted. Moreover, because many countries find it difficult to provide adequate financing for these public institutions, the quality of training has often been poor and the effect on productivity minimal. The record shows, however, that training can be cost effective and can result in high placement rates when it responds to market forces.

The policy paper's recommendations clearly have implications for current and future Bank investments in vocational education.

Vocational education and technical education have been the cornerstones of Bank lending in the sector, representing 40 percent of education lending in the period 1963–76 and about one third since 1977. More than 80 percent of this lending has supported pre-employment public vocational education and training for wage employment in the modern sector.

The policy paper's framework and strategy clarifies for developing-country governments and the Bank the criteria for decisions on investments in skills development. And the Bank stands ready to support countries that want to move their training policy in the suggested directions.

---

[1] The first building block—a policy study on primary education—was the subject of a discussion by the executive board in fiscal 1990. The study's conclusions were reported in the World Bank's *Annual Report* for fiscal year 1990 (pages 59 and 60). Work is planned on two other subsectors, secondary and higher education, and on three themes—education and employment, education-sector management, and education financing.
[2] Reimbursement programs, the study notes, should be strictly monitored to protect against fraud; they also should be considered as transitional devices for building up training capacity.

In fiscal 1991, WID coordinating units were established in all four operational regions of the Bank. The units provide conceptual analysis, policy guidance, and operational support to improve the quality and range of gender-responsive economic and sector work and lending operations.

By the end of the fiscal year, the Africa region had completed fourteen WID country assessments, and, over the course of the next

Box 3-5. How to Get Girls to School (and Keep Them There)

Education for women helps families escape the "poverty equilibrium" of low income, high fertility, illness, and ignorance. In any country, education raises male or female productivity in the workplace and at home. Educated men and women earn more in self-employment or the labor force and have greater labor mobility.

Education for women—more than education for men—also leads to smaller, healthier, and often better-educated families. As education opens up new opportunities that compete with childbearing, women tend to opt to have fewer children, slowing the population growth that underlies the abundance of labor. The potential for greater productivity and economic growth, as well as the social benefits, justifies far greater investment in female education than has been provided in the past.

Although the total returns from female education are high, many societies invest less in educating women than in educating men, especially at the secondary level, where both the private and social returns to female education are particularly high. This paradox ought to be resolved.

The solution requires a deeper understanding of how parents, especially poor parents, view the benefits and costs of educating daughters. In most developing countries, education is not compulsory; parents decide whether to send children to school and for how long. They weigh the net advantages of keeping children home against the net advantages of sending them to school. For parents, though not for society, sons' education may be the better investment.

A vicious cycle ensues: Women earn less, so education flows mainly to boys while girls stay home to help the family meet immediate survival needs, and the girls cannot compete with boys or earn much when they grow up. Cultural traditions may develop that reflect and reinforce economic realities.

Remedies to promote girls' schooling can be instituted through education policies and through other policies that increase women's earning capability or save their time.

As for education policy, the experience of the past two decades suggests promising approaches. Because poor families believe that they cannot afford the direct and opportunity costs of educating girls, it is vital to deal with those costs as parents see them and to reduce them. The more the family depends on daughters for work at home, the harder it is to increase girls' enrollment and keep girls in school.

Progress can be achieved by designing school systems and curricula better-suited to families' present economic circumstances and culture and by improving the quality of education so as to satisfy whatever limited demand may already exist. Then, as more girls start, or stay in, school, social attitudes may shift and tip more decisions toward sending girls to school. Policies must be tailored to country circumstances, but the following measures often deserve consideration: "awareness campaigns" to encourage parents to educate daughters, recruitment of more female teachers, protection of girls' privacy in coeducational settings, more flexible school schedules and hours so that girls can combine schooling with chores, and allowing girls who are mothers or are pregnant to remain in, or return to, school. Where the enrollment of girls is very low, scholarships or other incentives may be important and economically justifiable on the grounds that society would reap the broad gains from female education. Often a "package approach" addressing several constraints to female schooling is more efficient than provision of one or two incentives.

A recent $159.3 million project in support of general education in Bangladesh illustrates an innovative package approach: 60 percent of newly hired teachers will be women (the Bank will help finance their salaries); satellite schools will be set up closer to children's homes; textbooks and teaching methods will be improved to remove gender stereotypes and to enhance the self-image of girls; and nongovernmental-organization programs of nonformal education, with flexible scheduling, will be supported.

three to five years, it will have completed assessments (or more-narrowly focused issues papers) for all the countries of the region. A $2.2 million stand-alone pilot WID project in Côte d'Ivoire was also approved. Increased attention to WID concerns is evident in the application of the population/agriculture/environment "nexus" in several countries, as well as in the growing number of operations that explicitly identify WID objectives.

In Asia, WID issues are brought into the mainstream of activities by capitalizing on opportunities to treat WID cross-sectorally, and a few freestanding WID projects are under consideration. For closer monitoring of WID-related activities, local full-time program officers are being recruited in Bangladesh, India, and Indonesia. All projects in the population, health, and nutrition sector, as well as urban-development and rehabilitation projects, addressed WID issues in fiscal 1991.

In the Europe, Middle East, and North Africa region, efforts to integrate women's concerns into the lending program in the population, health, and nutrition sector, as well as the education sector, have been as successful as in other regions of the Bank. The particular challenge for the region is to integrate these concerns in other sectors. Efforts are under way to integrate WID activities into social-fund projects, into emergency-recovery lending, and into agricultural projects. In the $140 million social-fund project in Egypt, for example, income-generating and micro-credit schemes involving the participation of women are being given priority, and representation of women on the boards of private voluntary organizations that are to benefit from the project is being encouraged.

Understanding of women and the factors affecting their life circumstances in Latin America generally suffers from dated and unreliable data, especially on income, and labor-force statistics have only recently been disaggregated by sex in many countries. As a result, the Bank could not obtain reliable information on women's labor-force participation, on their earnings relative to men, or on female-headed households. As the availability and quality of information have improved, several projects in the region have begun incorporating components that will benefit women; relatively few projects in the current lending portfolio are stand-alone WID projects. During the year, women's needs were specifically addressed in Colombia (two projects), El Salvador, Honduras, Mexico, and Venezuela.

Several Bank operations addressing women's needs have progressed to the point where results can be discerned. For instance, as part of its national effort to upgrade extension, the Nigerian government, several years ago, asked the Bank for help in initiating a program of agricultural-extension services for women farmers. Subsequently, a project combining research and operational support—designed by the Bank and financed by the United Nations Development Programme—was launched to develop and test ways, using existing structures, to help women farmers. This led to a women-in-agriculture (WIA) program.

Findings from the pilot project provided the basis for expanding the program in three participating Nigerian states. The Bank provided further support by assisting several state-level agricultural-development projects and by having one resident-mission staffmember work full time on the WIA program. Monitoring indicators, which compare interstate performance, were developed and formed the basis for periodic experience-sharing across states, thus helping to extend the approach to a larger number of states.

Nigeria's WIA program has made substantial progress. The number of WIA agents has increased from 425 in 1989 to more than 800. Priority has been given to improving their mobility and coverage by providing them with mopeds. The number of female contact farmers has more than tripled, especially in the northern states. Women's groups, once they begin to operate efficiently, are being encouraged to organize themselves into registered cooperatives so that they can gain access to bank credit. Several WIA programs have supported women's efforts to develop community woodlots; as a result, the women do not have to spend as much time as before gathering fuel.

The lessons learned from the WIA program—in diagnosing women's requirements, launching pilot efforts to modify the extension services to meet those requirements, and developing support from the Nigerian government through cross-fertilization of ideas and approaches among states—can be useful to other countries, in Africa and elsewhere. In the next several years, the Bank expects other projects to reach similar maturity, as its policy and research work on WID expands.

Population, health, and nutrition. The volume of lending in the population, health, and nutrition (PHN) sector continued to grow in fiscal 1991. Twenty-eight projects, with commitments totaling $1,568 million, were approved, reflecting a growth in the number of operations of 56 percent and in loan and credit amounts of 68 percent over the previous year. (In fiscal 1990, growth in the number of projects approved and lending volume over fiscal 1989 amounts was 64 percent and 70 percent, respectively.) In the five years (fiscal 1983–87) before the president of the Bank announced that lending for PHN would be doubled over a period of several years, commitments to the sector averaged $205 million.

About two-fifths of the projects approved in fiscal 1991 were in the Africa region, while six projects were approved for Middle Eastern and North African countries.

Of the twenty-eight projects, twenty-three can be categorized as straight population, health, and nutrition projects (valued at $1,332.9 million), while five were social-development projects, valued at $234.7 million. Social-development projects were approved for Egypt, Haiti, Honduras, Yemen, and Zaire. One beneficiary group of the $140 million project in Egypt, which provides funds for training, microenterprise creation, and labor-intensive public works, is the mass of workers who were forced to return to the country during the Gulf crisis.

There are a number of reasons for the momentum of actual and forecasted growth in PHN lending. First, while population issues have been accorded high priority by the Bank for many years, efforts are currently being intensified to stimulate a demand for, and a consequent increase in, operations in the sector. Second, the demand for family planning and other population interventions is expected to continue to grow, as more governments, particularly those in Africa, come to appreciate fully the negative effect that population growth has on development prospects, as well as the health benefits of family-planning services. Third, human development is accorded high priority, in the context of overall economic reform and development objectives, by both national policymakers and the Bank. Human development, in turn, is supported by various types of Bank interventions, including PHN operations, as well as PHN components in social-development projects and structural-adjustment and sector-adjustment operations.

Fourth, in keeping with *World Development Report 1990*'s analysis of poverty issues, the Bank is placing the highest priority on activities to reduce poverty, an important component of which is the provision of basic social services to the poor. Fifth, many countries' health sectors, in particular, are currently poorly organized and financed, and face both rapidly escalating service costs and expanding consumer demand. Finally, the growth in nutrition activities is accelerating and is expected to continue in terms of its presence in PHN lending, as well as its presence in other multi-sectoral operations and structural-adjustment lending.

Recent lending by the Bank in the PHN sector has been marked by a change in the way the Bank identifies potential investments.

The increased emphasis at the macroeconomic level on human-resource development and social-sector reforms, by the Bank and national governments alike, has set the stage for more prominent and promising Bank interventions in the PHN sector. A growing number of discussions on structural-adjustment operations have culminated in the launching of human-development programs that are supported directly by Bank lending.

Recent Bank investments also reflect an increasing appreciation of the unequivocal importance of strong institutional capacity and sound management skills and practices in achieving PHN-sector objectives. Virtually all PHN projects approved during both fiscal 1990 and 1991 included some provision for improving the efficiency of programs and services through interventions to strengthen management.

Bank investments in the PHN sector are financing, in general, larger proportions of recurrent-cost components than they have in the past. The focus of Bank work has been on improving the effectiveness and efficiency of priority activities and services, and expanding them prudently when their financial sustainability can be reasonably ensured.

The Environment

The Bank's environmental strategies have three interconnected dimensions: the relationship between environmental degradation and poverty; the effect that today's resource-use patterns have on the development options of future generations; and the interdependence of environmental problems on a transnational scale.

Adverse environmental effects are felt immediately by the poor, urban and rural: through health consequences of urban air and water pollution; crop losses from increasing erosion due to deforestation; consumption losses as a result of forgone production of minor forest products, caused by the loss of forest cover; increased labor costs of gathering water and fuelwood; and crop losses and damage to irrigation systems due to the destabilization of hydrological patterns. In turn, the persistence of poverty, combined with rapid population expansion, contributes to environmental pressures by forcing the poor to exert unsustainable demands on natural resources through overgrazing in reduced common spaces, deforestation to expand the agricultural frontier or to obtain fuelwood, and pollution from systems of waste disposal and energy use.

Environmental degradation also forces intractable choices between the needs of the current generation and those of the unborn. The risks to the planet of current production and consumption patterns are subject to considerable technical debate. Yet there is little doubt that substantial adjustments are needed in technologies, policies, and institutions to achieve environmental sustainability.

Environmental problems transcend national boundaries, and awareness about them is increasing. It is thought that about 100 species become extinct daily. Concentrations of discharged chlorofluorocarbons in the atmosphere, which are believed to be growing at about 5 percent annually, result in the depletion of the ozone layer and increase exposure to damaging ultraviolet rays. Other forms of modification of the atmosphere may be contributing to global warming. Finally, there is the growing problem of transboundary pollution and hazardous-waste disposal, particularly in marine environments.

Responsibility for the generation, as well as the solution, of global environmental problems is shared by developing and industrial countries; thus, for example, while past accumulations of "greenhouse" gases have largely come from industrial countries, future growth is likely to come increasingly from the developing countries. This common responsibility highlights the necessity of multilateral arrangements for remedial action and burden sharing (see Box 3-6).

While lack of information and appropriate methodologies still stand in the way of swift action in some environmental areas, much is known today, and research is under way to expand knowledge. Five clusters of priority environmental problems in the coming decade have emerged: destruction of natural habitats, including tropical moist forests; land degradation; degradation and depletion of fresh-water resources; urban, industrial, and agricultural pollution; and degradation of the global commons.

The development of environmental awareness, the lowering of population growth rates in many developing countries, the identification and solution of country-specific environmental problems, and the coordination and design of funding channels to address local costs of global environmental problems will be important elements of the development agenda for the 1990s. Work on *World Development Report 1992,* which focuses on the relationship between development and the sustainable use of environmental resources, is under way and will cover many of the concerns that will be raised at the United Nations Conference on Environment and Development, to be held in Brazil in 1992.

At its September 1990 meeting, the Development Committee reiterated the importance of integrating environmental concerns into the Bank's operations. The integration of these concerns into Bank operations continued throughout the past fiscal year. Consequences of this are that the distinction between environmental and other work in the Bank—whether research or lending operations—is becoming increasingly blurred, and that concern and responsibility for environmental work, as well as the relevant expertise, are now widely diffused throughout the institution.

Formal responsibility for environmental work in the Bank continues to be shared among several units. The Environment Department is responsible for setting overall strategic objectives, carrying out the necessary research, preparing guidelines, conducting staff training, and handling external-relations issues relating to the Bank's environmental work. It has also the newly acquired responsibility of administering the Global Environment Facility. Environmental divisions located in the technical departments of each of the regions have day-to-day responsibility for ensuring the quality of Bank operations, focusing not only on individual projects but also on more strate-

gic approaches to addressing environmental problems on a country or regional basis. As far as the total effort of the operations complex is concerned, this is only the tip of the iceberg. Increasingly, country-operations departments and other technical-department divisions are taking responsibility for environmental work and for recruiting staff, who are given specific environmental responsibilities. Evaluation of environmental aspects of Bank operations is also of growing significance in the work of the Operations Evaluation Department and the Economic Development Institute (see pages 88 and 89, respectively).

Estimates of the amount of staff effort devoted to environmental work in the Bank are difficult to make, in large part because of the extent to which environment is now becoming integral to a wide range of Bank activities. There are currently 106 high-level and thirty-four support staff in the Environment Department and the four regional environment divisions. These staff include economists, sociologists, engineers, land-use planners, ecologists, foresters, anthropologists, and institutional experts. There are also a number of operational divisions that have specific environmental functions. Overall, based on time recorded by staff, approximately 270 staffyears were devoted to forestry or environment in fiscal 1991, corresponding to about 10 percent of total Bank staff time.

Of the 229 projects approved in fiscal 1991, eleven were categorized as having diverse and significant environmental effects (category A), while another 102 were characterized as having the potential for more limited and specific environmental effects (category B).

Project assessments are meant to ensure that development options are environmentally sound and sustainable (participation of local communities is therefore central to the process) and that any environmental consequences are recognized early in the project cycle and are taken account of in project design.

Continued progress in integrating environmental concerns into the Bank's operations is illustrated by the number of projects with environmental components or objectives approved in fiscal 1991. In all, fourteen of the projects approved had primarily environmental objectives (projects are deemed to be "primarily" environmental if either environmental costs or benefits exceed 50 percent of total costs or benefits). The fourteen projects represent total lending of about $1.5 billion. In addition, many projects were approved during the year which, while not primarily environmental, addressed one or more environmental

Box 3-6. The Global Environment Facility

Responsibility for the amelioration of environmental problems is shared by industrialized and developing nations alike. Past accumulations of "greenhouse" gases, for example, have largely come from the former, while future growth in emissions is likely to come increasingly from the latter group. Developing countries will need assistance in taking steps to protect the "global commons."

But what is to be done when a country must bear the costs for environmental protection, while a portion of the benefits accrues to the global community? Under certain circumstances, might not there be a need for concessionary financing?

The establishment of a separate facility to do just that was proposed by France—and supported by Germany and other nations—at the Development Committee discussions in 1989. As a result, twenty-five developed and developing nations agreed in November 1990 to establish a Global Environment Facility (GEF), to be run jointly by the Bank, the United Nations Development Programme (UNDP), and the United Nations Environment Programme.

With total financing available of about $1.5 billion, the GEF will become operational in mid 1991.

The goal of the three-year pilot program is to provide resources to help finance innovative programs and projects affecting the global environment that would not normally be funded, and to do so in a manner that explores how developing countries can deal pragmatically with these issues, at low cost, and without impeding development. It is expected that the relevant experience derived from its operations in dealing with global environmental challenges will be taken into consideration in the World Bank's regular operations.

Four areas were selected for the operations of the facility.

Protecting the ozone layer. Developing countries will be assisted in making the transition from the use and production of chlorofluorocarbons and other gases—which contribute to the deterioration of the ozone layer—to available substitutes and alternatives.[1]

Limiting greenhouse-gas emissions. Areas for action by the facility include the adoption of cleaner fuels and technologies in the energy, agriculture, and industry sectors, as well as some reforestation and forest conservation.

Protecting biodiversity. The richest remaining sources of ecological systems and diversity of species—which contribute to a wide range of goods and services, including harvestable medicines or industrial products, genetic resources for food production, and the regulation of climatic and rainfall patterns—are in developing countries. The facility will support efforts to preserve specific areas.

Protecting international waters. The facility will support programs to enhance contingency planning for marine oil spills; to abate industrial and wastewater pollution that affects international marine and freshwater resources; to improve reception facilities for removing ballast from ships in ports; to prevent and clean up toxic-waste pollution along major rivers that affect international watercourses; and to conserve unique water bodies.

All developing countries with UNDP programs and that had a per capita gross national product of $4,000 or less in 1989 will be eligible for GEF funding for investment projects and technical assistance.

While most projects will be country specific, some regional projects (biodiversity in adjacent areas in two countries, for instance) will also qualify. Projects will be designed so as to ensure that there is a clear distinction between GEF and regular development programs and projects.

In addition, to qualify, projects must be consistent with global environmental conventions and with country-specific environmental strategies or programs, and be both cost effective and of high priority from a global perspective.

The three implementing agencies will develop work programs of investments, scientific and technical support, and technical assistance that follow these guidelines.

The GEF will be composed of a core fund, to which contributions on a voluntary basis and in convertible currency may be made in the form of grants, and a cofinancing agreement, funded through concessional loans or grants provided on a bilateral basis, to cofinance activities supported by the core fund.

The countries that have provided contributions are Austria, Brazil, China, Denmark, Egypt, Finland, France, Germany, India, Indonesia, Italy, Japan, Mexico, the Netherlands, Norway, Pakistan, Spain, Sweden, Switzerland, Turkey, and the United Kingdom. The United States has pledged to provide parallel funds to support GEF types of investments. At the end of the fiscal year, contributions to the GEF amounted to about $371 million.

---

[1] The GEF's work in this area will be coordinated with the implementation of the Montreal Protocol to phase out the use of substances harmful to the ozone layer. The Montreal Protocol already has an Interim Multilateral Fund as part of a financing mechanism established by its contracting parties. Specific procedures for the functions of this fund have already been agreed to by the contracting parties. Resources allocated to the World Bank for investment-project financing will be included under the GEF in an Ozone Projects Trust Fund, which would be kept separate from the GEF's core fund. Funding for ozone-related projects will normally be drawn from the Ozone Projects Trust Fund, which would apply only to countries that are signatories to the Montreal Protocol.

issues. Excluding projects whose environmental costs or benefits amount to less than 10 percent of total costs or benefits, almost 40 percent of projects approved in fiscal 1991 had significant environmental components.

The supervision of several projects approved in earlier years, some of which have been controversial, continued to command considerable staff effort during the past year. Such projects included the National Land Management and Livestock project in Botswana; the Sardar Sarovar Dam project in India; the Singrauli Thermal Power project, also in India; the Kedung Ombo project in Indonesia; the Carajás Iron Ore project in Brazil; and the Northwest III Settlement (Polonoroeste) project in Brazil. This supervision has been concerned with measures to protect the environment and to mitigate the potential adverse effects of certain investments on local populations.

Fiscal 1991 saw the completion of the *Environmental Assessment Sourcebook*.[9] This 800-page reference manual, published in three volumes, codifies all the Bank's environmental policies and guidelines into one source. The sourcebook is aimed primarily at borrowers' environmental-assessment teams that need to know how to implement Bank environmental-assessment policies and how the Bank expects the environmental-assessment process to be conducted. All relevant sectors and all types of projects with potential for major environmental effects are addressed, with emphasis on large infrastructure projects. Effects are outlined in energy, agriculture, industry, transportation, urban development, and water-supply and sewerage projects.

The Bank also responded to the importance attached by the Development Committee to initiatives to provide greater protection for tropical forests and to promote energy efficiency and conservation in developed and developing countries.

A draft forest-policy paper, which suggests ways in which the international community can work together to check deforestation and increase fuelwood supplies, was prepared in fiscal 1991. The paper also proposes specific actions by the Bank, including a total ban on the financing of commercial logging activities in primary tropical moist forests. The draft policy study was the subject of an executive-board seminar. A revised version of the paper will be presented to the board in fiscal 1992.

A Bank task force on energy efficiency and conservation was set up during fiscal 1991. The task force is reviewing the potential options for securing greater energy efficiency, conservation, and accompanying technology transfer in a developing-country context. It is also gathering and summarizing relevant Bank experience, identifying gaps in knowledge, and targeting major areas of opportunity. The information generated by the task force is to be used to strengthen a forthcoming Bank policy paper on energy-sector issues.

During the past year, it became increasingly evident that the Bank's four operational regions are going in different ways in integrating environmental concerns into their work programs. This outcome is to be expected, for environmental concerns vary from region to region.

In Africa, for instance, the large number of developing member countries has dictated that emphasis be placed on the development of national environmental-action plans (NEAPs). NEAPs have been completed or are nearing completion in Burkina Faso, Ghana, Guinea, Lesotho, Madagascar, Mauritius, Rwanda, and the Seychelles. Other countries—including Benin, Burundi, The Gambia, Guinea-Bissau, Nigeria, Togo, and Uganda—have begun to take steps in the same direction.

The NEAP process provides a framework for integrating environmental considerations into a nation's economic and social development. The process is "demand driven"—that is, it is initiated in response to requests from countries and starts with a comprehensive review of environmental issues to determine national priorities. It is a product of local participation within the various parts of the government, as well as with local administrations, civic groups, research and academic institutions, nongovernmental organizations, and other private-sector actors. Many international partners are also involved. The Bank's Africa region provided the initial impetus and stimulation to such activities as a service to its member countries. But special care has been taken to avoid the temptation, so often faced in development assistance, to take over the work and "do the job" for the country.

During fiscal 1991, a "Club of Dublin" was formed to provide support for the NEAP process and, specifically, to contribute to the full incorporation of environment issues into development in Africa. While not directly involved in fund raising, the club, which is made up of African nations and interested donors, is expected to be instrumental in mobilizing discussion, review, and support for actions and programs for which it will build a consensus.

During fiscal 1991, many of the environmental problems that relate especially to Asia were

9 World Bank, *Environmental Assessment Sourcebook* (Washington, D.C., 1991).

addressed. These problems include soil degradation (half of India's arable land is degraded through erosion, compaction, and salinization), disappearing forests (at the rate of 2 million hectares a year), and poor air quality (especially in the region's largest cities).

A $155.6 million loan to India was approved to control industrial pollution. Although the main focus of the project is on strengthening the government's monitoring and enforcement agencies, the project also helps industry to mend its polluting ways through the construction of waste-treatment plants and the like. In the Philippines, a $224 million sectoral-adjustment loan was designed to deal with some of that country's most pressing environmental problems in rural areas concerning the sustainability of forests, fisheries, and upland agricultural areas. Industrial pollution in the Philippines is the target of another project still in preparation. Two projects in China, addressing urban environmental concerns (in Beijing and Liaoning), are in advanced stages of preparation.

Work also began on a report that is looking at what lies behind the region's environmental problems; the study has been designed to provide the basis for a comprehensive strategy to deal with them. Work on the $2.5 million Metropolitan Environmental Improvement Programme—established in late 1989 by the United Nations Development Programme and the Bank—intensified; the program's focus is on how better management can reverse the process of urban environmental decline in Beijing, Bombay, Colombo, Jakarta, and Manila.

In the Europe, Middle East, and North Africa region, the focus is on environmental rehabilitation in Eastern Europe and implementation of the Mediterranean Environmental Technical Assistance Program (METAP), a major component of the Environmental Program for the Mediterranean. METAP is funded by the Commission of the European Communities, the European Investment Bank, the United Nations Development Programme, and the World Bank.

In accordance with METAP priorities, programming of activities is focused on the southern and eastern Mediterranean countries, where financial-resource constraints, particularly of foreign exchange, are the tightest and where development problems stem from unsustainable levels of resource use. Mediterranean countries need to adopt more stringent pollution-control measures, hazardous-waste programs, coastal-zone management plans, and wildlife-conservation programs.

Reflecting the importance of local participation to the ultimate implementation and sustainability of environmental-policy measures, particular emphasis has been placed on the establishment of close dialogue at the regional, national, provincial, and local levels. METAP is active in ten countries (Algeria, Cyprus, Egypt, Greece, Israel, Malta, Spain, Tunisia, Turkey, and Yugoslavia).

The Bank's environmental-assistance strategy in Eastern Europe has been based on initial economic work that has led to subsequent policy and project-lending programs. A variety of approaches has been designed to meet differing country needs and to explore alternative assistance mechanisms. However, governments and the Bank are recognizing the importance of such policy-reform measures as increased energy prices and the need to strengthen environmental institutions. These initiatives are seen as the first step to rehabilitating the environment.

Environmental-assistance strategies in this subregion are being made part of the larger picture of economic reform and are an inseparable part of the restructuring process in the industrial and energy sectors. Environmental concerns are integral to the reform process because they relate directly to the quality of life and the political perception of social progress under reform. Thus, in Poland, the Bank is financing a project that provides technical assistance to help that country to strengthen its ability to analyze and design a series of policy, regulatory, institutional, and investment actions it plans to undertake to improve environmental quality.

In Latin America and the Caribbean, institutional strengthening has become the dominant theme in environmental-assistance strategies. The Bank has prepared overview papers on the environmental issues facing all of its borrowing countries in the region. The papers pinpoint the main environmental problems, explore their underlying causes, and propose possible solutions. A common theme in many of the studies is the need to strengthen the national and provincial authorities responsible for regulating and policing the environment. Until the institutional framework is adequate, it will be difficult to attain the Bank's broader aim of reducing poverty and restoring growth in a way that ensures that natural resources are neither used up nor polluted beyond the environmental point of no return.

The landmark Bank-supported program in Brazil, begun in fiscal 1990, assists the country's national environment program by strengthening the central environment authority and four state-level environment-protection bodies. Experience gained in Brazil is now being applied in new Bank-supported programs to bolster national environment agencies in Ecuador and Mexico. Similar efforts are under way in Bolivia, the Caribbean region, Chile, Colombia, Paraguay, and Venezuela. The Bank, together with the government of Brazil and the Commission of the European Communities, prepared a proposal for a pilot program to protect the tropical rainforests of the Amazon region. This action was requested by the heads of state of the seven major industrialized countries at the 1990 economic summit, held in Houston. A national forestry policy is being prepared as part of this initiative.

The World Bank and the Environment, the Bank's first annual report to the public on its environmental activities, was published in September 1990. It covers activities that took place in fiscal 1990. The second annual report will be published early in fiscal 1992.

Debt and Debt-service Reduction: A Review of Progress

In fiscal 1989, the executive directors approved the use of World Bank resources to support debt-reduction and debt-service–reduction (DDSR) operations for heavily indebted, middle-income countries. Conditions for Bank support in the financing of such operations, and guidelines for the extent of such participation, were set.[10]

When the program was approved, directors requested that regular reviews and evaluations be conducted. The first such review was undertaken by the directors in fiscal 1990; a second review took place in March 1991.

Since the start of the program, a total of five DDSR operations have been supported—in chronological order, for Mexico, the Philippines, Costa Rica, Venezuela, and Uruguay.

The objectives of the program are to help debtors resolve problems of excessive debt and restore country creditworthiness.

Countries using the program have succeeded in obtaining debt relief while also materially enhancing their prospects for restoring growth, subject to their continued pursuit of appropriate adjustment policies and avoidance of adverse external shocks. Early evidence in the cases of Mexico and Venezuela suggests that creditworthiness is also beginning to be restored. Capital repatriation and foreign direct investment seem to have increased following the conclusion of debt-reduction operations coupled with successful adjustment programs.

It is too early, however, to determine whether voluntary lending will be resumed on a more general basis. That will depend both on debtors' continued sound policies and on the strategies of lenders. The banking community generally has been able to "quarantine" its developing-country exposure. Nevertheless, certain challenges to the program remain.

Of twenty middle-income countries identified as severely indebted,[11] only five have benefited from World Bank support, and the addition of other countries to the list of beneficiaries continues to prove slow and difficult.[12] Realistically, however, protracted negotiations should be expected. The instruments are complex, and, in some cases, new. Several of the outstanding cases also involve starting positions characterized by large arrears and the absence of a track record of adjustment.

The existence of large and widespread arrears makes it harder to reach additional agreements and increases the Bank's need to exercise careful judgment when providing support for DDSR operations. The Bank's role of supporting debtors through its policy dialogue, as well as through its general and structural-adjustment lending, is vital to the continued success of the program, as is the IMF's role of encouraging macroeconomic reforms.

Despite these difficulties, progress has been made under the debt strategy. Two countries—Egypt and Poland—have received exceptional debt relief from the Paris Club; five countries—Argentina, Brazil, Bolivia, Ecuador, and Poland—are at various stages of discussions with their banks; five are beneficiaries as has been reported earlier; Morocco has an agreement in principle with the banks; and two countries—Chile and Morocco—have used, or are expected to use, multilateral resources in support of debt reduction.

In their fiscal 1991 review, the executive directors generally agreed that the program was working according to its objectives and that no

---

[10] For details, see pages 49 and 50 of the World Bank's *Annual Report* for fiscal year 1989.

[11] Argentina, Bolivia, Brazil, Chile, the Congo, Costa Rica, Côte d'Ivoire, Ecuador, Egypt, Honduras, Hungary, Mexico, Morocco, Nicaragua, Peru, the Philippines, Poland, Senegal, Uruguay, and Venezuela.

[12] Morocco may be the closest. It signed an agreement with its Bank Advisory Committee in June 1990 providing for a rescheduling of commercial-bank debt. In addition, the agreement included waivers that allow Morocco to buy back debt at market prices and implement a debt-equity swap program. The banks have indicated that they would participate in a debt-reduction and debt-service–reduction operation if the country agrees to an Extended Fund Facility program with the International Monetary Fund (IMF) prior to December 31, 1991.

Outside the framework of the Brady initiative, banks have responded to Chile's strong economic performance by rescheduling $1.87 billion of amortization payments from the 1983–84 and 1985 reschedulings that would have begun to fall due between 1991 and 1994. Debt-equity swaps continue to be an important vehicle for reducing commercial-bank debt, and there has been a shift toward use of swaps for privatization.

changes in the guidelines were necessary, although a number of directors noted that continued flexibility in implementation of the guidelines will be needed in future cases. The more widespread existence of arrears was viewed with particular concern by the directors, who cautioned that the utmost care should be exercised when the Bank considers lending to countries in arrears. The appropriateness of the case-by-case approach was confirmed.

Some directors also noted with concern the slow pace of debt and debt-service agreements, while recognizing the circumstances causing the pace. Directors emphasized the need for the Bank to continue to monitor debt-reduction negotiations closely and, at appropriate times, to communicate to the negotiating parties the modalities of the potential support from its set-aside funds, from its direct-lending arrangements that a borrower can use for approved debt-reduction and credit-enhancement programs, from its guarantees of interest payments, or from waivers of its negative-pledge clause (see Box 3-7). They reaffirmed that sustainable macroeconomic and financing plans must be an inseparable part of any operation aimed at reducing debt and debt-service obligations in order to ensure a viable situation after that operation, and that all involved parties must be seen as carrying their fair share of the burden.

In fiscal 1992, a further review of the program will be presented to the board, which will evaluate the merits and impacts of the program in order to recommend its possible extension beyond the initial three years.

Lower-middle-income countries with high levels of official debt. The DDSR program is aimed at middle-income countries with large private debt. Concerns have been raised, as well, about the situation of heavily indebted, lower-middle-income countries that are mainly indebted to official creditors. The large share of debt to official creditors means that market-based reduction of private debt can play only a limited role in the financial strategy of these countries, even though a substantial reduction of existing commercial-bank debt and debt service could help alleviate payments difficulties—in some cases, significantly.

The experiences of the group of fifteen countries that are mainly indebted to official creditors and that have had Paris Club reschedulings since 1982[13] differ widely with respect to growth, the stance of policies, economic performance, and development prospects. In defining strategies to deal with the problems of their indebtedness, the experiences of those countries that have maintained or reestablished normal relations with creditors under-

score the critical importance of two elements. One is the need for comprehensive, medium-term adjustment programs, with particular emphasis on structural changes to restore investor confidence and generate the private inflows that will be essential for the success of growth-oriented reforms. The other is the need to maintain access to those sources of financing that are willing to support adjustment and development efforts while rebuilding access to other financing sources that can underpin growth in the future.

Some progress has been made with respect to these countries, as well. The Paris Club has begun to offer longer maturities as a follow-up to the 1990 Houston economic summit's admonition to consider options to address the official debt problem. Four lower-middle-income countries (the Congo, El Salvador, Honduras, and Morocco) and one low-income, oil-exporting country (Nigeria) have benefited from longer maturities and grace periods on reschedulings.[14]

Recent, more far-reaching understandings with Poland and Egypt through the Paris Club provide for reducing the net present value of future debt-service payments by 50 percent. Over and above this relief, individual creditors may convert part of the debt into local-currency obligations through debt-for-equity, debt-for-environment, or debt-for-development swaps. The programs for Poland and Egypt are seen as being unique, however.

Paris Club discussions have demonstrated the potential—given the requisite commitment and determination on the part of both creditors and debtors—of attaining, through a careful case-by-case review, substantial debt relief (through options for debt and debt-service reduction or for a package of new money) for those lower-middle-income countries that are pursuing sound economic reform.

In addition, a number of individual bilateral official creditors have made important contributions by implementing their own debt-relief and debt-forgiveness measures for countries in this group. Despite these achievements, however, many lower-middle-income countries

---

[13] Cameroon, the Congo, Costa Rica, Côte d'Ivoire, the Dominican Republic, Ecuador, Egypt, El Salvador, Honduras, Jamaica, Jordan, Morocco, Peru, the Philippines, and Poland. The Paris Club is the name given to the ad hoc meetings of creditor governments that, since 1956, have arranged, when necessary, for the renegotiation of intergovernmental debt and of officially guaranteed private export credits.

[14] In March 1991, Nigeria also signed an agreement in principle with its commercial-bank advisory committee. The amount of commercial debt affected by the agreement is about $4.5 billion.

Box 3-7. The IBRD's Negative-pledge Policy and Debt and Debt-service Reduction Operations

Negative-pledge clauses are concerned with the granting of security interests by a borrower over its assets to its creditors. By the terms of such a clause, the borrower agrees with a creditor or group of creditors to restrictions on its granting, or otherwise permitting to exist, security interests in favor of other creditors.

Negative-pledge clauses are usually standard in Bank loan documents. The reverse is also true: The Bank does not seek, in making loans, special security from its borrowers.

The Bank has always recognized, however, that given the far-reaching scope of the negative-pledge clause, it has to be administered with some flexibility. Most of the time, waivers of the clause have been granted in only two types of situations: when the waiver was not considered to pose any risk to the Bank as a creditor and in case of liens created by government-owned or government-controlled entities on their own assets and as security for their own borrowings.

Developments in the overall debt strategy have led borrowers from the Bank to seek waivers in circumstances and involving magnitudes that may have major implications for the Bank.

In late 1987, the Bank was asked to grant a limited waiver to Mexico in relation to the issuance by Mexico of bonds in exchange for a larger principal amount of commercial-bank loans.

The Bank had to be concerned about the possible adverse effect the waiver would have on its status as a preferred creditor and the possible negative consequences for the Bank's borrowing program. But it also had to be concerned about the effects on its requesting borrowing member: If the waiver were granted, would it be reasonable to expect that, as a result, the country's creditworthiness would be improved?

In the case of Mexico, the Bank concluded, for a variety of reasons, that the waiver was justified.

Subsequently, in May 1990, the Bank agreed to provide a limited waiver of its negative-pledge clause for Costa Rica, even though no Bank financing was provided for the country's debt and debt-service reduction (DDSR) operation. The case was deemed to be unique in that the timing of the operation prevented the Bank from providing direct financial support. The circumstances precluding Bank funding were, however, viewed as temporary, and the Bank decided that a waiver was justified in this case just as it would have been had the Bank been directly supporting the operation. And in December 1990, the Bank granted a waiver of the negative-pledge restriction in its loan agreements with Venezuela up to an amount equivalent to $2,000 million for collateral provided for bonds issued under that country's 1990 financing plan. Under that plan, Venezuela's commercial-bank creditors agreed to exchange eligible debt for new instruments involving DDSR and to provide new money.

As countries seek to obtain financial-relief agreements with their commercial creditors under the revised debt strategy or to obtain new credits after completing DDSR operations, it is likely that they will request the Bank to provide waivers in situations that are less than clear-cut. Requests for waivers of the negative-pledge clause in respect of DDSR operations for which the Bank is not providing financing are likely to continue. Sovereign borrowers may seek waivers from the Bank in order to obtain secured new money borrowings. Countries with severe debt problems may also seek to raise additional capital from increasingly reluctant international markets. It is likely, in such cases, that creditors will seek special protection for any loans as a condition of lending. In these circumstances, member countries may seek waivers in order to secure these borrowings.

Early in fiscal 1991, the executive directors reviewed the Bank's policy of granting waivers to the Bank's negative-pledge clause in respect of DDSR operations.

There was a consensus that the Bank should continue to grant waivers for DDSR operations on a case-by-case basis according to its current policy. In addition, directors endorsed a recommendation to permit waivers, also, for such transactions within certain limits in cases in which the Bank was not providing financial support in order to permit efficient follow-on transactions for DDSR.

It was agreed that the Bank should continue to refuse to grant waivers for new-money transactions that were part of concerted-financing packages. As for other new-money waivers, the directors agreed to keep the matter under review.

with substantial amounts of official debt continue to experience severe debt-servicing problems.

Severely indebted, low-income countries. Progress continues to be made in reducing the burden of debt for this group of countries through debt-relief measures provided by their major creditors—the official bilateral lending and credit-guarantee agencies. Many of these creditors have converted official development assistance loans to grants, and the Paris Club has provided reschedulings with concessional options.

Between October 1988 and July 1991, fourteen countries obtained Paris Club reschedulings of $5.3 billion in debt on the basis of a menu of options (so-called "Toronto terms") that includes reduced interest, very long grace and repayment periods (at commercial rates), or partial write-offs of debt-service obligations during the consolidation period (with the rest rescheduled at commercial rates).

Commercial debt of these countries constitutes a relatively small portion of their total external debt. However, due to the nonconcessional nature of the terms of this debt compared with the more concessional official debt, the contractual-service burden for commercial debt is often relatively large. There are, moreover, few mechanisms for easing the burden of this commercial debt, in contrast with Paris Club arrangements for bilateral official debt. One mechanism that came into play for the first time in fiscal 1991 was the Debt Reduction Facility for IDA-only Countries, which was established during the previous year and whose finances are derived from the transfer to it of $100 million of fiscal 1989 IBRD net income.

The first grant from the facility was approved—to the Banque centrale des états de l'Afrique de l'Ouest for Niger's debt-reduction program. The grant consisted of two elements: $10 million from the resources contributed to the facility by the IBRD and $3 million contributed to the facility by Switzerland. In addition, France made a parallel grant of $10 million.

Following approval of the grant by the Bank's executive directors, an exchange offer was made to Niger's creditor banks in January 1991. The operation was completed two months later, and virtually all of that country's commercial-bank debt was eliminated. In May 1991, a second grant of $10 million from the facility was made to Mozambique. That amount, together with contributions of up to $12.87 million from France, the Netherlands, Sweden, and Switzerland, would allow Mozambique to repurchase its outstanding debt owed to commercial creditors at a substantial discount of the face value of its principal debt of $193 million. Fourteen other low-income countries—the total combined debt under discussion is about $2 billion—have requested the use of this facility. The discussions are the furthest along for Bolivia.

These developments are encouraging. Yet, they have not been sufficient to resolve the debt difficulties of most of the severely indebted, low-income countries. Actual debt service is less than half the scheduled debt service for this group of countries. Although reschedulings on Toronto terms have helped, they have an implicit grant element of but about 20 percent—low for countries that need highly concessional assistance.

In this regard, the recent proposals made at the Trinidad meeting of the Commonwealth by John Major, then U.K. Chancellor of the Exchequer, and by Jan P. Pronk, the Netherlands Minister for Development Cooperation, would represent a deepening of concessionality in the existing debt-relief measures.

The Trinidad terms, if accepted and implemented, would reduce the stock of outstanding debt owed to Paris Club creditors by two thirds.[15] This would increase the grant element of official bilateral debt and debt-service reduction from about 20 percent to 67 percent. Mr. Pronk's proposal would cancel all bilateral official debt of the poorest developing countries facing severe debt problems, conditional on their implementing sound economic policies.

Private-sector Development: Strengthening the World Bank Group's Effort

Private initiative and competitive markets play a critical role in fostering dynamic and flexible economies. Support for private-sector development (PSD), therefore, is an essential element in efforts to achieve the World Bank Group's fundamental objective—to raise standards of living and reduce poverty.[16]

The World Bank Group's support for private-sector development is long-standing. Its focus was articulated anew in the action program adopted in 1989, which laid out ways in which the Bank could help its member countries define proper boundaries between the public and private sectors in developing countries and foster private-sector development as a means of promoting equitable growth.[17]

The action program identified four key activities to help promote PSD:

• creating business environments conducive to maximizing the private sector's contribution to development;

• restructuring public sectors to improve efficiency and to concentrate on services complementary to private activity;

• improving resource mobilization and allocation through financial-sector development; and

• directly fostering private enterprise through resource transfers and providing other support for entrepreneurial efforts.

The business environment. The creation of a supportive business environment, including the appropriate legal and regulatory framework, continues to be a primary objective of recent adjustment operations. Some 73 percent of the adjustment operations approved in the two-year period calendar 1989–90 have had PSD components addressing the business environment. There has also been a large increase during the

---

[15] For details, see footnote on page 46.

[16] The World Bank Group includes the World Bank, the International Finance Corporation, and the Multilateral Investment Guarantee Agency.

[17] For details, see pages 55–58 of the World Bank's *Annual Report* for fiscal year 1989.

past two years in the proportion of investment operations that work to enlarge the range of activities open to private agents, including noncommercial voluntary organizations.

Public-sector restructuring. Public-sector restructuring components have become increasingly important in Bank adjustment operations, as well, as countries move from basic policy reforms to institutional reforms. Adjustment operations are the major vehicle for Bank involvement in public-sector restructuring: Some 70 percent of the adjustment operations approved in calendar years 1989 and 1990 included divestiture components. Besides divestiture, the Bank supports a host of government efforts to increase the role of the private sector, including both commercial (for-profit) and nonprofit organizations (nongovernmental organizations, for example), in the production, delivery, and financing of public goods and services. The mechanisms employed to expand private participation include regulatory reform, as well as a variety of contractual arrangements in areas as diverse as road maintenance, provision of primary health care, education, water supply, and energy generation.

Financial-sector development. An efficient and dynamic financial sector is crucial to a growing market-oriented economy. In the context of Bank operations, financial-sector restructuring and policy reform are often necessary to raise the efficiency and effectiveness of resource mobilization from, and allocation to, the private sector. Implementation of the recommendations of the 1989 task force on financial-sector operations has resulted in a renewed emphasis on the importance of financial-sector policies, on the preconditions in the macroeconomic, incentive, and institutional environment for successful policy reform, and on a reassessment of the goals and design of Bank lending to financial intermediaries.

Resource transfers and entrepreneurial development. Operations in this area are increasingly being designed to have a broader effect on the efficiency of the financial system as a whole through the development of sound, competitive, market-based intermediary institutions, support for sector policy and institutional reforms, and the removal of obstacles that have prevented creditworthy borrowers and activities from gaining access to normal credit on market terms. A decline in the past few years in the volume of Bank financial-intermediary lending to large-scale industries has been partially counterbalanced (in terms of the number of financial-intermediation operations) by increased Bank support for small and medium-scale private enterprises.

At its September 1990 meeting, the Development Committee welcomed the progress made under the Bank Group's action program and reiterated the call it had made earlier on the Group to give a very high priority to private-sector development in its operations and to continue to expand the scope of its activities in this area, including new approaches and instruments as may be needed. Committee members emphasized the need to keep under review the roles, policies, and lending programs of the Bank and its affiliates, the balance between their advisory and operational functions, and the need for systematic coordination within the Bank Group. At that meeting, the president of the Bank noted that the Bank Group's efforts in the private sector must be strengthened—through additional resources for the International Finance Corporation (IFC) and through improved collaboration between the IFC and the Bank. The president of the Bank told committee members that efforts would also include those that sensitized the Bank at all levels to the potential contribution the private sector offers for growth.

A subsequent review of the implementation of the PSD action program concluded that cooperation within the World Bank Group could be strengthened on the basis of the shared objectives of promoting efficient market-based economies and dynamic private sectors. This required the Bank Group to reinforce its effort and expand its capacity to promote PSD, to define more clearly the functions of each member of the Group, and to improve procedures for cooperation.

Accordingly, several actions were taken by the management of the Bank in fiscal 1991 to clarify management's intentions with regard to further implementation of the PSD action program, including strengthened coordination between the Bank and the IFC and an expansion of the IFC's activities. The actions, which neither set new policies nor modified existing policies, included the following:

• The existing Private Sector Development Committee, whose function is to (a) assist the president of the Bank in providing policy guidance and in coordinating the work of the World Bank Group and (b) encourage new approaches and the development of more effective instruments in support of PSD, was reconstituted and strengthened. Chairmanship of the committee, composed of top management of the Bank, the IFC, and MIGA, was assumed by the president.

• Selected divisions throughout the Bank were restructured, expanded, and staffed to assume additional responsibility for supporting private-sector development.

• Guidelines for cooperation between the Bank and the IFC were issued that set out broad principles for the division of responsibility between the two institutions and that pinpoint opportunities for intensified and systematized collaboration at all stages of issue identification and decisionmaking.

• PSD strategies, identifying priority areas for Bank Group efforts, are being developed jointly by the Bank, the IFC, and MIGA. They cover, among other things, the policy and institutional environment, financial-sector development, privatization, and the promotion of both domestic and foreign investment. To ensure that Bank operations enhance, whenever appropriate, the contribution of the private sector to development, management has identified key approaches and criteria to be considered in the design of country strategies and of relevant operations. Private-sector assessments, which detail the opportunities and obstacles faced by the private sector and the role of the Bank in fostering its development, will be prepared, in consultation with the governments concerned, and will serve as a basis for the formulation of the Bank's strategy and work program of private-sector development. The first twenty assessments are scheduled to be completed by the end of fiscal 1993.

• As part of the overall effort to ensure that the IFC's experience and knowledge are made available to the Bank Group and are reflected in operations supporting PSD, a central coordinating unit in the IFC is being established to enable the IFC to make a more effective contribution to the work on private-sector assessments and country-assistance strategies.

• Detailed principles and procedures have been prepared to ensure that all World Bank Group operations fostering financial-sector reform or lending to the private sector are carried out in the context of a coherent strategy and take the best advantage of the kinds of expertise offered by the Bank and the IFC.

• In the case of private-sector projects that can appropriately be financed on market terms, or joint ventures that meet the IFC's ownership guidelines and that can appropriately be financed without government guarantees, the IFC will be the vehicle for providing and/or mobilizing the necessary resources. The IFC will seek investment opportunities in competitive sectors where protection and other distortions are relatively low or are being reduced significantly, and will generally avoid investing in sectors that have high levels of protection and other distortions without meaningful prospects for reduction. Where the scale of operations is such that IFC financing, coupled with other mobilized funds, may not be

sufficient, and the government is willing to provide the necessary guarantee, Bank participation, either directly or through intermediaries, may be warranted. In such cases, the Bank and the IFC will closely coordinate their involvement.

• As regards lending through financial intermediaries, in countries and operations where the support of the World Bank Group can appropriately be provided without significant government involvement or guarantee of repayment, the IFC would normally be expected to play the lead role. Conversely, where an important element of an operation is concerned with government policy changes (therefore forming a significant element in the Bank's dialogue with the government), the Bank would normally be expected to take the lead. When preparing financial-intermediary lending operations by either the Bank or the IFC, the staff of the initiating institution will consult, and take account of, comments the other may make. The Bank and the IFC will price comparable loans to comparable clients on a market basis wherever possible, and in any case will price their loans so as to ensure that Bank and IFC funds are regarded as equally attractive by financial intermediaries and final borrowers.

• The Bank plans to expand further its capacity to engage in a policy dialogue and its capacity to provide advice to governments on privatization policy and strategies. The IFC will increase its capacity to advise on, and invest in, privatization transactions and will, as appropriate, provide advice to the Bank as it responds to government requests for assistance.

• The Bank's research program will increasingly address PSD issues. Research is addressing broad issues, as well as sectoral, regional, and country-specific ones. The IFC, meanwhile, has been enhancing its research capabilities, with the aim of complementing its financing and advisory activities. A committee, chaired by the Bank's chief economist, has been created to ensure coordination and cross-fertilization in research.

The executive board reconfirmed its consensus on the importance of private-sector development as one of the Bank Group's priority areas of activity and of the need to pursue the PSD action program within the context of the Bank's established objectives of poverty reduction, human-resource development, and environmental sustainability. The board reaffirmed the integrity of this policy orientation with the predominant goal of raising the standard of living and reducing poverty. Adjustment, human-resource development, and environmental protection fit into this policy framework. Also confirmed was the contribution of private-sector development to the mutual reinforcement of the Bank Group's agenda. The board took note of management's intentions with regard to reinforced implementation of the PSD action program, for which there is the necessary support to proceed with its implementation. At the same time, it was agreed that any new policy issues that may arise in the course of implementation of the action program will be presented to the board. Directors also emphasized that the IFC—the Bank Group's focal point for its private-sector activities—should continue to make every effort to use its capital efficiently and effectively, while at the same time maintaining its commitment to achieving its basic developmental mandate. The IFC is strongly committed to strengthen its project selection and contribute to the developmental objectives of its clients.

Section Four
World Bank Finances

Fiscal 1991 saw the IBRD achieve financial targets and undertake programs designed to improve its ability to facilitate the funding of economic development projects and programs in member countries in the years ahead.

The IBRD's financial achievements include:

• Reaching its goal in March 1991 of having the currency composition of its loan pool in targeted proportions, thereby improving borrowers' ability to manage their attendant exchange risks.

• Strengthening its reserves-to-loan ratio by reaching 11.2 percent, the upper range of the current target (see Figure 4-1).[1] The increase largely resulted from the allocation in fiscal 1990 (effective in fiscal 1991) of $750 million of that year's net income to the general reserve, bringing reserves at the end of fiscal 1991 to $10.0 billion.

• Diversifying and globalizing the trading and risk-management techniques utilized in investing the IBRD's liquid-assets portfolio.

• Borrowing the equivalent of $10.9 billion of medium-term and long-term funding on attractive terms in the world's financial markets (see Table 4-1).

• Achieving a level of net income—$1.20 billion in fiscal 1991—that enabled the IBRD to realize its key financial objectives.

Financial Policy Actions

During fiscal 1991, the executive directors established policy guidelines for the annual allocations of IBRD net income. The guidelines provide that:

• The first claim against net income will be an allocation to the general reserve sufficient to achieve the reserves-to-loan target ratio (currently 11 percent) at the end of the following fiscal year.

• If net income exceeds the amount needed for allocation to the general reserve, consideration will first be given to a waiver, beginning July 1, 1991, of up to twenty-five basis points of the interest-rate spread on the borrower's semiannual debt-service payments to the IBRD. To qualify, a borrower must have made all its loan-service payments owed to the IBRD

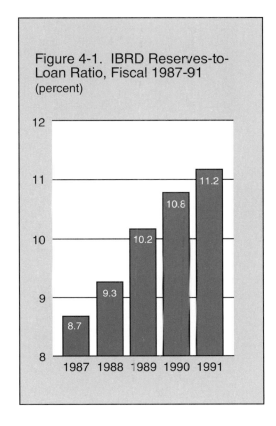

Figure 4-1. IBRD Reserves-to-Loan Ratio, Fiscal 1987-91
(percent)

during the previous semester within thirty days of their due dates. This twenty-five basis-points reduction would be in addition to a continuation during fiscal 1992 of the reduction of the commitment fee on undisbursed loan balances to 0.25 percent.

• Any net income not required to implement the twenty-five basis-points waiver of interest charges will be transferred to surplus; thereafter, it could be allocated for specific purposes consistent with the IBRD's Articles of Agreement.

---

[1] The reserves-to-loan ratio is the sum of general and special reserves and cumulative currency translation adjustments divided by the sum of total loan principal outstanding and the value of callable guarantees less accumulated loan-loss provisions.

Table 4-1. IBRD Borrowings, Fiscal Year 1991
(amounts in millions)

Type	Issue	Currency of issue		US-dollar equivalent[a]
Medium- and long-term public offerings				
Germany	9.0% ten-year bonds, due 2000	DM	750	504.8
	8.50% ten-year bonds, due 2001	DM	200	142.3
Hong Kong	9.50% five-year bonds, due 1995	HK$	600	77.4
Japan	7.0% seven-year bonds, due 1997	¥	30,000	192.6
New Zealand	12.50% seven-year bonds, due 1997	$NZ	250	149.3
Spain	13.75% five-year bonds, due 1995	Ptas	10,000	100.9
	13.625% five-year bonds, due 1996	Ptas	15,000	166.8
Switzerland	7.25% ten-year bonds, due 2000	Sw F	150	114.9
	7.50% five-year bonds, due 1995	Sw F	200	162.4
	7.0% ten-year bonds, due 2001	Sw F	600	483.6
Eurobond Market	13.50% five-year notes, due 1995	$A	100	84.1
	11.50% five-year bonds, due 1995	Can$	150	131.1
	9.125% five-year bonds, due 1996	F	1,000	185.5
	12.0% five-year notes, due 1995	£	100	199.0
	11.125% ten-year notes, due 2001	£	100	194.3
	12.125% five-year bonds, due 1995	Lit	300,000	261.7
	12.125% seven-year bonds, due 1998	Lit	300,000	269.1
	11.625% seven-year bonds, due 1998	Lit	600,000	487.0
	8.25% five-year bonds, due 1995	¥	30,000	220.5
	7.625% five-year bonds, due 1995	¥	50,000	406.2
	6.75% ten-year bonds, due 2001	¥	50,000	358.7
	9.25% ten-year bonds, due 2000	f.	300	182.6
	13.875% five-year notes, due 1995	SKr	400	71.1
Global	8.625% five-year bonds, due 1995	US$	2,000	1,990.8
	8.125% ten-year bonds, due 2001	US$	1,500	1,487.7
Total medium- and long-term public offerings				8,624.4
Medium- and long-term placements with central banks and governments				
Germany	8.71% note, due 1995	DM	152	93.8
	9.02% note, due 1996	DM	250	168.2
International[b]	7.875% two-year notes, due 1992	Sw F	300	233.9
	7.25% two-year notes, due 1993	Sw F	263	190.9
	8.34% two-year bonds, due 1992	US$	200	200.0
	7.71% two-year bonds, due 1992	US$	138	138.0
	7.36% two-year bonds, due 1993	US$	143	143.0
	6.97% two-year bonds, due 1993	US$	146	145.5
Total medium- and long-term placements with central banks and governments				1,313.3
Medium- and long-term other placements				
Japan	7.60% loan, due 2011	¥	10,000	67.4
	7.65% loan, due 1995	¥	10,000	77.1
	6.94% loan, due 1998	¥	10,000	75.2
	7.10% loan, due 1998	¥	10,000	73.6
	7.50% loan, due 1998	¥	10,000	73.5
Switzerland	7.0% seven-year notes, due 1997	Sw F	200	145.0
	7.50% five-year notes, due 1995	Sw F	100	79.0
	7.50% seven-year notes, due 1998	Sw F	100	80.6
United States	Continuously Offered Longer-term Securities (COLTS) Program	US$	114	114.4
International	20.0% five-year notes, due 1995	$A	50	48.0
	7.0% four-year bonds, due 1995	¥	15,000	111.9
Total medium- and long-term other placements				945.7
Total medium- and long-term borrowings, fiscal 1991				10,883.4

Type	Issue	Currency of issue		US-dollar equivalent[a]
Short-term borrowings outstanding[c]				
Central bank facility		US$	2,583	2,583.0
Continuously offered payment rights in Swiss francs (COPS)		Sw F	53	34.2
Discount notes		US$	2,750	2,749.8
Short-term borrowings outstanding as of June 30, 1991				5,367.0

a. Medium- and long-term amounts based on gross proceeds, expressed at exchange rates prevailing at the time of launch.
b. These issues were placed with central banks, government agencies, and international organizations.
c. Maturing within one year.

The executive directors also approved a modification of the IBRD's repayment terms for middle-income borrowers. The change is applicable to new loans committed during the period fiscal 1992–94. Borrowers will have an option of having either an extended grace period of five years, with loan amortization based on level repayments of principal, or a grace period of four years for lower-middle-income countries or three years for upper-middle-income countries with an annuity type of level-payment arrangement (in which a generally rising proportion of payments is applicable to the retirement of principal).

The IBRD approved a new approach, effective July 1, 1991, to encourage borrowers to make timely loan payments. If a payment becomes thirty days overdue, no new loans to the borrower will be presented to the executive board for approval or will be signed, and the borrower will become ineligible for any applicable waivers of the commitment and interest spread. If a loan payment from a nonsovereign borrower becomes forty-five days overdue (and the country is not itself the delinquent borrower), no new loans to, or to be guaranteed by, that country will be presented to the board for approval, and no previously approved loans to, or guaranteed by, that country will be signed. Further, the borrower and the country will be sent notice that a suspension of disbursements on other previously approved and signed loans will begin fifteen days later. (In the past, the fifteen days' notice of suspension, which also covered the nonconsideration of new loans and the nonsigning of previously approved loans, was sent on the sixtieth day following the due date of the loan payment.)

In May 1991, the IBRD adopted a policy regarding additional support for workout programs in countries with large and protracted arrears. The objective is to assist a country that has a demonstrated record of cooperation with the IBRD in mobilizing sufficient resources to support a sustainable growth-oriented adjustment program over the medium term. This IBRD initiative would be comparable to what is known at the International Monetary Fund (IMF) as a "rights approach" program.

During a preclearance "performance period," which may last several years, the borrower will have to meet four conditions. It must:

• implement a structural-adjustment program agreed to by the IBRD, with time-phased action targets and with monitoring by the IBRD during the preclearance performance period;

• begin implementing a stabilization program, endorsed and monitored, if necessary, by the IMF;

• service its debt to the IBRD falling due during the preclearance performance period and give comparable debt-service treatment to other multilateral development banks and the IMF where there is to be parallel clearance (unless sequential clearance is mutually agreed upon); and

• agree to a financing plan that provides for full clearance of arrears to the IBRD and normalization of relations with the IMF and creditor multilateral development banks prior to the resumption of IBRD disbursements.

The country would establish a track record on adjustment measures over the preclearance performance period. During the period, the IBRD would develop and process loans, but would not sign them, make them effective, or disburse any funds against them. After the performance period is over, and following the clearance of arrears, the country would receive disbursements on loans approved during the performance period, as well as on previous loans that had been suspended. The scale of IBRD lending activity would be commensurate with its support for any strong program in countries not in arrears.

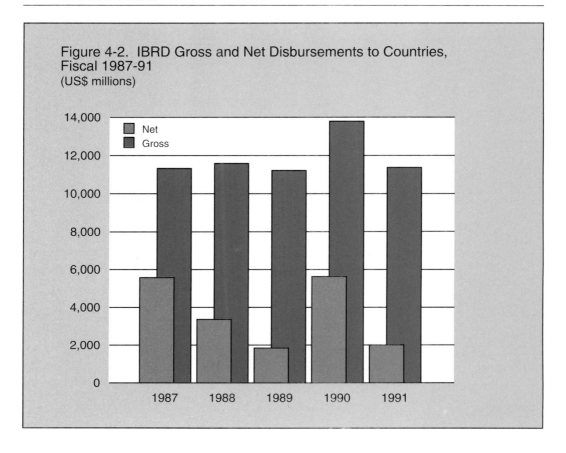

Figure 4-2. IBRD Gross and Net Disbursements to Countries, Fiscal 1987-91
(US$ millions)

During the performance period, a support group of other lenders or donors would be essential to provide sufficient funding to support the needs of the economy and facilitate the country's current servicing of debt outstanding to the IBRD and the IMF.

Loans

Disbursements. Gross disbursements by the IBRD to countries were $11.4 billion, down from fiscal 1990's $13.9 billion. Net disbursements were $2.1 billion, compared with $5.7 billion during the previous year (see Figure 4-2).

Lending rate. The IBRD's semiannual variable-lending rate was 7.72 percent and 7.73 percent, respectively, for the first and second semesters of fiscal 1991. By comparison, the other variable-lending rate—applicable to loans for which invitations to negotiate were sent before May 18, 1989, and not converted by borrowers to the new system—was 7.70 percent for both semesters. The difference between the rates is due to differences in allocations of borrowings to lending and/or to investments and to the weights applied to currency-specific costs.

Declining interest-rate risk. Interest-rate risk from possible increases in the IBRD's refinancing costs of prefiscal 1983 fixed-rate loans continues to decline because such loans represent a shrinking percentage of the outstanding loan portfolio—33 percent at the end of 1991, compared with 41 percent a year earlier. The amount remaining to be disbursed on fixed-rate loans is $374 million, compared with $53 billion on variable-rate loans.

Loans in nonaccrual status. Eight countries were in nonaccrual status at the end of fiscal 1991. Six were holdovers from the prior fiscal year—Liberia, Nicaragua, Panama, Peru, Sierra Leone, and the Syrian Arab Republic. The seventh, Guatemala, entered nonaccrual status in July 1990, while the eighth, Iraq, entered that status in December 1990. Zambia, which had been in nonaccrual status since August 1987, cleared its arrears in March 1991 with a payment of $319 million. Since $147 million of this amount was interest and commitment charges due prior to fiscal 1991, the payment increased the IBRD's fiscal 1991 net income by that amount.

Provisioning. The IBRD raised its consolidated provision for possible loan losses to $2.0

Table 4-2. **IBRD Borrowings, after Swaps, Fiscal Year 1991**
(amounts in US$ millions equivalent)

Item	Before swaps			Currency swaps (amount)	After swaps			
	Amount	%	Maturity (years)		Amount	%	Maturity (years)	Cost (%)
Medium- and long-term borrowings								
U.S. dollars	4,219.4	39	6.6	300.0	4,519.4	42	6.7	8.45
Japanese yen	1,656.7	15	7.2	−405.2	1,251.5	11	7.6	7.20
Deutsche mark	909.1	8	8.6	2,184.9	3,094.0	28	6.6	8.46
Swiss francs	1,490.3	14	6.5	486.0	1,976.3	18	6.5	7.02
Others[a]	2,607.9	24	6.4	−2,565.7	42.2	0	6.4	11.14
Total	10,883.4	100	6.8		10,883.4	100	6.7	8.06
Short-term borrowings outstanding								
Central bank facility (U.S. dollars)	2,583.0	48	1.0					6.27
COPS (Swiss francs)[b]	34.2	1	0.3					7.63
Discount notes (U.S. dollars)[c]	2,749.8	51	0.3					5.96
Total as of June 30, 1991[d]	5,367.0	100	0.6					6.12

NOTE: Details may not add to totals because of rounding.

a. Represents borrowings in Australian dollars, Canadian dollars, French francs, Hong Kong dollars, Italian lire, Netherlands guilders, New Zealand dollars, pounds sterling, Spanish pesetas, and Swedish kronor.

b. Continuously offered payment rights in Swiss francs.

c. Includes other short-term market borrowings in U.S. dollars.

d. Short-term borrowings outstanding on June 30, 1990, totaled $5,306.7.

billion, which, together with its "special reserve," equals 2.5 percent of its entire outstanding loan portfolio. This increase represents an evaluation of risks—specific risks associated with countries currently in nonaccrual status and general risks in the entire portfolio. The result is, in effect, an increase of the provisions to $2.3 billion at June 30, 1991, from $1.5 billion a year earlier. The prior provisioning policy was concerned only with loans in nonaccrual status.

Liquid-assets Investments

Six areas were targeted in the management of the IBRD's liquid-assets investments: (1) development of efficient benchmark portfolios, new products, and new trading models; (2) further improvement of its risk-management systems; (3) creation of a global money-markets group to focus internationally on cash management and credit-risk monitoring; (4) expanded diversification of fixed-income trading approaches to include mortgage-backed securities, volatility trading, intermarket spread trades, long-term positioning, covered forward trading in the money markets, and computer-guided trading, as well as resuscitation of bills, agencies, and strips trading; (5) the tightening of credit criteria regarding commercial banks and securities-dealer counterparties; and (6) provision of financial technical assistance to developing member countries and the promotion of exchanges of views with other money managers.

The IBRD's fiscal 1991 financial return on investments was 9.23 percent. In fiscal 1990, the financial return on investments was 8.15 percent.

At the end of fiscal 1991, the IBRD's liquidity totaled $20.0 billion, equivalent to about 51 percent of anticipated net cash requirements for the next three fiscal years, compared with $17.2 billion at the end of fiscal 1990. The IBRD's primary objective in holding such liquidity is to ensure flexibility in its borrowing decisions should borrowing be adversely affected by temporary conditions in the capital markets.

Resources

Borrowings. Borrowings were principally fixed-rate and were diversified by currency, country, source, and maturity. Medium-term and long-term (MLT) funding at the end of fiscal 1991 amounted to $84.7 billion equivalent and represented 94 percent of total outstanding debt. As of June 30, 1991, the average remaining life of total debt was 6.3 years, and its average cost, after swaps, was 7.35 percent. In fiscal 1991, the IBRD borrowed $10.9 billion, excluding refinancings of $5.4 billion of short-term debt, at an average cost, after swaps, of 8.06 percent equivalent and an average life of 6.7 years (see Table 4-2 and Figure 4-3).

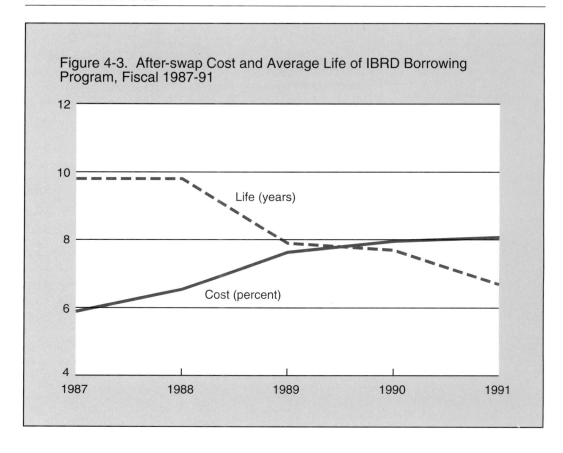

Figure 4-3. After-swap Cost and Average Life of IBRD Borrowing Program, Fiscal 1987-91

After swaps, all of the year's borrowings were in the so-called core currencies of the IBRD's loan pool—U.S. dollars, Japanese yen, and the deutsche mark group (including Swiss francs). This composition enabled the IBRD to achieve by March 1991, and thereafter to maintain, the targeted loan-currency-pool ratios, approved by the executive directors in January 1990, of 1 U.S. dollar to 125 Japanese yen to 2 deutsche mark (or their equivalent in deutsche mark, Swiss francs, and Netherlands guilders) for at least 90 percent of the loan-currency pool.

Other funding objectives achieved were preserving the inherent long-term value of diversification of funding sources by borrowing in fourteen currencies; achieving savings in core currencies by using swap-arbitrage opportunities derived from market borrowings in eleven currencies; maintaining core-currency borrowing relationships with official sources; and building on the lesson learned in developing and offering, in fiscal years 1989 and 1990, its U.S.-dollar global-bond issues—that cost savings can be realized by offering products that are responsive to investors' asset preferences.

During the fiscal year, the IBRD sought to reduce its cost of funding by offering benchmark issues in U.S. dollars, deutsche mark, and Swiss francs in response to investors' preferences for enhanced liquidity. These included two U.S.-dollar issues, aggregating $3.5 billion, through its global-bond issues, which are now the core instrument in the IBRD's medium-term to long-term U.S.-dollar funding program (the total volume outstanding of such issues since their inception in September 1989 amounts to $6.5 billion); a DM750 million issue, providing investors liquidity and an opportunity for portfolio diversification; and a Sw F600 million issue, the largest of its kind, designed to overcome the traditional illiquidity of Swiss franc bonds through broadened trading arrangements. In addition, as the first nondomestic borrower in the domestic New Zealand market, the IBRD launched a $NZ250 million issue designed to bring both foreign and domestic interest to bear on a single instrument. This issue can be viewed as a prototype for transactions that could help the IBRD to extend its comparative advantage as a borrower in smaller vehicle-currency markets and thus continue to access swap savings there as market liberalization proceeds.

At the end of the fiscal year, short-term borrowings outstanding were $5.4 billion equivalent, an increase of $60 million over the end of fiscal 1990. The short-term borrowings consisted of $2.6 billion from official sources through the central bank facility, $2.7 billion from the U.S.-dollar discount-note program and other short-term U.S.-dollar borrowings, and $34 million equivalent in short-term Swiss franc borrowings. Outstanding short-term borrowings and floating-rate funding, after swaps, aggregated $5.5 billion equivalent at the end of fiscal 1991 and represented about 6 percent of total debt.

Capital. On June 30, 1991, total subscribed capital was $139.1 billion, or 80 percent of authorized capital of $174.7 billion. During fiscal 1991, subscriptions to the $74.8 billion general capital increase (GCI), approved in April 1988, continued smoothly: Twenty-two countries subscribed an aggregate of $12.7 billion. A total of 356,412 GCI shares ($43 billion, or 57 percent of total allocations) have now been subscribed by fifty members; 266,560 shares ($32.2 billion) remain to be subscribed. At the end of fiscal 1991, the permissible increase of net disbursements, that is, "headroom," was $61.7 billion, or 40 percent of the IBRD's lending limit.

Reserves. On June 30, 1991, reserves totaled $10.0 billion. and the reserves-to-loan ratio amounted to 11.2 percent.

Liability Management

Swaps. The average notional savings the IBRD generated from currency swaps on MLT borrowings in fiscal 1991 was fifty basis points. Currency swaps totaled $3.0 billion equivalent. They were linked principally to borrowings in noncore, vehicle currencies so as to provide lower costs than direct market borrowings in deutsche mark, Swiss francs, and, to a lesser extent. U.S. dollars.

The IBRD contracted interest-rate swaps into fixed rates and variable rates. It used interest-rate swaps to separate the timing of borrowings in vehicle currencies from the timing of interest-rate fixing in target currencies. The IBRD was thereby able to complete vehicle-currency borrowings linked to currency swaps when arbitrage opportunities arose. It used interest-rate swaps either to lock in more attractive rates or to spread rate fixings within the fiscal year; in doing so, the IBRD would thereby not be bound to the absolute level of

target currency rates at the time of vehicle-currency transactions.

Interest-rate swaps were also used to create fixed-rate MLT funding from borrowings originally contracted on a floating-rate basis. The IBRD also used interest-rate swaps to a modest extent to effect forward-swap strategies, fixing the cost of a borrowing for a shorter term than its original maturity with a view toward resetting it at the then-prevailing cost for the remaining life of the borrowing.

Deferred rate setting and anticipatory rate setting. Deferred rate setting (DRS) is another technique the IBRD used in fiscal 1991 to delink the timing of cost fixings from that of the time of issuance of its U.S.-dollar global-bond issues. Just as in the case of interest-rate swaps, DRS enabled the IBRD to phase rate fixing over the course of several months. In addition, the executive directors authorized the use of anticipatory rate-setting arrangements, which allow for cost fixings to be undertaken in advance of issuance. The IBRD did not use this technique in fiscal 1991.

IDA Finances

Fiscal year 1991 marked the beginning of the commitment period of the ninth replenishment of IDA resources (IDA-9). Donor contributions to IDA-9, amounting to SDR11.7 billion, will finance commitments to IDA borrowers in the period fiscal 1991–93. The replenishment became effective on January 23, 1991, when Instruments of Commitments—the formal notification of participation in the replenishment—received from donors reached 80 percent of the total contributions to IDA-9 from contributing members.

Prior to the replenishment's effectiveness, credit approvals were financed through commitment authority provided under the Advance Contribution Scheme. This scheme became operational on July 19, 1990, when the association received Instruments of Commitments from ten donors (Canada, Denmark, France, Japan, Korea, New Zealand, Norway, South Africa, Sweden, and Yugoslavia) whose contributions aggregated 20 percent of the IDA-9 total contributions of contributing members.

During the course of the fiscal year, the association received the Instruments of Commitments from the following donors: Australia, Austria, Brazil, Finland, Germany, Hungary, Iceland, Ireland, Kuwait, Luxembourg, Mexico, Poland, Saudi Arabia, Spain, Turkey, the United Kingdom, and the United States.

IDA commitment authority. During the year, IDA approved 103 credits amounting to SDR4.55 billion. The commitment authority to finance these credits was derived from three sources—donor contributions, reflows, and transfers from the IBRD.

• The release of approximately one third of donors' contributions to IDA-9, amounting to SDR3.28 billion, was made available for lending in fiscal 1991.

• Funds available from future reflows during the year amounted to SDR1.07 billion. These supplement resources provided by donors through the regular replenishment. The SDR1.07 billion amount included (a) advance commitments of SDR575 million for general IDA credits; (b) "annual allocations," in the amount of SDR122 million, to supplement adjustment credits to IDA-only countries with outstanding IBRD debt; (c) a special allocation of SDR48 million to supplement operations for IDA-only countries that are undertaking debt workouts; and (d) a carry-over balance of about SDR193 million from the prior fiscal year. Additionally, in December 1990, the executive directors approved further advance commitments of SDR130 million to partially meet the incremental financing requirements of IDA countries affected by the Gulf crisis.

• Some SDR200 million was transferred to IDA from the IBRD's net income retained as surplus. This transfer was also intended to help finance IDA's efforts to alleviate the effect of the Gulf crisis on IDA recipients.

IDA's incremental requirements for assisting countries adversely affected by the Gulf crisis amount to about SDR600 million. As mentioned previously, this amount will be partially financed through advance commitments of reflows of SDR130 million and the transfer of IBRD income of SDR200 million. The balance, SDR270 million, will be financed through the carry-over from fiscal 1990 of SDR190 million and reprogramming of IDA-9 resources (SDR80 million).

IDA commitment fee. Since the current service charge of disbursed and outstanding amounts was expected to be sufficient to meet IDA's projected administrative expenses for the fiscal year, the fiscal year 1991 commitment fee was set at 0 percent for all outstanding credits financed by IDA, the Special Fund, and the Special Facility for Sub-Saharan Africa. Late in fiscal 1991, the executive directors approved a recommendation that IDA's commitment fee for fiscal 1992 continue to be set at zero and that, after fiscal 1992, the commitment fee be set at zero annually until such time as the directors decide to change it.

Cofinancing

The vice presidency for cofinancing and financial advisory services (CFS) was created in 1989 to strengthen the Bank's role as a catalyst for increasing the flow of financial resources to developing countries from non-Bank sources. The CFS helps mobilize financial resources by providing general coordination of official and private-sector cofinancing of Bank projects.

The volume of cofinancing anticipated in support of World Bank–assisted operations approved in fiscal 1991 was $8,985 million, some $4,495 million off the record-setting pace of fiscal 1990 (see Table 4-3). Roughly 55 percent of all Bank-assisted projects and programs attracted some form of cofinancing. By region, 27 percent of the cofinancing volume was for operations in Asia, 25 percent in Africa, 24 percent in the Europe, Middle East, and North Africa region, and 24 percent in Latin America and the Caribbean. In terms of number of cofinanced operations, the distribution by region indicates that 43 percent was in Africa, 21 percent in Asia, 19 percent in the Europe, Middle East, and North Africa region, and 17 percent in Latin America and the Caribbean.

The largest source of cofinancing in fiscal 1991 continued to be official bilateral and multilateral development institutions, which, together, accounted for $7,057 million, down from $9,307 million in fiscal 1990. This is attributable primarily to a slowdown in operations as a result of the Gulf crisis and delay in certain large cofinanced operations because of prolonged negotiations on debt issues and other difficult policy matters. Official cofinancing from Japan, through the Overseas Economic Cooperation Fund and the Export-Import Bank of Japan, continued to account for the largest share of official cofinancing in support of Bank-assisted operations. Cofinancing from the two agencies aggregated $1,405 million equivalent for twelve projects approved in fiscal 1991.

There was also a marked decline in the volume of export-credit cofinancing planned for projects approved during the year—from $3,519 million in fiscal 1990 to $1,495 million. The main reason for the decline was that Bank lending for sectors that attract a substantial proportion of export-credit financing (power, transportation, and telecommunications, for example) decreased significantly during the year. The volume of private cofinancing remained modest, at $434 million, reflecting the continued reluctance of private lenders to take on new exposure in most developing countries.

The new export-credit enhanced leverage (EXCEL) program is now being implemented. This program was developed in fiscal 1990 in close collaboration with a working group of the International Union of Credit and Investment Insurers (the Berne Union). The objective of

Table 4-3. **World Bank Cofinancing Operations, by Region, Fiscal Years 1990–91**
(amounts in millions of US dollars)

Region and year	Projects cofinanced No.	Projects cofinanced Amount	Official[b] No.	Official[b] Amount	Export credit No.	Export credit Amount	Private No.	Private Amount	World Bank contribution IBRD	World Bank contribution IDA	Total project costs
Africa											
1990	64	3,035.6	63	2,986.7	2	16.7	3	32.2	843.9	2,274.7	7,994.0
1991	54	2,216.8	53	1,974.5	2	147.0	3	95.3	650.7	1,848.2	6,170.7
Asia											
1990	29	4,513.0	28	2,685.1	5	1,245.6	2	582.3	3,166.7	714.3	16,790.3
1991	27	2,480.4	26	1,641.8	2	820.6	1	18.0	1,969.3	982.7	8,850.4
Europe, Middle East. and North Africa											
1990	17	1,489.4	16	1,267.1	3	182.3	1	40.0	1,875.0	161.0	8,982.4
1991	24	2,166.0	22	1,707.8	2	226.9	2	231.3	3,114.0	250.6	8,855.7
Latin America and the Caribbean											
1990	18	4,442.1	17	2,368.2	3	2,073.9	0	0.0	2,436.0	183.0	15,290.5
1991	21	2,121.4	21	1,732.4	1	300.0	1	89.0	2,044.0	105.7	5,800.9
Total											
1990	128	13,480.0	124	9,307.1	13	3,513.5	6	654.5	8,321.6	3,333.0	49,057.1
1991	126	8,984.6	122	7,056.5	7	1,494.5	7	433.6	7,778.0	3,187.2	29,677.6

NOTE: The number of operations shown under different sources add up to a figure exceeding the total number of cofinanced projects because a number of projects were cofinanced from more than one source. Details may not add to totals because of rounding.

a. These statistics are compiled from the financing plans presented at the time of approval of the World Bank loans by the board of executive directors. The amounts of official cofinancing are in most cases firm commitments by that stage; export credits and private cofinancing amounts, however, are generally only estimates since such cofinancing is actually arranged as required for project implementation and gets firmed up a year or two after board approval. The statistics of private cofinancing shown here for any fiscal year do not necessarily reflect market placements in that year.

b. These figures include cofinancing with untied loans from the Export-Import Bank of Japan.

the program is to mobilize export-credit support for medium-sized private enterprises in selected developing countries, where such enterprises currently have limited access to medium-term and long-term export credits. The first EXCEL facility, for approximately $75 million, is being put in place for an industrial-restructuring project in the Philippines.

The expanded cofinancing operations (ECO) program is intended to support eligible World Bank borrowers seeking to gain access to capital markets (both through public issues and private placements) and to improve their access to medium-term credit facilities. In fiscal 1991, the executive board approved one transaction under this program. A World Bank guarantee was used to support a ten-year, fixed-rate Eurodollar bond issue for $200 million by the State Development Institute of Hungary. The ECO enabled Hungary to gain access to the Eurodollar fixed-rate bond market for the first time and helped reaffirm its credit standing in the international capital markets.

Development of subsequent ECO transactions was deferred, pending a review, re-

quested by some executive directors, of the pilot program. In January 1991, the executive directors approved continuation of the program on a pilot basis for a further period of between twelve and eighteen months; a pipeline of prospective ECO operations is being developed.

In October 1990, the second phase of the special program of assistance (SPA), designed to support adjustment programs in low-income, debt-distressed countries of sub-Saharan Africa, was launched. In fiscal 1991, the fourth year of this multidonor program, $1.8 billion was provided to eligible countries in the form of cofinancing of IDA adjustment operations, as well as coordinated financing.

In addition to cofinancing, the donor community provided substantial support for the Bank through trust funds and other arrangements that directly or indirectly benefited recipient countries. To date, consultant trust funds have been established with twenty-five donors. Under this program, donors have allocated about $86 million in grant funds to support the Bank's operational work. In addition, special arrangements have been established with eight donors in support of environment-related activities, and discussions are under way with other prospective donors. The Bank has also received support from eight donors for work in member countries of Eastern and Central Europe.

On July 30, 1990, a special fund for policy and human-resource development (the PHRD Fund) was established within the IBRD and IDA, funded by Japan's Ministry of Finance. The PHRD Fund became the umbrella for five previously existing funds that the Bank administered on behalf of Japan. Japan's contribution of $300 million equivalent in grants is to be made over the period covering Japan's fiscal years 1990–92 to finance technical assistance, studies, and training.

Disbursements by Source of Supply

Projects financed by the World Bank require procurement from foreign and local sources to achieve project goals. Disbursements are made primarily to cover specific costs for foreign procurement, and some local expenditures.

The procurement rules and procedures to be followed in the execution of each project depend on the individual circumstances. Three considerations generally guide the Bank's requirements: the need for economy and efficiency in the execution of the project; the

Table 4-4. IBRD and IDA Foreign and Local Disbursements, by Source of Supply
(amounts in millions of US dollars)

Period	IBRD and IDA						
	Foreign[a]		Local		Net advance disbursements[b]		Total amount
	Amount	%	Amount	%	Amount	%	
Cumulative to June 30, 1986	64,627	63	35,537	35	2,290	2	102,454
Fiscal 1987	8,715	59	5,356	36	708	5	14,779
Fiscal 1988	8,562	56	6,077	40	714	5	15,353
Fiscal 1989	9,054	60	5,811	39	201	1	15,066
Fiscal 1990	11,184	63	5,909	33	697	4	17,790
Fiscal 1991	9,159	57	6,643	42	186	1	15,988
Cumulative to June 30, 1991	111,301	61	65,333	36	4,796	3	181,430

NOTE: IBRD figures exclude disbursements on loans to the IFC and "B" loans. IDA figures include Special Fund and Special Facility for Sub-Saharan Africa credits. Details may not add to totals because of rounding.

a. Amounts include disbursements for debt reduction.

b. Net advance disbursements are advances made to special accounts net of amounts recovered (amounts for which the Bank has applied evidence of expenditures to recovery of the outstanding advance).

Table 4-5. IBRD and IDA Foreign Disbursements, by Source of Supply
(amounts in millions of US dollars)

Period	IBRD							IDA				
	Part I		Part II		DR[a]		Total amount	Part I		Part II		Total amount
	Amount	%	Amount	%	Amount	%		Amount	%	Amount	%	
Cumulative to June 30, 1986	43,782	90	5,054	10	—	—	48,836	13,429	85	2,362	15	15,791
Fiscal 1987	5,421	80	1,345	20	—	—	6,766	1,607	82	342	18	1,949
Fiscal 1988	4,546	74	1,616	26	—	—	6,162	1,851	77	549	23	2,400
Fiscal 1989	5,157	76	1,609	24	—	—	6,766	1,753	77	535	23	2,288
Fiscal 1990	5,320	59	1,499	17	2,160	24	8,979	1,586	72	619	28	2,205
Fiscal 1991	4,963	76	1,225	19	313	5	6,501	1,843	70	807	30	2,650
Cumulative to June 30, 1991	69,189	82	12,348	15	2,473	3	84,010	22,069	81	5,214	19	27,283

— Zero.

NOTE: IBRD figures exclude disbursements on loans to the IFC and "B" loans. IDA figures include Special Fund and Special Facility for Sub-Saharan Africa credits, but exclude debt-reduction disbursements of $8 million in fiscal 1991. Net advance disbursements are excluded for the IBRD and IDA. Details may not add to totals because of rounding.

a. Disbursements for debt reduction.

Table 4-6. **IBRD and IDA Payments to Selected Supplying Part II Countries for Foreign and Local Procurement in Fiscal 1991**
(millions of US dollars)

Part II country	Local procurement	Foreign procurement	Total amount	Percentage of total disbursements[a]
India	1,241	98	1,339	8.4
Brazil	648	207	855	5.4
Mexico	697	82	779	4.9
China	541	163	704	4.4
Indonesia	598	23	621	3.9
Morocco	314	9	323	2.0
Korea, Republic of	99	149	248	1.6
Turkey	213	30	243	1.5
Pakistan	204	16	220	1.4
Chile	181	20	201	1.3
Malaysia	175	19	194	1.2
Argentina	141	51	192	1.2
Philippines	177	6	183	1.1
Singapore	—	161	161	1.0
Bangladesh	149	3	152	1.0
Colombia	108	18	126	0.8
Yugoslavia	67	51	118	0.7
Thailand	75	42	117	0.7
Nigeria	63	34	97	0.6
Venezuela	—	88	88	0.6
Tunisia	78	8	86	0.5
Spain	—	83	83	0.5
Iran, Islamic Republic of	—	68	68	0.4
Sri Lanka	61	—	61	0.4
Ecuador	56	1	57	0.4
Hungary	34	23	57	0.4
Kenya	34	23	57	0.4
Côte d'Ivoire	41	14	55	0.3
Saudi Arabia	—	46	46	0.3
Senegal	42	3	45	0.3
Jordan	24	20	44	0.3
Uruguay	39	5	44	0.3
Portugal	9	33	42	0.3
Cameroon	31	9	40	0.3
Iraq	—	37	37	0.2
Poland	—	34	34	0.2
Malawi	34	—	34	0.2
Algeria	27	3	30	0.2
Niger	21	8	29	0.2
Paraguay	14	14	28	0.2
Total	6,222	1,702	7,938	50.0

— Zero.

NOTE: Details may not add to totals because of rounding.

a. Refers to the Part II country's share of all IBRD and IDA payments for fiscal 1991, which totaled $15,980 million.

Table 4-7. IBRD and IDA Payments to Part I and Selected Part II Countries for Foreign Procurement
(amounts in millions of US dollars)

Supplying country	IBRD cumulative to June 30, 1991 Amount	%	IBRD fiscal 1991 Amount	%	IDA cumulative to June 30, 1991 Amount	%	IDA fiscal 1991 Amount	%
Part I countries								
Australia	842	1.0	106	1.6	297	1.1	14	0.5
Austria	929	1.1	148	2.3	173	0.6	22	0.8
Belgium	1,198	1.4	115	1.8	752	2.8	80	3.0
Canada	1,920	2.3	139	2.1	527	1.9	34	1.3
Denmark	440	0.5	54	0.8	208	0.8	19	0.7
Finland	290	0.3	20	0.3	80	0.3	13	0.5
France	5,655	6.7	508	7.8	2,733	10.0	258	9.7
Germany	9,433	11.2	765	11.8	2,845	10.4	254	9.6
Iceland	8	*	2	*	1	*	—	—
Ireland	94	0.1	5	0.1	47	0.2	11	0.4
Italy	4,771	5.7	356	5.5	1,260	4.6	106	4.0
Japan	12,329	14.7	637	9.8	3,498	12.8	189	7.1
Kuwait	218	0.3	8	0.1	165	0.6	51	1.9
Luxembourg	59	*	3	*	27	0.1	2	0.1
Netherlands	1,491	1.8	151	2.3	668	2.5	75	2.8
New Zealand	126	*	3	*	55	0.2	12	0.4
Norway	230	0.3	24	0.4	83	0.3	17	0.6
South Africa	297	0.4	16	0.2	351	1.3	86	3.2
Sweden	1,355	1.6	78	1.2	339	1.2	19	0.7
Switzerland	3,405	4.0	209	3.2	721	2.6	45	1.7
United Arab Emirates	482	0.6	45	0.7	305	1.0	5	0.2
United Kingdom[a]	6,343	7.4	412	6.3	3,997	14.7	378	14.2
United States	17,272	20.6	1,159	17.8	2,935	10.8	156	5.9
Total	69,189	82.3	4,963	76.3	22,069	80.9	1,843	69.5
Part II countries								
Argentina	658	0.8	43	0.7	51	0.2	8	0.3
Brazil	1,096	1.3	180	2.8	177	0.6	27	1.0
China	385	0.5	69	1.1	481	1.8	94	3.5
Hungary	120	0.1	21	0.3	18	0.1	2	0.1
India	367	0.4	38	0.6	443	1.6	60	2.3
Indonesia	273	0.3	16	0.2	33	0.1	7	0.3
Iran, Islamic Republic of	85	0.1	14	0.2	100	0.4	54	2.0
Iraq	458	0.5	36	0.6	28	0.1	1	*
Kenya	31	*	1	*	141	0.5	22	0.8
Korea, Republic of	774	0.9	108	1.7	491	1.8	41	1.5
Mexico	388	0.5	80	1.2	63	0.2	2	0.1
Nigeria	119	0.1	14	0.2	108	0.4	20	0.8
Panama	326	0.4	17	0.3	15	0.1	4	0.2
Poland	66	0.1	23	0.4	23	0.1	11	0.4
Portugal	44	0.1	3	*	141	0.5	30	1.1
Romania	272	0.3	21	0.3	55	0.2	5	0.2
Saudi Arabia	345	0.4	32	0.5	148	0.5	14	0.5
Singapore	664	0.8	76	1.2	400	1.5	85	3.2
Spain	826	1.0	67	1.0	169	0.6	15	0.6
Thailand	114	0.1	8	0.1	214	0.8	34	1.3
Turkey	239	0.3	17	0.3	28	0.1	13	0.5
Venezuela	358	0.4	37	0.6	58	0.2	51	1.9
Yugoslavia	801	1.0	38	0.6	147	0.5	13	0.5
Other	3,538	4.2	266	4.1	1,682	6.2	194	7.3
Total	12,348	14.7	1,225	18.8	5,214	19.1	807	30.5
Disbursements for debt reduction	2,473	3.0	313	4.8	8	*	8	*
Total foreign disbursements	84,010	100.0	6,501	100.0	27,291	100.0	2,658	100.0

* Less than 0.05 percent.   — Zero.
NOTE: Table excludes net advance disbursements for the IBRD and IDA. Details may not add to totals because of rounding.
a. United Kingdom includes Hong Kong.

Table 4-8. **IBRD and IDA Payments to Part I and Selected Part II Countries for Foreign Procurement, by Description of Goods, Fiscal 1991**
(amounts in millions of US dollars)

Supplying country	Equipment		Civil works		Consultants		All other goods		Total disbursements	
	Amount	%	Amount	%	Amount	%	Amount	%	Amount	%
Part I countries										
Australia	30	0.7	—	—	12	2.1	78	2.3	120	1.3
Austria	95	2.2	2	0.5	1	0.2	73	2.1	171	1.9
Belgium	79	1.8	33	7.8	10	1.8	73	2.1	195	2.1
Canada	68	1.5	1	0.2	52	9.1	52	1.5	173	1.9
Denmark	45	1.0	4	0.9	12	2.1	12	0.3	73	0.8
Finland	20	0.5	2	0.5	1	0.2	10	0.3	33	0.4
France	402	9.1	51	12.1	94	16.5	219	6.3	766	8.4
Germany	613	14.0	41	9.7	35	6.2	330	9.6	1,019	11.1
Iceland	1	*	—	—	—	—	1	*	2	*
Ireland	1	*	—	—	6	1.1	9	0.3	16	0.2
Italy	266	6.1	62	14.7	10	1.8	124	3.6	462	5.0
Japan	682	15.5	15	3.6	17	3.0	112	3.2	826	9.0
Kuwait	—	—	—	—	—	—	59	1.7	59	0.6
Luxembourg	—	—	—	—	1	0.2	4	0.1	5	0.1
Netherlands	93	2.1	5	1.2	25	4.4	103	3.0	226	2.5
New Zealand	1	*	1	0.2	5	0.9	8	0.2	15	0.2
Norway	7	0.2	—	—	1	0.2	32	0.9	40	0.4
South Africa	39	0.9	1	0.2	1	0.2	61	1.8	102	1.1
Sweden	70	1.6	—	—	4	0.7	23	0.7	97	1.1
Switzerland	142	3.2	10	2.4	15	2.6	87	2.5	254	2.8
United Arab Emirates	2	*	2	0.5	—	—	46	1.3	50	0.5
United Kingdom[a]	440	10.0	19	4.5	101	17.8	229	6.6	789	8.6
United States	625	14.2	2	0.5	100	17.6	588	17.0	1,315	14.4
Total	3,721	84.7	251	59.5	503	88.4	2,333	67.5	6,806	74.4
Part II countries										
Argentina	26	0.6	5	1.2	—	—	20	0.6	51	0.6
Brazil	60	1.4	3	0.7	1	0.2	143	4.1	207	2.3
China	70	1.6	51	12.1	1	0.2	41	1.2	163	1.8
Hungary	17	0.4	1	0.2	—	—	5	0.1	23	0.3
India	76	1.7	3	0.7	5	0.9	14	0.4	98	1.1
Indonesia	1	*	—	—	—	—	22	0.6	23	0.3
Iran, Islamic Republic of	—	—	—	—	—	—	68	2.0	68	0.7
Iraq	—	—	—	—	—	—	37	1.1	37	0.4
Kenya	9	0.2	—	—	1	0.2	13	0.4	23	0.3
Korea, Republic of	92	2.1	21	5.0	3	0.5	33	1.0	149	1.6
Mexico	22	0.5	12	2.8	—	—	48	1.4	82	0.9
Nigeria	1	*	—	—	—	—	33	1.0	34	0.4
Panama	7	0.2	—	—	—	—	14	0.4	21	0.2
Poland	16	0.4	5	1.2	—	—	13	0.4	34	0.4
Portugal	8	0.2	3	0.7	12	2.1	10	0.3	33	0.4
Romania	23	0.5	1	0.2	—	—	2	0.1	26	0.3
Saudi Arabia	2	*	—	—	—	—	44	1.3	46	0.5
Singapore	57	1.3	3	0.7	4	0.7	97	2.8	161	1.8
Spain	22	0.5	17	4.0	1	0.2	42	1.2	82	0.9
Thailand	14	0.3	2	0.5	—	—	26	0.8	42	0.5
Turkey	5	0.1	1	0.2	—	—	24	0.7	30	0.3
Venezuela	3	0.1	—	—	—	—	85	2.5	88	1.0
Yugoslavia	33	0.8	11	2.6	—	—	7	0.2	51	0.6
Other	109	2.5	32	7.6	38	6.7	281	8.1	460	5.0
Total	673	15.3	171	40.5	66	11.6	1,122	32.5	2,032	22.2
Disbursements for debt reduction	—	—	—	—	—	—	—	—	321	3.4
Total foreign disbursements	4,394	100.0	422	100.0	569	100.0	3,455	100.0	9,159	100.0

* Less than 0.05 percent.   — Zero.
NOTE: Details may not add to totals because of rounding.
a. United Kingdom includes Hong Kong.

Table 4-9. **IBRD and IDA Foreign Disbursements by Description of Goods, Fiscal 1989–91**

Item	1989 Part I	Part II	Total	1990 Part I	Part II	Total	1991 Part I	Part II	Total
				Millions of U.S. dollars					
Adjustment lending[a]									
Agricultural inputs	292	124	416	220	36	256	162	61	223
Civil works	4	2	6	3	—	3	4	1	5
Consultants	14	3	17	15	1	16	19	3	22
Equipment	665	203	868	1,052	223	1,275	949	249	1,198
Raw materials[b]	892	599	1,491	1,577	681	2,258	1,301	708	2,009
All other goods	497	314	811	366	229	595	629	224	853
Total	2,364	1,245	3,609	3,233	1,170	4,403	3,064	1,246	4,310
Investment lending									
Agricultural inputs	97	6	103	83	35	118	38	40	78
Civil works	308	216	524	281	235	516	245	168	413
Consultants	560	72	632	499	77	576	471	63	534
Equipment	2,818	493	3,311	2,515	509	3,024	2,720	425	3,145
Raw materials[b]	246	47	293	71	20	91	89	54	143
All other goods	488	93	581	219	73	292	184	31	215
Total	4,518	927	5,445	3,667	949	4,616	3,747	781	4,528
Total disbursements									
Agricultural inputs	389	130	519	303	71	374	200	101	301
Civil works	312	218	530	284	235	519	249	169	418
Consultants	574	75	649	514	78	592	490	66	556
Equipment	3,483	696	4,179	3,567	732	4,299	3,669	674	4,343
Raw materials[b]	1,138	646	1,784	1,648	701	2,349	1,390	762	2,152
All other goods	985	407	1,392	585	302	887	813	255	1,068
Total	6,882	2,172	9,054	6,900	2,119	9,019	6,811	2,027	8,838
				Percent[c]					
Agricultural inputs	75	25	6	81	19	4	66	34	3
Civil works	59	41	6	55	45	6	60	40	5
Consultants	88	12	7	87	13	7	88	12	6
Equipment	83	17	46	83	17	48	84	16	49
Raw materials[b]	64	36	20	70	30	26	65	35	24
All other goods	71	29	15	66	34	9	76	24	13
Total	76	24	100	77	23	100	77	23	100

— Zero.

NOTE: The table excludes disbursements for debt reduction of $2,160 million in fiscal 1990 and $321 million in fiscal 1991. It also excludes net advance disbursements and IBRD disbursements on loans to the IFC and "B" loans. Details may not add to totals because of rounding.

a. Operations under this heading include structural-adjustment loans, sector-adjustment loans, and hybrid loans. Hybrid loans support policy and institutional reforms in a specific sector by financing both a policy component disbursed against imports and an investment component, which sometimes includes civil works and consultant services.

b. Raw materials include chemicals and commodities.

c. All of the percentages are based on the dollar amounts shown under the total disbursements section. These percentages show both the breakdown between Part I and Part II countries for individual goods categories and the share of each goods category compared with total disbursements.

Bank's interest, as a cooperative institution, in giving all eligible bidders from developing and developed countries an opportunity to compete in providing goods and works financed by the Bank; and the Bank's interest, as a development institution, in encouraging the devel-

opment of local contractors and manufacturers in the borrowing country.

In most cases, international competitive bidding is the most effective method of procurement. The Bank prescribes conditions under which preference may be given to domestic or regional manufacturers and, where appropriate, to domestic contractors. Through the end of fiscal year 1991, 61 percent of IBRD and IDA disbursements covered goods and services provided directly by foreign suppliers located outside the borrowing country. While most foreign procurement comes from suppliers in developed member countries and Switzerland, suppliers from developing countries have become increasingly effective in winning contract awards. Through the end of fiscal year 1986, 11 percent of foreign procurement was awarded to Part II supplying countries. During fiscal year 1991, Part II suppliers' share was 22 percent of the total foreign disbursements.

Table 4-4 shows consolidated foreign and local disbursements for IBRD and IDA, through the end of fiscal 1986 and for each of the next five fiscal years to the end of fiscal 1991. Advance disbursements consist of payments made into special accounts of borrowers, from which funds are paid to specific suppliers as expenditures are incurred. Because balances in these accounts cannot be attributed to any specific supplying country until expenditures have been reported to the Bank, these are shown as a separate category in the table.

Table 4-5 provides details of foreign disbursements by Part I and Part II countries for IBRD and IDA separately. Disbursements for debt reduction are not attributable to specific

suppliers and are therefore shown as a separate category.

Table 4-6 shows disbursements made in fiscal year 1991 by the IBRD and IDA for local procurement from selected Part II countries and disbursements made for goods, works, and services procured from them by other Bank borrowers for projects funded by the Bank.

Table 4-7 shows the amounts disbursed from IBRD and IDA separately for foreign procurement of goods and services from Part I and selected Part II countries in fiscal year 1991 and cumulatively through fiscal 1991. Selection criteria are based on the extent of procurement from each of the Part II countries in fiscal year 1991.

Table 4-8 shows the proportion of foreign disbursements from IBRD and IDA for specific categories of goods and services provided by Part I and selected Part II countries in fiscal year 1991.

Table 4-9 provides a summary listing of the amounts paid to Part I and Part II suppliers in each fiscal year from 1989 to 1991. Amounts disbursed towards adjustment and investment projects are compared with respect to the significant categories of goods procured from foreign suppliers. The extent to which Part I and Part II countries participated in supplying these major categories of goods in each of the past three fiscal years is also compared.

Maintenance undertaken at a natural-gas terminal in Bang Pakong, Thailand. Bank lending for oil, gas, and coal is nearing the $10 billion mark.

Section Five
World Bank Activities, IFC, MIGA, and ICSID

Operations Evaluation

The basic purpose of operations evaluation in the World Bank is to assess the efficiency and effectiveness of Bank-supported development projects and programs. It provides the Bank's shareholders with full accountability for past operations, while informing operational managers of relevant experience and helping them to sharpen the objectives of current programs.

Demand for operations evaluation has been rising within and outside the Bank, reflecting the scarcity of resources for development, concern for efficiency in their use, and the need for accountability and transparency in the more open societies of the 1990s. The effects of the Bank's decentralization include a renewed search for quality in operations that draws on cross-country experience; for refined analytical tools and empirical data to arrive at more realistic expectations of future costs and benefits; and for evidence on the effect of past operations on people and the environment.

The director-general, operations evaluation (DGO), has overall responsibility for evaluation. He reports directly to the Bank's executive board, with an administrative link to the president, and is supported by the Operations Evaluation Department (OED). The Joint Audit Committee (JAC) of the board oversees the work of the OED. In fiscal 1991, as in the past, the findings and recommendations of the JAC were reviewed by the full board, as was the fiscal 1990 annual report of the DGO and the department's annual review of evaluation results for 1989.

Most of the OED's work falls into two categories: audits of completed Bank-supported operations and studies that address broader development issues at the country and sectoral levels. The OED also works to bring borrowers more closely into the evaluation process and to help them strengthen their own evaluation capacity.

During fiscal year 1991, the OED:
• enhanced the value of its audits, putting more emphasis on the lessons to be drawn from experience;

• produced studies on topics relevant to operations and policy;
• took steps to make its findings more accessible to potential users; and
• helped developing countries and other donor organizations to build up or strengthen their evaluation systems.

Audits. The OED audits all adjustment-lending operations and 40 percent of the Bank's investment operations. For those operations that are not audited, the OED reviews the project-completion reports (PCRs), which are prepared by the Bank's operational staff, to ensure their quality and facilitate the transfer of experience to new Bank lending operations; it then forwards these PCRs to the executive board.

The OED received 293 PCRs in fiscal 1991 and audited 129 of them, of which 117 were for investment projects and 12 for adjustment operations. The cumulative total of Bank operations subjected to *ex post* evaluation reached 2,000 at the end of the fiscal year.

Nearly two thirds of the fiscal 1991 audits were undertaken in clusters—for example, on a series of agricultural-extension projects within one country or on comparable energy-exploration projects across countries. Clustering allows more broadly based conclusions to be drawn, with wider applicability for future operations.

Studies. To carry out its mandate, the OED must evaluate the Bank's policies and their appropriateness, procedures and their integrity, processes and their adherence to established rules, and effectiveness in promoting lasting development in borrowing member countries.

In designing its studies program, the OED takes into account the analytical work being done elsewhere in the Bank and focuses on topics in which its independence, institutional memory, or time perspective give it a comparative advantage. Its most basic criterion is that of relevance to the concerns of the Bank's board, management, and staff. The OED keeps in touch with these evolving concerns through its contacts with the board of executive directors and by keeping abreast of debates on policy, practice, and research results through-out the Bank.

The OED's mandate to evaluate only completed operations and their effects sometimes limits its ability to respond to current concerns. But, at the same time, it is also often a source of strength. Development projects have a long gestation, and the perspective of time is essential to find out about their effects, particularly on people. Ultimately, the Bank's development effectiveness is measured by outputs after many years, rather than by reassessment of inputs and by reestimation of benefits at project closing. Even then, evaluation evidence contributes new questions or answers of its own. It points to trends, or to hypotheses about what makes development work, that with further study yield guidance on how to shape policies, programs, methods of analysis, or practical choices. And often, because it is empirically based, it substantiates what was already suspected, or argued on the basis of theory, and thus makes it easier to see what actions need to be taken.

In fiscal 1991, the OED sent eight studies to the board. Topics included the Bank's assistance for trade-policy reform and for structural adjustment in a range of borrower countries; support for industrialization in semi-industrialized countries; sustainability in education projects; education lending in Indonesia; lessons from Bank-supported population programs in different country circumstances; and lending for small and medium-sized industry.

Environmental issues—particularly the importance of national forestry strategies in borrowing countries, and the need to understand the interplay among natural resources, economic incentives, and traditional cultures—were central to a study, completed in fiscal 1991, of Bank policies and practices in forestry development. Three continuing studies assess the environmental impact of Bank projects in Brazil, the use and management of natural resources in Nepal and Bolivia, and the environmental, economic, and social effects of involuntary settlement resulting from Bank energy and agricultural projects.

Other topics of special concern, particularly poverty alleviation and women in development, continued to be addressed in various studies across sectors and regions.

Evaluation Results for 1989, which was published in March 1991, reviewed and synthesized the results of operations that were evaluated in that year.

Project analysis methodology. Prompted by the findings reported in the OED's *Evaluation Results* for 1988 and 1989, the Bank's management and the OED began, during the past fiscal year, a broad review of the Bank's methods of project selection, appraisal, and evaluation. The first phase of this review sought to identify practical ways to improve the analysis of key issues of concern, such as poverty alleviation and sustainability, and ways to use the lessons of experience to assess the risks of different types of operations better, and thus to improve their design.

Application of findings. Guidelines issued in 1989 require the Bank's operational staff to seek out evaluation findings and apply them in future operations. In fiscal 1991, operational departments experimented with new procedures for systematically identifying relevant findings early in the project cycle; the OED assisted in these ventures. Management responses continued to be prepared on all major evaluation reports.

The OED took steps to sharpen its messages and to improve access to findings within and outside the Bank. Within the Bank, for example, it began a series of abstracts summarizing the findings of major audits and studies, and made available a user-friendly, searchable, computerized textbase containing summaries of all its reports. Outside the Bank, it began distributing its reports more effectively to those able to act on the findings.

Some OED reports were followed up in seminars arranged by borrowers. For example, a study of the Bank's support of the Colombian power sector—undertaken in response to a request from the government of Colombia—was reviewed by a panel of senior representatives from that country. The OED provided the principal speakers, and regional Bank staff participated as observers.

Help to developing countries. The OED's evaluation-capability development program (ECDP), now in its fifth year, helps those developing member countries of the Bank that are committed to strengthening their evaluation capacity. Having an evaluation capacity of one's own enables borrowers to assess the developmental effectiveness of their investments and to inform donors on how their aid has been used. Activities are arranged in response to the interests of individual countries as part of a general concern to strengthen public-sector management. During the past year, the program was active in Brazil, Colombia, Morocco, and Zimbabwe; it also assisted the West African Development Bank. The Bank's regional departments and resident offices provided support.

Other activities. The department participated as an observer in meetings of the Development Assistance Committee's expert group on aid evaluation. (The committee, or DAC, was established in 1961 as part of the original structure of the Organisation for Economic Co-operation and Development. Its mandate is to secure an expansion of the aggregate volume of resources made available to developing countries and to improve the effectiveness of those resources.) Staff attended workshops and seminars with evaluators from other international organizations and donor countries to compare work programs and discuss possibilities for cooperation.

OED staff continued to participate as "resource persons" in Economic Development Institute seminars on the monitoring and evaluation of development projects, and in seminars on project sustainability.

Economic Development Institute

An important source of technical assistance is the Bank's staff college, the Economic Development Institute (EDI). The EDI trains people from borrowing member countries to create and carry out development programs. In recent years, the Bank has focused on growth that promotes both equity and financial and environmental sustainability. That combination of goals has generated the priority the EDI now assigns to issues of poverty reduction, human-resource development, concern for the environment, debt and adjustment, public-sector management, and private-sector development. The fiscal 1991 training program of the institute directly reflected these issues.

Thus, the EDI has expanded coverage of poverty among its offerings. A detailed three-year poverty-related training program, which will involve as many as forty distinct activities, has been prepared for submission to potential funding sources. The program addresses both poverty-reduction and gender issues.

The EDI is also undertaking a number of training programs that directly address the issue of recognizing and increasing the contribution of women to the development process. These programs, initially confined to the Africa region, focus on the training needs of women managers in both the formal and informal sectors.

Environmental issues were the central theme of a worldwide seminar on energy policy that was held at the EDI in October 1990. A follow-up seminar was held in France. These two seminars addressed environmental considerations relating to urban and industrial water supply and waste disposal. In addition, a series of national workshops on environmental assessment, started in fiscal 1990, has been continued in Egypt and Latin America, with subregional workshops in the Caribbean and Central America.

In addition, the EDI has begun a three-year program of regional and country workshops on collaboration among governments, nongovernmental organizations (NGOs), and international agencies. The program, which is being carried out in partnership with the government of Japan, is designed as a joint learning process, with EDI organizing workshops and seminars in which participants can review projects on which NGOs and governments have collaborated successfully, assess roles of NGOs in participatory planning and policy development, review policy and operational aspects of collaboration, and draft action guidelines and recommendations.

The regional and sectoral distribution of fiscal 1991 activities is shown in Table 5-1. Within the regional activities, Africa accounted for slightly more than one third of the total. Of the nineteen activities in the Europe, Middle East, and North Africa region, eight were held in Eastern Europe. The rapid pace of economic liberalization in Eastern Europe has created quicker-than-expected demands for new EDI courses and seminars. These activities have dealt with the subregion's immediate problems of economic liberalization—inflation and stabilization, financial-sector reform, and privatization. Other activities have included courses concerned with concepts of market economics, housing and transport policy, and management of state-owned enterprises.

Overall, the largest number of activities was in the field of development management, while activities in the other sectors were closely balanced. Well over half of all activities were policy-oriented seminars that addressed issues of macroeconomic management or sector management. About one fifth of the activities were senior policy seminars, 10 percent were for training of trainers at EDI partner institutions, and about 5 percent were technical or project-analysis activities.

In the recent past, special emphasis has been placed on developing case studies of African policy issues, in particular, on structural adjustment. While development of materials related to adjustment issues remains important, the EDI has shifted its attention to developing training materials related to questions of poverty and employment. Other training materials begun during the year included a manual on tax reform that draws on the results of a recent Bank research project, an updating of existing materials on project analysis and agroindustrial development, and a set of teaching cases based on studies by the Operations Evaluation Department.

Although the institute continues to produce mainly printed materials, it has also developed

Table 5-1. **Fiscal 1991 EDI Training Activities, by Region and Sector**

Sector	Nonregional	Africa	Asia	Europe, Middle East, and North Africa	Latin America and the Caribbean	Total
Agriculture	1	5	3	3	1	13
Development management	3	10	8	4	2	27
Finance and industry	6	5	5	4	0	20
Human resources	1	4	4	1	2	12
Infrastructure	1	3	4	5	2	15
Macroeconomics	2	4	3	2	4	15
Total	14	31	27	19	11	102

interactive computer-based materials that make use of the Bank's program for achieving consistency in making macroeconomic projections. Work has begun on the development of computer software and documentation on project management and project analysis. The EDI has launched a publicity campaign to promote the wide use of its training materials; the campaign has resulted in an increase in requests for materials of nearly 60 percent over fiscal 1990.

One of EDI's long-standing objectives has been to strengthen local training institutions through technical assistance, including assistance in mobilizing external funding. In recent years, the institute has maintained relationships with more than 100 training institutions in developing countries. Of the seventy-three institutions with which EDI worked in fiscal 1991, 55 percent were in Africa, 25 percent in Asia, 12 percent in the Europe, Middle East, and North Africa region, and 8 percent in Latin America and the Caribbean.

The EDI's relationships with partner institutions vary widely in terms of resource use. With certain institutions, the EDI maintains formal multiyear agreements for substantive, wide-ranging assistance intended to strengthen the partner institutions (or networks) to help them become effective, independent training institutions. Good progress was made in fiscal 1991 in strengthening some of these networks. One of the most promising is the UNEDIL network in sub-Saharan Africa, dedicated to strengthening management-training institutions. (The acronym stems from the fact that the network is cosponsored by the United Nations Development Programme, the EDI, and the International Labour Organisation.) The EDI's assistance to UNEDIL is being carefully coordinated with another important institution-building program in Africa, launched with Bank assistance during fiscal 1991—the African capacity-building initiative (ACBI).

A second institution-building effort launched recently is directed at training institutions in Africa's five Portuguese-speaking countries. In mid 1990, the EDI participated in a needs-assessment survey of local training institutions. A networking approach was judged to be the most promising means of assistance. A five-year program has been drawn up identifying twenty-four activities to be undertaken, ten of which will be priorities for the first two years (1991–92).

The growth of cofinancing in the 1980s has made possible the large increase in EDI activities. Cofinancing has also generated important secondary benefits by establishing closer contacts with a wide range of bilateral and multilateral aid agencies and with training institutes in industrial countries. It has also provided access to additional sources of teaching materials and speakers, drawn from EDI's financing partners. This has proven to be particularly true in multiyear cofinancing arrangements that give both parties a greater stake in going beyond an ad hoc funding relationship.

The institute administers two programs for postgraduate study, largely but not exclusively limited to the area of economic development: the McNamara Fellowships Program and the World Bank Graduate Scholarship Program. The McNamara fellowships are for nondegree postgraduate study, which need not be at a university. The World Bank scholarships are for postgraduate study leading to an advanced degree. Candidates for both programs must come from, and must pursue their studies in, a Bank member country.

Early in 1990, fifteen new fellowships—compared with ten in the previous year—were awarded for studies to begin in fiscal 1991. This was the largest number of awards made to date under the program, with women outnumbering men for the first time. Of the sixteen individuals covered by the fifteen awards, six were from Asia, three were from Africa, one from

Latin America, and six were from industrialized countries. There were 382 candidates in the past year's application cycle, a 6 percent increase over the previous year.

The World Bank Graduate Scholarship Program is funded by the Japanese government. Now in its fourth year, the program has awarded scholarships to 234 scholars from seventy-one countries. In the 1990–91 academic year, 157 scholars are being supported; 90 are receiving first-year grants, while 67 are in their second or third year of study. Over the four years of the program, 112 grantees have elected to study economics, 54 have chosen finance and administration, and 16 planning and policy. Others have studied agricultural sciences, environment, public health, demographics, energy, and law. Twenty-four percent of the scholarships have gone to women. In fiscal 1991, as a result of a sizable increase in the Japanese contribution, the program processed between 2,500 and 3,000 applications for 100 new scholarships in the 1991–92 academic year. In addition, it is expected that between 80 and 100 scholars will receive continuing funding.

The EDI's five-year strategic plan, covering the years 1990–94, calls for a systematic review of training activities. Fiscal year 1991 has seen the beginning of a more comprehensive review of activities than was possible during the recent years of the EDI's rapid expansion. The review has focused on assessing the accomplishments of course objectives and on the improvement of training methods. An analysis of participant-evaluation reports for activities conducted in fiscal 1991 indicates a continued record of relatively high satisfaction among participants with regard to relevance, usefulness, and the attainment of objectives. The EDI has also begun to evaluate its programs of longer-term institutional-development assistance to partner institutions, and its senior policy seminars. The first of these reviews was completed in fiscal 1991; it focused on the institute's relationship with the Center for Integrated Rural Development for Asia and the Pacific.

Research at the World Bank

The World Bank's project and program-loan portfolio is supported by its program of economic and social research. This research is intended to broaden understanding of the development process, to strengthen the foundation of Bank policy and advice, to support Bank lending, and to develop the research capacity of the Bank's developing members.

The research program is reviewed annually by the executive directors of the Bank. Research priorities are established by the Research and Publications Policy Council, and individual projects are funded by departmental monies or approved by the Research Committee and funded by the research support budget. Most research projects are undertaken in the policy, research, and external affairs complex of the Bank; about one fifth are conducted in the operations and finance complexes.

The research program addresses the program objectives determined by the Bank's senior management and the areas of emphasis set by the Research and Publications Policy Council. The objective areas are adjustment and debt; financial intermediation; poverty reduction; human-resource development; private-sector development and public-sector reform; the environment; natural resources; and infrastructure and urban development. Research emphasis areas are the environment, private-sector development, and the reform of socialist economies.

The transformation of socialist economies has engendered a range of analytical work for the development community, generally, and for the research program of the World Bank, in particular. A World Bank seminar on "Implementation Problems of Privatization in Eastern Europe" was held in Yugoslavia, and six Eastern European countries and the Soviet Union participated. A review of the experience and challenges to date in trade, privatization, agriculture, finance, fiscal policy, poverty, and social safety nets, and of the Bank's activities in socialist Europe, is contained in the paper "Transformation of Economies of East and Central Europe." Research staff were heavily involved throughout the year in operational missions to Eastern and Central Europe, China, and Ethiopia.

The World Bank, the Organisation for Economic Co-operation and Development, the International Monetary Fund (IMF), and the European Bank for Reconstruction and Development cooperated in a joint study of the Soviet economy. The objective of this study was to make recommendations to the Soviet Union on economic reforms and to the major industrialized countries on criteria for assistance. The Bank managed two task forces on systemic and sectoral reform; the first dealt with prices, enterprise management and reform, privatization, finance, and law, while the second analyzed the manufacturing, agricultural, and housing sectors.[1]

Closely related to problems in transition from centrally managed economies are issues

---

[1] For details, see page 43.

in private-sector development and public-sector management. Bank research staff worked jointly with the Chinese Systems Reform Commission to stage a week-long symposium, "Alternative Forms of Public Sector Ownership." A review of the experience of seven countries was incorporated in the paper "Enterprise Reform and Privatization in Socialist Economies." Several other papers on public-sector management were completed, including policy studies on the history of tax systems in developing countries, tax reform, management of urban development, and technology development in East Asia.

The central issues in reform of socialist economies are also similar in many aspects to those addressed for decades by the Bank in advising developing countries on economic reform. Central in these have been policies on macroeconomic adjustment, trade, and debt. Staff from the Bank and the IMF worked jointly on three research studies on the prospects for economic growth in developing countries in the credit-constrained 1990s. These are "The Impact of Industrial Countries' Trade, Agricultural, and Industrial Policies on Developing Countries," "The Role of Foreign Direct Investment in Development," and "Implementation of the Debt Strategy and Its Impact on the Development Prospects of All Severely Indebted Countries."

The Bank completed the 1990 edition of *World Debt Tables,* which is a major reference work and an important item on the Bank's ongoing research agenda. A project was also completed comparing alternative approaches for stopping high inflation in hyperinflationary and long-term, high-inflation countries. The results were widely disseminated at conferences and seminars in Latin America, Europe, and the United States and will appear in journals and a forthcoming book.

Several international seminars on financial issues were sponsored by the Bank's research departments, including two on industrial and financial-sector policy (Paris and Seoul) and one, "African External Finance in the 1990s," which reported on sixteen papers produced as a collaborative effort by the research and African operations sections of the Bank.

The Bank has been involved in many efforts to advise on reform, negotiations, and international agreements on trade. A recently completed project, "Trade Reforms in SALs: A Positive Analysis of Performance and Sustainability," analyzed the trade-offs between short-run performance and longer-term distribution, investment, and revenue effects. The Bank and the U.S. Department of Agriculture cosponsored a conference, "EC 1992: Implica-

tions for World Food and Agricultural Trade." Another joint conference, "The European Community and the Caribbean in the 1990s," discussed the European Community's Single Market Act, the Lomé IV Convention negotiations, the Uruguay Round negotiations, and changes in Eastern European markets, and the implications of these events and circumstances for developing countries. The results of the research project, "Industrial Competition, Productive Efficiency, and Their Relation to Trade Regimes," were disseminated at conferences at the National Bureau of Economic Research, the World Institute for Development Economics Research, and Harvard and Georgetown Universities.

A renewed emphasis on poverty reduction was reflected in the program and output of the research complex during the year. *World Development Report 1990* focused on the circumstances and size of the poor population in developing countries, and on critical factors in poverty alleviation. The lessons of the report are being disseminated internationally and implemented in Bank policy. Seminars on the book's analysis were held in the most populous developing member countries of the Bank (China, India, and Indonesia), and the Economic Development Institute drafted a poverty training strategy that will be implemented over the next three years. Research staff are preparing a poverty handbook to guide country-assistance programs for poverty reduction, and two new research reports analyze the cost-effectiveness of government programs to alleviate poverty—"Reaching the Poor through Public Employment Schemes: Arguments, Evidence, and Lessons from South Asia" and "Financial Implications of Development Policies Aimed at Poverty Reduction."

An issue integrally related to poverty alleviation is human-resource development. During the year, the research program included a wide range of work on improving the quality of life of women, on labor training and employment, and on health. Work specifically oriented to the needs of women included an issues paper, "Enhancing the Economic Role of Women in Development," presented to the Development Committee; the initiation of a "Women's Management Training Outreach Program" for leaders of women's groups; participation in the Pan African Institute for Development, which is intended to develop local training delivery systems for women in the informal sector; and the publication of *Women's Work, Education, and Family Welfare in Peru.*

Other work on human-resource development completed during the year included a report, "Skills Training for Productivity: Policies for Vocational Education and Training in Developing Countries," the management of a seminar in Indonesia on "Health Financing and Health Insurance in Asia," training workshops for Bank staff on population projects and on textbook production, and a workshop in Geneva on vocational education and training for donor staff.

Because development projects can disrupt the livelihood and culture of indigenous peoples, research staff have been involved in an ongoing attempt to encourage the development of participant groups of affected peoples and protection of them. A paper on such strategies formed the basis of a revised operational directive on indigenous peoples.

Development projects, specifically, and economic growth, more generally, have been seen as a source of environmental degradation. The World Bank has been increasingly involved in environmental and natural-resource management and in the development of environmentally sustainable economic policy; increased activity is reflected in the expansion of research on these issues. Central in this work has been the role of the Bank in coordinating international efforts at ecological protection. In this regard, the World Bank's research staff are now responsible for the administration of the Ozone Projects Trust Fund, which is to fund work by developing countries to honor their Montreal Protocol commitments to reduce production and use of chlorofluorocarbons and other ozone-depleting gases. Bank research staff are also preparing issues papers for the Global Environment Facility's Scientific and Technical Advisory Panel on a proposed "small projects window," on international waters, and on three topics pertaining to the protection of biodiversity.

The importance of the agricultural sector for economic growth, poverty reduction, and food security makes it the focus of continued research in the Bank. Various studies completed during the year addressed land tenure and agricultural-supply response in sub-Saharan Africa and price projections for, and risk management of, basic commodities produced in developing countries. A review of the results of a comprehensive cross-country comparison of agricultural pricing was compiled in "The Political Economy of Agricultural Pricing Policies," published in fiscal 1991, and a more general reassessment of agricultural policy was reflected in the paper "Redefining the Role of Government in Agriculture for the 1990s."

The Bank's Eleventh Annual Agricultural Symposium, "Agriculture in the 1990s," was a forward-looking analysis of technical development, the Uruguay Round negotiations, and the changes in Eastern European agriculture and agroindustry in this decade. A seminar sponsored jointly with the National Bank of Hungary focused more specifically on "Agricultural Reform in Eastern Europe and the USSR."

The Bank's long-term experience with infrastructure and urban-development projects is reflected in a range of reports and training programs under way in fiscal 1991. The major work in this area was "Urban Policy and Economic Development: An Agenda for the 1990s," which outlined strategies for infrastructure provision, financial services, and environmentally sustainable activities, and suggested new research and development needs for urban development. The approach developed in the paper on "Impacts of Infrastructure Deficiencies on Nigerian Manufacturing" may provide a basis for application in other developing countries. Several other ongoing projects address issues in housing policy, the power sector, road pricing, and the relative efficiency of utilities that use diesel fuel rather than other types of energy.

The Bank held the third in the series of annual conferences on development economics, focusing in fiscal 1991 on the transition in socialist economies, the role of military expenditures in development, challenges in urbanization, and the role of governance in development. In his paper on privatization in Eastern and Central Europe, Professor Jeffrey Sachs emphasized the urgent need to maintain momentum in the transition process; Robert S. McNamara argued for reductions in military expenditures worldwide and for redirection of expenditures toward critical human and physical investments in developing countries; Professor A. L. Mabogunje outlined a paradigm for dealing with urban growth and productivity; and Edgardo Boeninger drew on his experience of governance in Chile to address a broad range of practices that can enhance or debilitate governance. These four papers from the plenary sessions, together with discussant comments, eight additional papers, and a roundtable debate, will be published in the *Proceedings of the World Bank Annual Conference on Development Economics,* a supplement to *The World Bank Economic Review* and *The World Bank Research Observer.*

Technical Assistance

Technical-assistance components in Bank operations are used primarily to support investment lending. In calendar year 1990, these components totaled $1.4 billion, representing a 24 percent increase in value over 1989 amounts. Technical-assistance components, as a percentage of investment lending, have also grown, from 7 percent in 1989 to 9 percent in 1990.

In calendar 1990, nine freestanding technical-assistance loans were approved for a total of $130 million, up slightly from the year before. During the year, the Bank approved a freestanding technical-assistance loan to Poland. The loan is helping finance an environment-management project that is addressing key environmental problems through policy, management, and program coordination; industrial efficiency and environmental reviews; air-quality management; and water-resources management. The Bank is also supporting the technical-assistance needs of other Eastern and Central European countries; freestanding technical-assistance loans were approved in late fiscal 1991 for Bulgaria and Romania, and one for Czechoslovakia is being prepared.

Eighty-three advances under the Project Preparation Facility (PPF) were approved during calendar year 1990 for a total of $65.6 million. The PPF was created in 1975 to help overcome weaknesses in borrowers' capacity to complete project preparation and to support the entities responsible for preparing or carrying out the projects. Under the facility, the Bank can advance up to $1.5 million per project either to meet gaps in project preparation ($750,000 limit) or to assist in institutional strengthening ($750,000 limit) so that project implementation can begin before the loan or credit becomes effective.

During the year, the Bank's executive directors approved amendments to the facility that address the changing needs of PPF borrowers. In recent years, requests for institutional-strengthening assistance have become far more common than requests for assistance in project preparation. Among other things, therefore, the amendments remove the distinction between the two types of PPF activities and allow the Bank's four operational regions to authorize one or more advances up to the limit of $1.5 million a project.

In contrast to PPFs, which are either subsequently refinanced through Bank loans or are repaid by the borrower, the Special Project Preparation Facility (SPPF) is one of the few technical-assistance grant instruments in the Bank. (Reimbursement is required only when a Bank-financed project results within five years from the date the SPPF is approved.) The SPPF was established in 1985 to help IDA-eligible member countries in sub-Saharan Africa finance preparation activities (including preparation of project proposals for financing by other donors) that could not be financed from other sources.

In calendar 1990, twenty-seven advances were made for $3 million. A review of SPPF activities over the past three years shows that more than three quarters of all SPPF grants are helping to finance the preparation of projects involving the environment, debt, financial intermediation/adjustment, human-resource development, poverty reduction/food security, public-sector management, and private-sector development.

Some 196 projects, which cost $307 million and are assisted by the United Nations Development Programme (UNDP), were being executed by the Bank at the end of the calendar year. In most of these cases, the Bank acts as sole executor; in some cases, however, the Bank is responsible only for the execution of components of projects that are another entity's responsibility (either the government or another agency). The UNDP is shifting its operational approach from the present arrangement, which relies heavily on exogenous executing agencies, to one that will rely on local entities for project execution. The changes will go into effect in January 1992. The implications for the Bank as executing agency for the UNDP are not yet clear.

The number of projects funded by trust funds continued to grow during the year. At the end of 1990, the Bank was administering 850 operations (including those of the UNDP) for a total of $3,197 million equivalent in donor commitments. Total disbursements during the year were $574 million, 53 percent of which were for cofinancing of Bank projects. The remainder of the disbursements was for such activities as preinvestment studies, environment studies, the Consultative Group on International Agricultural Research, the Special Program for Research and Training in Tropical Diseases, and the Onchocerciasis Control Program.

On July 30, 1990, a special fund for policy and human-resource development (the PHRD Fund) was established within the IBRD and IDA. Funded by Japan's Ministry of Finance, the PHRD Fund encompasses and extends several existing programs of support and collaboration between Japan and the Bank.

Japan has pledged approximately $300 million equivalent, over the three-year period covering Japan's fiscal years 1990–92, in support of Bank-assisted projects and programs, including those for the environment, training and training-related activities of the Economic Development Institute, and the provision of scholarships under the Bank's Graduate Scholarship Program. During the course of Japan's 1990 fiscal year (April 1990 to March 1991), Japan committed approximately $85 million in grant funding for technical assistance, primarily for the preparation of Bank-supported projects and programs. Of this amount, about $15 million supported environmental technical assistance.

Substantial technical assistance for the alleviation of transboundary environmental concerns (biodiversity preservation, global warming, pollution of international waters, and protection of the ozone layer) will be provided through the newly formed Global Environment Facility (GEF). Participating governments have committed about $1.5 billion for GEF activities during its initial three years. The Bank has been given responsibility for administering the GEF, in partnership with the UNDP and the United Nations Environment Programme.[2] The billion-dollar-plus fund, which was established in November 1990, already has a $273 million portfolio in its tranche of projects for fiscal 1992. Eleven projects, valued at $59 million, are primarily for technical assistance and are to be managed by the UNDP. The balance of the tranche is composed of fifteen investment projects that are to be managed by the Bank. However, substantial technical-assistance activities, integral to the success of the investments, are contained in this $214 million commitment.

Interagency Cooperation

Stepped-up activities by the United Nations and associated agencies have focused increasingly on strengthening the capacity of developing countries to implement and sustain policy reform.

One initiative, sponsored jointly by the African Development Bank, the United Nations Development Programme (UNDP), and the World Bank, has as its objective the expansion of African capacities in the key areas of policy analysis and development management. The African capacity-building initiative (ACBI), formally launched in February 1991, is designed to help develop the kinds of skills and institutional know-how needed to manage economic change. Under the ACBI, national and regional institutions will be strengthened, government and private-sector capabilities will be enhanced, and graduate-level and in-service training will be supported. The ACBI represents a broad partnership between sub-Saharan African countries and the international donor community.[3]

Complementing the ACBI's focus on policy analysis and economic management is a program jointly sponsored by the UNDP, the World Bank's Economic Development Institute, and the International Labour Organisation that has as its goal the strengthening of

African training institutions. The program, called UNEDIL, is fostering civil-service improvements, public-enterprise reform, and private-sector development. UNEDIL works closely with regional associations and a consortium of donors.

Support for economic transition in Eastern and Central Europe has become a major commitment of the United Nations (U.N.) system. The Bank is collaborating with other international agencies to help Eastern and Central European countries meet their three fundamental challenges—economic transformation, social protection, and environmental clean-up. Following up on the request of the seven major industrialized countries and the president of the Commission of the European Communities at the July 1990 Houston economic summit, the Bank participated with the International Monetary Fund, the Organisation for Economic Co-operation and Development, and the European Bank for Reconstruction and Development in a detailed study of the Soviet economy.[4]

Increased interagency cooperation on the environment reflected the heightened international concern with the link between environment and development. The UNDP, the United Nations Environment Programme (UNEP), and the Bank have joined forces to manage a Global Environment Facility (GEF) to channel technical, scientific, and financial resources to middle-income and lower-income countries to help finance programs and projects affecting the global environment. The GEF will be implemented under a tripartite arrangement that may well serve as a model for future interagency collaboration on issues of major interest to the international community.[5] Work proceeded during the year on a major restructuring of the Tropical Forestry Action Plan, a five-year, $8 billion program cosponsored by the Food and Agriculture Organization of the U.N. (FAO), the UNDP, the World Resources Institute, and the Bank. Several recent studies of the plan—by nongovernmental organizations, as well as by an independent panel appointed by the FAO—have identified severe shortcomings in the plan's implementation.

A high-level international commission recently evaluated the role and operations of the joint UNDP/World Bank Energy Sector Management Assistance Programme (ESMAP) and

---

[2] For details, see page 61.
[3] For details, see page 115.
[4] For details, see page 43.
[5] For details, see page 61.

recommended a strategic reorientation of the focus and management of the program to reflect energy-sector priorities in the 1990s. The priorities include energy efficiency, environmental linkages, long-term investment planning, investment financing, technology transfer, and institutional strengthening. Other issues identified for special consideration include end-use efficiency, least-cost supply investments, gender issues and poverty linkages, the encouragement of private-sector involvement, and long-term capacity building. Further changes to the program include recasting the annual donors' meeting into a broader consultative group and a strengthening of relations with regional development banks.

Increasingly, Bank initiatives aim at strengthening measures to protect future development projects from potential catastrophes and to arrest environmental degradation that could spark further natural disasters. The Bank and the United Nations Centre for Human Settlements (Habitat) are collaborating on a program to mitigate the effects of disasters in metropolitan areas and to promote preparedness in disaster-prone developing countries.

Habitat's collaboration with the Bank has continued to expand over the years. A main vehicle for collaboration is the joint Habitat/UNDP/World Bank Urban Management Programme (UMP), the first major concerted multilateral effort to support developing countries worldwide in improving urban management. The UMP places strong emphasis on the links among research, operational activities, and the policymaking process and seeks to develop and promote appropriate policies and tools for land management, provision of infrastructure, operations and maintenance, municipal finance and administration, and urban environmental management. The overriding concern in all UMP activities is to help build urban-management skills.

Relations with nongovernmental organizations. The Bank continues to foster cooperation with nongovernmental organizations (NGOs) worldwide. The challenge of meeting the needs of the world's poor, together with a heightened sense of urgency about global environmental degradation, has prompted institutions of many different types to cooperate in finding ways to protect, conserve, and develop the world's human and natural resources. The Bank and its borrowers are expanding their interaction with NGOs of many kinds—for example, community associations, private voluntary organizations, religious groups, and environmental organizations—to ensure that grassroots insights and expertise are taken into account at both the project and policy levels.

In fiscal 1988, the Bank began a systematic effort to increase NGO involvement in the operations it supports. Since fiscal 1988, the average annual number of Bank-assisted projects that involve NGO participation has tripled. Eighty-two projects approved by the Bank's executive directors in fiscal 1991 involved NGOs. As in previous years, sub-Saharan Africa continued to have the largest share of NGO-associated projects, but the shares in Asia and Latin America and the Caribbean have increased in recent years, as well. Historically, most of the projects involving NGOs have been in the agriculture and rural-development sector, but, in the past two years, NGOs have been engaged more frequently in Bank-supported social-dimensions-of-adjustment and education projects (see Table 5-2).

The Bank has sought to involve local NGOs in its operations largely for their firsthand knowledge and capacity to organize low-income people. About 86 percent of the NGO-associated projects approved in fiscal 1991 involved either indigenous intermediary NGOs or grassroots groups. The Bank's senior management has also encouraged staff to engage beneficiary groups and local NGOs early in project planning and design, as experience has shown that successful poverty-focused programs have usually involved the poor, both at the design stage and during implementation. A list of projects in the pipeline in which Bank staff see potential for NGO involvement is now regularly updated to facilitate interaction with NGOs and implementing agencies in the early stages of project preparation.

The Bank-supported Third Jabotabek Urban Development Project in Indonesia—approved in fiscal 1991—illustrates the Bank's stepped-up efforts to involve local NGOs in project design.[6] The project builds on the twenty-five-year-old *kampung*-improvement project (KIP), which, as the largest urban community-upgrading program in the world, has helped improve the basic living conditions of about 8 million low-income residents in some 200 cities and towns throughout the country.

The traditional KIP has been effective in providing basic infrastructure, but its top-down approach has revealed some significant weaknesses. Inadequate investments have been made in sanitation and health education; communities have not been fully involved in

---

[6] Jabotabek is the Indonesian government's mnemonic for the urban region consisting of the province of DKI Jakarta and the surrounding local governments of Bogor, Tangerang, and Bekasi. The population of Jabotabek is about 15 million.

Table 5-2. **Patterns in World Bank–NGO Operational Collaboration, Fiscal 1973–91**

	1973–88		1989		1990		1991[a]		Total, 1973–91[a]	
Item	No.	%	No.	%	No.	%	No.	%	No.	%
By region (number of projects)										
Africa	111	51	27	59	22	44	39	48	199	50
Asia	51	24	8	17	14	28	23	28	96	24
Europe, Middle East, and										
North Africa	16	7	4	9	3	6	9	11	32	8
Latin America and the Caribbean	40	18	7	15	11	22	11	13	69	18
Total	218	100	46	100	50	100	82	100	396	100
By sector (number of projects)										
Adjustment-related	2	1	4	9	8	16	9	11	23	6
Agriculture/Rural development	102	47	15	33	18	36	21	26	156	39
Education/Training	20	9	4	9	5	10	11	13	40	10
Environment	2	1	2	4	4	8	3	4	11	3
Industry/Energy	22	10	4	9	1	2	7	9	34	9
Infrastructure/Urban										
development	41	19	8	17	5	10	14	17	68	17
Population/Health/Nutrition	26	12	7	15	9	18	16	20	58	15
Relief	3	1	2	4	0	0	1	1	6	1
Total	218	100	46	100	50	100	82	100	396	100
By type of NGO (number of NGOs)										
Grassroots	75	30	29	41	30	42	56	30	190	33
Indigenous intermediary	75	30	28	40	26	36	104	56	233	40
International	104	40	13	19	16	22	25	14	158	27
Total	254	100	70	100	72	100	185	100	581	100
By function (number of functions)										
Advice	75	27	7	10	7	8	26	15	115	19
Cofinancing	10	3	5	7	8	10	21	12	44	7
Design	33	12	11	16	19	22	29	17	92	15
Implementation	162	58	42	59	46	54	78	45	328	54
Monitoring and evaluation	1	0	6	8	5	6	18	10	30	5
Total	281	100	71	100	85	100	172	100	609	100

a. Preliminary.

planning and deciding on the location of facilities; and operation and maintenance have been poor. Demand has been increasing for a more flexible, community-based program to respond directly to communities' concerns in such areas as loans for individual and group sanitation facilities, as well as home improvements, advice to small businesses, and strengthening of sanitation and public-health components.

Under the new KIP, which the third Jabotabek project is supporting, NGOs—mainly Indonesian developmental NGOs—are working with *kampung* committees to inform the community of the project and establish community development-action groups. The problems and needs of the community will be identified, and, together with the development-action groups, *kampung*-improvement plans will be devel-

oped and funding negotiated with KIP implementing units; water and sanitation users' associations will be organized and trained to manage and operate public sanitation facilities; small-scale credit will be made available to individuals and groups for home improvements and small-business support; and implementation of project components and facilities will be monitored. By the end of project implementation (around 1998), it is expected that the new community-based approach of the KIP will have been firmly established and that NGO skills in community development will have been developed to the extent that NGOs can be accepted as full partners with the government in other, similar kinds of operations.

Other member governments of the Bank have become interested in the ways in which the nonprofit, voluntary sector can assist in national development. In some cases, borrowers have sought advice from the Bank on the most effective ways to promote government-NGO cooperation in their countries. The Bank has studied the process by which the Indian government provides grants to NGOs in the population sector, and is now analyzing the Indian government's experience in providing grant funds to NGOs in general. Analysis may suggest how government funding of NGOs can best be managed.

The expansion of NGO involvement in Bank-assisted operations has occurred against a backdrop of intensified policy discussion between NGOs and the Bank. The Bank appreciates exchanges of information, experience, and viewpoints with NGOs on policy issues related, in particular, to the social and environmental aspects of development. Many NGOs, in both developed and developing countries, want to contribute their perspectives to influence Bank thinking. Nongovernmental organizations are becoming better organized into coalitions and networks, and their collective voice is consequently gaining greater notice in the Bank and among borrowers.

Nongovernmental organizations, with the authorization of their governments, can be granted visitors' status to attend the annual meetings of the Bank and the International Monetary Fund. In addition, parallel seminars for NGOs on Bank policies have become a regular feature of these meetings. The topics of NGO seminars organized by the Bank during the annual meetings in September 1990 included environmental assessment, *World Development Report 1990,* the GEF, and the Bank's forestry policy. As a follow-up to discussions surrounding the last-named topic, the Bank organized, in April 1991, a consultation with NGOs to discuss the Bank's draft forestry policy paper. Fifty-five representatives of environmental groups and development NGOs, including more than twenty-five from developing countries, participated in the meeting, which represented the Bank's most significant effort to date to involve NGOs in the development of an operational policy document.

The most important Bank-NGO forum—in terms of longevity, breadth, and depth of the discussion—is the NGO–World Bank Committee. Formed in 1982, the committee provides a formal, international forum for policy discussions between senior Bank managers and NGO leaders from around the world. At the committee's tenth annual meeting (held in Washington on October 31 and November 1, 1990), the main topics discussed were *World Development Report 1990,* areas of agreement and disagreement between the Bank and NGOs on

broad outlines of development policy, and popular participation in development decisionmaking.

Increased Bank involvement in recent years in aspects of popular participation has helped set the stage for the initiation by the Bank in fiscal 1991 of a program of action and learning on popular participation.

The three-year program has several components. One involves the continued monitoring of the participatory aspects of environmental assessments and the Bank's collaboration with NGOs. A second involves a selective review to determine how faithfully Bank guidelines that invoke popular participation are being implemented; in addition, aspects of participation in new operational directives will be scrutinized. A third component seeks to sensitize operational staff on aspects of popular participation through interactive reviews of twenty Bank projects that involved popular participation. An "expert group" of Bank staff has been formed to guide this part of the program. The group will draw on analytical work on participation that is being carried out in various parts of the Bank and elsewhere. One particular focus will be on ways in which the Bank may need to modify its operational policies to encourage popular participation more widely in its projects and economic and sector work.

Cooperation with the Organisation for Economic Co-operation and Development. The Bank actively pursues a dialogue on policies and practices of mutual concern to bilateral and multilateral aid donors with the Organisation for Economic Co-operation and Development (OECD) and its Development Assistance Committee (DAC). Data are regularly exchanged between the Bank and the DAC, especially regarding aid flows, debt, and financial transfers. The Bank participates in DAC working groups concerned with improving aid coordination, evaluation, and practices, as well as financial and statistical reporting. In this regard, Bank staff helped write the Principles of Program Assistance, Technical Cooperation, and Aid Evaluation, which were designed to facilitate aid coordination and consistency among donors.

As an official observer on a number of OECD committees, notably the DAC, the Bank was active in discussions on issues of current concern, including popular participation; aspects of governance (such as accountability, openness, and the legal environment); the coordination of aid to countries affected by the crisis in the Gulf; environmental issues; creation of an enabling environment for the private sector; and the development of market economies in Eastern Europe. Increased aid effectiveness and sustainability were important goals of all these meetings.

The first high-level meeting of donor governments' environment and development ministries, an initiative aimed at better formulation of policies affecting developing countries, was convened at the OECD in February 1991. The Bank also participated in the development of environmental-policy guidelines that were designed to create more consistency among donors and facilitate planning by aid recipients. Research by the OECD on global modeling and the issue of taxes on carbon-dioxide emissions is providing useful background for the Bank's work on the environment, particularly for the forthcoming *World Development Report 1992,* which focuses on the relationship between development and the sustainable use of environmental resources.

The annual ministerial-level meeting of the OECD in early June and the twice-yearly meetings of the OECD's Economic Policy Committee, which focus on industrial-country concerns such as economic recovery, inflation, competition, trade, public expenditures, and unemployment, are important fora in which the Bank can point out how various industrial-country policies affect developing countries.

Cooperation with the regional development banks. The World Bank maintains close relationships with the three major regional development banks—the African Development Bank, the Asian Development Bank, and the Inter-American Development Bank.

The Bank's relationship with the African Development Bank (AfDB) has intensified in recent years. The Bank has been involved in numerous joint initiatives with the AfDB, and the AfDB's cofinancing of Bank-assisted projects has more than tripled since the mid 1980s, from about $170 million in 1985 to more than $525 million in 1990. The World Bank also collaborates closely with the Asian Development Bank (AsDB). During 1990, six projects in five countries were cofinanced; AsDB cofinancing amounted to more than $600 million. Economic and operational information is routinely shared, and joint missions and sector work have become common. The AsDB's entry into policy lending underscores the need for structured coordination on sector policies, as well as for cooperative efforts in the areas of special operational emphasis that are shared by the two institutions.

The Bank and the Inter-American Development Bank (IDB) have had a close relationship since the IDB began its operations in 1961. Those relations have been strengthened and intensified since April 1989, when the board of governors of the IDB approved a seventh capital replenishment. At that time, the governors authorized the management of the IDB to initiate programs of sector-adjustment and structural-adjustment lending and encouraged the institution to seek cofinancing for such programs from the World Bank. In fiscal 1989, five Bank-assisted projects were cofinanced by the IDB for a total of $346 million; in fiscal 1991, fourteen operations were cofinanced for a total of $1.4 billion. Cooperation has strengthened substantially in other areas, as well. Since 1990, staff of both institutions have participated in several preparation, preappraisal, appraisal, and economic-sector review missions. Consultations have also been fostered: Information sharing and policy consultations, as well as formulation of initiatives, are an integral part of the two institutions' working relations. The senior managements of the institutions meet periodically to consult on operational matters, as well.

To determine the longer-term cooperation and cofinancing possibilities between the World Bank and the newly formed European Bank for Reconstruction and Development (EBRD), officials of the two institutions have met several times in both Washington, D.C., and Paris; the EBRD has expressed interest in cofinancing with the Bank in the areas of enterprise restructuring, privatization, and financial-sector development, as well as projects in the energy, telecommunications, and environment sectors. In June 1991, the EBRD cofinanced a Bank-assisted heating-supply project in Poland designed, among other things, to encourage energy conservation and reduce environmental pollution. The two institutions have also expressed interest in sharing country- and project-specific information. During fiscal 1991, the EBRD also participated, along with the Bank, the International Monetary Fund (IMF), and the OECD, in a major study of the economy of the Soviet Union.

Cooperation with the International Monetary Fund. The Bank and the International Monetary Fund share the broad objectives of promoting sustained growth and development of member countries, and they have been assigned differing but complementary roles in pursuing this objective. The two institutions are expected to ensure close collaboration in order to serve members with maximum effectiveness.

Guidelines for collaboration between the Bank and the IMF have been in place since 1966, and they have been periodically reviewed since then, the most recent review having taken place in March 1989, when additional or more formal administrative and procedural steps were agreed upon.

A review of recent experience in collaboration concluded that the procedures governing collaboration were working reasonably well and that recent collaborative practices have been more uniform and systematic than previously. Specifically, the review noted that:

• extensive staff contacts have been maintained for both country-related matters and general policy aspects of common interest;

• regular sessions for planning country strategies and review by the senior staffs and the two managements have helped create a more transparent operational framework for the staffs at the working level and have helped maintain a common ground in the approaches of the two institutions;

• collaboration in support of members' adjustment efforts has been extensive;

• in general, divergences of views, when they arose, were identified and resolved at an early stage;

• financial support to member countries by the Bank and the IMF has been coordinated even though resource flows in the context of adjustment programs remained difficult to predict with precision;

• through collaboration between the staffs and practical experience gained by country authorities, the process of formulating policy-framework papers has evolved to serve the papers' original purpose better;[7]

• collaboration has been particularly intensive in the area of debt, at the country-specific level, as well as on general policy matters; and

• collaboration has also continued with respect to research and related activities, primarily through joint participation in seminars and projects.

In their discussion of the report on collaboration between the two institutions, the executive directors of the Bank emphasized the need for, and importance of, continued close collaboration and noted that in the area of support of adjustment, early identification and resolution of differences of views had contributed to improved country dialogue on policies and more consistent advice to member countries. In the areas of debt strategy and arrears, the directors welcomed the close cooperation between the two institutions and the positive results achieved so far. Many stressed, however, the need for continuing efforts both to prevent countries from falling into arrears and to help those that have fallen into arrears to become current with both institutions.

Overall, the directors agreed that the March 1989 framework for enhanced collaboration had proven to be useful and that no immediate need for revised or additional procedures had emerged.

Cooperation on agricultural research. The Consultative Group on International Agricultural Research (CGIAR) is an informal association of forty public and private-sector donors that supports a network of sixteen international agricultural-research centers. The Bank is a cosponsor of the CGIAR, together with the Food and Agriculture Organization of the U.N. and the United Nations Development Programme.

Programs carried out by CGIAR-supported centers fall into six broad categories: productivity research (technology generation), management of natural resources, improvement of the policy environment, institution building (strengthening national agricultural-research systems in developing countries), germplasm conservation, and facilitating linkages between developing-country institutions and other components of the global agricultural-research system.

Research at CGIAR centers covers commodities that provide 75 percent of food energy and a similar share of protein requirements in developing countries. Production in developing countries would be poorer by several hundred million tons of staple food annually without CGIAR-supported research.

Some 45,000 agricultural scientists have been trained at CGIAR centers during the past nineteen years. The types of training provided by the centers range from mid-level regional courses to postdoctoral programs. The many alumni of CGIAR centers form the nucleus of, and provide leadership to, national systems of agricultural research.

In 1990, thirty-three donors contributed a total of $234.9 million to the centers' core programs, an increase from $224.5 million in 1989. The Bank contributed $34.3 million. Sixty-nine percent of the contributions came from donor countries, while international or regional organizations contributed 30 percent. The balance was provided by two foundations. The average contribution amounted to $7.1 million, compared with $6.2 million in 1989—when there were thirty-six donors—reflecting, in part, the effect of exchange-rate fluctuations.

Reorientation of programs and expansion of the system. In 1990, the CGIAR made a number of landmark decisions that stemmed from proposals contained in a report from the

---

[7] A policy-framework paper is a three-year comprehensive report prepared by the national authorities with the assistance of the staffs of the Bank and the IMF. It identifies the sources of a country's problems, describes the proposed remedies, and provides estimates of the associated financing requirements and the role of the major aid agencies.

A Colombian farmer packing peeled cassava for the market. The CGIAR's first facility devoted to biological control—the International Institute of Tropical Agriculture's Biological Control Center—has helped reverse the spread of the cassava mealybug, an insect pest responsible for $5.5 billion of damage to Africa's cassava crop.

group's Technical Advisory Committee on a possible expansion of the CGIAR system. The report was the result of a two-year deliberative process that began when the group decided at its 1988 mid-term meeting to review the desirability of admitting into the CGIAR all or some of the international research centers that were then outside the CGIAR system. Donors sub-sequently expressed the view at the group's 1989 mid-term meeting that the mandate of the CGIAR should be expanded to include agroforestry and forestry research.

Although the Technical Advisory Committee had been asked to review whether the ten "nonassociated centers" should be included within the system, the committee felt that it could not approach the task as a simple matter of recommending the inclusion or exclusion of new institutions. The committee saw the potential expansion of the CGIAR as the starting point for systemic restructuring.

The report consequently contained proposals for integrating agroforestry and forestry into the CGIAR system, for a major expansion of the system, for a substantial restructuring of the system in the medium term, and for the long-term evolution of the system.

To reorient research carried out at the international centers, the CGIAR:

• strongly endorsed the concept of eco-regional activity within the CGIAR system as a means of merging productivity concerns with natural-resource management;

• called for a continuing examination of a series of natural-resource management themes— such as the relationship between soil and water, soil fertility, and plant protection—and of the institutional changes required to ensure that those themes were encompassed in CGIAR-supported research;

• decided that a number of commodities of particular importance for poor people should be included in future research programs within the CGIAR framework; and

• emphasized that the full benefits of international agricultural research could not be attained unless national agricultural-research systems were significantly strengthened.

The immediate consequence of these decisions was that two nonassociated centers joined the CGIAR system. The new centers are the Colombo, Sri Lanka–based International Irrigation Management Institute and the International Network for the Improvement of Banana and Plantain, headquartered in Montpellier, France.

To ensure that agroforestry and forestry research is firmly established within the CGIAR, the International Council for Research in Agroforestry (ICRAF) in Nairobi, Kenya, was admitted into the system with responsibility for agroforestry. A new institution, to be established shortly, will undertake forestry research.

A working group, consisting of representatives from Australia, Brazil, the International Development Research Centre, the Rockefeller Foundation, and Sweden, was formed to develop proposals for the second institution. The working group reported to the CGIAR mid-term meeting in May 1991 on the spectrum of research to be undertaken by the new entity, options for location and staffing, and the relationship between the new entity and ICRAF.

The group also broadly agreed that vegetables research should be a constituent element of the work of the system, and it recognized the global contribution that has been made by the Asian Vegetable Research and Development Center, based in Taiwan. At the same time, however, the group appreciated the need for political developments to mature before any final decision could be made.

Award for biological control. The Nigeria-based International Institute of Tropical Agriculture (IITA) and the Colombia-based Centro Internacional de Agricultura Tropical (CIAT) have achieved much success in controlling, through biological means, one damaging African food pest and are making progress towards controlling another.

Success in controlling the cassava mealybug has benefited more than 200 million Africans for whom cassava is a staple food. The benefit-cost ratio of the cassava-mealybug program has been calculated at 149 to 1—$149 worth of food saved for every $1 invested in research and development.

Swift action against the mango mealybug, which, three years ago, threatened mango production across much of West and Central Africa, was patterned after the successful program against the cassava mealybug.

The mango mealybug-control program included identification of the rapidly spreading pest as an accidental import from Southeast Asia, the discovery in India of natural enemies of the pest, and the release of two promising parasitic wasps following their quarantine, testing, and mass-rearing. Several affected countries, where natural enemies of the mealybug were released in 1988, enjoyed a good mango crop in 1989, following an almost total loss of production during the previous two years.

For their work on biological-control programs, IITA and CIAT were awarded the CGIAR King Baudouin Award in 1990.

The CGIAR King Baudouin Award is given every two years to a CGIAR-supported agricultural-research center for a particular technology or discovery that has improved the lives of farmers in developing countries.

In 1980, the CGIAR itself won the King Baudouin Prize for International Development, established in commemoration of the first twenty-five years of the Belgian monarch's reign. The original prize of $50,000 is held in trust. The CGIAR King Baudouin Award is made from the earnings accrued. Winners are selected by members of the CGIAR Technical Advisory Committee.

Personnel and Administration

The Bank's administrative budget for fiscal 1991, as approved by the executive directors

Table 5-3. **World Bank Budget by Expense Category and Work Program, Fiscal Years 1988-92**
(millions of US dollars)

Item	Actual				1992 program
	1988	1989	1990[a]	1991	
Expense category					
Staff costs	441.9	479.3	558.1	608.4	700.3
Consultants	58.4	59.2	69.2	78.0	82.6
Contractual services	18.4	26.7	29.8	31.0	33.4
Operational travel and representation	76.7	79.4	90.8	99.5	103.0
Overhead/contingency	113.0	112.5	127.9	138.2	148.6
Direct contributions to Special Grants Program	46.0	52.6	52.6	57.0	58.9
Reorganization implementation	21.7	..	..	..	..
Reimbursements	(21.1)	(31.6)	(41.3)	(48.3)	(57.8)
Total	755.0	778.1	887.1	963.7	1,069.0
Work program					
Operational	279.2	280.2	319.4	352.4	374.2
Financial	31.4	33.0	35.5	38.7	40.3
Policy, research, and external affairs	69.8	72.7	87.6	90.3	94.2
Operations evaluation	5.2	5.6	6.5	7.0	7.5
Administrative support	50.4	53.5	58.7	64.5	66.8
Boards, corporate management, and legal services	35.5	36.7	40.3	45.6	50.6
Total regular programs	471.6	481.7	548.1	598.4	633.6
Reimbursable programs	12.1	15.0	16.9	20.9	29.5
Special programs[b]	59.8	66.5	68.5	73.0	75.5
Overhead/benefits	232.5	246.5	294.7	319.8	378.1
President's contingency[c]	..	..	..	..	10.2
Reimbursements	(21.1)	(31.6)	(41.3)	(48.3)	(57.8)
Total	755.0	778.1	887.1	963.7	1,069.0
Memorandum item					
Total in millions of fiscal 1992 dollars	979.9	979.6	1,015.2	1,041.4	1,069.0[d]

.. Not applicable.

NOTE: Details may not add to totals because of rounding.

a. Excludes budget supplement of $149.8 million, approved by the board on May 31, 1990, to fund the Retired Staff Benefits Plan.

b. Includes investment operations.

c. Allocations from the president's contingency have been included under the respective work programs for fiscal 1988–91.

d. $705.0 million for the IBRD and $364.0 million for IDA.

late in fiscal 1990, totaled $969.1 million, including a supplement of $7.0 million for the May 1991 compensation adjustment.

Late in fiscal 1991, the executive directors approved a budget for fiscal 1992 of $1,069 million (see Table 5-3), a rise of 2 percent in real terms over the fiscal 1991 administrative budget. Staff salary increases, together with related increments in benefits, accounted for most of the rise in the administrative budget.

The substantive priorities of the fiscal 1992 budget are to make poverty reduction the centerpiece of Bank work (continuing the emphasis on human-resource development, the environment, and private-sector development, as well as promoting more efficient use of resources at the country level); meet the needs of new member countries and of emerging programs in currently inactive countries; and improve implementation of development programs and projects through more supportive supervision and through advisory services of high quality.

At the end of fiscal 1991, World Bank regular and fixed-term staff on board numbered 5,900, of which 3,776 were higher-level staff of about 125 nationalities. This was an increase of 2.4 percent over the previous year's total. Of the higher-level staff, 58 percent were from the industrialized Part I countries, while the remaining 42 percent were from the developing Part II countries; women formed 27 percent of the total. Efforts continued to diversify the composition of staff by nationality and gender, consistent with securing the highest standards of technical competence and efficiency. However, compared with fiscal 1990, there were only modest improvements in the overall distribution, by nationality and gender, of staff. Of the 197 higher-level staff who joined the Bank during the year, 59 percent were from Part I countries. Some 26 percent of the newly hired higher-level staff were women. Twenty-six of the new recruits were selected through the Young Professionals Program. Fourteen were from Part II countries; eleven were women.

Programs to maintain and improve the caliber of management and professional and technical standards of staff were continued. In this regard, redesigned and strengthened training programs have been implemented. Results from the fourth Bankwide Attitude Survey, conducted at the end of fiscal 1990, were analyzed, and necessary follow-up actions to address areas of concern have been initiated.

The survey revealed a high degree of satisfaction with work and personal accomplishment, with the immediate managers of staff, and with physical resources in the workplace (office technology, for example). However, considerable dissatisfaction was expressed with career development, communications from senior management, and, to a lesser extent, with the decentralization of personnel teams. A joint working group with representatives of the Staff Association has been established to address career-development issues. Following the recommendations of the Support Staff Action Steering Group, a number of changes in personnel policies were approved to organize and manage office work better and improve the career prospects for, and job satisfaction of, support staff.

Following the quadrennial staff-benefits survey completed earlier, the structure of benefits policies, including the medical-insurance plan, was reviewed, and certain improvements have been implemented to rationalize these policies and maintain the international competitiveness of the overall package of benefits necessary to attract and retain the highest caliber of staff.

Work progressed on the review of other benefits applicable to staff who are not U.S. citizens, the tax allowance to U.S. staff, and the introduction of a flexible benefits system. In fiscal 1990, the executive board approved a temporary special-assistance program to protect non-U.S. staff and their spouses from major changes in the U.S. estate-tax provisions. Because efforts to get U.S. authorities to change these adverse provisions have not yet been effective, the executive board approved a one-year extension of the program and, to some extent, widened its coverage. The annual staff-compensation survey was completed according to the general principles of the revised compensation system adopted by the executive board, and appropriate salary adjustments for 1991 were approved.

The project to rehabilitate the Bank's main complex of buildings began on schedule. This project, to be undertaken in three phases over a period of seven years at a cost of $211 million, will almost entirely replace the Bank's original buildings, which were obsolete and inefficient and which posed potential health hazards. The project will permit the accommodation of a larger number of staff on Bank-owned property and, thus, will achieve considerable savings in leased-space and building-operating costs. The first phase of the work, consisting of the selection of the building's design on the basis of international competition, the demolition of two buildings, and the beginning of foundation and structural works, has been completed according to schedule and within the approved budget.

A major management event was the decision by the Bank's seventh president, Barber B. Conable, not to seek another term of office and the election of Lewis T. Preston as president to succeed him. To allow for an orderly transition, Mr. Conable will continue in office through August 1991.

Internal Auditing

The Internal Auditing Department (IAD) acts as an independent appraiser that reviews and evaluates Bank operations and activities. It is headed by an auditor-general who reports functionally to the president of the Bank and administratively to the vice president, corporate planning and budgeting.

To achieve its overall objective of assisting management throughout the Bank in the effective discharge of its responsibilities, the IAD has continued to revise its work program in consultation with members of the President's Council. This helps to ensure that the most critical activities and operations receive priority coverage and that audit reviews address issues that are of the most relevance to concerned management.

In response to requests from Bank management, the IAD focused more attention in fiscal 1991 on the procedures relating to the decentralization of accounting. In addition to participating in discussions that have been held to enhance communication between the concerned departments and to improve the planning process, the IAD undertook audits of computerized systems and administrative procedures that are being transferred. This work was closely coordinated with the reviews being undertaken by the Bank's external auditors in order to avoid a duplication of effort and to maximize the audit coverage of this important process.

The Bank has a wide range of services provided to it by external contractors and consultants. To ensure that these services are provided and obtained in a cost-effective and efficient manner, the IAD performed a number of audits of this aspect of Bank activities in the past year.

These included reviews of payments made to one company for compensation-comparator information, and to another for food services, as well as of payments made to contractors involved in the rehabilitation of the Bank's main complex of buildings. Where it has been considered necessary and appropriate, these reviews included audits of the contractor's financial records and procedures.

The Bank has made, and continues to make, significant progress in applying information technology to meet its global objectives, transforming its environment from one that was almost exclusively mainframe-based to one that involves a worldwide network of interconnected computers. Reflecting this increased reliance on information technology, the IAD conducted a series of technical audits addressing management and control issues pertaining to the three principal computing elements within the Bank. The IAD also performed a number of audits addressing efficiency, effectiveness, and control of critical applications that are about to be implemented or are currently being developed.

International Finance Corporation

The International Finance Corporation (IFC), a member of the World Bank Group, promotes private enterprise in its developing member countries. It does this by financing sound private-sector projects, mobilizing debt and equity financing in the international markets for private companies, and providing technical assistance and advisory services to businesses and governments.

Fiscal year 1991 was one of continued growth for the IFC. The corporation approved financing (loans, guarantees, and equity and quasi-equity investments) for its own account of $1.5 billion for 152 projects, with total costs of $10.7 billion. In addition, the IFC approved a record $1.3 billion in syndicated loans. It also underwrote debt and securities issues totaling $33 million for four companies. The corporation executed three currency-swap intermediations for clients in developing countries that normally do not have access to such services. Disbursements reached $1.2 billion.

The IFC's financial position was also strengthened during fiscal 1991. Net income, at $166 million, was the second highest in its history. The IFC borrowed a total of $598 million in the international markets during the year. Its largest borrowing in fiscal 1991, and its third large public issue in the Euromarkets, was a $300 million Eurobond issue. Since it first received triple-A ratings (or its equivalent) for its debt securities in fiscal 1989, the IFC has established itself as a highly regarded supranational in the public Eurobond markets. Other market borrowings during the year included issues in yen, Spanish pesetas, and Portuguese escudos.

The number of member countries increased by six to 141 during the year. New members of the corporation are Algeria, the Central African Republic, Czechoslovakia, Mongolia, Namibia, and Romania. In response to growing demand for its financial and advisory services in all regions, the IFC opened up new Regional Missions in Cameroon and Zimbabwe and Resident Missions in Brazil, Czechoslovakia, and Hungary. The IFC also created a new position—a capital-markets regional representative in Eastern and Central Europe—that is based in Prague.

Project finance approved for the IFC's own account increased in all regions except Latin America and the Caribbean, with the biggest increase registered in Asia. Projects spanned a number of industries and sectors, including tourism, banking, mining, printing and publishing, pulp and paper, petrochemicals, power, oil and gas exploration, telecommunications, and agroindustries.

In recent years, the IFC's capital-markets program has expanded rapidly. In fiscal 1991, the IFC helped establish thirty financial institutions, many of which provide products or services that are new to the host countries. For example, the IFC helped establish Hungary's first investment bank and one of its first private insurance companies. It also helped finance a joint-venture commercial bank in Poland and the first private housing-finance institutions in Botswana and Pakistan.

In fiscal 1991, the mobilization rate—the ratio of the amount of financing provided by other lenders and investors to financing approved for the IFC's own account—increased to 5.9:1.0, compared with 5.2:1.0 in the year before. In recent years, the IFC has increased its resource-mobilization activities, in many instances raising substantial amounts of debt and equity financing for companies with relatively small outlays of its own funds.

In addition to raising funds through cofinancing, loan syndications, and underwritings, the IFC also mobilizes funds by sponsoring, underwriting, or investing in country and debt-conversion funds. In fiscal 1991, the corporation was involved in three new investment funds—one debt-conversion fund (in Egypt); a fund that will invest in convertible-debt and equity securities in Mexico; and a fund that will invest in equities in developing Commonwealth countries. The IFC also approved investments in five venture-capital companies.

As many countries around the world move toward economic liberalization and encourage private-sector activity, demand for the IFC's advice and technical assistance is increasing. In fiscal 1991, the IFC established its Polish Business Advisory Service, which is based in Warsaw and which will provide advice to local entrepreneurs. The South Pacific Project Facility (SPPF), which was approved in fiscal 1990, opened an office in Sydney, Australia, during the year. The SPPF, which is modeled on the IFC's successful project-development facilities for Africa and for the Caribbean and on the Business Advisory Service for the Caribbean and Central America, will advise entrepreneurs in the South Pacific island countries. Within the corporation's Engineering Department, the IFC established a Technical Advisory Service to provide fee-based advice to companies and governments on a variety of subjects, including technical restructuring, market and feasibility studies, and strategic planning.

The Corporate Finance Service Department, which specializes in restructurings and privatizations, provided advice to the governments of Morocco, Poland, and Portugal on privatization and advised firms in Brazil, Czechoslovakia, Greece, the Philippines, and Yugoslavia on restructuring and privatization. The Foreign Investment Advisory Service, a joint operation of the IFC and the Multilateral Investment Guarantee Agency, advised the governments of twenty-six countries on foreign direct investment.

Late in the fiscal year, the executive directors of the corporation agreed to submit a proposal to the board of governors calling for a $1 billion capital increase—from $1.3 billion to $2.3 billion. The governors are expected to adopt the increase in the coming months. The increase would provide the IFC with the capacity to meet a reasonable level of the substantial demand for finance and advisory services in Latin America and Asia; establish and maintain a strong presence in Eastern and Central Europe that would enable the corporation to make a significant contribution to these countries' transition to market economies; substantially expand the IFC's role in the Middle East; and make an enhanced effort in sub-Saharan Africa.

Full details of the IFC's fiscal year can be found in its annual report, which is published separately.

Multilateral Investment Guarantee Agency

The mandate of the Multilateral Investment Guarantee Agency (MIGA) is to encourage the flow of foreign direct investment (FDI) for productive purposes to and among developing member countries.

Established in 1988, MIGA offers investment insurance to mitigate political risk through its guarantee program and provides promotional and advisory services to assist member countries in their efforts to attract or retain FDI.

During fiscal 1991, MIGA's executive board, which is separate from the boards of the International Finance Corporation and the Bank, reviewed and approved modifications to the agency's operational regulations, reviewed and approved the agency's work program and budget, and concurred with the president's decisions on twenty-four insurance projects conveyed to it.

The board carefully examined the proposed insurance contracts to ensure that MIGA's operations support the environmental and developmental objectives of the World Bank Group.

Guarantee program. MIGA's guarantee program protects investors against losses arising from the noncommercial risks of currency transfer, expropriation, war and civil disturbance, and investment-related breach of contract by host governments. In addition to new projects, MIGA can insure the expansion of existing ones, including privatizations and financial restructurings. Projects must be registered with MIGA before the investments are made or are irrevocably committed. No minimum investment is required to be eligible for MIGA insurance.

Eligible investments include equity, loans made or guaranteed by equity holders, and certain forms of nonequity direct investment. MIGA may insure a loan made by a financial institution if the agency is also insuring a shareholder's investment in the project. The standard policy of MIGA covers investments for fifteen years, although, in exceptional cases, coverage may be extended to twenty years. MIGA also cooperates with national investment-insurance agencies and private insurers to coinsure or reinsure eligible investments. In the past year, MIGA reinsured projects with two national agencies, the Export Development Corporation of Canada and the Overseas Private Investment Corporation of the United States.

In fiscal 1991, MIGA more than doubled its volume of insured projects over 1990 totals. MIGA issued eleven guarantees with a maximum contingent liability of $58.9 million for ten projects, representing a total of $922 million in direct investment. These projects are expected to generate an estimated 3,681 new jobs in host countries by the fifth year of operation. The insured investors are Chiyoda and Marubeni of Japan for a large fertilizer facility in Bangladesh; Millicom of Luxembourg and Motorola of the United States for separate cellular-phone operations in Chile; McDonald's of the United States for four joint-venture restaurants in Chile; Holding Savana of France for three separate companies that will operate hotels in Madagascar; Bering Netherlands, a Dutch company, for a potato and grain-processing operation in Poland; Rio Algom Limited of Canada for a copper mine in Chile; and SAS Service Partner of Denmark for an airline-catering and restaurant company in Turkey.

MIGA's efforts to broaden awareness of its programs and services met with considerable success. At the end of fiscal 1990, preliminary applications for guarantees that were registered and eligible for coverage totaled 116; at the close of fiscal 1991, the total was 274. Notable was the rising interest in MIGA shown by European and Japanese investors and the diversity of registered projects across industry sectors, including manufacturing, mining, agribusiness, energy, and services. The volume of these applications demonstrates the increasing demand for MIGA guarantees.

Policy and advisory services. Policy and advisory services (PAS) assists developing member countries to create attractive investment environments in several major ways: promotion, research, and advisory assistance to governments.

To alert the international business community to the favorable investment climate and specific commercial opportunities in Hungary and Jamaica, PAS organized two successful investment-promotion conferences cosponsored with the governments of the two countries. Foreign investors met with domestic entrepreneurs, discussed issues with senior government officials, and made visits to local enterprises. These conferences resulted in the finalization of several joint ventures. Some of the deals have also involved businesses from other developing countries, thus achieving an important MIGA objective: to facilitate investment flows not only from developed to developing countries but also among developing countries.

PAS's main research activity in fiscal 1991 resulted in the report "Review of the Policies of Some Industrialized Countries Affecting the Outflow of Private Investment to Developing Countries."

In addition, twenty-one advisory projects were carried out through the Foreign Investment Advisory Service (FIAS). Jointly operated by MIGA and the IFC, FIAS provides member governments with advice on policy and institutional issues affecting FDI flow. Almost half of the active projects during the year were diagnostic studies. Activities with repeat clients included more in-depth work on specific investment policies and institutional development. FIAS provided advice on investment-promotion strategies to the governments of Kenya, Lesotho, Madagascar, Morocco, the Philippines, Uruguay, and Venezuela. FIAS also sponsored two United Nations Development Programme–supported regional conferences on investment-policy issues. The first, which focused on attracting more investment to Central America and the Caribbean, assembled thirty-five participants from twenty countries. The second examined the future of foreign investment in Asian developing countries and was attended by twenty-five government officials and prominent professionals from the business and academic communities, representing fifteen countries.

Member relations. In fiscal 1991, sixteen additional countries signed the MIGA convention, increasing the number of signatories to 101. It is expected that countries that have signed but have not yet completed all the membership requirements will soon do so to become full members of MIGA. Latin American countries were the primary focus of the membership drive, which was led by MIGA's Legal Department; a majority of Latin American countries have now signed the MIGA convention. MIGA membership is open to all member countries of the World Bank and Switzerland.

Details of MIGA's activities in fiscal 1991 appear in its annual report, which is published separately.

International Centre for Settlement of Investment Disputes

The International Centre for Settlement of Investment Disputes (ICSID) is a separate international organization established under the Convention on the Settlement of Investment Disputes between States and Nationals of Other States (the convention), which was opened for signature in 1965 and entered into force on October 14, 1966.

ICSID seeks to encourage greater flows of international investment by providing facilities for the conciliation and arbitration of disputes between governments and foreign investors. To further its investment-promotion objectives, ICSID also carries out a range of research and publications activities in the field of foreign-investment law.

In the course of the fiscal year, Argentina, Bolivia, Chile, Czechoslovakia, Grenada, Mongolia, and Zimbabwe signed the convention, bringing the number of signatory countries to 106. In addition, Australia, Grenada, and Mongolia ratified the convention, bringing to ninety-five the number of signatory countries that have completed the process of joining ICSID.

There are currently four disputes pending before the centre. These include one proceeding for the annulment of an award and three arbitration cases. During the fiscal year, the disputes in two other cases submitted to the centre were amicably settled.

ICSID's foreign-investment law publications include a semiannual law journal, *ICSID Review—Foreign Investment Law Journal,* and multivolume collections of *Investment Laws of the World* and *Investment Treaties.* Two issues of the law journal and three releases of the investment laws and treaties collections were published in fiscal 1991.

Details of ICSID's activities in fiscal 1991 appear in its annual report, which is published separately.

Section Six
1991 Regional Perspectives

Africa

The overall economic situation in sub-Saharan Africa (SSA) remains difficult. For many countries, the external environment continues to be hostile, as reflected by the adverse effects of debt overhang, capricious weather, sluggish growth in export demand, and steady declines in terms of trade. A few countries are even suffering internal strife and famine conditions.

The overall rate of growth of gross domestic product (GDP) in the region was only 1.1 percent in 1990—significantly lower than 1989's growth rate of 3.0 percent. External factors such as an increase in oil prices and unfavorable weather for agriculture contributed to the poor growth performance of the region in 1990, a year during which growth rates of other developing regions (Asia excepted) also slowed.

Variations in GDP growth during the past year, however, clearly show that adjustment measures and donor support are making a difference. Low-income SSA economies that are pursuing structural adjustment under the

Table 6-1. **Africa: 1989 Population and Per Capita GNP of Countries That Borrowed during Fiscal Years 1989–91**

Country	Population[a] (thousands)	Per capita GNP[b] (US dollars)	Country	Population[a] (thousands)	Per capita GNP[b] (US dollars)
Angola	9,700	610	Lesotho	1,700	470
Benin	4,600	380	Madagascar	11,300	230
Botswana	1,200	1,600	Malawi	8,200	180
Burkina Faso	8,800	320	Mali	8,200	270
Burundi	5,300	220	Mauritania	1,900	500
Cameroon	11,600	1,000	Mauritius	1,100	1,990
Cape Verde	361	780	Mozambique	15,300	80
Central African Republic	3,000	390	Niger	7,400	290
Chad	5,500	190	Nigeria	113,800	250
Comoros	458	460	Rwanda	6,900	320
Congo	2,200	940	São Tomé and Principe	120	340
Côte d'Ivoire	11,700	790	Senegal	7,200	650
Djibouti	411	—[c]	Somalia	6,100	170
Equatorial Guinea	407	330	Sudan	24,500	—[d]
Ethiopia	49,500	120	Tanzania	23,800	130[e]
Gabon	1,100	2,960	Togo	3,500	390
Gambia, The	849	240	Uganda	16,800	250
Ghana	14,400	390	Zaire	34,500	260
Guinea	5,600	430	Zambia	7,800	390
Guinea-Bissau	960	180	Zimbabwe	9,500	650
Kenya	23,500	360			

NOTE: The 1989 estimates of GNP per capita presented above are from the "World Development Indicators" section of *World Development Report 1991.*

a. Estimates from mid 1989.

b. *World Bank Atlas* methodology, 1987–89 base period.

c. GNP per capita estimated to be in the $581–$2,334 range.

d. GNP per capita estimated to be below $580.

e. Estimate refers to mainland Tanzania only.

special program of assistance (SPA) achieved a growth rate of 3.8 percent in 1990. In contrast, economic output in those countries not implementing reforms or in countries that reversed policies—countries that are outside the framework of the SPA—declined by 2.4 percent in 1990. Among the non-SPA countries, Sudan, Ethiopia, Somalia, and Zaire did particularly poorly owing to a combination of internal strife and poor policies. The combined output of this group of countries declined by 3.6 percent in 1990.

Although performance varies among SPA-eligible countries, the overall growth of adjusting countries confirms that strong policy reforms, coupled with adequate donor support, can lead to better economic performance and also help ease some of the social problems caused by earlier economic and financial crises. Within the SPA group, countries in which economic management is considered well above average—Ghana, Madagascar, Malawi, and Togo—show the greatest improvement. The average annual GDP growth of these countries, where programs of structural adjustment have been sustained over several years, steadily accelerated during the last half of the

1980s, especially during the period 1988–90. Growth of output, of between 3.6 percent and 5.3 percent annually, was significantly higher than in other SPA countries. For example, a group of recently adjusting countries or average performers among SPA countries (Benin, Mali, Mauritania, and Niger) had output growth of 1.2 percent during 1987–89 and 1.4 percent in 1990.

The SPA program has helped those low-income, debt-distressed sub-Saharan African countries that have pursued reforms vigorously and consistently. Reforms have helped the exports of these countries to grow strongly (at about 6 percent a year during 1988–90), and this, along with increased foreign assistance, has allowed imports and investments to grow (at about 4 percent and 8 percent a year, respectively, during 1988–90).

While results from SPA-eligible reforming countries are especially impressive, the overall progress in expanding the Bank's policy dialogue with countries is no less striking. Out of a total of forty-seven countries in sub-Saharan Africa, thirty are implementing programs of economic adjustment. There is a growing consensus on what the main elements of structural

Table 6-2. **Lending to Borrowers in Africa, by Sector, Fiscal Years 1982–91**
(millions of US dollars)

Sector	Annual average, 1982–86	1987	1988	1989	1990	1991
Agriculture and Rural Development	470.6	519.2	562.3	754.8	997.4	504.9
Development Finance Companies	104.9	518.0	232.5	311.6	127.6	138.8
Education	95.3	104.9	178.2	88.2	350.7	265.9
Energy						
Oil, gas, and coal	69.3	35.0	—	31.2	—	311.0
Power	158.9	69.3	88.0	138.4	230.0	155.0
Industry	72.6	—	150.5	81.4	105.1	—
Nonproject	293.3	232.0	525.0	1,019.0	271.6	832.6
Population, Health, and Nutrition	44.1	30.8	121.4	81.3	232.7	432.8
Public-sector Management	3.3	75.0	165.0	—	45.6	5.7
Small-scale Enterprises	21.4	16.0	—	270.0	130.0	—
Technical Assistance	59.7	50.7	95.7	144.6	56.0	70.9
Telecommunications	50.2	27.8	—	103.3	225.0	12.8
Transportation	306.3	226.7	618.6	248.7	543.6	309.5
Urban Development	81.8	130.5	146.5	414.0	360.4	98.3
Water Supply and Sewerage	89.7	61.8	45.0	238.2	257.2	256.0
Total	1,921.5	2,097.7	2,928.7	3,924.7	3,932.9	3,394.2
Of which: IBRD	815.0	865.8	725.1	1,560.6	1,147.0	662.9
IDA	1,106.5	1,231.9	2,203.6	2,364.1	2,785.9	2,731.3
Number of operations	79	78	80	81	86	77

— Zero.
NOTE: Details may not add to totals because of rounding.

Irrigating fields in Cape Verde—a necessity in a country whose development is hindered by a poor natural-resource base and by long cycles of drought.

adjustment should be—a remarkable change from five years ago, when most governments resisted structural reforms because of fear of the political consequences and some doubts about their justification. The policy dialogue in recent years has also deepened: In fiscal 1991, most of the Bank's adjustment lending, for example, was for sector-adjustment operations.

The Bank's overall lending program for sub-Saharan Africa has been increasing steadily in recent years, from an average $1.9 billion over the period fiscal 1981–85, to nearly $3 billion a year over the period fiscal 1986–90. Total commitments reached $3.9 billion in fiscal 1990 and $3.4 billion in fiscal 1991; about 80 percent of this amount was for concessional assistance from IDA.

Subregional Perspectives

West Africa. The oil-exporting countries of West Africa grew by 3.3 percent in 1990, somewhat slower than in 1989 (3.7 percent). In Nigeria, the overall GDP growth rate increased from 4.9 percent in 1989 to 5.0 percent, led by an expansion of oil production during the Gulf crisis. Nonoil GDP rose by 4.5 percent, resulting largely from growth in agriculture of around 4 percent and a pickup in services.

Manufacturing is estimated to have recovered somewhat from stagnation in 1989 and is growing at around 2 percent. The overall commitment of the current government to reforms remains strong. However, weak implementation capacity and pressures from interest groups have caused occasional lapses. For the next few years, the challenge facing Nigeria's government is to sustain the reform process while adhering to sound fiscal and monetary policies during the period of transition to civilian rule.

The GDP of Gabon grew at a rate of 3.1 percent during the period 1987–90, reflecting mostly the expansion of the oil sector. By contrast, Cameroon's economic crisis continued to worsen in 1990—a process that started in 1985–86. In real terms, GDP per capita has fallen by 25 percent since 1985–86. The decline was triggered by decreasing oil production and, more important, by falling oil prices during the mid 1980s, which was followed by a drop in agricultural-export prices. The government is implementing an initial structural-adjustment program that is being supported by a Bank structural-adjustment loan and an economic-management project designed to facilitate the implementation of the adjustment program and to build institutional capacity. The economic situation in the Congo, the other oil-exporting country, remains depressed, as the country continues to suffer from large financial gaps and a considerable debt overhang. Even after the substantial gain realized from higher oil prices during the Gulf crisis, the 1991 budgetary financing gap remains large, the result of a substantial increase in the civil-service wage bill granted in the last quarter of 1990.

During the past eighteen months, the Sahelian countries continued efforts to implement economic reforms and to establish a basis for higher GDP growth. Six of the eight countries— Burkina Faso, The Gambia, Mali, Mauritania, Niger, and Senegal—are actively implementing Bank-supported adjustment programs. In another country, Chad, the reform program has slowed because of recent political turmoil and a change of government. Despite adverse external developments such as the oil-price increase, economic developments over the past eighteen months have been positive in these countries. Overall, GDP growth of 2.7 percent in 1990 was significantly higher than in the previous year (about 1 percent). Nonetheless, per capita income growth remains negative. Growth rates in 1990 varied considerably among countries—ranging from 4.5 percent in The Gambia to only 0.3 percent in Mali and Mauritania.

Agricultural output in the countries of the Sahel increased by only 1 percent, as rainfall distribution was poor in a number of countries, particularly Burkina Faso and Niger. Aggregate export volumes increased by over 9 percent, rebounding strongly from a decline in 1989. As a result of this strong export performance, and despite a small deterioration in the terms of trade, the aggregate current-account deficit of the eight countries declined slightly, from 13.4 percent of GDP in 1989 to 12.1 percent in 1990. Developments over the past year continue to underline the inherent fragility of the Sahelian economies and their great sensitivity to, and dependence on, external factors. In fiscal 1991, the Bank focused its attention on addressing long-term growth issues, particularly human-resource development, poverty alleviation, natural-resource management, and the enabling environment for private-sector development. Debt issues also continued to receive particular attention, and debt-reduction packages, the first to make use of the Debt Reduction Facility for IDA-only Countries, were approved and successfully implemented in Niger and Mozambique.[1]

Economic performance in the rest of West Africa was mixed. In Ghana, the momentum of growth of recent years of 6 percent a year slowed to about 4 percent, partly reflecting stagnant agricultural output caused by bad weather and the adverse effect of higher oil prices. The commitment of the government and the donor community to the country's structural-adjustment program, however, remains strong. Increased financing from concessional sources helped to reduce Ghana's debt-service ratio from 60 percent in 1989 to 36 percent in 1990. The foreign-exchange markets were unified in April 1990; twenty-three state enterprises were either divested or liquidated; the banking system was restructured; and the government took steps to improve the business environment by reducing taxes on corporate income, capital gains, and dividends. Togo is another country with a successful adjustment program. Despite adverse weather, gains in output were about 2 percent during the year, down from between 3 percent and 4 percent during 1989. During the fiscal year, the Bank approved a fourth structural-adjustment credit that seeks to build up institutional capacity and mitigate the social costs of adjustment.

Guinea is yet another country in the subregion that has attained encouraging, if not dramatic, results from its economic-reform program: In 1990, its GDP grew by 4.7 percent. To sustain this growth, the Bank is working with the government to design measures that will increase the domestic savings rate, promote private investment, and improve financial intermediation. Benin, which experienced a GDP decline in 1989, showed a positive growth rate of over 1 percent in 1990. The outlook for the future looks promising because the new government has launched reforms that, if implemented resolutely, could ultimately raise revenue and restore conditions for growth.

Côte d'Ivoire's continued macroeconomic and financial crises—whose root causes lie in a large structural deficit, a lack of competitiveness in the productive sectors, and adverse movements of terms of trade—led the government to prepare a new adjustment program for support by the Bank and the International Monetary Fund (IMF), to enable it to move towards public-finance equilibrium and reduce domestic-payment arrears. During the past year, the government had difficulties in implementing its stabilization program, but undertook structural-reform programs in the agriculture, energy, and water-supply sectors. In addition, key reforms in the financial sector, in privatization and the restructuring of public enterprises, in the regulatory and tax systems, and in human-resource development are under

---

[1] For details, see page 67.

way. Important administrative reforms have also taken place.

Over the past eighteen months, the government of Sierra Leone, in consultation with the IMF and the World Bank, has implemented substantial reforms in its fiscal, monetary, trade, and exchange-rate policies, as well as structural changes in the mining and agricultural sectors. It has also resumed debt-service payments to both the IMF and the World Bank and cleared its payment arrears to the African Development Bank. The IMF is negotiating a rights-accumulation program, an agreement on which will open the way for the Bank to resume lending to Sierra Leone after its arrears to the Bank are settled.

Eastern and Central Africa. Although the overall growth rate of this subregion was close to zero in 1990, some countries did quite well. Uganda has remained a strong, consistent reformer since 1987, and its growth performance continues to be impressive. Overall, GDP growth has been between 6 percent and 7 percent, reflecting a marked recovery in both agricultural production and manufacturing output. In 1990, however, growth fell below 5 percent, and the terms of trade worsened, the result of drought, rising oil prices, and falling coffee exports. The government continued to pursue significant fiscal and monetary reforms to ensure a continued strong performance of the economy. In mid 1990, the parallel market for foreign exchange was legalized—a policy step that will help export growth. In addition, fiscal adjustment is being pursued through several expenditure measures—such as the elimination of "ghost" workers and the reduction of temporary workers—and through a reduction of unwarranted tax exemptions.

The GDP growth rate of Kenya also fell below 5 percent during 1990 as terms of trade worsened, oil prices rose, and receipts from tourism dried up. The government continues to pursue a flexible exchange-rate policy and tighter fiscal and monetary measures.

Madagascar, which has a liberalization program to which the government is fully committed, grew by about 4 percent in 1990. In March 1990, the government prepared, in collaboration with the Bank and the IMF, a new three-year policy-framework paper that outlines new policies to promote private-sector development while preserving competitiveness and further improving public-resource management. The government also took corrective steps in exchange-rate management, including a 13 percent devaluation of the Malagasy franc in early 1991. Burundi, another country that has been pursuing, with success, a long-standing adjustment program, has stabilized both

fiscal and balance-of-payments imbalances. Its growth rate has been over 4.5 percent during 1980–89. and its recent slowdown in growth (3.3 percent in 1990) is attributable to deteriorating terms of trade and drought-related stagnation in agricultural production.

Elsewhere in the subregion, the picture was discouraging: The economies of Sudan, Ethiopia, and Somalia continued to hemorrhage as a result of internal strife and insecurity. It is estimated that GDP fell by 5.8 percent in 1990 in Sudan, while in Ethiopia, output dropped by about 2.5 percent. In Somalia, the economic situation continued to deteriorate. The civil war has had devastating effects on the economy, and rehabilitation will be slow and difficult.

The central African states of Rwanda and Zaire also experienced negative growth in 1990. In Rwanda, the recent civil hostilities resulted in extensive damage to the infrastructure and increased defense expenditures. Furthermore, the price of coffee (which accounts for around 90 percent of Rwanda's exports) hit an all-time low in 1990. All these factors contributed to a further deterioration of the financial and economic situation, and GDP declined by nearly 3 percent. The government recently launched a reform program that included an initial devaluation of the Rwanda franc by 40 percent. The overall goal of the reform program—for which the government has received help from the Bank and the IMF—is to rely more on market forces and the private sector to attain sustainable economic growth. This new strategy represents a clear break from policies pursued in the 1980s.

In 1990, Zaire's overall economic situation deteriorated markedly. Stabilization and adjustment efforts were discontinued, the inflation rate soared to 35 percent a month during the last quarter of 1990, export earnings declined by 9 percent, and GDP fell by nearly 3 percent.

Southern Africa. Economic performance in the Southern Africa subregion remained strong in response to adjustment efforts in a number of countries. Aggregate growth in this subregion averaged 3.2 percent in 1990, down somewhat from 1989 (4 percent). The Malawi economy showed continued strength as the government's program of economic adjustment stayed on track. Gross domestic product grew at 4.8 percent, and inflation slowed considerably. The Malawi government continued to implement a number of economic reforms in 1990, of which import liberalization was of particular significance. Lesotho had another year of impressive growth, repeating 1989's rise of almost 8 percent. Lesotho also took a pioneering step towards the long-term conservation of its environment by integrating a national environment-action plan with an ongoing adjustment program supported by the Bank and the IMF. In Zimbabwe, GDP growth fell to 4 percent in 1990 (compared with an average of 5.7 percent in the previous two years), and inflation increased from 10 percent to 16 percent. In response to these troublesome events, the government initiated a comprehensive economic-reform program designed to move the economy away from regulation and control toward greater reliance on market forces. The economic-reform program combines trade liberalization, tariff reform, fiscal adjustment, public-enterprise reform, a relaxation of domestic controls, and the loosening of labor-market restrictions with appropriate exchange-rate and monetary policies.

Tanzania and Mozambique continued their resolute implementation of adjustment programs. The Tanzanians pursued reforms in key areas (such as trade liberalization) and sectors (agricultural, industrial, and financial). Gross domestic product grew by more than 4 percent in 1990, the fifth consecutive year of increased per capita income. Inflation, which reached 30 percent in 1989, declined to about 20 percent. Although Mozambique continued to demonstrate a firm commitment to implementing its economic-reform program and to moving towards a multiparty system, GDP growth was only 3.1 percent because of several adverse external factors (in particular, high oil prices, adverse weather, and internal strife). In Zambia, considerable progress was made in implementing the government's year-old economic-reform program, especially in decontrolling domestic prices, lowering the budget deficit, liberalizing international trade, and moving to a market-determined exchange rate. Although Zambia's GDP growth in 1990 was low (only 1 percent), with continued reforms and favorable weather conditions, the outlook for economic recovery seems brighter than at any point in the past decade. Good progress in regularizing its position with bilateral and multilateral donors was also made during the year: With arrears to the Bank cleared in March 1991, an IDA credit, the first since 1987, was approved.

Special Programs

A number of special programs complement and underpin the Bank's lending operations in sub-Saharan Africa. The special program of assistance (SPA), discussed in detail on pages 44–47, is one such program. Others—in the areas of population planning, environment, agricultural development and food security, social dimensions of adjustment, education, and

women in development—were reported on in the World Bank's *Annual Report* for fiscal 1990.

The expansion and strengthening of these programs, and others as well, were cited as necessary to Africa's development in the World Bank study *Sub-Saharan Africa: From Crisis to Sustained Growth—A Long-Term Perspective.* Long-term development strategies, the study argued, should be people-centered; human-resource development and meeting basic needs were therefore declared as "top priorities."

The study became a basic document of the high-level conference held in Maastricht, the Netherlands, in July 1990 under the auspices of the Dutch government. Co-chaired by Quett Masire, President of Botswana, Jan P. Pronk, the Netherlands' Minister for Development Cooperation, and Robert S. McNamara, former head of the World Bank, the meeting was attended by virtually all the finance and planning ministers in sub-Saharan Africa, as well as the ministers in charge of aid to Africa from donor countries.

The study's conclusions were couched in general terms. It noted, "Each country must develop the approach that suits its particular circumstances." One recommendation emanating from the Maastricht conference was that African countries should begin preparing national long-term perspective studies.

Some progress toward that end was made during the past fiscal year. The United Nations Development Programme (UNDP) has made funding available to support national efforts to carry out country studies. Twenty-six countries have confirmed their decision to undertake their national perspective studies, and twelve others have already taken steps to launch the exercise. In addition, to help design and carry out these studies, work is under way at the subregional level; a three-year training and research program is being prepared at two national institutions, one in Benin and the other in Senegal; and two management teams of experts are being set up, one in Abidjan and the other in Harare.

The long-term perspective study also clearly identified closer regional integration as a key ingredient for stronger growth over the long run. The Bank is now processing an operation to provide closer economic integration among countries that are members of the Central African Customs and Economic Union (Cameroon, Central African Republic, Chad, the Congo, Equatorial Guinea, and Gabon). The Bank is also working with the Economic Community of West African States on a study of barriers to trade and factor movements

Table 6-3. **Net Transfers to Africa**
(millions of US dollars; fiscal years)

Item	Nigeria		Sudan		Côte d'Ivoire		Total region	
	1991	1987–91	1991	1987–91	1991	1987–91	1991	1987–91
IBRD and IDA commitments	821	3,630	—	364	2	718	3,394	16,867
Gross disbursements	208	1,943	100	467	236	1,027	2,848	13,149
Repayments	245	929	12	51	141	546	974	3,377
Net disbursements	−36	1,014	88	416	95	480	1,874	9,772
Interest and charges	265	1,114	8	42	155	691	979	3,840
Net transfer	−301	−100	80	374	−60	−210	895	5,931

— Zero.

NOTE: Disbursements from the IDA Special Fund and the Special Facility for Sub-Saharan Africa are included. The countries shown in the table are those with the largest amounts of public or publicly guaranteed long-term debt. Details may not add to totals because of rounding.

among its member states (Benin, Burkina Faso, Cape Verde, Côte d'Ivoire, The Gambia, Ghana, Guinea, Guinea-Bissau, Liberia, Mali, Mauritania, Niger, Nigeria, Senegal, Sierra Leone, and Togo). The countries of Southern Africa have a strong sense of regional identity and common purpose, which was manifested in the creation in 1980 of the Southern African Development Coordination Conference (SADCC), whose membership now includes ten countries,[2] with a seat reserved for a post-apartheid South Africa. The World Bank, through its investment operations in individual SADCC countries, has given major support to the SADCC's goals of greater regional cooperation and harmonization. The Bank has also provided long-standing technical assistance to the SADCC's secretariat in Gaborone, and—in collaboration with the SADCC—has carried out several studies of regional significance.

Achieving closer economic integration is a long-term endeavor. While it is vital to have a clear statement of objectives at the outset— monetary integration, for example—the process itself will consist of many small steps by countries, such as standardizing trade procedures and simplifying financial transactions (including investment), as well as greater harmonization of domestic economic policies and lowering of trade barriers. The process of adjustment currently ongoing in many countries of the region offers useful opportunities for such harmonization to take place.

The long-term perspective study also emphasized the need to build up Africa's institutional capacity, and its recommendation became a reality when, in February 1991, the African capacity-building initiative (ACBI) was launched.

The ACBI focuses on the critical need to strengthen African skills and institutions for economic policy analysis and macroeconomic management. Cosponsored by the World Bank, the UNDP, and the African Development Bank (AfDB), the ACBI will draw—during its four-year pilot phase—from a fund of about $100 million pledged by international agencies, donor nations, African governments, and private sources (the World Bank's contribution to the fund will not exceed 15 percent of the expected $100 million).

The ACBI will be implemented through an African Capacity Building Foundation, to be based in Harare, Zimbabwe. The foundation will provide grants to strengthen public-policy analysis and development-management programs in institutions of higher education and will seek to improve regional institutions providing instruction in development issues so as to bolster the human and institutional capacity of African countries to plan and carry out their development programs. Fellowships will be made available to outstanding African civil servants, business leaders, and academics, which would permit them not only to undertake additional training but also to pursue independent economic research and analytical work. Given the emphasis now attached to the private sector as an engine of growth, local consulting firms and professional associations will be strengthened: In addition to providing funds, the ACBI will work to raise awareness of the potential of these firms and associations and will help establish regional consulting net-

[2] Angola, Botswana, Lesotho, Malawi, Mozambique, Namibia, Swaziland, Tanzania, Zambia, and Zimbabwe.

works. An international executive board, consisting of public-policy and development-management experts from Africa and elsewhere (along with representatives from the three sponsoring agencies) will guide the ACBI's program.

It is hoped that, by building up local capacity for economic analysis and management, Africa's dependence on technical assistance from industrial nations can be reduced, thereby helping the region to manage economic change better. The goal of the ACBI is to foster the creation, within twenty years, of a critical mass of African professional policy analysts and managers, as well as institutions, to provide training and advice in policy analysis and development management.

The Bank's long-term perspective study also called for a "global coalition" to facilitate the dialogue between African governments and their foreign partners. The initiative was formally agreed to at the Maastricht conference and was later endorsed by the Organization of African Unity (OAU) in July 1990.

Important objectives of the global coalition include (a) bringing together various political leaders and experts from Africa and the donor community, who will meet on a regular basis to help build a consensus and better coordinate international support for Africa's continued development; (b) monitoring progress in various areas of development and developing new ideas; and (c) ensuring that global attention remains focused on this difficult development challenge.

Issues likely to receive attention from the coalition include ways to overcome the nexus of weak agricultural production, rapid population growth, and environmental degradation; international and domestic-resource mobilization; the issues of accountability and transparency in governing; human-resource development; capacity building; regional cooperation and integration; and poverty reduction.

A number of industrialized countries and international agencies have made specific proposals to sponsor action in these key areas.

The global coalition has been incorporated as a nonprofit corporation in Washington, D.C., and is headed by an executive secretary from Africa. It will be supported and guided by a high-level advisory committee consisting of eight Africans of ministerial rank and a like number of officials from among donor countries and representatives of international organizations, including the executive secretary of the Economic Commission for Africa, the secretary-general of the OAU, the president of the AfDB, the head of the UNDP's African Bureau, and the World Bank's regional vice president for Africa.

Asia

The developing countries of Asia passed through a particularly turbulent and disruptive period over the past twelve months as a result of volatile conditions in the global economy and domestic developments of an economic and political character. In particular, a sudden rise in oil prices, loss of workers' remittances, and other Gulf-related shocks in 1990 imposed serious strains on the external position of several Asian countries. Governments responded in a uniformly agile and timely way by passing through higher oil costs so as to contain the accumulation of internal and external deficits. Despite these difficulties, the rapidly industrializing middle-income economies sustained their growth momentum, which is based on prudent economic management, continuing structural reforms, and sound long-term investments. Their overall prospects are still comparatively bright.

A second group of Asian countries with a more clouded outlook faces several problems, some of which are recent and others long-standing: the rise of serious macro imbalances, accentuated by the events in the Middle East; an increasingly ominous interaction between widespread poverty and population growth; and accelerating environmental deterioration that threatens to undermine the productive base of society. The challenges confronting this Asian subgroup are cause for a tempering of the near-term optimism typically bestowed on the region's developing countries.

Rapidly Industrializing Economies

A large part of the success of Asia has been the result of the continued good performance of the rapidly industrializing open economies of Asia, which now comprise not only the Republic of Korea but also Thailand, Malaysia, and Indonesia. During the 1980s, these countries registered high growth rates of per capita income, and the percentage of population below the poverty line declined to less than 20 percent by 1989. In these countries, an increasingly favorable environment has been created for private-sector development, with governments playing an active role in building physical, social, legal, regulatory, and technical infrastructure. At the beginning of the 1990s, these countries were well positioned to handle shocks and maintain this growth performance, while, at the same time, reducing poverty.

Korea and Thailand are heavily dependent on foreign sources of petroleum, but, as a result of underlying strengths in reserves and exports, both countries weathered the sudden rise in oil prices in late 1990 either by passing through the price hikes to consumers (Thailand) or by using an ample oil-price stabilization fund to absorb the additional costs (Korea).

Table 6-4. **Asia: 1989 Population and Per Capita GNP of Countries That Borrowed during Fiscal Years 1989–91**

Country	Population[a] (thousands)	Per capita GNP[b] (US dollars)
Bangladesh	110,700	180
China	1,113,900	350
Fiji	740	1,650
India	832,500	340
Indonesia	178,200	500
Korea, Republic of	42,400	4,400
Lao People's Democratic Republic	4,100	180
Malaysia	17,400	2,160
Maldives	210	420
Nepal	18,400	180
Papua New Guinea	3,800	890
Philippines	60,000	710
Sri Lanka	16,800	430
Thailand	55,400	1,220
Tonga	98	910
Vanuatu	152	860
Western Samoa	163	700

NOTE: The 1989 estimates of GNP per capita presented above are from the "World Development Indicators" section of *World Development Report 1991.*

a. Estimates from mid 1989.

b. *World Bank Atlas* methodology, 1987–89 base period.

Korea's prospects remain tied to the evolution of its competitiveness in terms of labor costs and access to technology. Despite a balance-of-payments deficit and an inflation rate that was higher than in the mid 1980s, growth in 1990 was about 9 percent. Thailand's economy continued its double-digit growth performance in 1990. Manufacturing expanded rapidly, and, with vigorous promotion, exports from this sector have grown significantly as a share of merchandise trade and gross domestic product (GDP). Exports of manufactures have helped to rectify basic imbalances on both the fiscal and external accounts and to lower the debt-service ratio on long-term debt, further enhancing Thailand's creditworthiness. Bottlenecks, however, have been felt in the power, telecommunications, and transport sectors, while rapid industrialization has contributed to growing air and water pollution and related health problems.

Malaysia, as an oil exporter, reaped a brief but substantial windfall from the Gulf crisis, and the country's economic prospects continue to be favorable. Malaysia's recent economic success has two salient features: achievements in poverty eradication and a remarkable adjustment effort in the early 1980s that cut back public spending and brought about macroeconomic stability, exchange-rate alignment, and economic liberalization.

Indonesia, while benefiting from higher oil prices over the past year, continued to implement the structural-adjustment program that it began in 1983. Measures introduced in 1990 involved additional efforts to deregulate the economy and promote the private sector. Major reforms were announced in the financial sector, involving the phasing out of subsidized credit, and in the trade sector, involving further reductions in nontariff barriers, tariffs, and export restrictions. In parallel with trade-policy reform, the government intensified its efforts to improve domestic incentives and the regulatory environment by extending deregulation in investment procedures to agriculture and the pharmaceutical industry.

These actions have contributed to growth in private investment, especially in export-oriented activities: Total private investment grew by almost 20 percent in real terms in 1990. The strong private-sector response to deregulation was associated with a surge in imports, mainly of capital goods. Although there was some

Table 6-5. **Lending to Borrowers in Asia, by Sector, Fiscal Years 1982–91**
(millions of US dollars)

Sector	Annual average, 1982–86	1987	1988	1989	1990	1991
Agriculture and Rural Development	1,543.5	817.7	1,966.3	1,162.0	1,203.7	2,044.1
Development Finance Companies	298.0	302.0	—	1,102.8	243.0	153.5
Education	380.6	—	355.7	484.5	902.7	899.1
Energy						
Oil, gas, and coal	464.1	527.0	358.0	340.0	86.0	517.2
Power	1,216.3	1,926.8	1,095.9	1,993.5	1,503.3	475.0
Industry	364.6	197.4	632.1	656.0	500.0	1,031.6
Nonproject	357.6	840.0	500.0	452.5	344.4	257.0
Population, Health, and Nutrition	101.9	—	74.5	290.2	192.5	507.5
Public-sector Management	—	—	—	—	—	32.0
Small-scale Enterprises	142.6	166.5	185.0	160.0	—	185.0
Technical Assistance	12.8	30.7	—	—	—	30.0
Telecommunications	43.1	359.5	—	12.7	391.7	57.0
Transportation	882.7	449.1	1,486.3	1,136.8	504.7	411.1
Urban Development	247.9	837.0	1,015.8	41.5	86.2	543.1
Water Supply and Sewerage	173.5	284.0	—	—	438.9	347.7
Total	6,229.1	6,737.7	7,669.6	7,832.5	6,397.1	7,490.9
Of which: IBRD	4,485.5	4,890.4	5,751.6	5,657.1	4,174.8	4,583.0
IDA	1,743.6	1,847.3	1,918.0	2,175.4	2,222.3	2,907.9
Number of operations	69	57	65	62	55	62

— Zero.
NOTE: Details may not add to totals because of rounding.

Fishermen straightening nets near Manila. A project approved in fiscal 1991 seeks to preserve what remains of the country's biological diversity, including species of fish.

slowdown of nonoil exports, overall growth in nonoil GDP remained strong in 1990 at nearly 8 percent.

China and India Show Mixed Results

China and India have recently encountered serious macro imbalances. The Gulf crisis played a significant role in India, whereas China was not as directly affected. To restore stability and accelerate growth, both countries will need to act upon their respective agendas for structural reform.

During the past two years, China's macroeconomic policies have been primarily devoted to addressing inflationary conditions that peaked in 1988. Underlying these imbalances were excessive monetary expansion, rising price and enterprise subsidies, and a declining ratio of government revenue to GDP. The last two combined to raise the fiscal deficit from 0.5 percent of gross national product (GNP) in 1985 to an estimated 2.5 percent in 1988. The anti-inflationary policies that were introduced in late 1988 included administrative guidelines to cut state investment, as well as a tightening of credit expansion and interest rates. These policies proved successful, as inflation was

reduced from 18 percent in 1988 to 2.1 percent in 1990. Inevitably, income growth, which had approached 11 percent in 1988, slowed to a still respectable 5 percent in 1990. However, unemployment increased in this period, and several million transient urban workers returned to the countryside. Macro policy was eased in the second half of 1990, which quickened the tempo of growth, while generating some concern over renewed inflation.

Overall, the Chinese economy performed well on the external front during the period 1989–90: Partly as a result of the strong austerity program, which reduced imports, China enjoyed sizable trade and current-account surpluses in 1990. Furthermore, levels of debt, as well as the debt-service ratio, continue to be stable. While evidence of recovery is mounting, the large number of loss-making state enterprises, inventory buildup, and sluggish retail sales warrant continuing attention. The fiscal situation also remains worrisome, since central-government revenue is highly inelastic, while expenditures may expand under the pressure of financing enterprise losses, procurement of a record grain harvest in 1990, and price subsidies. These issues once again bring to the foreground the need for China to address, through reform, the many distortions and imbalances in its economic system.

The number of people living in absolute poverty in China has been reduced from 196 million in 1981 (about 20 percent of the population) to an estimated 67 million (6 percent of the population) by 1989. Continued progress in poverty reduction, however, will require attention both to measures that can generate sufficient productive employment opportunities for the rural poor and to reforms that will increase the flexibility of the labor market, along with policies that ensure the cost-efficient provision of basic social services to the population at large. Similarly, economic reforms that rationalize energy prices can help reduce the use of energy and other resources that currently are sources of environmental pollution.

For India, the 1980s was a decade of higher growth performance and improved social indicators. The eradication of poverty was, and remains, the basic objective of the government. Economic growth and price stability, combined with effective implementation of anti-poverty programs, led to a significant reduction in the incidence of absolute poverty during the decade. It is estimated that the proportion of the population living below the poverty line declined from about 37 percent in 1983–84 to about 30 percent in 1987–88. Those living in poverty in rural India declined from 40 percent of the population to about 33 percent, and those in urban India from 28 percent to 20 percent. Given the enormity of the problem, this was a major achievement.

The sustained rate of growth and the improvement in the living conditions of the people were associated, however, with the emergence of macroeconomic imbalances.

The recent Middle East oil shock precipitated, therefore, an economic crisis with origins long before 1990. Foreign-exchange reserves had fallen to seven weeks of imports by the end of July 1990, causing major bond-rating agencies to review and subsequently downgrade India's credit rating. The oil shock itself was not as severe as those of 1973–74 or 1979–80, but it hit the Indian economy when it was already on the verge of a foreign-exchange liquidity crisis. The substantial additional import costs of higher oil prices, lost remittances, and other factors through March 31, 1991, aggravated the country's fiscal 1991 current-account deficit.

Although the economy continued to grow during India's 1991 fiscal year (April 1, 1990 to March 31, 1991), the expectations for the current fiscal year are more conservative. Many pitfalls await the new government, which will

need to manage this crisis with skill and dispatch, while also addressing the many structural-reform issues inhibiting growth in the economy. The onset of serious macroeconomic difficulties, accompanied by continuing political uncertainties, has already exerted a dampening effect on the progress of key economic-policy reforms to deregulate industry, liberalize the trade regime, and improve the overall environment for private-sector activity.

Slower-growth Economies

For a large group of Asian countries, the 1980s was a decade of low and declining growth rates. These countries—Bangladesh, the Lao People's Democratic Republic, Myanmar, Nepal, the Philippines, Sri Lanka, and Viet Nam—face uncertain or clouded prospects for the first years of the new decade, as well. Although their development constraints vary in intensity and composition from country to country, they all share, to some degree, an ominous convergence of rapid population growth, ecological vulnerability, large numbers of absolute poor, and deeply rooted domestic and external macroeconomic problems. Exceptional skills will be needed in managing economic policy and infrastructure investments if these problems are to be addressed effectively. Resolute redirection of public expenditure toward family planning, rural social services, and environmental rehabilitation and preservation of forests, soils, and water is also needed.

Although the economy of the Philippines suffered major disruptions and setbacks in 1990, both natural and man-made, bolder policy moves by the government at the end of the year and into 1991 promise improvement in the near future.

During 1990, a series of shocks weakened the fragile economic recovery that had begun in 1987. A prolonged drought through the first half of the year reduced agricultural production and led to serious power shortages. A devastating earthquake in July killed nearly 1,600 people and resulted in asset losses approaching 1 percent of GDP. Then, the crisis in the Gulf placed severe pressures on the balance of payments because of lost income from the 50,000 Philippine workers returning from Kuwait and Iraq, as well as higher oil prices.

Tentative policy responses by the government during 1990 compounded the difficult economic situation, and a slowdown in growth resulted. Gross domestic product grew by only 2.5 percent in 1990 (which implies stagnant per capita income), and inflation accelerated to 14 percent. In the last months of 1990, however, the government began to take corrective policy actions such as raising domestic oil prices and devaluing the exchange rate. In January and February 1991, the government formulated a stabilization program that embodies serious efforts to improve the fiscal balance and control money supply. This program received support in February 1991 from the International Monetary Fund (IMF) in the form of an eighteen-month standby arrangement. Soon after, at the consultative-group meeting in Hong Kong, foreign-aid donors pledged to provide $3.3 billion in 1991 in support of the government's adjustment program and development projects. These recent developments steer the Philippines towards a path of higher growth and improved macroeconomic balances.

In the Lao People's Democratic Republic, GDP grew at the much lower (but still respectable) rate of 5.3 percent in 1990, down from 10 percent in the previous year when a dramatic recovery in crop output took place. At the same time, inflation declined considerably, from 68 percent at the end of 1989 to 22 percent in 1990. Both changes resulted largely from a drastic tightening in monetary policy. Although exports to industrialized countries continued to grow, imports rose substantially as well, in part reflecting the carryover of external assistance unused in 1989 and higher oil prices in the latter part of the year. Through a combination of a leveling off of petroleum prices and continued improvements in agriculture and public infrastructure, it is expected that GDP in 1991 will continue to grow moderately.

Growth in Viet Nam has picked up in the past two years, following poor macroeconomic performance—characterized by weak resource mobilization and low efficiency of investment—throughout most of the 1980s. Despite recent dramatic changes initiated by its far-reaching economic-reform program, Viet Nam remains one of the poorest countries in Asia. Although faced with difficult stabilization and reform requirements, recent policy changes have resulted in a large and fast-growing (but still mostly small-scale) private sector. Viet Nam continues to operate under difficult external conditions: Soviet aid is declining rapidly, and there is no immediate prospect of official financing from traditional donor countries to take its place.

Despite an upturn in the economy of Bangladesh (foodgrain production increased substantially following good weather and an improved agricultural-policy environment), short-term macroeconomic indicators deteriorated in late 1989 and into 1990. Expansionary domestic policy led to a surge in imports, and foreign-exchange reserves fell sharply to about $450 million (equivalent to 1.5 months of imports) in March 1990. In response, the government initiated a short-term program to stabilize the balance of payments and the budget. These efforts, which included a flexible exchange-rate policy, were successful in restoring financial stability and improving external competitiveness.

Shortly after initiating its reform program (supported by funds from the IMF's enhanced structural-adjustment facility), however, the government was faced with high imported-oil prices and the need to repatriate workers from Iraq and Kuwait in the wake of the Gulf crisis. The government's policy response to the crisis was prompt, both in terms of increasing domestic petroleum prices and taking measures to restrain current expenditures. At the same time, it managed the difficult task of resettling displaced workers. More recently, the balance-of-payments position has improved as a result of a contraction in imports.

Economic growth in 1991 was expected to be lower than in the previous year even before the devastating May cyclone struck. It is estimated that at least 125,000 people were killed, and millions of others were left homeless. Agricultural production and storage facilities in the area struck by the cyclone (along the southeast coast of the country, starting from north of Chittagong and running south for about 100 miles) were devastated. Vital public infrastructure was crippled, hampering immediate relief efforts and, later, economic recovery. The port of Chittagong, the country's only major outlet, was clogged with sunken ships and suffered extensive damage to shipping facilities. Roads, bridges, irrigation works, flood-control structures, and other social infrastructure were all hit hard. The damage to infrastructure and production will have a negative effect on the country's macroeconomic situation: The storm had a serious impact on the Chittagong export-processing zone and on the export products awaiting shipment in port; shrimp farms and fish nurseries, both export industries, were also severely hurt.

Over the past year, a number of external and domestic developments adversely affected Nepal's economic performance. Although the trade-and-transit treaty impasse with India was resolved in June 1990, its effects lingered on; the Gulf crisis directly increased import costs of oil and slowed receipts from tourism; and in early 1990, Nepal underwent a major political transformation from an absolute to a constitutional monarchy.

These events contributed to a slowdown in GDP growth to 2 percent during the period mid July 1989 to mid July 1990, well below the

Table 6-6. **Net Transfers to Asia**
(millions of US dollars; fiscal years)

Item	China 1991	China 1987–91	India 1991	India 1987–91	Indonesia 1991	Indonesia 1987–91	Total region 1991	Total region 1987–91
IBRD and IDA commitments	1,579	6,635	2,049	12,804	1,638	7,344	7,491	36,128
Gross disbursements	1,114	4,853	1,901	9,996	1,259	6,549	5,828	29,419
Repayments	236	477	595	2,202	605	2,294	2,665	12,677
Net disbursements	878	4,376	1,306	7,794	653	4,255	3,164	16,742
Interest and charges	236	818	742	2,866	786	3,199	2,693	11,889
Net transfer	642	3,558	564	4,928	−133	1,056	470	4,853

NOTE: Disbursements from the IDA Special Fund are included. The countries shown in the table are those with the largest amounts of public or publicly guaranteed long-term debt. Details may not add to totals because of rounding.

population growth rate of 2.7 percent. Progress in implementing structural reforms that were begun in 1989 continued, however, and the government has generally maintained macroeconomic stability despite increasing fiscal pressures from recent wage concessions, price controls, and higher subsidies. Economic growth during Nepal's current fiscal year is expected to be around 3.5 percent. Thus, over the past three years, there has been no increase in per capita incomes. Government commitment to reducing population growth (which is at the core of Nepal's development problem), fostering human-resource development, and strengthening key development-management institutions will be essential in raising per capita income and reducing poverty.

In Sri Lanka, the government is faced with simultaneous challenges: restoring peace in the north and the east, shouldering the additional costs to the economy resulting from the Gulf crisis, and maintaining economic stability through sound macroeconomic management while moving forward on growth-oriented structural reforms supported by the IMF and the Bank. Growth in GDP, which hovered around 2 percent during 1987–89, reached 6 percent in 1990.

In addition to these immediate tasks, the government has started to address underlying development issues. These include measures to reduce the level of central-government expenditures; a program to restructure or privatize public-sector enterprises; measures to restore the confidence of private investors; and steps to target better the large volume of income transfers and subsidies towards the poorest of the population, as well as to restructure poverty-alleviation programs in the direction of increasing the productivity of the poor.

Pacific Island Economies and the Maldives

Over the past year, the government of Papua New Guinea made good progress in implementing the financial-stabilization and structural-adjustment program that it embarked on in early 1990 in response to the closure of the Bougainville copper mine and a sharp deterioration of its external terms of trade. Prompt adjustments in macroeconomic policies allowed the domestic and external financial impact of these shocks to be effectively contained. At the same time, measures were undertaken to improve public-resource management and reform the incentive and regulatory framework to spur the development of the private sector. The central objective of this program of structural reform is to promote the development of the nonmining economy to underpin sustained and more broadly based growth of income and employment over the medium term. As a result of the shocks felt by the economy and the adjustments made in response to them, GDP fell by about 1.5 percent in 1990; however, it is expected to rebound strongly in 1991, supported by the development of new mineral operations and advances in the nonmining economy (growth in the nonmining economy is projected to rise to 3.5 percent a year during 1992–95).

Performance in the island countries of the Pacific was mixed. Propelled by enhanced competitiveness and a greater outward orientation, growth in Fiji accelerated to nearly 10 percent in 1990. Double-digit growth rates were recorded in manufacturing and tourism, and advances in agriculture and services were steady. Led by tourism that was spurred by improved air links, growth in Vanuatu was exceptionally strong. In Western Samoa, Tonga, and Kiribati, growth rates were low, partly reflecting the effects of the February 1990 cyclone in Western Samoa and the downturn in copra prices, which affected Tonga and Kiribati. In the Solomon Islands, growth was strong, in part the result of an expansionary fiscal policy that contributed to continued pressures on domestic prices and the external position.

Growth in the Maldives remained impressive. As a result of continuing strong performance by the fisheries and tourism sectors, real national product has increased by nearly one third over the past two years.

Bank Operations and Strategy

Led by a $989 million increase in lending to China, commitments by the IBRD and IDA to the region in fiscal 1991 totaled $7,491 million, up 17 percent from last year's total.

Bank operations in Asia continued their focus on the priority development challenges in the region: restoring macro balance and sustaining structural reform so as to spur private-sector–led growth; designing sectoral and targeted operations aimed at reducing levels of absolute poverty and limiting rapid population growth; building analytical understanding of environmental processes and supporting programs to arrest and reverse environmental losses; and developing the necessary physical and institutional infrastructures in support of these objectives.

Overall, the level of adjustment lending in Asia continued to be modest, reflecting the region's relative freedom from financial crisis. During the year, macroeconomic adjustment operations approved in past years continued to be implemented; with the exception of loans to Indonesia and the Philippines, no new operations were approved. Two important studies of macroeconomic management were recently completed for China and India, while an analysis of adjustment and the role of the private sector was discussed with the government of Sri Lanka.

The Bank continued to be active in the area of private-sector development and public-sector reform. An Asia-wide study recommended policy measures and regulatory frameworks to encourage private participation in the power and coal sectors. Country economic work on Indonesia had a special focus on issues of private-sector development, while a major study of infrastructure bottlenecks in that country also addressed private-sector concerns. A second private-sector development loan provided support for key structural reforms and helped mobilize almost $1 billion

from other donors in balance-of-payments support. In addition, two credit operations are supporting expansion of private-sector investment, and projects in the urban and power sectors are improving the physical setting for industry.

In China, rationalization of the state-owned sector is being addressed by two projects: a rural industrial-technology operation and an urban industrial-restructuring project. In Sri Lanka, the Bank is supporting an aggressive public-sector privatization and restructuring program through recent analytical work and a $120 million IDA credit that supports the commercialization and privatization of public manufacturing enterprises. In Korea, a health-technology project will onlend $60 million to private hospitals for expansion of capacity to treat chronic and degenerative diseases.

Bank operations for industrial restructuring of the private sector and development of cottage-industry exports, as well as investments in highways and irrigation, have underpinned the Philippines' strategy for private-sector growth. In the high-growth economies of East Asia, the Bank's analytical work and lending are supporting land titling (Thailand) and vocational education (Korea) to strengthen the enabling environment for the private sector.

In the areas of poverty reduction and population, the region's analytical work has included a study of access by the poor to India's social services and poverty programs. A regional comparative study of population programs has also been undertaken. A study of poverty in Nepal was completed, and the Bank's first analysis of Papua New Guinea's health and population sector was discussed with the government. Lending operations included within the region's core poverty program of targeted and sectoral assistance were approved for Bangladesh, China (three operations), India, Indonesia (two loans), the Philippines (two operations), and Sri Lanka.

In Papua New Guinea, a project supporting special interventions to alleviate the social costs of the ongoing adjustment program was initiated. Project components addressing the constraints faced by women, particularly in South Asia, have been incorporated in a growing number of the region's investment operations. In India, for example, an agricultural project in Tamil Nadu state will support women farmers through involvement of nongovernmental organizations in extension, participatory planning, and common-property resource management. A strategy for consolidating and expanding the gains women have achieved in Indonesia was the subject of a study discussed with the government.

In the region's core environment program, operational output increased substantially. In the Philippines, a pioneering project in natural-resource management is directly addressing the economic issues involved in preserving the country's hardwood forests. An industrial project in India is providing institutional, policy, and investment support for industrial pollution-control efforts, while the Bank's first rural water-supply project in India incorporates an environmentally sound sanitation component.

The Bank produced its first regional economic report for the Pacific island countries during the year. The report reviewed the economic performance of these countries during the 1980s, assessed the factors underlying their relatively weak performance (compared with growth in the small Indian ocean and Caribbean countries), and suggested strategies for accelerated and sustained growth in the 1990s.

The need for stronger promotion of the private sector in these countries was emphasized. The report's findings were discussed at a Bank-organized seminar attended by high-level government and donor representatives. In the future, the regional economic report (to be updated every two years) will play an important role in aid coordination within the framework of the United Nations Development Programme roundtables.

In addition to the regional report, a study on the incentives framework for private-sector investment in Fiji was completed. Working together with the Asian Development Bank and bilateral donors, Bank staff are targeting lending operations to fill key gaps in infrastructure and social services. An investment credit in low-cost housing in Vanuatu was approved during the year, and work continued on a fisheries-sector project in the Maldives.

Europe, Middle East, and North Africa

The Europe, Middle East, and North Africa region is one that is characterized by great cultural, political, and economic diversity. Notwithstanding differences in levels of income and social development, economic organization, and the role of the state, the countries of the region share, in varying degrees, three common, long-term economic challenges: those of the transition to a market economy (faced not only in the reforming socialist econ-

omies of Eastern and Central Europe, but in Algeria and Egypt, as well); the challenge of accelerating the pace of social progress (which exists not only in relatively poor countries such as Pakistan and Yemen but in Egypt and Morocco, as well); and the heavy burden of debt, not only in Eastern Europe (notably Bulgaria, Hungary, and Poland) but also in the Maghreb (Algeria and Morocco) and the Middle East (Egypt and Jordan).

The drive towards economic reform further strengthened in the region during the past year. Unfortunately, the massive adverse external economic shocks arising from the Gulf crisis and the collapse of the Council for Mutual Economic Assistance (CMEA) trading arrangement between the Soviet Union and Eastern Europe greatly complicated orderly adjustment and resulted in sharp declines in economic output in many countries. While Algeria and Iran benefited from higher oil prices in 1990, the cumulative negative impact of the Gulf crisis on Turkey, Egypt, and Jordan is estimated to be in the range of $12 billion to $15 billion through June 1991.

For the Eastern and Central European economies, the Gulf crisis exacerbated the disruption in trade and payments arising from the loss of exports to the Soviet Union and a deterioration in terms of trade resulting from the elimination of the CMEA. It is estimated that the impact of these shocks will be about $20 billion in calendar year 1991. It is not surprising, therefore, that under the weight of both strong stabilization efforts and a large negative shock, GDP levels in Eastern and Central Europe fell by 10 percent in 1990 and are expected to show a further decline of 5 percent in 1991. Strong growth in Turkey, Pakistan, and the Maghreb countries helped to limit the decline in the regionwide GDP to less than 2 percent.

Performance in Pakistan and Turkey

Macroeconomic performance in Pakistan was uneven, reflecting slow implementation of policy reforms that had started in 1988 as part of the government's medium-term adjustment

Table 6-7. Europe, Middle East, and North Africa: 1989 Population and Per Capita GNP of Countries That Borrowed during Fiscal Years 1989–91

Country	Population[a] (thousands)	Per capita GNP[b] (US dollars)
Algeria	24,400	2,230
Bulgaria	9,000	2,320
Cyprus	695	7,040
Czechoslovakia	15,600	3,450
Egypt	51,000	640
Hungary	10,600	2,590
Iran, Islamic Republic of	53,300	3,200[c]
Jordan	3,900	1,640[d]
Morocco	24,500	880
Pakistan	109,900	370
Poland	37,900	1,790
Portugal	10,300	4,250
Romania	23,200	—[e]
Tunisia	8,000	1,260
Turkey	55,000	1,370
Yemen, Republic of	11,200	650
Yugoslavia	23,700	2,920

NOTE: The 1989 estimates of GNP per capita presented above are from the "World Development Indicators" section of *World Development Report 1991*.

a. Estimates from mid 1989.

b. *World Bank Atlas* methodology, 1987–89 base period.

c. Data provided by the government subsequent to the publication of *World Development Report 1991* put per capita GNP at $2,550.

d. Estimate refers to East Bank only.

e. GNP per capita estimated to be in the $2,335–$5,999 range.

program that aimed at restoring resource balance to sustainable levels and at improving the efficiency of the economy. The changes in government that occurred in August and November 1990 may have contributed to the delay in the implementation of the policy-reform measures. Real GDP growth was about 5 percent, and while inflation had decelerated to 6 percent by the end of June 1990, it started to rise towards the end of the year to 8.4 percent. This increase was caused partly by further acceleration of monetary growth during the second half of 1990 and partly by the rise in the prices of petroleum products during the Gulf crisis. The government was able to achieve a modest reduction in its budget deficit, from 7.3 percent to 6.6 percent of GDP, mainly through a restraint on already low development expenditures.

Despite a better-than-expected performance of exports during the latter half of 1990, coming mainly from raw cotton and cotton-based manufactures, the combination of an increase in world oil prices and the nondisbursement of policy-based aid led to a considerable gap in the balance of payments. Improvement in the current-account deficit in fiscal 1991 was tempered by the Gulf crisis, and it is estimated to be 4.1 percent of GNP.

The events in the Gulf weakened Pakistan's resource position and demonstrated the country's vulnerability to external shocks. The negative impact of the crisis on Pakistan's current account (estimated at about $600 million through the end of June 1991) was mainly caused by the increased cost of oil imports and reduced workers' remittances. Delays in passing through the international oil-price increases to domestic consumers put additional pressure on the government budget; financing the budget deficit and energy-price increases accelerated inflation. The crisis accentuated an already deteriorating economic performance by putting additional pressure on the government's budget.

In early 1991, the new government took several important steps to resume and broaden the adjustment effort. Energy-related prices were adjusted to reflect the movement of international prices, as were railway tariffs. The government also did away with investment and import licensing, liberalized the exchange-control system, and privatized several public enterprises. Agreement was also reached on the

Table 6-8. Lending to Borrowers in Europe, Middle East, and North Africa, by Sector, Fiscal Years 1982–91
(millions of US dollars)

Sector	Annual average, 1982–86	1987	1988	1989	1990	1991
Agriculture and Rural Development	747.7	398.4	560.5	1,411.4	599.3	216.8
Development Finance Companies	387.9	362.9	580.0	300.0	430.0	715.0
Education	139.8	250.0	241.8	251.0	233.2	491.4
Energy						
Oil, gas, and coal	194.0	21.0	30.1	365.5	—	642.0
Power	346.4	597.0	400.0	165.0	587.5	714.0
Industry	194.5	166.0	377.0	385.1	190.5	751.4
Nonproject	279.3	240.0	150.0	200.0	1,050.0	1,310.0
Population, Health, and Nutrition	15.6	13.3	—	79.5	119.0	290.0
Public-sector Management	—	—	—	—	130.0	—
Small-scale Enterprises	54.0	54.0	328.0	—	—	26.0
Technical Assistance	7.0	7.0	—	23.0	26.0	197.0
Telecommunications	51.0	295.0	36.0	—	—	270.0
Transportation	284.7	545.8	327.0	296.0	708.0	553.4
Urban Development	76.4	176.6	90.0	58.0	105.5	250.0
Water Supply and Sewerage	226.1	559.6	238.0	233.0	228.0	136.7
Total	3,004.5	3,686.6	3,358.4	3,767.5	4,407.0	6,563.7
Of which: IBRD	2,746.2	3,437.4	3,133.3	3,511.8	4,131.2	6,079.1
IDA	258.3	249.2	225.1	255.7	275.8	484.6
Number of operations	47	42	35	39	40	46

— Zero.
NOTE: Details may not add to totals because of rounding.

Carrying water in Morocco. The Bank is currently engaged in an environmental assessment of Morocco that aims at finding ways to manage the country's natural resources, particularly its water resources.

sharing of water and of fiscal revenues among the provinces. These measures add up to an impressive beginning in policy reform that emphasizes private-sector development.

The Turkish economy experienced rapid growth in 1990, despite being adversely affected by the post-August 1990 events in the Gulf. Gross national product (GNP) grew by an estimated 9.2 percent, reflecting a recovery in agriculture from the drought-induced slump of 1989, as well as a strong expansion in manufacturing output. The stimulus to growth came from the demand side and resulted, in part, from gains in real wages, including increases in wages and salaries in the public and state-enterprise sectors. While consumption rose, causing investment's share in GNP to fall, fixed investment increased in real terms. A tight monetary program, the continuing appreciation of the real exchange rate, and recovery in agricultural output combined to reduce wholesale-price inflation from 62.3 percent in 1989 to 48.6 percent in 1990. Less progress was made, however, in reducing consumer-price inflation. On the fiscal side, growth in public expenditure was faster than gains in revenue in spite of the quick pass-through of the price effect of the oil shock and a further rise in value-added tax rates. As a result, the public-sector borrowing requirement increased to about 10 percent of GNP.

Turkey's external accounts deteriorated in 1990—even before the negative effects of the Gulf crisis had started to be felt—in part because of a surge in imports following the liberalization of the import regime. Still, it is estimated that much of the $2.4 billion (2.2 percent of GNP) current-account deficit for 1990 was due to the incremental effect of the events in the Gulf. Financing was adequate, nevertheless; indeed, official reserves at the end of 1990 had increased by $1.3 billion to $7.4 billion (including gold), or approximately four months of imports.

Growth in the Maghreb Countries

In Algeria, despite another poor harvest, GDP grew at the modest rate of 1.1 percent in 1990. The combination of fiscal restraint and higher revenues —driven by the recovery of oil prices in the second half of the year—generated an estimated budget surplus of over 3.5 percent of GDP. Most of this surplus was used to repay Treasury debts to the central bank. Consequently, the banking system was able both to retire foreign debt and to replenish reserves while slowing money growth. Reflecting higher oil prices, the balance of payments showed a current-account surplus of about 3 percent of GDP. Exchange-rate adjustments and price liberalization continued throughout 1990 and into early 1991, contributing to a significant rise in consumer-price inflation, to almost 17 percent (as compared with 9 percent in 1989). A full two percentage points of this increase occurred in December 1990, when devaluation accelerated.

Algeria also embarked on some key institutional and political reforms. While the domestic political situation continues to evolve, the government remains committed to holding the country's first multiparty national legislative elections since independence. Key institutional reforms included the adoption of a new money and credit law, as well as several laws pertaining to the labor market. The money and credit laws granted the central bank full autonomy to formulate and implement monetary, external-debt, and foreign-exchange policies. It also removed controls on foreign direct investment in most sectors, allowing, among other things, 100 percent foreign ownership of new investment projects and unrestricted joint ventures between foreign concerns and Algeria's private sector. In preparation for trade liberalization, the central bank devalued the dinar by about 100 percent between mid November 1990 and the end of April 1991. In April 1991, Algeria introduced a major liberalization of its external trade that complements the already far-reaching measures taken to liberalize domestic trade. The new labor legislation lays the groundwork for a more competitive labor market, allowing the creation of autonomous labor unions and specifying procedures for the resolution of labor-management disputes.

In Morocco, prudent monetary and budgetary policies, followed by a 9.25 percent nominal devaluation of the exchange rate in May 1990, resulted in good macroeconomic performance for 1990 despite the Gulf crisis. Gross domestic product grew at slightly above 3 percent in 1990 (compared with 4.1 percent during the period 1985–89). The budget deficit declined from 5.5 percent of GDP in 1989 to about 2.1 percent. Following the transitory deterioration in 1989 of the current-account deficit (which resulted from a commercial dispute related to sales of phosphoric acid), exports recovered, and, in the first half of 1990, workers' remittances, manufactured exports, and tourism receipts increased significantly, allowing international reserves to rise to a record $2 billion at the end of 1990. The Gulf crisis had a substantial, adverse effect on Morocco's economy in terms of higher oil prices, as well as losses of tourism income and work-

ers' remittances. However, these losses were somewhat offset by higher official transfers from the Gulf states.

The international financial community gave support to Morocco's stabilization and adjustment efforts in 1990, as agreement was reached on the rescheduling of the country's commercial and official debts. The agreement with the London Club of commercial creditors consisted of a block rescheduling of the entire $3.2 billion owed to commercial banks. In addition, Morocco obtained a rescheduling agreement from the Paris Club of official creditors in September of 1990. The combined effects of the two agreements will save Morocco about $1.9 billion in debt-service payments in 1990 and around $500 million in 1991.

Tunisia's economy performed well in 1990, and the implementation of liberalization measures, which had been slowed in 1988–89, accelerated. Following a long drought in 1989, good rainfall in 1990 allowed agricultural output to grow by 27 percent, accounting for almost half of the year's 6.5 percent growth rate (as compared with 3.5 percent in 1989). A strong recovery in exports of manufactures and tourism was the driving force behind the growth of industry and services. Demand pressures were kept under control by tight monetary policy, which succeeded in holding the inflation rate to 6.6 percent (as against 7.7 percent in the previous year). The government budget deficit was kept on target (4 percent of GDP), thanks to reductions in consumer subsidies permitted by the good crop. Higher demand for imports, mainly for intermediate and capital goods for export industries, was mainly responsible for the current-account deficit that rose to about 4 percent of GDP. The economy was severely affected by the Gulf crisis, however. In net terms, the loss of foreign-exchange receipts, caused by reduced exports of goods and services and transfers, is estimated at about $675 million, or some 5 percent of projected 1991 GDP.

Economic Developments in Four Middle Eastern Countries

For Jordan, the year began on an optimistic note, with the government pressing ahead with its adjustment program, which was being supported by an International Monetary Fund (IMF) standby arrangement, agreements with the Paris and London Clubs, and a $150 million industry and trade-policy adjustment loan from the Bank. Further progress was made in early 1990 towards reduction of the budget deficit, when prices for water and electricity were selectively increased and a program to reduce food subsidies was launched.

The Gulf crisis, however, disrupted the implementation of Jordan's adjustment program and caused a dramatic deterioration in its economy through losses of export markets, workers' remittances, and income from tourism; the burden of returning workers on the government budget; and loss of income in the transit sector. Preliminary estimates indicate that in 1990, Jordan's GDP fell by 8 percent from its 1989 level; nearly all of the decline was concentrated during the last four months of the year (implying that GDP was falling at an annual rate of roughly 25 percent during the period September–December 1990).

Balance-of-payments difficulties, serious even before August 1990, were exacerbated by the crisis, increasing the size of the current-account deficit by about $700 million for 1990. There was also a similar deterioration in the 1990 budget, despite a number of measures adopted in the first half of the year to contain expenditures and enhance revenues. Post-August 1990 increases in subsidies and in extra-budgetary expenditures related to the crisis led to an additional budget deficit of almost 7 percent of GDP, increasing the overall deficit (excluding grants) to almost 25 percent in 1990.

The Egyptian economy continued to experience a slowdown in growth, with real GDP rising by only about 1 percent in fiscal 1990, far below the rate of population growth (over 2.5 percent). However, the deficits in the balance of payments and in the government's budget showed some improvement as a result of a robust recovery of nonoil exports and restrictive budgetary expenditures. Revenue-raising measures were also launched, as the government implemented a wide range of fiscal measures, including upward adjustment of petroleum and electricity prices and increases in taxes. In March 1990, the government began implementation of its economic-reform and structural-adjustment program (recently supported by an IMF standby arrangement and a $300 million World Bank structural-adjustment loan) that focuses on (a) stabilization to restore macroeconomic balance and reduce inflation, (b) structural adjustment to stimulate and sustain medium-term and long-term growth, and (c) accelerated implementation of current social policies to minimize the effect of economic reforms on the poor. This last-named focus was supported by a $140 million IDA credit for the establishment of an emergency social fund.

The effects of the Gulf crisis on Egypt were severe. Losses of export markets and workers' remittances, as well as declines in tourism receipts and Suez canal fees for 1990 and 1991, were estimated by the Bank and the IMF to total more than 35 percent of Egypt's exports of goods and nonfactor services. The budgetary impact was smaller, as the most negative effects were felt in the private sector (tourism and workers' remittances); in contrast, some revenue gains actually accrued to the government from increased receipts from the state petroleum company. There was also a significant increase in international financial support to Egypt. Some of this exceptional financial support, resulting from deliberations of the Gulf Crisis Financial Coordination Group, included debt forgiveness by a number of Arab countries, as well as by the Paris Club of official creditors, which decided to forgive half the $20.2 billion that was owed to them by Egypt.

The Republic of Yemen, formed in May 1990 through unification of the Yemen Arab Republic and the People's Democratic Republic of Yemen, inherited all the economic difficulties of its two constituent parts: an unsustainable budget deficit, a structural balance-of-payments deficit, intense inflationary pressures, and rising unemployment. These difficulties were aggravated by the process of amalgamating two governmental administrations and the additional expenses associated with it, as well as by the Gulf crisis. The crisis resulted in the return home of some 750,000 Yemenis (migrant workers and their children), whose remittances have been the most important source of foreign exchange for Yemen in the past two decades. It also significantly reduced external trade in goods and services, as well as external assistance to the country.

In response to the deteriorating situation, the government has recently taken a number of steps to stabilize the economy, the most important of which relate to some liberalization of the foreign-trade and exchange regime, whereby import licensing was relaxed and private-exchange markets were freed from government controls. The government also doubled the price of gasoline and raised by 50 percent the price of diesel fuel. These measures, although significant, have not yet led to improvements in the economic conditions of the country. Preliminary data indicate that no economic growth took place in 1990. The government has agreed to work with IDA to formulate a medium-term economic framework that would satisfy the requirement for the restoration of viable macroeconomic stability over the medium term.

Since the end of its war with Iraq in 1988, the government of Iran has been focusing more attention on economic policies and the management of its economy. The country's first five-year development plan, which was approved in January 1990, emphasizes fiscal discipline, export promotion, private-sector development, and the progressive liberalization of pricing policies. Economic performance, which had began to turn around in 1989, continued to improve. For 1990 as a whole, economic growth was 10.1 percent (compared with 4 percent in 1989); oil revenues—benefiting from higher volume, as well as prices—increased sharply; the budget deficit, reflecting additional relief and reconstruction expenditures for the devastating earthquake of June 1990, was 1.8 percent of GDP (4 percent in 1989); and the external current account had a surplus of around $1 billion (compared with a $3.5 billion deficit in 1989).

Economic Developments in the Gulf Cooperation Council Countries

The first half of 1990 witnessed the confirmation of the 1989 recovery in the six countries that are members of the Gulf Cooperation Council (GCC). In particular, daily oil output rose by more than 10 percent. Economic developments in the second half of 1990, however, were dominated by the events that followed in the wake of Iraq's invasion of Kuwait. While the economic effect of the crisis varied from country to country, all GCC countries (except Kuwait, of course) saw their oil-export receipts increase due to higher output and prices (the combined oil receipts of the five countries are estimated to have exceeded $70 billion in 1990, an increase of more than 60 percent over 1989). This increase in income was more than offset, however, by additional military-related costs arising from the crisis and by provision of substantial financial assistance to countries affected by the crisis. Heavy capital flight occurred in August 1990 but slowed afterwards. While domestic private investment decreased considerably, major public projects such Saudi Arabia's petrochemical-expansion projects, Qatar's North gas field, and aluminum projects in Bahrain and Dubai continued to be implemented as previously planned.

Economic Developments in Reforming Europe

The dramatic social and political changes that are occurring in Eastern and Central Europe show that the countries in this subregion are committed to a thorough transformation of their economic systems. The transformation process—which includes macroeconomic stabilization; reform of incentives and price systems; enterprise reform, privatization, and financial-sector development; the abolition of state monopolies on foreign trade, foreign exchange, and production; the installation of

legal frameworks that are necessary for the development of market economies; and the development of social safety nets—is proceeding against the backdrop of large external shocks associated with the collapse of the CMEA, the shrinking of the Soviet market, the Gulf crisis, and, for some countries, a heavy burden of external debt. The result was a sharp decline in economic output in these countries.

Bulgaria, which is especially dependent on CMEA trade, particularly with the Soviet Union, experienced severe terms-of-trade, export-market, and payments-disruption losses that were estimated to be about 18 percent of GDP in 1990. Consequently, the current-account deficit widened substantially, even with a further decline in import volumes, and output fell by a steep 12 percent.

In February 1991, a new stabilization and reform program was launched in Bulgaria. Many subsidies were eliminated, most restrictions on the setting of retail and wholesale prices were lifted, and the exchange-rate system was freed. Tight wage, fiscal, and monetary policies (including a sharp rise in interest rates) were adopted. An agrarian-reform bill was also passed, providing for the return of land to its former owners.

In Czechoslovakia, following the country's return to democracy in late 1989 and national elections in mid 1990, the government prepared an economic and social program to transform the economy into a market economy. To achieve this objective, stabilization and structural-reform policies are being implemented simultaneously. Retail subsidies on food were removed in July 1990, and other measures such as a substantial currency devaluation and price increases for gasoline, industrial energy, and transport were introduced in the second half of 1990.

In January 1991, Czechoslovakia's transformation program was intensified. A balanced budget and a tight monetary policy were pursued to maintain macroeconomic stability and support structural adjustment. Foreign trade and prices were liberalized; a privatization program, covering thousands of small retail outlets and service enterprises, was launched, and one for medium-sized and large enterprises was at an advanced stage of preparation; and a social safety net to protect the people most adversely affected by the transition to a market economy was being put in place. The government's program is being supported by an IMF standby arrangement, as well as by a $450 million structural-adjustment loan from the Bank. The government's reform program is also being supported by the European Community and the group of twenty-four industrial-

Table 6-9. **Net Transfers to Europe, Middle East, and North Africa**
(millions of US dollars; fiscal years)

Item	Egypt		Turkey		Poland		Total region	
	1991	1987–91	1991	1987–91	1991	1987–91	1991	1987–91
IBRD and IDA commitments	524	827	900	4,069	1,440	2,221	6,564	21,783
Gross disbursements	105	683	594	3,234	139	159	3,015	13,667
Repayments	203	774	684	2,401	—	—	2,324	11,868
Net disbursements	−98	−91	−90	833	139	159	691	1,800
Interest and charges	151	701	526	2,484	3	3	1,673	8,202
Net transfer	−248	−792	−616	−1,651	136	156	−982	−6,403

—Zero.

NOTE: Disbursements from the IDA Special Fund are included. The countries shown in the table are those with the largest amounts of public or publicly guaranteed long-term debt. Details may not add to totals because of rounding.

ized countries. Notwithstanding the country's strong domestic adjustment, the country's financing needs—caused by the severe effect of external shocks—have not diminished.

In Hungary, measures were taken during the past year to correct the large external and internal imbalances that had emerged in 1989. These measures were complemented, in mid 1990, by a wide-ranging program of structural reforms that were supported by an IMF standby arrangement and a $200 million World Bank–financed structural-adjustment loan. Adherence to macroeconomic stabilization policies, after some mid-year corrections, led to a significant improvement in the country's convertible-currency current-account balance. Despite unfavorable exogenous shocks—including the worst drought experienced by the country in this century and higher oil prices on world markets—the current account recorded a $127 million surplus.

Economic growth, however, was weaker than expected, mainly due to the steeper-than-projected decline in exports to the Soviet Union and the drought. Real GDP fell by 5 percent in 1990, and consumption dropped by almost 6 percent. Inflation accelerated and reached 30 percent, partly the result of higher oil prices. The government's reform program deepened and accelerated in 1991 and was supported by an extended arrangement from the IMF and a $250 million structural-adjustment loan from the Bank.

In Poland, the government launched its economic-transformation program in early 1990 with the objective of stabilizing the economy, transforming it according to market-oriented principles, and reintegrating it into the world economy. In support of this program, Poland secured an IMF standby arrangement, as well as a $300 million structural-adjustment loan from the Bank, and was able to negotiate a Paris Club rescheduling of foreign debts. Initial results of the economic-transformation program are promising: Prices are now freely determined, and most barriers to international trade have been removed. Inflation has slowed; nonetheless, it remains excessive (between 5 percent and 6 percent a month) and continues to be the main threat to the program. The program also resulted in a large trade surplus due to strong export expansion and reserve accumulation, a sharp drop in GDP (−12 percent), a budgetary surplus of more than 3 percent of GDP in 1990, and a rise in unemployment to an estimated 6.1 percent.

Poland also launched a number of systemic and structural reforms during the past year. Privatization legislation was passed, and a new Ministry of Ownership Transformation was established. Over 20,000 small shops and service outlets, as well as a number of large enterprises, have been privatized, and plans are under way to privatize a further 150 to 200 large enterprises. An Antimonopoly Office is vetting the privatization process to ensure that public monopolies are not transformed into private monopolies. Unemployment and welfare systems have been established. Restructuring options are now being studied for the energy sector. In May 1991, the government devalued the zloty by about 14 percent and announced a new exchange-rate system that would tie the zloty to a basket of currencies that is subject to daily change along international parities.

Following the December 1989 revolution, the new government of Romania declared its commitment to economic reform and restructuring on a market-economy basis. Since then, many institutional changes have taken place: Ministries have been reduced in number, a two-tiered banking system has been introduced, farm-procurement prices have been increased, and private farmers are now permitted to sell at market-determined prices. Privatization legislation has been prepared, autonomy has been given to enterprises, and two phases of price liberalization were implemented, in November 1990 and April 1991. Reform of the tax regime and of external tariffs is also under preparation.

In addition, the legal framework to permit the country's transition to a market economy has been created; a new fiscal system has been adopted; and budgetary activity now emphasizes expenditures for health, education, and other social services rather than industrial investments. A new foreign-exchange regime has been adopted (with a dual foreign-exchange system), and a land law has been approved by the parliament under which land is being returned to its former owners.

The government's programs are being supported through an IMF standby arrangement, as well as through pledged assistance, totaling about $1 billion, from the European Community and the wider group of twenty-four industrialized countries. Late in fiscal 1991, the Bank approved a $180 million loan to finance the importation of essential spare parts and equipment; technical assistance, designed to support the ongoing economic-reform process, is also being provided.

However, deep-seated structural difficulties, coupled with the general uncertainty caused by the dismantling of the command system, a shortened work week, and a reduction in energy supplies to industries, caused real GDP to decline by 10 percent in 1990. Industrial output, accounting for over 50 percent of GDP, declined nearly 20 percent, while industrial labor productivity fell by 23 percent in the first half of 1990. Declines in domestic output, the demise of CMEA trading arrangements, and the rise in oil prices led to a large current-account deficit in 1990 of about 8 percent of GDP.

In January 1990, Yugoslavia began to implement a strong stabilization program with the aim of sharply reducing inflation. This program, supported by an IMF standby arrangement and a structural-adjustment loan from the Bank, was based on a tight monetary and fiscal policy, liberalized imports and prices (except for some basic products), a fixed nominal-exchange rate for a convertible dinar, and a comprehensive freeze of wages and public expenditures. The implementation of the program recorded initial success, in spite of some slippages in the wage-freeze component by a number of republics. By mid June 1990, inflation was reduced to zero, exports were buoyant, and foreign-exchange reserves were at an all-time high ($9 billion). However, industrial production dropped by nearly 2.5 percent, and the agriculture sector was hit hard by a severe drought.

By the third quarter of 1990, inflation reappeared, and trade performance weakened in the wake of a deterioration in the implementation of stabilization policies. While inflation decelerated in the fourth quarter following a tightening of monetary policy, other economic indicators continued to deteriorate. Industrial output declined steeply as retail sales slumped. Meanwhile, the Gulf crisis had a far-reaching negative effect, not only through higher oil prices but also through losses of export contracts and payments, including workers' remittances. For the year as a whole, industrial production declined by 10 percent, and the gross social product fell by 7.2 percent. The rate of inflation soared to 118 percent (against a 20–30 percent rate planned under the program). The current account with convertible-currency countries had a deficit of $1 billion, compared with an initially projected surplus of $1 billion, and foreign-exchange reserves declined to about $7 billion. In Yugoslavia, any significant economic recovery is now linked to the resolution of political difficulties.

World Bank Operations, Fiscal Year 1991

Fueled by a dramatic increase in lending to its borrowing member countries in Eastern and Central Europe, Bank lending to the region reached a record high of $6.6 billion for forty-six projects in sixteen countries. Commitments to Eastern and Central European countries totaled $2.9 billion, up from $1.8 billion in fiscal 1990. Almost half of the amount—$1.4 billion—was committed to Poland. In addition, Bulgaria and Czechoslovakia received loans for the first time from the Bank ($17 million and $450 million, respectively), while lending resumed to Romania after a hiatus of nine years.

Projects designed to mitigate the adverse economic effects caused by the flood of workers returning from the Gulf were approved for Egypt, Jordan, and Yemen; in addition, the Bank approved a $250 million loan to Iran to assist that country in the aftermath of the June 1990 earthquake that killed or injured 100,000 people and left another half million homeless.

Latin America and the Caribbean

Economic performance in the Latin America and the Caribbean region in 1990 continued to be depressed. There was a small decline in total output for the region as a whole, and per capita output fell for the third year in a row. As a result, per capita income in the region today is about 10 percent below the level attained in 1980. These aggregate numbers, however, do not reflect the profound political and economic changes that are taking place within many countries. These changes could lay the foundation for future growth.

Many governments have recently instituted economic-policy reforms that are radically different from the patterns that were followed in recent decades. The movement has been away from a broad role for government, highly protected industrial development, extensive regulation of the private sector, public ownership of productive assets, and large budgetary deficits. The new pattern of economic policy emphasizes smaller and more efficient governments, privatization of government enterprises, more open foreign-trading regimes, deregulation of financial and commodity markets, and reductions in public-sector expenditure imbalances. There is also a greater awareness of the relationship between the environment and economic development, and increased emphasis on broadening opportunities for the less privileged and providing safety nets for the poor during the adjustment process.

Regional aggregates tend to obscure the wide range of individual country performance. For instance, the overall numbers combine countries with positive per capita income growth, such as Colombia, Costa Rica, El Salvador, and Paraguay, with countries having declines in total output, such as Argentina, Brazil, and Peru.

In some cases, growth is low or negative because countries have only very recently begun to undertake major stabilization and adjustment programs; in other cases, it is low because restructuring has not yet taken place. For example, in Argentina and Peru, negative growth is the product of hyperinflation and the initial impact of stabilization efforts. Significant structural reforms, including restructuring of the public sector and trade liberalization, have just begun and have had an initial negative effect on growth. In Chile, rapid growth during both 1988 and 1989 was accompanied by

Table 6-10. Latin America and the Caribbean: 1989 Population and Per Capita GNP of Countries That Borrowed during Fiscal Years 1989–91

Country	Population[a] (thousands)	Per capita GNP[b] (US dollars)
Argentina	31,900	2,160
Bahamas, The	249	11,320
Bolivia	7,100	620
Brazil	147,300	2,540
Chile	13,000	1,770
Colombia	32,300	1,200
Costa Rica	2,700	1,780
Dominican Republic	7,000	790
Ecuador	10,300	1,020
El Salvador	5,100	1,070
Guatemala	8,900	910
Guyana	796	340
Haiti	6,400	360
Honduras	5,000	900
Jamaica	2,400	1,260
Mexico	84,600	2,010
St. Kitts and Nevis	41	—[c]
St. Lucia	148	1,810
St. Vincent and the Grenadines	113	—[d]
Trinidad and Tobago	1,300	3,230
Uruguay	3,100	2,620
Venezuela	19,200	2,450

NOTE: The 1989 estimates of GNP per capita presented above are from the "World Development Indicators" section of *World Development Report 1991*.

a. Estimates from mid 1989.

b. *World Bank Atlas* methodology, 1987–89 base period.

c. GNP per capita estimated to be in the $2,335–$5,999 range.

d. GNP per capita estimated to be in the $581–$2,334 range.

a resurgence of inflation in the range of 30 percent annually. Efforts to tighten monetary policy in 1990 reduced inflation but also temporarily reduced growth. The economy is expected to recover significantly in 1991, however. In Brazil, negative growth is a result of intermittent efforts to stabilize fiscal finances and to control credit policy.

Performance in the region has also been affected by changes in the international environment, including higher oil prices, and a slowing of growth in the developed countries, particularly the United States, which has slowed growth in demand for manufactured exports. The sudden increase in oil prices after August 1990 significantly raised the cost of oil imports in many Latin American countries, although it also benefited oil exporters such as Mexico, Trinidad and Tobago, and Venezuela. Some of the countries most seriously affected by higher oil prices tended to be those smaller and poorer countries in the region that are highly dependent on imported petroleum, such as Belize, the Dominican Republic, Guyana, Jamaica, and Nicaragua.

Patterns of Reform, 1983–91

While each country is unique, the patterns of reform being followed by countries in the Latin America and the Caribbean region contain many similarities. In order to summarize this experience, it is possible to group countries into four broad categories:

• those with a record of sustained reform during the latter half of the 1980s (Bolivia, Chile, and Mexico, for example);

• those that lately have shown increased commitment to policy and institutional change, in some cases after a series of failed programs of adjustment (Argentina, Brazil, Colombia, Ecuador, Jamaica, Paraguay, Uruguay, and Venezuela, for example);

• those having economies severely eroded by economic mismanagement and internal strife, but whose governments have recently initiated major economic reforms (El Salvador, Guyana, Honduras, Nicaragua, and Peru); and

• those in which programs of reform and restructuring are still being developed (Dominican Republic, Guatemala, Haiti, and Panama).

Table 6-11. **Lending to Borrowers in Latin America and the Caribbean, by Sector, Fiscal Years 1982–91**
(millions of US dollars)

Sector	Annual average, 1982–86	1987	1988	1989	1990	1991
Agriculture and Rural Development	995.7	1,195.0	1,404.8	161.8	855.7	941.5
Development Finance Companies	262.1	1,115.0	970.0	1,164.3	471.1	844.5
Education	89.3	84.9	88.3	140.0	—	595.3
Energy						
Oil, gas, and coal	165.9	104.4	—	94.0	—	260.0
Power	595.6	423.8	423.0	736.0	897.5	—
Industry	63.6	55.0	1,065.0	860.0	—	200.0
Nonproject	267.3	1,040.1	250.0	692.0	1,378.0	422.3
Population, Health, and Nutrition	40.0	10.0	109.0	99.0	389.2	337.3
Public-sector Management	—	—	—	500.0	350.0	604.0
Small-scale Enterprises	246.8	185.0	—	155.0	77.5	—
Technical Assistance	21.1	15.5	—	50.7	59.0	68.8
Telecommunications	14.0	—	—	45.0	—	—
Transportation	480.5	524.3	210.6	149.3	1,029.0	114.0
Urban Development	180.1	335.0	491.0	675.0	450.0	364.0
Water Supply and Sewerage	166.4	64.0	252.3	320.0	7.7	485.0
Total	3,558.5	5,152.0	5,264.0	5,842.1	5,964.7	5,236.7
Of which: IBRD	3,542.9	4,994.6	5,152.0	5,703.7	5,726.7	5,067.2
IDA	45.6	157.4	112.0	138.4	238.0	169.5
Number of operations	42	58	37	43	41	44

— Zero.

NOTE: Details may not add to totals because of rounding.

This boy in San Salvador may be among the more than 1 million beneficiaries of a project, approved in fiscal 1991, that will provide basic health and education services to the poor.

In general, reforms in the first group of countries have covered such areas as reduction of tariffs and elimination of quantitative restrictions on foreign trade, liberalization of financial-sector regulations (including controls on interest rates), privatization of public enterprises, and appropriate adjustment in taxes, public-sector prices, and expenditures to reduce public-sector deficits.

Chile is the most advanced country in this group, having been one of the first to start the process. It has had a steady growth for the past six years, and the investment rate is now at an historical peak. In Bolivia and Mexico, the rate of growth attained so far has been more modest than in Chile, although the reforms have been very impressive. In Mexico, over 900 public enterprises have been closed or privatized since 1982, including the two largest airlines, the telephone company, and the largest copper mine. The privatization of commercial banks is in an early stage of implementation. In Bolivia, after years of economic mismanagement and hyperinflation, major reform has been implemented since 1985. Fiscal imbalances have been kept under control, and inflation has stabilized at around 15 percent a year. Import tariffs have been reduced to about 10 percent, prices have been liberalized, and a flexible exchange rate is in place.

In the second group, the changes under way in Argentina, Brazil, Colombia, and Venezuela are probably the most substantial. In Venezuela, key prices, such as exchange and interest rates, have been freed, subsidies have been heavily curtailed, trade is being liberalized, a reform of public enterprises and the financial system is in progress, the public-sector deficit has been virtually eliminated, and an agreement reducing debt service to commercial banks has been implemented. In Colombia, the government has decided to open the economy, deregulate and reform public enterprises, and liberalize the financial system. The first steps in each have already been taken. In both Venezuela and Colombia, the combination of a rich natural-resource base and recent policy reforms makes for very favorable growth prospects.

In Argentina, a highly visible and determined effort is being made to change the structure of the economy. Privatization of major public enterprises is a key element in the reform program. The program of privatization and debt-equity conversion has already reduced Argentina's commercial debt by $7 billion, or about 20 percent of its long-term debt to commercial banks. In addition, a program of tax reform is being implemented, and the fiscal deficit has been reduced sharply. Government expenditures are being cut through administrative reforms and an early-retirement scheme for government workers. The financial system is gradually being rehabilitated, and interest rates are now set by market forces. In foreign trade, quantitative restrictions have largely been eliminated, and the maximum tariff has been lowered to 24 percent. In Brazil, the government has reduced the fiscal deficit of the central government, and public employment has been cut. Trade reform has eliminated most quantitative trade restrictions and will reduce tariffs. Inflation remains high, however, and the government has been unable to control monetary expansion.

Countries in the third group are those that are just beginning reform programs after a period of unorthodox policies or long periods of internal strife.

Peru has suffered a significant erosion of economic institutions, policies, and infrastructure during the past several years. Since August 1990, the new government has been implementing a major stabilization and adjustment program designed to deal with inflation through more restrictive monetary and fiscal policies, as well as to liberalize foreign trade and deregulate the economy. Payments of current debt service to multilateral institutions (including the World Bank) have been resumed, and, as a result, arrears to international organizations have been frozen. Although the initial effect of the new economic policies has been positive, Peru still faces daunting problems, particularly in consolidating its stabilization effort, rebuilding the base of infrastructure, restoring social services, and finding solutions to deal with arrears owed to foreign creditors. While the new economic program has balanced the budget and reduced inflation considerably, inflation remains high (over 300 percent a year).

In Central America, Nicaragua faces a situation similar to Peru's; it needs to reestablish economic policies and institutions while it rehabilitates key infrastructure and facilities in order to facilitate a recovery of economic growth. Nicaragua and external donors are working together within the framework of a consultative group chaired by the Bank. In El Salvador and Honduras, the conditions faced by governments at the start of the reform process are somewhat better. Far-reaching changes to improve macroeconomic management, deregulate economies, and liberalize external trade have been initiated, and steps have been taken to reduce the burden of adjustment on the poor.

Costa Rica has largely avoided the sort of crises shared by other Central American countries. It has implemented, albeit with occasional slippages, a program of economic reform and has enjoyed modest but steady growth. Recently it concluded an agreement with commercial banks, substantially reducing the burden of debt service. Governments in Guatemala and Panama, however, are still attempting to define a viable recovery program and assemble the finance needed.

Economic performance and policy response on the part of the countries of the Caribbean region, by and large, have been relatively strong.

In Jamaica, the government has advanced the reform agenda in recent years. Trade is being further liberalized, the role of the public sector is being reduced, interest-rate subsidies are being eliminated, and the exchange-rate system is now market-based.

In Guyana, the government has introduced a radical change in economic management—from a system based on state intervention to a market-oriented one, with a much greater role for the private sector. The adjustment program is constrained, however, by shortages of manpower and external finance.

Overall, the countries of the Eastern Caribbean have grown steadily, helped by good economic management, preferential access of their exports to the European Community (EC), the United States, and Canada, and capital flows under the umbrella of the regional consultative group chaired by the Bank. Changes in access to the EC after 1992, however, could adversely affect these countries. Haiti's economy has suffered from a decade of stagnation and disequilibrium, caused in part by political instability. The recent inauguration of a new, democratically elected government provides an opportunity to begin to address the fundamental development issues of that country in a concerted way.

Lessons Learned

Economic change on such a wide scale, and over so short a time period, is unprecedented in the region. Clearly, the process has not been smooth or easy, and setbacks are likely to occur in the future. Even so, there are certain lessons to be learned.

First, the restoration of confidence takes time. In Mexico, it has taken eight years of sustained reform to restore public confidence and an adequate level of private investment. Today, domestic capital is returning from abroad, and real interest rates are declining. Restoration of economic growth also takes time. Fundamental restructuring of the relationships between the public and private sectors inevitably brings about a sharp reduction in output in the early years, and revival is slow as private-sector confidence returns and public infrastructure is rebuilt.

Second, the restructuring of the public sector and the elimination of large fiscal deficits are fundamental to a successful reform effort. Many initial attempts at reform failed because of inadequate efforts to eliminate the fiscal deficit. More important, however, successful reform of the public sector requires a fundamental rethinking of the role and responsibility of the public sector in the economy. Throughout Latin America, steps are being taken to improve the efficiency of the public sector, shift its activities to the private sector wherever possible, and reduce its overall size. Efficiency concerns relate not only to the way in which the public sector spends its resources but also to the way it raises resources from the private sector. These concerns have led to major programs of tax reform. The restoration of fiscal discipline may also require institutional changes that affect the relationship among different parts of the public sector—including central and regional governments, public enterprises, autonomous agencies, central banks, and so forth.

Third, domestic and external economic management are both highly interdependent and mutually reinforcing. Thus, programs of public-sector restructuring have to be combined with programs for liberalizing trade and resolving external-debt problems. In Argentina and Brazil, for instance, early efforts at reform were undertaken while external-trade restrictions and distorted incentive regimes were maintained, both of which added to domestic inflationary pressures. At the same time, the absence of an agreement with external creditors increased skepticism about the success of stabilization programs. In contrast, reform programs in Bolivia, Chile, and Mexico have all been accompanied by workouts with commercial banks that reduce debt-service burdens.

Finally, since adjustment is a prolonged process and growth is slow to recover, special measures have to be adopted to protect the less-privileged groups, maintain essential social programs, and implement specific basic health and education programs targeted to reach the poor and the vulnerable. In many cases, the Bank has directly assisted these efforts (see Box 6-1).

Debt and Trade

Progress continues to be made on resolving the problems of high levels of debt and debt service. Agreements were reached between Venezuela and Uruguay and their commercial-bank creditors in 1990. Both agreements included debt buybacks, debt exchanges, and new-money/debt-conversion facilities.

The Uruguay agreement covers the entire $1.6 billion of rescheduled commercial-bank debt, while the Venezuela agreement covers about $20 billion of its external commercial debt of $35 billion. Brazil reached an agreement with its commercial-bank creditors in April 1991 on the refinancing of $8 billion in payment arrears. The settlement of the arrears problem is the first step toward a possible debt-financing package. For Chile, the commercial banks agreed to reschedule $1.9 billion of repayments falling due during 1991–94 and to subscribe to $320 million in new-money bonds over the next two years. Colombia successfully negotiated with its commercial creditors for the refinancing of debt service falling due during 1991–94 in lieu of debt rescheduling. Official debts were also rescheduled during the year through the Paris Club for El Salvador, Guyana, Honduras, and Panama.

Some progress was also made during the year in strengthening regional trading arrangements. Argentina, Brazil, Paraguay, and Uruguay agreed in July 1990 to establish a full common market (Mercosur) by the end of 1994, two years ahead of the original target. Although the Mercosur was preceded by several unsuccessful attempts at regional integration, prospects for success are better now, given the rapid increase in trade among these countries since 1985 and the strong commitment to liberalization and deregulation in the region.

Mexico began negotiations in 1991 with the United States and Canada, its most important trading partners, for the possible establishment of a free-trade agreement among the participating countries. Chile is making preparations to begin similar negotiations. Under the Enterprise for the Americas program, the United States has indicated its willingness to broaden this approach to cover other countries in the region, with the eventual goal of establishing a comprehensive free-trade agreement for all of Latin America. The enterprise initiative will also provide additional support for privatization, liberalization of investment regimes, and debt reduction, largely funneled through the Inter-American Development Bank.

Box 6-1. Poverty Alleviation through Targeted Programs in the Social Sectors

Bank projects address regional poverty concerns in a variety of ways, including macroeconomic adjustments that, in the medium to long term, increase the demand for labor and social-sector projects that increase the human-capital potential of the poor. The effects that arise from such adjustments and projects, however, tend to occur over the longer term. The Bank is also supporting projects with a more immediate and direct impact that help prevent significant declines in the standard of living of the poor through targeted interventions in the social sectors. These interventions aim to improve directly the quality of life of the poor by providing, for instance, improved nutrition, primary health care, water and sewerage services, and food to those below a threshold consumption level. The key considerations in the design of these projects are to minimize the leakage of targeted programs to unintended beneficiaries and to minimize administrative costs.

These projects take on a variety of shapes and attributes. For instance, the child-care and nutrition project in Colombia (approved in fiscal 1990) aims at strengthening the country's existing community day-care program and ensuring its sustainability. This program provides training and housing improvements for women who provide day-care services in their homes for poor working mothers. Enrolled children receive improved nutrition and care and take part in preschool learning activities. The program is targeted to the poorest urban neighborhoods and permits participating mothers to seek employment outside of the home. The Bank loan is financing supplies, equipment, and housing improvements for the program, as well as training and technical assistance.

In Mexico, the Bank-assisted basic health-care project aims to strengthen and extend health-care services to 13 million poor people in forty-seven health jurisdictions. Besides providing for equipment, furniture, and basic medical supplies, the project also supports institutional improvements to strengthen management capability to enhance the efficiency and effectiveness of the health-care system and strengthen the implementation of sectoral reforms. These reforms aim at decentralizing budgetary, management, and operational responsibilities from the federal level to the states.

In Brazil, children in poor urban communities have high school-dropout and repetition rates because of poor facilities, poor health and nutrition, and lack of supportive home environments. The São Paulo innovations in basic education project, approved in fiscal 1991, is designed to address these problems. Planned reforms include a new curricular approach, school construction in poor neighborhoods, a longer school day, teacher training, expanded meal programs, a preschool support fund, reform of the school health program, and educational television directed toward poor children.

A major vehicle for targeting assistance to the poor has been Bank support for social funds that provide financing for small-scale, employment-creating projects, often in the social sectors. To date, the Bank has supported the establishment of such funds in Bolivia, Guatemala, Haiti, Honduras, Jamaica, and Venezuela. Bolivia's emergency social fund (ESF) was one of the first to be established. The ESF, begun in 1986, was designed to provide finance for income-generating and employment-generating projects, as well as social-assistance activities. The main objective of the ESF was to provide employment promptly. A similar program, the social investment fund, was subsequently established. It provides a more permanent vehicle for funding small-scale projects in the social sectors, is better integrated into the country's overall public-investment program, and is more closely coordinated with line ministries. Over the past five years, the Bank has supported these funds with three IDA credits.

Targeted programs can also be developed as part of larger adjustment operations. For instance, two agricultural-sector adjustment loans to Mexico (approved in fiscal 1988 and fiscal 1991) support a number of reforms in the agricultural sector, including rationalization of public investment and privatization of parastatals. Untargeted subsidies, in the form of controls on food prices, are being eliminated, and the present system of targeted subsidies is being improved to eliminate leakages to those who are not poor and to expand coverage in rural areas. In addition, the government is increasingly using the health system to identify eligible beneficiaries for its food and nutrition programs.

In the case of Venezuela, targeted programs were developed within the ambit of a structural-adjustment loan approved late in fiscal 1989. Indirect food subsidies operating through a multiple exchange-rate system were phased out and direct transfer programs, including one that provides direct cash grants to poor households with children in school in the *barrios*, were introduced or expanded. The loan also provided technical assistance for the establishment of a pilot program of health and nutritional assistance for vulnerable groups. Food distribution for the nutrition component was effected through private-sector contractors. These programs were expanded and extended through the Bank's follow-up social-development project, approved during the past year.

The structural-adjustment loan to El Salvador also includes programs aimed at the most nutritionally vulnerable groups, including babies at the weaning stage. The government plans to introduce three pilot programs during 1991–92: Provisions in the programs include the distribution of nutritionally fortified cookies to primary-school children, the distribution of weaning food, and the distribution of food coupons.

Table 6-12. **Net Transfers to Latin America and the Caribbean**
(millions of US dollars; fiscal years)

Item	Brazil		Mexico		Argentina		Total region	
	1991	1987–91	1991	1987–91	1991	1987–91	1991	1987–91
IBRD and IDA commitments	955	5,852	1,882	10,428	680	3,158	5,237	27,460
Gross disbursements	822	5,270	1,314	8,421	457	2,539	4,288	22,883
Repayments	1,318	5,022	894	3,418	294	1,040	3,647	13,721
Net disbursements	−496	247	420	5,004	162	1,499	641	9,162
Interest and charges	734	3,434	860	3,038	200	785	2,701	11,236
Net transfer	−1,230	−3,186	−440	1,966	−37	714	−2,060	−2,073

NOTE: Disbursements from the IDA Special Fund are included. The countries shown in the table are those with the largest amounts of public or publicly guaranteed long-term debt. Details may not add to totals because of rounding.

Other initiatives aimed at establishing free-trade areas in the region include those of the Andean Pact (Bolivia, Colombia, Ecuador, Peru, and Venezuela), which plans to achieve an almost total free-trade area among its members beginning in January 1992; the Group of Three (Colombia, Mexico, and Venezuela), which is negotiating an agreement on trade and investment aimed at the liberalization of trade and deregulation among its three members; and Chile, Mexico, and Venezuela, which began negotiations in 1990 on ways to achieve free trade in the near term.

Activities of the Bank, Fiscal 1991

In the context of the rapid changes taking place in the region, the Bank has played a multifaceted role, providing economic advice, in-depth economic and sector analysis, and financial assistance to support adjustment programs, as well as debt and debt-service reduction schemes. In many cases, the level and extent of the Bank's involvement cannot be measured in terms of loans extended or economic reports produced, as it often consists of informal advice and suggestions provided over a long period of time. As adjustment programs are gradually being carried out, the Bank has been able to shift its resources from adjustment lending to other high-priority tasks, including sector and project lending for environmental protection and human-resource development.

In fiscal 1991, total new loan commitments of $5.2 billion, involving forty-four operations, were provided to the region. This was a slight reduction from the level of $6 billion achieved in the previous year. The drop is partly explained by a decline in lending for debt reduction, which slipped from $1.3 billion in fiscal

1990 to $215 million. Disbursements during the year were $4.3 billion, and repayments to the Bank were $3.6 billion, yielding net disbursements of $641 million, an amount considerably lower than in the previous year (see Table 6-12). This is a result of the high level of gross disbursements achieved in fiscal 1990 when large amounts of adjustment lending (including a debt-reduction exercise) were committed to Mexico.

Adjustment lending, which amounted to 30 percent of total lending in fiscal 1991, remains an important instrument for supporting major reforms being undertaken in the region. In general, adjustment lending has shifted away from broad structural-adjustment lending to one that places greater emphasis on sector adjustment, particularly in such areas as public-sector and financial-sector reform. Major adjustment loans undertaken during the past year included the public-enterprise reform loan in Argentina ($300 million), a public-sector reform loan in Colombia ($304 million), and, in Mexico, export-sector development ($300 million) and agriculture-sector adjustment loans ($400 million).

Structural-adjustment loans in El Salvador and Honduras supported major reforms in trade liberalization and public-expenditure redirection. In El Salvador, the Bank's structural-adjustment loan is supporting a program of economic revival and poverty reduction that is being put in place despite the problems associated with a decade-long civil conflict. Lending to Honduras was suspended in 1989, and the country was placed in nonaccrual status. The installation of a new government in 1990, however, led to the definition of a new program of adjustment, the clearing of arrears to international financial institutions, and the resumption of lending by the Bank. In addition, the Bank continued in fiscal 1991 to support debt-restructuring programs with loans to Venezuela and Uruguay for debt and debt-service reduction.

Traditional Bank project lending continued to constitute the majority of Bank operations in the region, totaling more than 65 percent of the year's lending. Mexico and Brazil were the largest recipients of project loans. In addition to traditional project lending for water-supply systems, agriculture, and transportation, lending in the region increasingly emphasizes health and human-resource development, municipal development and decentralization, and the development of science and technology.

Project loans during the past year for Mexico, for example, provided support for water-supply and sanitation improvements, basic health services, and decentralization and regional development. An innovative loan of $150 million to Brazil is supporting scientific research and training by providing grants, awarded on a competitive basis, for university research in various sciences, as well as the development of support services for this research. Social-development funds, which provide support for small, employment-creating, investment projects in poverty areas, are being supported in Haiti, Honduras, and Venezuela.

Cooperation and Cofinancing

The Bank continued to act as chairman for consultative groups for several countries of the region. Consultative-group meetings were held for Bolivia, the Caribbean Group, El Salvador, Honduras, and Nicaragua, including subgroup meetings for Guyana and Haiti.

The first-ever consultative-group meeting for Nicaragua met in Paris under Bank chairmanship in December 1990 and included representatives from seventeen countries. The initial focus of the group was on the reintegration of Nicaragua into the international financial community. The members reviewed Nicaragua's stabilization and adjustment objectives, its external-debt situation, and its technical-cooperation requirements, as well as mechanisms for the settlement of arrears to the World Bank and the Inter-American Development Bank (IDB). Subsequent donor meetings, including a second consultative-group meeting in May 1991, helped to firm up the arrears-clearing process and the external financing of the program.

The consultative-group meeting for Honduras, which took place in December 1990, followed a series of donor meetings that had taken place the previous year. The group focused on Honduras' external-financing needs for 1991 and on the government's poverty-alleviation efforts, particularly the establishment of the Honduran Social Investment Fund and the government's plan to restructure the social sectors.

The first consultative-group meeting for El Salvador took place in May 1991. The meeting reviewed the government's economic-stabilization and adjustment program, with particular emphasis on the social sectors. Donors expressed their satisfaction with the encouraging results of El Salvador's economic and social program to date and commended the thrust of the adjustment efforts. They especially noted the enhanced role of nongovernmental organizations and the private sector in the government's program, and emphasized their hope for a peaceful resolution to the civil conflict.

The fifth consultative-group meeting for Bolivia (November 1990) was encouraged by the continued commitment of the government to economic reform within a democratic framework, the maintenance of macroeconomic stability, and Bolivia's efforts to improve social conditions and preserve its environment. The Bolivian delegation presented a new antinarcotic development program that explicitly set the solutions to the problem of the coca economy within the broader context of the government's growth, poverty-alleviation, and environmental-protection strategies.

During the year, the volume of cofinancing to countries in the region was $2.1 billion for twenty-one projects, a drop from the unusually high level of the year before. The IDB was the region's largest source of cofinancing during the year. Cofinancing arrangements with the IDB included fourteen operations for a total of $1.4 billion. Japan remained the largest source of official bilateral cofinancing through the Export-Import Bank of Japan (three operations for a total of $275 million) and the Overseas Economic Cooperation Fund (two operations for $85 million). An export-credit enhanced leverage (EXCEL) program for up to $300 million for the export-sector loan to Mexico is being discussed with export-credit agencies.

Section Seven
Summaries of Projects Approved for IBRD and IDA Assistance in Fiscal 1991

Acronyms and Abbreviations Used in This Section

ADF—African Development Fund
AfDB—African Development Bank
AFESD—Arab Fund for Economic and Social Development
AGCD—Administration générale de la coopération au développement (Belgium)
AIDAB—Australian International Development Assistance Bureau
AsDB—Asian Development Bank
BADEA—Arab Bank for Economic Development in Africa
BITS—Swedish Agency for International Technical and Economic Cooperation
BOAD—West African Development Bank
CCCE—Caisse centrale de coopération économique
CEDEAO—Economic Community of West African States
CIDA—Canadian International Development Agency
DANIDA—Danish International Development Agency
DGIS—Directoraat Generaal voor Internationale Samenwerking
EBRD—European Bank for Reconstruction and Development
EC—European Community
EDCF—Economic Development Cooperation Fund (Republic of Korea)
EDF—European Development Fund
EIB—European Investment Bank
FAC—Fonds d'aide et de coopération
FINNIDA—Finnish International Development Agency
GEF—Global Environment Facility
GTZ—German Technical Assistance Corporation
ICEIDA—Icelandic International Development Agency

ICOD—International Centre for Ocean Development
IDB—Inter-American Development Bank
IFAD—International Fund for Agricultural Development
IFC—International Finance Corporation
IsDB—Islamic Development Bank
ITU—International Telecommunications Union
KFAED—Kuwait Fund for Arab Economic Development
KfW—Kreditanstalt für Wiederaufbau
MCD—Ministère de la coopération et du développement (France)
NDF—Nordic Development Fund
NIO—Netherlands Investment Organization
NORAD—Norwegian Agency for International Development
ODA—Overseas Development Administration
OECD—Organisation for Economic Co-operation and Development
OECF—Overseas Economic Cooperation Fund
OPEC—Organization of the Petroleum Exporting Countries
SCF—Save the Children Fund
SDC—Swiss Development Corporation
SIDA—Swedish International Development Authority
UNDP—United Nations Development Programme
UNFPA—United Nations Fund for Population Activities
UNICEF—United Nations Children's Fund
USAID—United States Agency for International Development
WFP—World Food Programme
WHO—World Health Organization
WWF—World Wildlife Fund

Agriculture and Rural Development

ARGENTINA: IBRD—$33.5 million. Agricultural services are to be strengthened through investments in physical facilities, institutional development, training, and technical assistance, thus improving the country's ability to produce, certify, and maintain high-quality agricultural products for export. Cofinancing is anticipated from the IDB ($30 million) and Japan ($950,000).

Total cost: $82.7 million.

BANGLADESH: IDA—$75 million. The average annual per capita income of more than half a million farm families is expected to increase as a result of a project that supports increased

---

Data used in this section have been compiled from documentation provided at the time of project approval.

investment by farmers in simple, low-cost minor irrigation equipment sold by private dealers for cash under the government's liberalized policy and institutional framework for private-sector–led minor irrigation development. Total cost: $126.7 million.

BANGLADESH: IDA—$54 million. Some 314,000 families may see their annual per capita incomes more than double as a result of a project designed to promote growth in agriculture through increased private-sector investment in minor irrigation facilities. Cofinancing ($88 million) is expected from the EC. Total cost: $171.1 million.

BANGLADESH: IDA—$35 million. Through a strengthening of agricultural-support services (breeder-seed operations and extension services, for instance), agricultural production will increase—especially of foodgrains—and a diversification process, aimed at introducing high-value export crops, will be initiated. Cofinancing ($14.7 million) is expected from the ODA. Total cost: $59.4 million.

BENIN: IDA—$12.3 million. The provision of agricultural services will be improved by restructuring the country's agricultural institutions. Cofinancing is anticipated from IFAD ($13.5 million), France ($10.8 million), the EDF ($9.8 million), the UNDP ($5.1 million), and the GTZ ($3 million). Total cost: $29.6 million.

BOLIVIA: IDA—$21 million. Some 2 million small and medium-sized farm families are targeted to benefit from a project that will establish mechanisms to coordinate research and extension activities and to develop technology to be used in association with key crops important to the majority of small farmers who live in the highlands. Institution-building assistance to the Bolivian Institute for Agricultural Technology is included. Cofinancing ($3.5 million) is expected from Switzerland. Total cost: $29.8 million.

BURKINA FASO: IDA—$16.5 million. Community land-management plans, using an innovative participatory and multisectoral approach, will be designed and implemented in an effort to stop and reverse the process of natural-resource degradation in order to meet the conditions essential for sustainable agricultural production. Cofinancing is being secured from Norway ($3.4 million), the GTZ ($2 million), and the CCCE ($1.5 million). Total cost: $25.2 million.

CHINA: IBRD—$147.1 million; IDA—$187.9 million. By improving and expanding irrigation schemes to permit greater productivity on low-yield and medium-yield areas in the North China plain, farm incomes will be increased, as will production of staple foods and cash crops. Total cost: $593 million.

CHINA: IBRD—$75 million; IDA—$200 million. About 90,000 full-time jobs will be created through a fourth rural-credit project that will provide funds to the Agricultural Bank of China and its affiliated rural-credit cooperatives for onlending to farmers, collectives, state farms, and enterprises. Technical assistance is included. Total cost: $550 million.

CHINA: IDA—$110 million. Rural incomes could double for some 630,000 poor farm families through crop diversification, increased yields, and livestock, fishery, and agroprocessing activities. In addition, about 8,500 female village farmer technicians will be recruited and trained to serve the special needs of women farmers. Total cost: $196 million.

CHINA: IDA—$64 million. Per capita incomes may increase by an average of 180 percent for 130,000 poor smallholder farm families in Sichuan and Hubei provinces through increases in production and marketability of fruit (mostly citrus) for both domestic consumption and export. Institutional support is included. Total cost: $136.9 million.

COLOMBIA: IBRD—$75 million. A time slice of the country's integrated rural-development investment program—consisting of small discrete projects in agricultural production and environmental protection and training and community organization, as well as projects to improve the rural infrastructure—will be financed, thus helping to support the country's decentralization reforms. Institution-building assistance is included. Cofinancing ($75 million) is expected from the IDB. Total cost: $250 million.

CONGO: IBRD—$15.8 million. More than half of the country's smallholders may benefit directly from a project that supports the government's efforts to increase production efficiency and smallholder incomes by facilitating the development and dissemination, particularly to women and youths, of relevant agricultural technology (primarily extension and adaptive research). Cofinancing is anticipated from the UNDP ($900,000) and the EDF ($500,000). Total cost: $21.7 million.

COTE D'IVOIRE: IBRD—$2.2 million. The two-year pilot phase of a medium-term program to establish a viable process for strengthening the institutional capacity of support services to better address women's issues (by increasing farm productivity, improving marketable skills, and changing the perception of the role of women in society) will be supported. Total cost: $3.7 million.

ECUADOR: IBRD—$59 million. Almost 200,000 people will benefit from the provision of infrastructure necessary for flood control and drainage in part of the Lower Guayas basin—as part of the long-term plan for the overall development of the basin—potentially the most productive agricultural region in the country. Measures that aim at building up the institutional capacities of agencies participating in agricultural development and environmental initiatives are included. Cofinancing ($7 million) is anticipated from the DGIS. Total cost: $97.5 million.

EQUATORIAL GUINEA: IDA—$6.3 million. The entire rural population of the country (35,000 families) is expected to benefit from a strengthened agricultural-extension service, while about half of that group will also be beneficiaries of private-sector marketing activities. Institution-building assistance is included. Cofinancing has been agreed upon with IFAD ($5 million), BADEA ($3.9 million), and the OPEC Fund for International Development ($1.5 million). Total cost: $18 million.

GHANA: IDA—$22 million. The long-term process of strengthening the country's agricultural-research system—with emphasis given to the development of processes and institutional arrangements to ensure that research priorities are in accord with national development priorities, the needs of farmers, and the sustainable use of the country's natural-resource base—will be initiated. Cofinancing ($1.8 million) is expected from the ODA. Total cost: $29.5 million.

GHANA: IDA—$16.5 million. Efficiency will be restored in the long-neglected noncocoa tree-crops subsector (coffee, oil palm, and rubber), and an enabling environment will be created for the development of pineapple and other horticultural crops. Total cost: $22.4 million.

INDIA: IBRD—$40 million; IDA—$170 million. In the wake of the May 1990 cyclone that caused an estimated $1,250 million in damage to infrastructure and productivity in Andhra Pradesh state, assistance will be provided for reconstruction operations and for strengthening institutional capabilities in cyclone preparedness and mitigation. Total cost: $380 million.

INDIA: IBRD—$23 million; IDA—$130 million. The institutional framework for ensuring dam safety will be strengthened at the central government level and in the states of Madhya Pradesh, Rajasthan, Orissa, and Tamil Nadu. In addition, safety features will be upgraded —through remedial works and the installation of flood-forecasting systems and other basic facilities—in and around selected dams. Total cost: $196.8 million.

INDIA: IBRD—$20 million; IDA—$92.8 million. Improved agricultural technologies—particularly for watershed management, livestock, forestry, and seed production—will be introduced in Tamil Nadu, and agricultural extension will be made more cost effective and relevant to the needs of diversified farming. Help in improving planning and in establishing investment priorities, along with institution-building assistance, is included. Total cost: $133.3 million.

INDONESIA: IBRD—$125 million. Potential benefits from irrigated agricultural development will be achieved by completing and fully developing ongoing small and medium-scale irrigation schemes in thirteen provinces in the Outer Islands. About 127,000 rural families may benefit directly as new areas are brought under irrigation, while the incomes of another 100,000 families already receiving irrigation service are expected to rise. Total cost: $215.4 million.

INDONESIA: IBRD—$15.5 million. A follow-up area-development project in Yogyakarta province seeks to help the government develop the processes, institutions, and technologies needed to foster sustainable development throughout the country's most critical upland watersheds with the objectives of protecting the environment from erosion and reducing poverty. Total cost: $25.1 million.

KENYA: IDA—$75 million. A second agricultural-sector adjustment operation seeks to improve incentives for smallholder maize producers, increase fertilizer availability among small farmers, and improve the efficiency of public expenditures. Targeted programs, based on the government's food-security program, will be promoted to protect vulnerable lower-income groups, and new initiatives will be developed to prepare for droughts. Institution-building assistance is included. Cofinancing, totaling $100 million, is anticipated from the AfDB, the KfW, the ODA, the DGIS, and the OECF.

KENYA: IDA—$24.9 million. A second national agricultural-extension project focuses on creating a strong and dynamic agricultural-extension system that effectively delivers technical messages particularly tailored to farmers' needs and that aims to increase yield levels for both staple food and export crops. Cofinancing ($6 million) is expected from IFAD. Total cost: $47.9 million.

KENYA: IDA—$19.9 million. A forestry-development project has been designed to promote, on a pilot basis mainly, tree farming through intensified extension services; improve indigenous forest conservation, protection, and management; improve the physical and financial management of existing industrial forest plantations; strengthen the capacity of the Forestry Department; and upgrade forest research and technical forestry education. Cofinancing is expected from the EC ($15.8 million), the ODA ($13.7 million), FINNIDA ($6 million), and the SDC ($5.6 million). Total cost: $83.8 million.

MADAGASCAR: IDA—$19.8 million. The government's reform program for the livestock sector will be supported through institutional strengthening, as well as through production-development components that include improved disease control and dairy development. Cofinancing is anticipated from the CCCE ($5.4 million), NORAD ($2.1 million), and the MCD ($1 million). Total cost: $38.6 million.

MALAWI: IDA—$8.8 million. A fisheries-development project seeks not only to increase fish production but also to (a) generate additional off-farm employment and income to help reduce poverty among women and the rural population and (b) conserve the natural-resource base of the country's water bodies and prevent environmental degradation. Institution-building assistance is included. Cofinancing is anticipated from the NDF ($3.5 million) and the ICEIDA ($1 million). Total cost: $15.5 million.

MALI: IDA—$24.4 million. As many as 450,000 farm families will benefit from improvements in the country's crop, livestock, and forestry extension services, and, through a functional literacy and numeracy training program for men and women, most rural villages will be provided with a core group of functional literates who would be able to manage the affairs of the village. Total cost: $27.1 million.

MAURITIUS: IBRD—$10 million. The successful approach to coordination and policy reform in the sugar sector will be expanded to include the nonsugar sector through a project that seeks to strengthen sectoral policymaking and management capacity, improve research and extension services, and develop improved irrigation services. Technical assistance and training are included. Total cost: $18.1 million.

MEXICO: IBRD—$400 million. The government's objectives of increasing the rate of growth in agriculture, raising productivity and improving the efficiency of the agricultural sector, and alleviating the poverty of the most vulnerable population groups through targeted food programs will be supported.

MEXICO: IBRD—$350 million. A project directed at poverty alleviation and decentralization of public services will help finance core infrastructure and social projects in the country's four poorest provinces (Chiapas, Guerrero, Hidalgo, and Oaxaca), thereby decreasing by an estimated 40 percent the gap in the population's access to roads, schools, and other basic social goods. Components aimed at environmental preservation, archeological protection, and institutional development are included. Total cost: $1,363 million.

MOZAMBIQUE: IDA—$15.4 million. Some 50,000 cashew nut producers may benefit from a project that seeks to rehabilitate and develop the cashew subsector and increase efficiency and profitability among medium-scale state and commercial agricultural enterprises. In addition, local capacity to formulate and implement long-term growth strategies for the irrigation and cashew subsectors will be strengthened. Total cost: $17.8 million.

NIGERIA: IDA—$78 million. The first stage of strengthening the country's agricultural-research system so that it is able to generate appropriate technologies and adapt them to meet the immediate needs of smallholder farmers under diverse agroecological conditions will be initiated. Total cost: $104.1 million.

PAKISTAN: IBRD—$36.3 million; IDA—$47.3 million. A quarter million farm families are expected to benefit from a project that seeks to increase agricultural production through effective use of water saved as a result of improved water-management practices. In addition, the government's financial obligations will be reduced through increased cost recovery from beneficiaries and encouragement of greater farmer involvement in the operation and maintenance of minor irrigation-distributory canals. Total cost: $155.5 million.

PAKISTAN: IDA—$20 million. Agricultural production, primarily in Punjab province, will increase through improved and timely availability of supplemental irrigation on a financially sustainable basis. More than 1,300 government-owned and government-operated tubewells, which are expensive to operate and are poorly maintained, will be replaced by 13,000 small-capacity private tubewells, thus facilitating the transfer of responsibility for future groundwater development and protection against waterlogging in the project area to the private sector. A pilot project will test the viability of the transition from the public to the private sector in Sindh province. Total cost: $48.5 million.

PHILIPPINES: IBRD—$158 million; IDA—$66 million. An environment and natural-resources sector-adjustment program—consisting of a quick-disbursing program based on policy and institutional reforms and an investment component in support of institutional strengthening and regional, community-based resource-management activities—seeks to preserve, or, wherever practicable, reestablish what remains of the biological diversity of the Philippines. Cofinancing is anticipated from the OECF ($100 million), the GEF ($20 million), Japan ($4.6 million), and the NDF ($1 million). Total cost: $369 million.

PHILIPPINES: IBRD—$150 million. The volume of credit to finance private investments in fixed assets, incremental working capital, and seasonal production for a broad spectrum of agricultural and other viable rural investments will be expanded. In addition, the rural banking system will be strengthened, both institutionally and financially, and assistance will be provided in implementing improved rural financial-sector policies. Total cost: $203.5 million.

PHILIPPINES: IBRD—$46.2 million. Through support for the communal-irrigation program of the National Irrigation Administration, which seeks to increase crop production through reliable irrigation and improved agricultural-support services, the incomes of about 20,000 low-income farm families are expected to be enhanced and stabilized. Total cost: $64.4 million.

POLAND: IBRD—$100 million. Private farmers will be supported and other private-sector activities in rural areas will be promoted, primarily through the restructuring of high-priority rural cooperatives. Technical assistance is included. Cofinancing is anticipated from the EC ($29 million) and others ($6 million). Total cost: $180.2 million.

SRI LANKA: IDA—$29.6 million. Average incomes of about 100,000 farm families are expected to increase through a project that will support a series of related actions designed to upgrade the level of services provided by existing irrigation schemes. Cofinancing ($4 million) is expected from the EC. Total cost: $49.8 million.

ST. KITTS AND NEVIS: IBRD—$1.5 million; IDA—$1.5 million. Efficient conditions for agricultural development will be established, in particular by replacing the one-year agricultural-lease system with thirty-five-year renewable leases, thereby removing a major deterrent to the development of the agricultural sector. In addition, the financial condition of the sugar industry will be stabilized prior to divestiture. Cofinancing ($800,000) is anticipated from bilateral donors. Total cost: $4.3 million.

TANZANIA: IDA—$16.1 million. Funds from IDA reflows will be provided to supplement the agriculture-adjustment credit, approved in fiscal 1990 in the amount of $200 million.

THAILAND: IBRD—$30 million. The second phase of the national cadastral-mapping and land-titling program, which aims to extend secure, documented land tenure to rural landholders, strengthen property valuation in urban areas, and improve revenue generation from land transactions, will be supported. Cofinancing ($5.2 million) is expected from the AIDAB. Total cost: $73 million.

UGANDA: IDA—$100 million. The government's adjustment program in the agricultural sector will be supported by facilitating financial stabilization (by controlling credit expansion through improved institutional arrangements for financing coffee-crop procurement, as well as through organizational and financial restructuring of market intermediaries) and promoting agricultural growth and diversification (by creating competitive systems for processing and marketing of export crops, improving institutional arrangements for agricultural research and extension, and increasing the efficiency of public instruments). Total cost: $101.6 million.

UGANDA: IDA—$21 million. As many as half a million households will benefit from a project whose objective is to reverse the decline in livestock numbers through support for an emergency national disease-control program and a tsetse fly–control program. In addition, the quality and cost-effectiveness of livestock services will be improved through institutional reform, retraining, and the privatization of veterinary services. Total cost: $24.7 million.

YEMEN, REPUBLIC OF: IDA—$13.2 million. A fisheries project seeks to expand fish production, improve processing and marketing of fish, improve the assessment and management of fish resources, and improve the position of women in fishing communities. Cofinancing is anticipated from the EC ($16.3 million) and IFAD ($6.5 million). Total cost: $39.8 million.

Development Finance Companies

BANGLADESH: IDA—$3.5 million. Funds from IDA reflows will be provided to help supplement the financial-sector adjustment credit approved in fiscal 1990 in the amount of $175 million.

BOLIVIA: IDA—$14.5 million. Funds from IDA reflows will be provided to help supplement the financial-sector adjustment credit approved in fiscal 1988 in the amount of $70 million.

BRAZIL: IBRD—$300 million. Efforts by the National Bank for Social and Economic Development (BNDES) to reorient its focus to the private sector and reduce its exposure to the public sector, to reduce credit segmentation (whereby credit lines are directed to specific targets), and to strengthen credit policies and procedures will be supported. Total cost: $1,198.5 million.

CENTRAL AFRICAN REPUBLIC: IDA—$11.3 million. Private-sector development will be stimulated by a project that will channel credit through participating financial intermediaries for the rehabilitation of existing private firms and the creation of new enterprises. A microenterprise scheme, consisting of a revolving fund for credit, institutional support, training, and studies, is also included. Total cost: $15.2 million.

CHINA: IBRD—$150 million. Organizational and technological restructuring, as well as policy reforms, will result in greater efficiency and better domestic and international competitiveness in four of Shanghai's priority industrial subsectors—electronic components, precision and scientific instruments, printing machinery, and electrical apparatus. Total cost: $319.6 million.

COLOMBIA: IBRD—$200 million. Capital and other support will be provided to assist the private sector in renovating existing industrial production capacity, increasing product quality and services, building new capacity, and, where necessary, phasing out capacity that is unlikely to produce acceptable long-run returns. Total cost: $500 million.

JAMAICA: IBRD—$30 million. The government's trade-reform measures, which are expected to result in cheaper and better consumer goods and a more efficient allocation of resources, will be supported, as will a financial-sector reform program, which should help reduce credit subsidies, improve the allocation of credit, and strengthen capital markets. Cofinancing ($50 million) is anticipated from the IDB and has been requested from the Export-Import Bank of Japan.

KENYA: IDA—$67.3 million. Funds from IDA reflows will be provided to supplement the financial-sector adjustment credit approved in fiscal 1989 in the amount of $120 million.

LESOTHO: IDA—$21 million. Private foreign and indigenous investment in the industrial and agroindustrial sectors will be promoted through promulgation of policy reforms aimed at deregulation of key aspects of the investment code, removal of distortions, and provision of incentives; increased access to loan and equity finance by indigenous enterprises; investment-promotion activities; more efficient agroindustrial parastatals; and institutional support. Total cost: $25.3 million.

MALAWI: IDA—$32 million. By assisting the government in further improving the investment environment and strengthening institutions engaged in term finance and investment promotion, efforts to expand exports and improve the policy and institutional framework relevant to private-sector investment will be supported. Cofinancing has been provided by the EC ($100,000), and indications of initial support from the UNDP, the EIB, and USAID, as well as further support from the EC, have been received. Total cost: $47.2 million.

MALAWI: IDA—$7.2 million. Funds from IDA reflows will be provided to supplement the industry and trade-adjustment credit approved in fiscal 1988 in the amount of $70 million.

MEXICO: IBRD—$300 million. Help in implementing trade and customs reforms (aimed at encouraging efficiency and expanding the tradables sector) and in assisting the Banco Nacional de Comercio Exterior to play a more efficient role in trade financing will be provided.

MOROCCO: IBRD—$235 million. A program of reforms in the financial sector will be supported, and medium-term and long-term financing will be provided to eligible firms for investment subprojects, mainly in private, export-oriented industries. Cofinancing for the investment component ($100 million) will be provided through an IFC-led syndicated loan, while arrangements for cofinancing the adjustment component are being pursued with multilateral and bilateral agencies.

POLAND: IBRD—$280 million. Poland's efforts to develop and implement a broad privatization program of state-owned enterprises and to implement restructuring across a major share of its industry will be supported. Technical assistance is included. Cofinancing ($69 million) is expected from the EC and the EIB, as well as from others. Total cost: $915 million.

POLAND: IBRD—$200 million. An action program on the policy, regulatory, and institutional fronts needed to support and extend ongoing reforms in the financial system, as well as to underpin its longer-term deepening and strengthening, will be supported. Institution-building assistance is included.

Education

ALGERIA: IBRD—$65 million. Interventions at three universities of science and technology (together enrolling more than 41 percent of the students in the science and technology streams, excluding medicine) are aimed at developing an institutional and operational framework to improve the quality, relevance, and responsiveness of higher education. Total cost: $130 million.

BRAZIL: IBRD—$245 million. As many as 120,000 preschool children and more than 670,000 first and second graders will benefit from a project that will finance programs to improve learning and reduce dropout and repetition rates among low-income children in primary and preprimary schools in Greater São Paulo. Total cost: $600 million.

BRAZIL: IBRD—$150 million. A time slice of a planned, eight-year program to strengthen scientific-research capacity and training in key scientific and support areas and consolidate ongoing institutional reforms will be financed. Total cost: $300 million.

BURKINA FASO: IDA—$24 million. A fourth education project will help improve the quality of, and increase access to, primary education; improve the quality of general secondary education; and provide support to key sectoral institutions. Cofinancing is expected from CIDA ($8.7 million), the EC ($7.3 million), and Norway ($3.8 million). Total cost: $46.4 million.

CHINA: IDA—$131.2 million. Support for improved scientific training and research will continue through a project designed to increase the output of researchers, enhance the quality and productivity of research in areas relevant to long-term economic and social development, strengthen research management, provide for a modern infrastructure, and encourage cooperation across institutional and national boundaries. Cofinancing ($1.6 million) is anticipated from the UNDP. Total cost: $238.6 million.

DOMINICAN REPUBLIC: IBRD—$15 million. A primary-education development project has been designed to improve the quality of primary education, increase enrollment (by as many as 80,000) of children from low-income families, and strengthen resource management. Total cost: $17 million.

GHANA: IDA—$14.7 million. More than 18,000 student places will be created through a project that is supporting about 140 communities in their efforts to construct senior secondary schools in educationally underserved areas. Total cost: $19.6 million.

HAITI: IDA—$12.6 million. A fifth education project seeks to maintain the gains made in basic education to date and to prepare for future progress. Transitional measures to support long-term improvements in access to, and in the quality and efficiency of, basic education, with emphasis on the first four years of schooling and on the rural and poorest schools, will be financed. Total cost: $14.5 million.

HUNGARY: IBRD—$150 million. The government will be assisted in its program to alleviate the unemployment impact of economic restructuring and to invest in human resources so as to promote economic and technological competitiveness. Total cost: $339.8 million.

INDIA: IDA—$307.1 million. A technician-education project, to be implemented in eight states and the Union Territory of Delhi, will expand capacity in the polytechnic system and improve its quality and efficiency, thereby providing the industrial sector with engineering technicians of suitable quality in the areas of civil, mechanical, electrical, computer, and electronics technologies. Emphasis will be placed on increasing the percentage of polytechnic students who are female. Total cost: $362.1 million.

INDONESIA: IBRD—$150 million. A second higher-education development project will provide further support for efforts to improve quality and efficiency, as well as planning and management, in both public and private universities. In addition, the number of students with science and engineering skills will be expanded, and the quality of natural science and mathematics education upgraded. Total cost: $282.4 million.

KOREA, REPUBLIC OF: IBRD—$60 million. The government's emphasis on technology-intensive industrial development will be reinforced through a project that seeks to strengthen industrial research and development and basic research capacity and to enhance the application of

industrial standards in order to raise the quality of products. Total cost: $92.2 million.

KOREA, REPUBLIC OF: IBRD—$30 million. The quality of skill training provided in vocational high schools will be upgraded, thus enhancing the value of school graduates to prospective employers, by increasing graduates' immediate usefulness and by improving their ability to adjust to technological change in the workplace. Total cost: $43.3 million.

MEXICO: IBRD—$152 million. The quality, efficiency, and relevance of the National System for Vocational and Technical Education (CONALEP) will be further improved by upgrading the quality of high-level skills training and middle-level technician training; selectively expanding the range of training activities in key sectors; and providing institution-building assistance. Total cost: $204.5 million.

MOROCCO: IBRD—$145 million. As many as 120,000 additional students will be enrolled in upper basic-education schools in rural areas through the construction, equipping, and furnishing of about 250 middle schools, as well as through provision of room and board scholarships. In addition, a national assessment program will be financed, as well as a comprehensive in-service teacher-training program. Cofinancing ($45 million) will be provided by the AfDB. Total cost: $238 million.

MOZAMBIQUE: IDA—$53.7 million. The quality and efficiency of the primary-education system, as well as of the University Eduardo Mondlane, will be enhanced through a second education project. Institution-building assistance to the Ministry of Education is included. Total cost: $67.9 million.

NIGERIA: IDA—$120 million. The country's underfinanced and inefficiently managed primary-education system will be improved by providing books and upgrading curricula, ensuring sustainable financing, and increasing enrollments. Institution-building assistance is included. Cofinancing ($4 million) is expected from Japan. Total cost: $158.4 million.

PAPUA NEW GUINEA: IBRD—$20.8 million. By supporting implementation of the government's national training policy, in-service training in the public and private sectors will be strengthened, and the supply of specialized high-level personnel to staff the government's policy and planning agencies will be increased. Total cost: $23.1 million.

PHILIPPINES: IBRD—$200 million. The government's three-year physical-investment program in elementary education will be supported, the groundwork for reducing the elementary-school dropout rate among children of poor families will be laid, and literacy training for out-of-school youths and adults who lack functional literacy will be expanded. Total cost: $410 million.

POLAND: IBRD—$100 million. The government will be assisted in developing improved employment policies, institutions, and programs to mitigate the negative effect of economic adjustment on the labor force and to contribute to a resurgence of economic growth. Total cost: $142.2 million.

RWANDA: IDA—$23.3 million. A first education-sector project has been designed to support government policies whose objectives include the consolidation and expansion of primary education, improvement in the quality of primary education, and a strengthening of sector management capacity. Cofinancing ($2 million) is expected from the UNDP. Total cost: $26.9 million.

TOGO: IDA—$9.2 million. The country's technical-education and vocational-training system will become more demand driven, employment oriented, and responsive to the needs of the productive sectors. Institution-building assistance to the Ministry of Technical Education and Vocational Training is included. Cofinancing ($3.7 million) is anticipated from the EC. Total cost: $15.7 million.

TRINIDAD AND TOBAGO: IBRD—$20.7 million. The social consequences of adjustment will be moderated by providing opportunities for as many as 10,000 youths annually over five years to acquire remedial education, marketable skills, work experience, and practical business training for employment or self-employment. Institution-building assistance for the government's Youth Training and Employment Partnership Program is included. Total cost: $31.9 million.

TUNISIA: IBRD—$12 million. An estimated 30,000 people will be placed in productive employment over an initial three-year period through a project that will provide more effective training and labor-market intermediation and consolidate existing human capital through development of in-company training activities. Cofinancing ($4.5 million) is expected from USAID. Total cost: $34.7 million.

YEMEN, REPUBLIC OF: IDA—$19.4 million. A foundation for raising the quality of teaching in secondary schools will be created by upgrading the cadre of teachers, putting them to more effective use in the classroom, and planning for future improvements. Cofinancing is anticipated from the OPEC Fund for International Development. Total cost: $35.1 million.

ZAIRE: IDA—$21 million. An education-sector rehabilitation project seeks to stop the deterioration of quality in primary education and to boost it by taking immediate steps to increase the availability of key educational inputs. Technical assistance is included. Cofinancing is

anticipated from the FAC ($4.2 million), UNICEF ($600,000), the UNDP ($500,000), and the WWF ($300,000). Total cost: $29.7 million.

Energy

BANGLADESH: IDA—$67.2 million. The country will be assisted in pursuing an economic and least-cost household-energy and commercial-energy supply strategy through the substitution of liquefied petroleum gas for imported kerosene and commercial fuelwood. Cofinancing ($1.9 million) is expected from CIDA. Total cost: $94.2 million.

BENIN: IDA—$15 million. By strengthening all facets of the management and operations of Société béninoise d'électricité et d'eau, as well as by rehabilitating and expanding its facilities, power reliability will be improved, losses reduced, and additional sales generated. Cofinancing ($13.2 million) is anticipated from the CCCE. Total cost: $36.5 million.

BRAZIL: IBRD—$260 million. The substitution of natural gas for other forms of energy will be enhanced, and the distribution costs of petroleum products will be reduced by substituting pipelines for road and water transport. Total cost: $623.1 million.

BURUNDI: IDA—$22.8 million. Rational energy policies will be promoted and the efficient management of energy resources strengthened through a project focusing on pricing reforms, institutional development, expansion of access to electricity, and reduction of the negative environmental effects of energy use through promotion of improved stoves that burn charcoal more efficiently. Total cost: $32.2 million.

CHAD: IDA—$11 million. Preparatory studies on ways to ensure the most efficient and least-cost execution of a proposed petroleum and power project (involving the construction of a petroleum pipeline, a refinery, and a power plant) will be financed. Cofinancing ($3 million) is anticipated from the EIB. Total cost: $14.5 million.

EGYPT: IBRD—$84 million. Pipeline and related equipment for expanding the existing gas-distribution system to households and businesses in Cairo will be financed, as will gas compressors, gas-treatment facilities, and the platform template required for the gathering of an extra 70 million cubic feet per day of gas for delivery to the national grid. Institution-building assistance to the Petroleum Gas Company is included. Cofinancing ($33 million) is expected from the EIB. Total cost: $285.5 million.

GUINEA-BISSAU: IDA—$15.2 million. The medium-term supply of key products in the commercial energy sector—petroleum products and electricity—will be improved through the rehabilitation and expansion of existing electricity-generation facilities and the rehabilitation of petroleum storage and handling facilities, the expansion of the electricity and petroleum-distribution network, and the establishment of a new petroleum facility. Technical assistance and training are included. Cofinancing is expected from the EIB ($4.7 million) and the EC ($2 million). Total cost: $23.2 million.

INDIA: IBRD—$450 million. The flaring of 12 million cubic meters of gas a day in the Bombay High oil field will be eliminated, thus increasing indigenous oil production by about 4 million tons a year. Institution-building assistance is included. Cofinancing is anticipated from the Export-Import Bank of Japan ($350 million), the AsDB ($300 million), and suppliers' credits ($745.6 million). Total cost: $3,184.3 million.

INDIA: IBRD—$200 million. Additional genera-tion, transmission, and distribution capacity will be provided to help meet increasing demand for electricity in Bombay and to maintain good ser-vice for consumers. Cofinancing (a $50 million A loan and a B loan of up to $18 million) is being provided by the IFC. Total cost: $653.3 million.

INDONESIA: IBRD—$275 million. The trans-mission facilities for the Java-Bali electric-power system will be expanded, strengthened, and upgraded so that electricity can be supplied to new consumers and the increased demand for electricity from existing consumers can be met. Technical assistance is included. Total cost: $415.7 million.

MOROCCO: IBRD—$114 million. About 462 villages in thirty-four provinces will be connected to the country's main power grid, and the costs of connecting about 170,000 customers will be met. Institution-building assistance to the Office national de l'électricité is included. Total cost: $220 million.

NIGERIA: IBRD—$218 million. Nigerian hydrocarbon exports will be increased through the development of the Oso condensate field, thereby significantly enhancing the country's foreign-exchange earnings. Institution-building assistance to the Nigerian National Petroleum Corporation is included. Cofinancing is expected from the IFC ($75 million), the EIB ($65 million), the export-import banks of the United States and Japan ($95 million and $47 million, respectively), and commercial banks ($95 million). Total cost: $885 million.

PAKISTAN: IBRD—$130 million. The government will be assisted in restructuring Sui Northern Gas Pipelines Limited with a view to increasing its autonomy and ability to mobilize resources from the financial capital markets and the general public, as well as to expanding the utility's transmission and distribution network at least cost. Total cost: $547 million.

PAKISTAN: IBRD—$60 million. Supplemental funds will be provided to help finance a corporate-restructuring and system-expansion project, approved in August 1990 in the amount of $130 million (see previous summary).

PAKISTAN: IBRD—$28 million. Supplementary funds for the ongoing investment program under the second energy-sector loan, approved in June 1989 in the amount of $250 million, will be made available to finance additional investments.

POLAND: IBRD—$340 million. The implementa-tion of comprehensive energy-sector restructur-ing will be supported, as will the commercializa-tion and privatization of restructured enterprises and of petroleum exploration and production activities. In addition, the life of existing heating assets will be extended through rehabilitation and the introduction of modern technologies and materials, thereby significantly reducing capital expenditures. Cofinancing ($50 million) is expected from the EBRD. Total cost: $619.3 million.

TANZANIA: IDA—$44 million. The availability of petroleum products throughout the country will be improved by enhancing—through reduced transport costs, a modernized and rehabilitated supply and distribution network, and strengthened institutions—the efficiency and effectiveness of the petroleum industry. Cofinancing is expected from the EIB ($8.9 million), the OPEC Fund for International Development ($6.1 million), the DGIS ($6.1 million), the EC ($6 million), and DANIDA ($2.5 million). Total cost: $103.6 million.

TOGO: IDA—$15 million. Detailed engineering studies, to be followed by the rehabilitation and extension of the Lomé electric-power distribution system, will be provided. Institution-building assistance to the Compagnie énergie électrique du Togo is included. Cofinancing ($15.5 million) is anticipated from the CCCE. Total cost: $38.5 million.

TURKEY: IBRD—$300 million. The restructuring of the Turkish Electricity Authority (TEK) will be supported, and the foreign-exchange costs of a time slice (1991–94) of TEK's least-cost investment program will be partially financed. Technical assistance is included. Total cost: $5,388 million.

UGANDA: IDA—$125 million. A third project will continue and build on the rehabilitation work of the ongoing second power project to prevent bottlenecks, which would otherwise hinder economic development, by providing urgently needed least-cost capacity additions to the country's power generation, transmission, and distribution facilities. The project will also help safeguard and strengthen the existing Owen Falls dam. Cofinancing is expected from the ADF ($45 million), Norway ($24.6 million), the IsDB ($20 million), and the BITS/SIDA ($15 million). Total cost: $335.1 million.

YUGOSLAVIA: IBRD—$300 million. To meet the growth in demand for electricity in Serbia, construction will begin on a 7 million tons-per-year lignite mine and a 700-megawatt power plant (including auxiliary facilities). Technical assistance is included. Suppliers' credits ($181.9 million) are anticipated. Total cost: $1,314.3 million.

Industry

ALGERIA: IBRD—$350 million. The government's program of reforms in the financial and industrial sectors during the transition from a centrally planned to a market economy will be supported.

CHINA: IBRD—$50 million; IDA—$64.3 million. Implementation in three diverse locations— Jiangsu province, Jilin province, and Chongming island, a rural county within the municipality of Shanghai—of an innovative program that has made a strong start in upgrading levels of technology and management in rural, nonstate enterprises will be supported. Cofinancing is expected from Japan ($1.7 million). Total cost: $222.1 million.

CYPRUS: IBRD—$30 million. The government will be assisted in undertaking a substantial adjustment of its industrial sector with a view to its gradual integration within the EC. Reforms in the financial sector will also support the process. Technical assistance is included. Total cost: $42.8 million.

INDIA: IBRD—$245 million. The plastics-production capacity of Indian Petrochemical Corporation Ltd. will be expanded and modernized, and the efficiency and quality of downstream plastics products will be improved through provision of technical assistance. Total cost: $587 million.

INDIA: IBRD—$124 million; IDA—$31.6 million. A cost-effective program for industrial-pollution monitoring, control, and abatement (to be concentrated in the states of Gujarat, Maharashtra, Tamil Nadu, and Uttar Pradesh) will be identified and implemented. Technical assistance and institutional strengthening are included. Total cost: $260 million.

INDONESIA: IBRD—$221.7 million. The government's efficiency-oriented objectives in the fertilizer industry will be supported through construction of a new ammonia and urea facility, modernization of existing fertilizer plants at the Gresik complex in East Java, and optimization investments in four other plants. Marketing and environmental studies are included. Total cost: $444.3 million.

JORDAN: IBRD—$15 million. The Arab Potash Company will expand its potash-production capacity through the optimization of existing facilities and the introduction of new technology, and new chemical industries, all based on Dead Sea brine and other local raw materials, will be developed, thus increasing the country's industrial production and export capacity. Technical assistance is included. Cofinancing ($16 million) is anticipated from the IsDB. Total cost: $121.3 million.

MEXICO: IBRD—$200 million. To help transform mining into a modern and dynamic sector of the economy, the government's program to deregulate the sector and stimulate private domestic and foreign investment will be supported; broader financial-market support to the mining industry will be built; and the surge in demand for investment funding, expected to result from the improved policy and institutional setting for mining operations, will be financed. Total cost: $436.5 million.

PAKISTAN: IBRD—$56.4 million. Supplemental funds will be provided to help finance a cement-industry modernization project approved in November 1987 in the amount of $96 million.

PHILIPPINES: IBRD—$175 million. Term funds, both in loans and lease finance, will be provided to help private-sector enterprises modernize, restructure, and expand their productive capacity. Cofinancing from bilateral sources (the BITS, the NDF, NORAD, and others) is anticipated, as are export credits, under the export credit enhanced-leverage program (EXCEL), in the amount of $75 million. Total cost: $541 million.

SRI LANKA: IDA—$120 million. The phased implementation of the government's program for reform of public manufacturing enterprises—it encompasses policy reforms in the sector's regulatory and institutional framework and incentive system, as well as measures (such as privatization) designed to enable specific enterprises to adjust to a commercial and increasingly competitive environment—will be supported.

TURKEY: IBRD—$200 million. Financially and economically viable private investments, especially in export-oriented activities, will be financed so as to increase the country's productive capacity in areas of comparative advantage under a reforming environment. Technical assistance is included. Total cost: $401 million.

TURKEY: IBRD—$100 million. The first phase of the government's program to encourage industrial-technology development—focusing on investment in a national framework for quality assurance consistent with OECD standards, the introduction of market forces into the research and development system, and catalyzing the supply of venture-capital finance—will be supported. Cofinancing is expected from the IFC ($5.1 million); the governments of Germany ($3.3 million), the United States ($500,000), and the United Kingdom ($200,000); and the UNDP ($1.5 million). Total cost: $262.2 million.

Nonproject

BENIN: IDA—$55 million. The second phase of the government's structural-adjustment program, designed to create the conditions for a sustainable recovery of economic activity and to improve the provision of basic social services while protecting vulnerable groups, will be supported.

BURKINA FASO: IDA—$80 million. A first structural-adjustment loan will support the country's overall adjustment program and will focus on implementation in two key areas—public-resource management and private-sector incentives. Cofinancing is anticipated from the EC ($30 million), the AfDB ($20 million), France ($17 million), Canada ($13 million), and Germany ($12 million).

COMOROS: IDA—$8 million. The foundation for economic growth will be laid by improving the enabling environment for private-sector activity while streamlining the public sector and restoring financial stability to the country. Cofinancing is expected from the ADF ($17 million) and the UNDP ($1 million). Total cost: $28 million.

CZECHOSLOVAKIA: IBRD—$450 million. The first phase of the country's rapid transition to a market economy will be supported. Cofinancing ($200 million) is anticipated from the Export-Import Bank of Japan.

EGYPT: IBRD—$300 million. The government's economic-reform and structural-adjustment program, which focuses on macroeconomic stabilization, structural adjustment to stimulate medium-term and long-term growth, and acceleration of social policies to minimize the effects of economic reforms on the poor, will be supported. Cofinancing is expected from the AfDB ($130 million) and the EC (between $79 million and $132 million).

EL SALVADOR: IBRD—$75 million. The government's structural-adjustment program, which aims to create a more liberalized, private-sector–led economy, and which focuses on reforms in the external, fiscal, monetary, financial, and agricultural sectors, will be supported.

GHANA: IDA—$120 million. A fourth adjustment credit will support the government's efforts to promote private investment and sustained development.

GHANA: IDA—$8.3 million. Funds from IDA reflows will be provided to supplement the second structural-adjustment credit, approved in fiscal 1989 in the amount of $120 million.

GUYANA: IDA—$18 million. Funds will be provided to supplement the structural-adjustment credit approved in fiscal 1990 in the amount of $74.6 million.

GUYANA: IDA—$4.3 million. Funds from IDA reflows will be provided to supplement the structural-adjustment credit approved in fiscal 1990 in the amount of $74.6 million.

HONDURAS: IBRD—$90 million. The government's structural-adjustment program, designed to accelerate export growth and increase domestic savings while creating the preconditions for a recovery of economic growth and employment, will be supported.

HONDURAS: IDA—$20 million. Supplemental financing, necessitated by the impact of higher oil prices and lower-than-expected banana earnings for 1990-91, will be provided to help support the government's structural-adjustment program (see above).

HUNGARY: IBRD—$250 million. The government's medium-term economic-reform program, which represents an acceleration and deepening of reforms implemented successfully since the beginning of 1990, will be supported by a second structural-adjustment loan.

INDONESIA: IBRD—$250 million. Private-sector expansion will be accelerated through a loan that supports the implementation of reforms undertaken by the government during 1989 and 1990, assists the government in maintaining a satisfactory pace of economic growth consistent with external and internal financial stability, and maintains the policy dialogue on further reforms to promote the efficiency and longer-term viability of the economy.

JORDAN: IBRD—$10 million. A set of core components (education, health, public transport, water supply and sewerage, and highways and roads) from the government's emergency-response program—designed to help meet the immediate and incremental needs for essential social services and physical infrastructure of as many as 400,000 workers returning from Iraq, Kuwait, Saudi Arabia, and other Gulf states—will be supported. Cofinancing is being provided by Switzerland ($25 million), Sweden ($10 million), Canada ($7.3 million), and Luxembourg ($1.3 million). Total cost: $60 million.

KENYA: IDA—$100 million. The government's strategy to diversify and expand nontraditional exports will be supported through an integrated package of policy reforms, investments, studies, and technical assistance. Total cost: $109.2 million.

MALI: IDA—$70 million. The government's structural-adjustment program will be supported through a loan that focuses on implementation in two key areas—private-sector initiatives and public-resource management. Cofinancing is anticipated from the EC ($20 million) and the AfDB ($18 million).

POLAND: IBRD—$300 million. The government's unprecedented economic-transformation program, which combines stabilization and structural change (including a radical liberalization of the trade regime, as well as of pricing policies), will be supported.

RWANDA: IDA—$90 million. The first phase of the government's economic-reform program will be financed. Cofinancing is expected from Switzerland (Sw F10 million) and Belgium (BF400 million); coordinated financing is being negotiated with the AfDB, the EC, Austria, Canada, France, Germany, and the United States.

SENEGAL: IDA—$7.1 million. Funds from IDA reflows will be provided to supplement the fourth structural-adjustment credit, approved in fiscal 1990 in the amount of $80 million.

SRI LANKA: IDA—$7 million. Funds from IDA reflows will be provided to help supplement the economic-restructuring credit approved in fiscal 1990 in the amount of $90 million.

TOGO: IDA—$55 million. Support will be provided to the government's fourth structural-adjustment program, which aims to increase real GDP growth to more than 4 percent by 1992, maintain inflation at around 3 percent a year, reduce the current-account balance relative to GDP, and enhance provision of social services.

UGANDA: IDA—$2 million. Funds from IDA reflows will be provided to help supplement the second economic-recovery credit, approved in fiscal 1990 in the amount of $125 million.

URUGUAY: IBRD—$65 million. The debt and debt-service reduction agreement reached between Uruguay and its commercial-bank creditors will be supported through disbursement of funds to reimburse Uruguay for a portion of the costs of the cash buyback and of the interest collateral of the par bond.

VENEZUELA: IBRD—$150 million. Interest support, to be utilized to purchase part of the collateral for par bonds issued by Venezuela, together with related measures (set-aside funds from adjustment loans and a waiver of negative-pledge restrictions in Bank loan agreements) will help the country implement its agreement, involving debt and debt-service reduction, with commercial-bank creditors.

ZAMBIA: IDA—$210 million. Import financing in support of the country's economic-adjustment program will be provided, thus alleviating constraints on Zambia's foreign-exchange cash flow at a time when arrears to the Bank are being paid. Cofinancing ($18.8 million) is expected from Germany and, possibly, other sources.

ZAMBIA: IDA—$27.2 million. Funds from IDA reflows will be provided to help supplement the economic-recovery credit described above.

Population, Health, and Nutrition

ALGERIA: IBRD—$16 million. To improve efficiency and effectiveness in the public health-care delivery system, a pilot program seeks to develop the necessary management tools to allow effective implementation of changes in systems management and operations that the government is gradually introducing at the central and local levels. Total cost: $26.7 million.

BANGLADESH: IDA—$180 million. The government's efforts to reach the qualitative and quantitative population and health targets laid out in the fourth five-year plan (in terms of fertility, child morbidity and mortality, maternal mortality, and nutrition levels) will be supported. Cofinancing is anticipated from the EC ($47.8 million), CIDA ($40.3 million), the KfW ($38.8 million), NORAD ($33.2 million), the DGIS ($24.8 million), the ODA ($23.7 million), SIDA ($13.4 million), the GTZ ($12.8 million), AIDAB ($9.6 million), the Japanese Economic Cooperation Bureau ($9.1 million), and the AGCD ($2.8 million). Total cost: $601.4 million.

EGYPT: IDA—$140 million. The first phase of an overall program aimed at addressing the immediate and pressing needs of those most vulnerable to the reform process and at facilitating the reintegration of workers returning from Kuwait and Iraq will be financed. Investments will focus on income-generating and employment-generating activities and the provision of essential physical infrastructure and public services. Cofinancing is anticipated from the EC ($140 million), USAID ($55 million), the AFESD ($50 million), the KFAED ($50 million), Switzerland ($30 million), Germany ($30 million), the Abu Dhabi Fund ($25 million), Denmark ($10 million), Canada ($10 million), France ($10 million), Sweden ($10 million), the Netherlands ($6 million), the UNDP ($4 million), and Norway ($2 million).

EL SALVADOR: IBRD—$26 million. The coverage and delivery of basic social services—primary health care and preprimary and primary education—targeted to about 1.1 million people in some of the poorest municipalities of the country will be improved. Institution-building assistance is included. Cofinancing is expected from USAID ($2.1 million) and UNICEF ($300,000). Total cost: $35.6 million.

GHANA: IDA—$27 million. A second health and population project has been designed to improve health-service quality and coverage (especially for poorer groups), the supply of essential drugs, and family-planning services. Total cost: $34.4 million.

HAITI: IDA—$11.3 million. An economic and social fund has been established to respond flexibly and efficiently—through a variety of grassroots organizations—to the basic needs (particularly primary health care and nutrition) of the country's poor. The government will also be aided in improving health, nutrition, and education services and providing physical infrastructure, employment opportunities, and other sources of income for the poor. Cofinancing ($10.4 million) is expected from the IDB. Total cost: $23.6 million.

HONDURAS: IDA—$20 million. Assistance will be provided to the Honduran Social Investment Fund (FHIS) to help protect and improve the standard of living of the poor—through provision of jobs and improved services (health, nutrition, and education)—during the current period of economic adjustment. Cofinancing is anticipated from the KfW ($12 million); USAID ($8 million); the DGIS, jointly with the UNDP ($2.1 million); and the UNDP ($600,000). In addition, other funds, totaling $1.8 million, have been approved by the GTZ, CIDA, UNICEF, Spain, and Japan. Total cost: $68 million.

INDIA: IBRD—$10 million; IDA—$96 million. An estimated 5 million relatively disadvantaged children under the age of seven and 3 million pregnant and nursing women in Andhra Pradesh and Orissa states will directly benefit from a project that seeks to reduce malnutrition among children, as well as lower infant mortality rates and the incidence of low birth weight. Total cost: $157.5 million.

INDONESIA: IBRD—$104 million. A fifth population project will help the government intensify its efforts to lower fertility (in part, by targeting family-planning services to specific groups that would not benefit otherwise) and maternal mortality (by improving the effectiveness of existing community midwives and training an additional 16,000) during the 1990s. Total cost: $148.4 million.

KOREA, REPUBLIC OF: IBRD—$60 million. The government's policy of responding to the increased demand for medical care resulting from national health insurance, rising incomes, technological innovations, the changing population structure, and the shift in the epidemiological profile from communicable to noncommunicable diseases will be assisted. Total cost: $81.2 million.

MADAGASCAR: IDA—$31 million. The government's health-sector program, which aims at reducing mortality and morbidity, moderating fertility levels, and improving the efficiency and sustainability of public expenditures for health, will be supported. Total cost: $42.5 million.

MALAWI: IDA—$55.5 million. The second phase of the government's efforts to reform and improve the population, health, and nutrition sector will be supported through a project that focuses on strengthening basic programs (primary health care, population programs, disease control, and nutrition interventions) and support services (staffing issues, pharmaceuticals, and information, education, and communications).

Cofinancing is expected from the EC ($11.1 million) and WHO/the Netherlands ($1.4 million). Total cost: $74.3 million.

MALI: IDA—$26.6 million. The government will be assisted in its efforts to improve the health of the Malian people (especially women and children), begin implementing a recently adopted population policy, and improve access to safe water by rural communities. Cofinancing is expected from the EDF ($12.3 million), USAID ($10.1 million), and Germany ($6.2 million), while the FAC may contribute up to $1.7 million equivalent. Total cost: $61.4 million.

MEXICO: IBRD—$180 million. Health-care services, including targeted nutrition assistance in selected areas, will be strengthened and expanded to about 13 million uninsured poor people in the country's four poorest states and in the Federal district. Institution-building assistance is included, and the implementation of sectoral reforms (involving decentralization) will be strengthened. Total cost: $249.8 million.

NIGERIA: IDA—$78.5 million. This long-range project seeks to strengthen the institutional framework and expand the basis for undertaking a large-scale, intersectoral national population program over the coming decades in fulfillment of Nigeria's ambitious population-policy goals. Total cost: $93.6 million.

NIGERIA: IBRD—$70 million. Health services will be improved for a wider base of the country's population through the creation of a wholesaling mechanism, the Health System Fund, to finance health-system improvements in a larger number of states than has been possible in the past. Cofinancing ($1.3 million) has been received from Japan. Total cost: $94.5 million.

PAKISTAN: IDA—$45 million. The health services available to some 80 percent of the total population of Sindh and North-West Frontier provinces (including 9 million women of childbearing age) will be improved through a project that will introduce an enhanced package of maternal health services (including family planning) and integrate and expand communicable disease-control activities. Comprehensive in-service training and institutional-development components are included. Cofinancing is anticipated from the ODA ($2.8 million) and the SCF ($1 million). Total cost: $62.9 million.

RWANDA: IDA—$19.6 million. A first population project seeks to help reduce the country's fertility rate, decrease child and maternal morbidity and mortality, and integrate the demographic dimension into the overall socioeconomic planning process. The project will complement other major donor interventions in the sector—in particular from USAID, UNFPA, and the GTZ. Total cost: $26.1 million.

SENEGAL: IDA—$35 million. Government efforts to control fertility and reduce the rate of population growth will be supported, as will efforts intended to improve the quality and increase the accessibility of basic health services. Total cost: $37.9 million.

SRI LANKA: IDA—$57.5 million. Income-earning opportunities among the poor will be increased, and the nutritional status of children under the age of three and pregnant and lactating mothers will be improved, through a project that will assist a newly created trust fund in financing credit operations, human-resource and infrastructure development, and nutrition-intervention activities of nongovernmental organizations and government agencies. Cofinancing ($10 million) is expected from the KfW. Total cost: $85 million.

TOGO: IDA—$14.2 million. The implementation of a comprehensive package of sector policy reforms in the area of population and health—aimed at ensuring a satisfactory level of primary health care and family-planning services to the population, especially in rural areas—will be supported.

TUNISIA: IBRD—$30 million. The implementation of the government's reform program to address major efficiency and service-quality issues in its public health-care network—the program's centerpiece is the organizational and managerial restructuring of the country's twenty-two largest hospital facilities—will be supported. Technical assistance and training are included. Total cost: $49.5 million.

TUNISIA: IBRD—$26 million. As many as 30,000 new family-planning acceptors will be reached annually, and more than 500,000 women will continue to be served with family-planning services as a result of a project that aims to reduce both fertility and mortality nationally by targeting the provision of basic health services to relatively underprivileged groups. Total cost: $63.2 million.

VENEZUELA: IBRD—$100 million. By increasing prenatal and postnatal health and nutrition-service coverage, as well as preventive health care for children under the age of six, and through expanded coverage of formal and informal preschool education, the negative effects of adjustment on the country's most vulnerable groups (poor women and their children) will be cushioned. Total cost: $320.9 million.

YEMEN, REPUBLIC OF: IDA—$33 million. The core components of the government's emergency-recovery program—designed to assist the 750,000 Yemenis who had to return to their country during the Gulf crisis—will be supported. The project will help expand essential social infrastructure and services and housing sites, support agricultural activities to maintain nutritional levels and living standards, and create employment opportunities for the returnees.

Cofinancing is anticipated from USAID ($15 million), Germany ($4.5 million), and the UNDP ($500,000). Total cost: $59.5 million.

ZAIRE: IDA—$30.4 million. A social-sector project seeks to protect the poor from the social effects of a deteriorating economic situation by establishing budgetary allocations targeted to basic medical care and primary education. And, with help from other donors, essential public health, nutrition, and family-planning programs will be strengthened. Project-preparation assistance is included. Cofinancing ($2.9 million) is expected from the UNDP. Total cost: $37 million.

ZAMBIA: IDA—$20 million. Community initiatives to protect the poor during the period of structural-adjustment implementation, involving rehabilitation and improvement of existing infrastructure and service delivery, will be financed. Cofinancing is anticipated from the EC ($15 million) and Norway ($2.2 million). Total cost: $46.3 million.

ZIMBABWE: IBRD—$25 million. A second family-health project seeks to improve maternal and child health; reduce the rate of population growth; ensure that households in target districts have access to basic health, population, and nutrition services; and increase the output of trained Zimbabwean health workers. Institution-building assistance is included. Cofinancing is anticipated from NORAD ($14.2 million), DANIDA ($8.3 million), the Netherlands ($5.8 million), the ODA ($4.7 million), and the EC ($3.7 million). Total cost: $116.9 million.

Public-sector Management

ARGENTINA: IBRD—$300 million. Funds will be provided to help the government either privatize or restructure public enterprises in the tele-communications, railways, and hydrocarbon sectors. Assistance in privatizing or overseeing additional public enterprises is included.

COLOMBIA: IBRD—$304 million. The management of public enterprises will be improved with the establishment of a performance-planning and evaluation system and efficiency improvements in resource allocation and use as a result of reform in the railway, port, shipping, agricultural-marketing, and housing sectors where the public sector has heretofore played a dominant role.

MADAGASCAR: IDA—$1.7 million. Funds from IDA reflows will be provided to supplement the public-sector adjustment credit approved in fiscal 1988 in the amount of $125 million.

MAURITANIA: IDA—$4 million. Funds from IDA reflows will be provided to supplement the public-enterprise sector adjustment credit approved in fiscal 1990 in the amount of $40 million.

THAILAND: IBRD—S32 million. The country's overall tax-collection system will be improved and its efficiency, effectiveness, and equity increased through a project that includes all hardware and related data-entry processing equipment, software, training, and technical assistance required by the Revenue Department. Total cost: $73.2 million.

Small-scale Enterprises

INDONESIA: IBRD—$125 million. Ongoing efforts by Bank Rakyat Indonesia to strengthen and expand its financially viable Unit Desa system—the only nationwide network that meets the needs of both small borrowers and savers—will be supported. Institution-building assistance is included. Total cost: $2,618 million.

PAKISTAN: IBRD—$26 million. A project that will channel funds to microenterprises through private leasing companies and nongovernmental organizations seeks to demonstrate that financial innovations and initiatives in the private sector can be sustained and that microentrepreneurs of both sexes can be creditworthy, even when subjected to market prices and practices. Cofinancing ($2.8 million) is anticipated from the Netherlands. Total cost: $36.6 million.

PHILIPPINES: IBRD—$15 million. The investment and working-capital needs of about 4,200 cottage firms will be financed through the use by the Development Bank of the Philippines of proceeds of the IBRD loan to rediscount subloans made by retail banks to members of approved mutual-guarantee associations. Cofinancing ($13.4 million) is anticipated from the KfW. Total cost: $44.7 million.

SRI LANKA: IDA—$45 million. Credit will be made available through eligible financial institutions for the partial funding of term loans to productive enterprises for new investments, balancing, modernizing, or rehabilitation, thus providing support to a significant number of new and growing private-sector operations. Institution-building assistance is included. Cofinancing ($30 million) is expected from the AsDB. Total cost: $145 million.

Technical Assistance

ANGOLA: IDA—$23 million. The government's capacity to formulate and implement, over both the medium and short term, sound economic policies and investment projects will be strengthened. Total cost: $26.1 million.

ARGENTINA: IBRD—$23 million. Technical assistance will be provided to strengthen the administrative and technical capabilities of the national administration to carry out its public-sector reform program. Total cost: $31.5 million.

ARGENTINA: IBRD—$23 million. The government's administrative and technical capability to carry out its public-enterprise reform program will be strengthened. In addition, further privatization programs will be prepared, and the institutional and regulatory framework for sectors in which public enterprises operate will be strengthened. Total cost: $32.9 million.

BENIN: IDA—$5.4 million. The immediate constraints on investments caused by the lack of properly prepared projects will be relieved, and the institutional capacity for identifying investment proposals and processing them through feasibility studies, for obtaining financing, and for establishing final project-execution plans will be created. Total cost: $6 million.

BOLIVIA: IDA—$11.3 million. The efficiency, effectiveness, and transparency of the country's resource-management system will be improved. Total cost: $22.3 million.

BULGARIA: IBRD—$17 million. The government will be supported in the implementation of its economic-reform program through the provision of technical assistance in private-sector development, bank restructuring and reform, human-resource development and strengthening of the social safety net, energy-sector reforms, and institutional development to support activities critical to the overall reform program. Cofinancing is anticipated from the EC's Program of Assistance for Reforming Economies in Eastern Europe ($13.2 million) and the Know-How Fund ($1.3 million) of the United Kingdom. Total cost: $33.5 million.

CENTRAL AFRICAN REPUBLIC: IDA—$6.5 million. The government will be helped in incorporating social dimensions of adjustment into its economic and sector policies through the strengthening of social policy and planning, support for the implementation of a national policy for the promotion of women, and implementation of an accelerated teacher-training program. Total cost: $7.1 million.

GHANA: IDA—$15 million. Improvement in the analytical and administrative capacity of the country's core economic-management agencies will contribute to stronger implementation capacity in the government, help ensure that public expenditures effectively support the country's growth strategy, and help sustain current structural reforms. Cofinancing ($3.9 million) is expected from the ODA. Total cost: $23 million.

INDONESIA: IBRD—$30 million. Technical assistance will be provided to enhance the government's project-evaluation capacity, particularly in areas that cut across sectors and cannot be addressed under existing project activities because they involve, for instance, private-sector participation. Total cost: $36 million.

JAMAICA: IBRD—$11.5 million. The efforts of the government to improve the efficiency of financial and human-resources management in the central administration will be supported. Total cost: $15.6 million.

ROMANIA: IBRD—$180 million. Foreign exchange will be made available for the import of essential spare parts and equipment so as to sustain output performance, which is threatened by serious foreign-exchange constraints and dislocations caused by the transition from a planned to a market economy. Technical assistance, designed to support the ongoing economic-reform process in the formulation and implementation of macroeconomic and sectoral-policy programs, is included. Cofinancing ($17.4 million) is expected from the EIB. Total cost: $262.4 million.

ZAMBIA: IDA—$21 million. The government will be helped in implementing an effective development strategy in the mining sector—in the short run, by making the sector more efficient and productive, and, in the longer term, by supporting the development of new copper mines by private investors and of noncopper mining-sector exports. Institution-building assistance to the Zambia Consolidated Copper Mines Ltd. is included. Total cost: $24 million.

Telecommunications

HUNGARY: IBRD—$150 million. A second telecommunications project consists of a three-year time slice of the Hungarian Telecommunications Company's investment program for 1991–93, including some preparatory work in 1990, combining physical expansion and modernization of the network with institutional strengthening through technical assistance and training. Cofinancing ($100 million) is anticipated from the EIB. Total cost: $1,354.7 million.

POLAND: IBRD—$120 million. A first telecommunications project seeks to strengthen and expand the national trunk network, as well as carry out selected improvements (primarily to help the business sector, in general, and export-oriented businesses, in particular) in the international and local networks. Technical assistance is included. Cofinancing ($90 million) is expected from the EIB. Total cost: $378.7 million.

RWANDA: IDA—$12.8 million. A second communications project aims at institutional reform and training (leading to autonomy in the postal sector and eventual privatization of telecommunications operations) and provision of key maintenance equipment for telecommunications, as well as buildings and equipment to improve postal services. Cofinancing is expected from the FAC ($4.7 million). Total cost: $17.2 million.

SRI LANKA: IDA—$57 million. Sectoral reform will be supported through the establishment of a new, commercially oriented autonomous operating entity, Sri Lanka Telecom (SLT), and through improvements in sector efficiency. In addition, help in financing SLT's initial investment program to expand and improve telecommunications services will be provided. Cofinancing is anticipated from the OECF ($44.1 million), the AsDB ($40 million), France ($4.4 million), and the UNDP/ITU ($1 million). Total cost: $204.1 million.

Transportation

BANGLADESH: IDA—$45 million. A third inland-waterway transport project seeks to improve waterway safety and environmental controls, passenger-transport infrastructure, capital-asset utilization, and the finances and operations of inland-water transport agencies. Provisions to reduce freight transport costs and for institution-building assistance are included. Cofinancing is anticipated from FINNIDA ($5 million) and Japan ($700,000). Total cost: $64.2 million.

BOTSWANA: IBRD—$14.9 million. Road links necessary for the development and integration of the Selebi-Phikwe area and its hinterland will be provided, thereby facilitating the effectiveness of this region as a marketing center. Institution-building measures are included. Cofinancing is expected from BADEA ($6.4 million) and the AfDB ($1.3 million). Total cost: $37.6 million.

CHINA: IBRD—$100 million; IDA—$53.6 million. The most serious constraints posed by Jiangsu province's inadequate transport infrastructure on its fast-developing economy will be mitigated. In addition, the province will be assisted in upgrading the planning, budgeting, and implementation of transport works and in developing more efficient construction entities. Technical assistance is included. Total cost: $312.8 million.

COMOROS: IDA—$6.6 million. A program of road maintenance seeks to stem the deterioration of the country's paved road network, half of which is in serious need of periodic maintenance. In addition, road safety will be improved and institutional support provided to the General Public Works Directorate. Cofinancing is anticipated from the FAC ($2 million) and the UNDP ($700,000). Total cost: $11.3 million.

DOMINICAN REPUBLIC: IBRD—$79 million. The initial three-year slice of the five-year investment program of the Secretariat of Public Works and Communications—major components include road rehabilitation, a program of periodic maintenance, rehabilitation of equipment, and highway-safety works—will be financed. Total cost: $111 million.

GHANA: IDA—$96 million. A second transport-rehabilitation project focuses on both road and railway rehabilitation and the strengthening of the country's transport-sector institutions. It also includes a pilot scheme (featuring involvement by nongovernmental organizations and participation of women) comprising labor-intensive road rehabilitation in about fifty villages and support for nonmotorized transport, hand-dug wells, and environmental improvements. Cofinancing, totaling $66 million, is being sought from the CCCE, the ADF, the ODA, BADEA, and the NIO. Total cost: $230.4 million.

JAMAICA: IBRD—$35 million. Managerial and technical strengthening of the Ministry of Construction (Works) will be financed, as will part of a $302 million, five-year investment program designed to upgrade and bring back to a condition of maintainability, and improve safety on, the nation's road infrastructure. Total cost: $50.3 million.

LAO PEOPLE'S DEMOCRATIC REPUBLIC: IDA—$45 million. A 266-kilometer-long section of Route 13 (the country's main north-south road artery) from Namkading to Savannakhet will be rehabilitated, thus improving access to the agriculturally rich southern part of the country. In addition, the foundation for the establishment of a systems approach to maintenance planning and execution will be established. Cofinancing ($5 million) is expected from the NDF. Total cost: $52.6 million.

MOROCCO: IBRD—$132 million. Assistance, provided under the ongoing project to improve the ports of Casablanca and Mohammedia, will be broadened to support better allocation of resources and modernization of existing port facilities. Total cost: $282 million.

PAKISTAN: IBRD—$91.4 million. Assistance will be provided to develop an appropriate strategy for the medium-term and long-term development of the port subsector, and port costs at Karachi will be reduced through improved cargo-handling productivity, accelerated cargo and document clearance, and improved landside access to the port. Institution-building assistance is included. Total cost: $143.1 million.

PHILIPPINES: IBRD—$125 million. The adverse economic effects of the July 1990 earthquake will be minimized through the reconstruction of essential infrastructure and other facilities. In addition, measures will be introduced to lessen the effects of future earthquakes. Total cost: $182.7 million.

SENEGAL: IDA—$65 million. The country's transport sector will be restored by modernizing the sector's administration, restructuring its parastatals, and halting the decay of transport infrastructure for road, rail, maritime, and air services. Cofinancing is anticipated from the EDF ($54.1 million), Italy ($32.6 million), the CCCE ($25.1 million), the AfDB ($23.8 million), BOAD ($18 million), the IsDB ($11.5 million), the CEDEAO ($5.4 million), Finland ($5 million), the FAC ($3.3 million), CIDA ($3.2 million), and the UNDP ($800,000). Total cost: $604.5 million.

SRI LANKA: IDA—$42.5 million. A third roads project seeks to reduce transport costs and delays of passengers and goods by restoring major trunk roads to better operational condition. In addition, priority road infrastructure damaged during the floods in May and June of 1989 will be repaired. Institution-building assistance is included. Cofinancing ($14.5 million) is expected from the EDCF. Total cost: $70.5 million.

TANZANIA: IDA—$76 million. A railways-restructuring project will help rehabilitate infrastructural assets, replace obsolete and uneconomical operational assets, and provide limited new investments consistent with the prospects for traffic growth. Institutional strengthening of the Tanzania Railways Corporation is included. Cofinancing is anticipated from the ADF ($31.2 million), the KfW ($18.3 million), the EDF ($18 million), CIDA ($10.3 million), the ODA ($8.5 million), and the WFP ($3.3 million). Total cost: $275.2 million.

TURKEY: IBRD—$300 million. Almost 1,000 kilometers of state and provincial roads will be either strengthened or improved, thus helping to keep transport costs low. Institution-building assistance will be provided to the General Directorate of Highways (KGM), and equipment and materials needed by the KGM for operations, road safety, and administration will be purchased. Total cost: $480 million.

YEMEN, REPUBLIC OF: IDA—$30 million. By providing equipment and materials to improve the 157-kilometer road between Harad and Huth, the important agricultural areas between the northeastern highlands and the Tihama coastal region will become more accessible. Institutional-strengthening measures and training are included. Total cost: $43 million.

ZAIRE: IDA—$12.4 million. The rehabilitation and maintenance of feeder roads will be tackled in an experimental manner through the use of labor-intensive techniques, reliance on existing local private-sector and nongovernmental institutions as executing entities, and pilot cost-recovery methods to improve long-term sustainability. Technical assistance and training are included. Cofinancing ($3.3 million) is expected from the UNDP. Total cost: $17.5 million.

ZIMBABWE: IBRD—$38.6 million. Support will be provided to the National Railways of Zimbabwe to implement a restructuring program to improve its operational and financial performance. Cofinancing is anticipated from USAID ($39.4 million), the KfW ($7.6 million), FINNIDA ($4.7 million), DANIDA ($3.7 million), the SDC ($2.3 million), and Austria ($1.8 million). Total cost: $263.4 million.

Urban Development

ARGENTINA: IBRD—$200 million. Financial support and incentives will be provided to provinces (meeting strict financial and other eligibility criteria) to undertake their own adjustment programs. Institution-building assistance is included. Cofinancing ($200 million) is expected from the IDB. Total cost: $575 million.

BURKINA FASO: IDA—$20 million. A program of small municipal works in the area of urban-infrastructure upgrading and rehabilitation will be financed, thereby creating, at least temporarily, substantial new employment opportunities in urban areas through the private sector. Cofinancing ($7.8 million) is being negotiated. Total cost: $30 million.

CHINA: IBRD—$79.4 million; IDA—$89 million. This first integrated urban-development project in China, which will introduce a wide range of improvements in planning, management, and design techniques based on conditions relevant to the country, will directly benefit, through the upgrading of urban services, about 1.8 million people living in the cities of Changzhou, Luoyang, and Shashi. Total cost: $277.2 million.

COLOMBIA: IBRD—$60 million. The government will be assisted in the implementation of its municipal-development program, which seeks to improve the coverage and quality of municipal services and urban infrastructure, promote more effective investment projects, improve the skills of sector personnel and local-government performance, and improve resource mobilization at the local level. Cofinancing ($44 million) is expected from the IDB. Total cost: $188.2 million.

DJIBOUTI: IDA—$11.2 million. Through continued policy and institutional strengthening and infrastructure investments, the basis for sustained urban development will be consolidated, job prospects will be expanded, and drainage, sanitation, and other physical environmental conditions will be improved for about 80,000 people. Cofinancing is anticipated from the EC ($10.5 million), the MCD ($8.1 million), the CCCE ($6.5 million), and the OPEC Fund for International Development ($1.9 million). Total cost: $45.5 million.

ECUADOR: IBRD—$104 million. Through a combination of institutional development and training and the provision of infrastructure, the fiscal autonomy of municipal governments will be increased and their capacity to deliver services efficiently and equitably will be strengthened.

Cofinancing is expected from the IDB ($104 million) and the GTZ ($4 million). Total cost: $300 million.

INDONESIA: IBRD—$180.3 million. The quality of urban infrastructure investments and service delivery on the part of forty-five local governments in East Java and Bali will be improved. In addition, strengthening of local revenue-mobilization and maintenance capabilities, as well as the preparation of future projects, will be supported. Cofinancing ($4.2 million) has been committed by Japan. Total cost: $373.4 million.

INDONESIA: IBRD—$61 million. Through extensive community participation in the government's *kampung*-improvement program, some 1.5 million people living in predominantly low-income areas in the Jakarta metropolitan region will benefit from the upgrading of basic urban infrastructure and utility services. In addition, measures will be instituted to strengthen environmental protection and pollution control in the region. Technical assistance is included. Cofinancing ($600,000) is anticipated from Japan. Total cost: $97 million.

IRAN: IBRD—$250 million. In the wake of the June 1990 earthquake, which left almost 100,000 people dead or injured and another half million homeless, finance will be provided for the medium-term and long-term recovery of the two sectors most heavily affected—agriculture and housing. In addition, the introduction of a national program for seismic-risk prevention and mitigation will be supported. Total cost: $4,172 million.

KOREA, REPUBLIC OF: IBRD—$100 million. Through support for an ongoing program of targeted lending by the National Housing Fund for low-income housing, some 15,000 additional housing units will be financed. Technical assistance and training for institutional strengthening in the sector are included. Total cost: $500 million.

MAURITIUS: IBRD—$12.4 million. Policy and institutional arrangements necessary to have physical planning, land-use control, infrastructure investments, and environmental protection managed in a coordinated and rational way will be put in place, and remedial measures designed to reverse the trend toward environmental degradation will be undertaken. Cofinancing ($400,000) is anticipated from the ICOD. Total cost: $20.5 million.

NIGER: IDA—$20 million. At least 12,000 man-years of temporary employment will be provided through a program, to be carried out under labor-intensive schemes by local contractors, of public facility and infrastructure rehabilitation and maintenance in urban areas. Cofinancing, totaling $10 million, is expected from the KfW and the

OPEC Fund for International Development. Total cost: $33.3 million.

PAPUA NEW GUINEA: IBRD—$30 million. About 10,000 man-years of productive jobs over a two-to-three-year period are to be provided through a program of investments in housing, industry, and road drainage, thus helping to alleviate urban and rural poverty and cushion the effects of the ongoing economic-adjustment program. Technical assistance for project management and monitoring is included. Total cost: $40.3 million.

SAO TOME AND PRINCIPE: IDA—$6 million. The social and economic effects of economic decline and structural adjustment will be mitigated through a project that will provide basic infrastructure to facilitate private economic activity, generate employment opportunities for urban and rural households, and raise living standards. Technical assistance is included. Total cost: $7.6 million.

UGANDA: IDA—$28.7 million. A first urban project seeks to improve living conditions and alleviate poverty in Kampala by restoring key infrastructure services and related maintenance activities. In addition, the revenue base of the Kampala City Council will be improved, and technical assistance will be provided to the Ministry of Local Government. Cofinancing is expected from the NDF ($4.6 million) and the GTZ ($600,000). Total cost: $38.5 million.

VANUATU: IDA—$3.4 million. About 400 middle-income and lower-income households (including squatters) will be provided with affordable serviced plots and houses, thus meeting about 20 percent of the estimated total demand in Port Vila and Luganville. In addition, the development of policies and standards leading to an improved supply response and enhanced private-sector involvement will be supported. Cofinancing ($180,000) is anticipated from Japan. Total cost: $5 million.

Water Supply and Sewerage

ARGENTINA: IBRD—$100 million. A water-supply and sewerage project seeks to promote greater sector efficiency and financial viability, expand service coverage, improve sector services while protecting the environment, and encourage private-sector participation. Cofinancing ($100 million) is anticipated from the IDB. Total cost: $250 million.

BOLIVIA: IDA—$35 million. About 1 million people are expected to benefit from water and sewerage subprojects in the country's three major cities, and the government will be assisted in introducing sector financial policies and upgrading its ability to regulate and oversee the sector. Cofinancing ($8 million) is expected from the KfW. Total cost: $57 million.

CHILE: IBRD—$50 million. A second water-supply and sewerage project seeks to optimize the operations of the existing water-supply system and improve water-supply conditions in the Greater Valparaiso area, as well as improve sanitary conditions in water streams, public beaches, and the marine environment. Total cost: $141.5 million.

CHINA: IDA—$77.8 million. The government of Liaoning province will be assisted in the initial phase of a long-term investment program aimed at addressing the shortages and poor quality of water supply in the three cities of Shenyang, Fuxin, and Yingkou, as well as shortcomings in urban transport in Shenyang. Technical assistance and training are included. Total cost: $128.6 million.

INDIA: IDA—$109.9 million. The health and productivity of about a million people living in 1,100 villages in Maharashtra state will improve as a result of a project that will expand access to rural water-supply systems, health education, and environmentally sound sanitation facilities. Total cost: $140.7 million.

INDONESIA: IBRD—$100 million. Urban infrastructure will be provided in selected cities in Sulawesi and Irian Jaya, with emphasis on increasing the access of households to water supply and solid-waste and sanitation services. Institutional assistance is included. Cofinancing ($700,000) is expected from Japan. Total cost: $188.2 million.

MEXICO: IBRD—$300 million. More than 3 million people are expected to benefit from a project whose major objective is to support the implementation of a sector-reorganization program designed to improve the quality and quantity of water-supply and sanitation services, promote sound pricing policies, progressively reduce the need for government funding, and improve environmental conditions throughout the country. Total cost: $650.9 million.

NEPAL: IDA—$60 million. Urban water-supply and sanitation services will be improved through a project involving rehabilitation and extension of water-supply facilities and improvements in sewerage and sanitation. Institution-building support will also be provided to the Nepal Water Supply Corporation. Cofinancing ($3.4 million) is expected from the UNDP. Total cost: $71 million.

NIGERIA: IBRD—$256 million. Water-supply rehabilitation subprojects—each comprising rehabilitation of existing facilities, leakage-detection and repair programs, and institutional strengthening at the state level—will be financed. Cofinancing ($4.5 million) is being provided by Japan. Total cost: $306.7 million.

PAKISTAN: IDA—$136.7 million. Rural productivity and health, particularly of women and children, will be improved through a project—designed to have a significant and positive impact on poverty alleviation in both the short and long term—that will finance the rehabilitation or construction of community-managed rural water-supply and sanitation infrastructure in Azad Jammu and Kashmir, Balochistan, and Sindh. Institution-building assistance and training are included. Total cost: $194.2 million.

Table 7-1. **Projects Approved for IBRD and IDA Assistance in Fiscal Year 1991, by Region**
(amounts in millions of US dollars)

Region and country	IBRD loans		IDA credits		Total	
	Number	Amount	Number	Amount	Number	Amount
Africa						
Angola	—	—	1	23.0	1	23.0
Benin	—	—	4	87.7	4	87.7
Botswana...........................	1	14.9	—	—	1	14.9
Burkina Faso	—	—	4	140.5	4	140.5
Burundi	—	—	1	22.8	1	22.8
Central African Republic	—	—	2	17.8	2	17.8
Chad...............................	—	—	1	11.0	1	11.0
Comoros	—	—	2	14.6	2	14.6
Congo..............................	1	15.8	—	—	1	15.8
Côte d'Ivoire	1	2.2	—	—	1	2.2
Djibouti	—	—	1	11.2	1	11.2
Equatorial Guinea	—	—	1	6.3	1	6.3
Ghana..............................	—	—	7	319.5	7	319.5
Guinea-Bissau......................	—	—	1	15.2	1	15.2
Kenya..............................	—	—	4	287.1	4	287.1
Lesotho	—	—	1	21.0	1	21.0
Madagascar.........................	—	—	2	52.5	2	52.5
Malawi	—	—	3	103.5	3	103.5
Mali	—	—	3	121.0	3	121.0
Mauritania.........................	—	—	—	4.0	—	4.0
Mauritius...........................	2	22.4	—	—	2	22.4
Mozambique........................	—	—	2	69.1	2	69.1
Niger	—	—	1	20.0	1	20.0
Nigeria.............................	3	544.0	3	276.5	6	820.5
Rwanda	—	—	4	145.7	4	145.7
São Tomé and Principe	—	—	1	6.0	1	6.0
Senegal.............................	—	—	2	107.1	2	107.1
Tanzania	—	—	2	136.1	2	136.1
Togo...............................	—	—	4	93.4	4	93.4
Uganda.............................	—	—	4	276.7	4	276.7
Zaire...............................	—	—	3	63.8	3	63.8
Zambia.............................	—	—	3	278.2	3	278.2
Zimbabwe	2	63.6	—	—	2	63.6
Total..........................	10	662.9	67	2,731.3	77	3,394.2
Asia						
Bangladesh	—	—	6	459.7	6	459.7
China	6	601.5	4	977.8	10	1,579.3
India...............................	8	1,112.0	2	937.4	10	2,049.4
Indonesia...........................	12	1,637.5	—	—	12	1,637.5
Korea, Republic of	4	250.0	—	—	4	250.0
Lao People's Democratic Republic ...	—	—	1	45.0	1	45.0
Nepal	—	—	1	60.0	1	60.0
Papua New Guinea	2	50.8	—	—	2	50.8
Philippines..........................	7	869.2	—	66.0	7	935.2
Sri Lanka...........................	—	—	6	358.6	6	358.6

(continued)

Table 7-1 (continued)

Region and country	IBRD loans		IDA credits		Total	
	Number	Amount	Number	Amount	Number	Amount
Asia (continued)						
Thailand.........................	2	62.0	—	—	2	62.0
Vanuatu.........................	—	—	1	3.4	1	3.4
Total.........................	41	4,583.0	21	2,907.9	62	7,490.9
Europe, Middle East, and North Africa						
Algeria..........................	3	431.0	—	—	3	431.0
Bulgaria.........................	1	17.0	—	—	1	17.0
Cyprus..........................	1	30.0	—	—	1	30.0
Czechoslovakia	1	450.0	—	—	1	450.0
Egypt...........................	2	384.0	1	140.0	3	524.0
Hungary.........................	3	550.0	—	—	3	550.0
Iran, Islamic Republic of	1	250.0	—	—	1	250.0
Jordan	2	25.0	—	—	2	25.0
Morocco	4	626.0	—	—	4	626.0
Pakistan.........................	4	428.1	3	249.0	7	677.1
Poland	7	1,440.0	—	—	7	1,440.0
Romania.........................	1	180.0	—	—	1	180.0
Tunisia..........................	3	68.0	—	—	3	68.0
Turkey	4	900.0	—	—	4	900.0
Yemen, Republic of	—	—	4	95.6	4	95.6
Yugoslavia.......................	1	300.0	—	—	1	300.0
Total.........................	38	6,079.1	8	484.6	46	6,563.7
Latin America and the Caribbean						
Argentina........................	6	679.5	—	—	6	679.5
Bolivia	—	—	3	81.8	3	81.8
Brazil	4	955.0	—	—	4	955.0
Chile............................	1	50.0	—	—	1	50.0
Colombia........................	4	639.0	—	—	4	639.0
Dominican Republic	2	94.0	—	—	2	94.0
Ecuador.........................	2	163.0	—	—	2	163.0
El Salvador......................	2	101.0	—	—	2	101.0
Guyana..........................	—	—	—	22.3	—	22.3
Haiti	—	—	2	23.9	2	23.9
Honduras........................	1	90.0	2	40.0	3	130.0
Jamaica	3	76.5	—	—	3	76.5
Mexico..........................	7	1,882.0	—	—	7	1,882.0
St. Kitts and Nevis	1	1.5	—	1.5	1	3.0
Trinidad and Tobago..............	1	20.7	—	—	1	20.7
Uruguay.........................	1	65.0	—	—	1	65.0
Venezuela	2	250.0	—	—	2	250.0
Total.........................	37	5,067.2	7	169.5	44	5,236.7
Grand total	126	16,392.2	103	6,293.3	229	22,685.5

— Zero.

NOTE: Supplements are included in the amounts, but are not counted as separate lending operations.

Joint IBRD/IDA operations are counted only once, as IBRD operations.

Table 7-2. **Projects Approved for IBRD and IDA Assistance in Fiscal Year 1991, by Sector**
(millions of US dollars)

Sector[a]	IBRD	IDA	Total
Agriculture and Rural Development			
Argentina—Agricultural credit	33.5	—	33.5
Bangladesh—Agricultural credit	—	35.0	35.0
Bangladesh—Irrigation and drainage	—	75.0	75.0
Bangladesh—Irrigation and drainage	—	54.0	54.0
Benin—Agriculture sector loan	—	12.3	12.3
Bolivia—Research and extension	—	21.0	21.0
Burkina Faso—Agricultural credit	—	16.5	16.5
China—Agricultural credit	75.0	200.0	275.0
China—Area development	—	110.0	110.0
China—Area development	—	64.0	64.0
China—Irrigation and drainage	147.1	187.9	335.0
Colombia—Area development	75.0	—	75.0
Congo—Research and extension	15.8	—	15.8
Côte d'Ivoire—Agriculture sector loan	2.2	—	2.2
Ecuador—Irrigation and drainage	59.0	—	59.0
Equatorial Guinea—Agriculture sector loan	—	6.3	6.3
Ghana—Perennial crops	—	16.5	16.5
Ghana—Research and extension	—	22.0	22.0
India—Agricultural credit	40.0	170.0	210.0
India—Area development	20.0	92.8	112.8
India—Irrigation and drainage	23.0	130.0	153.0
Indonesia—Agricultural credit	15.5	—	15.5
Indonesia—Irrigation and drainage	125.0	—	125.0
Kenya—Agriculture sector loan	—	75.0	75.0
Kenya—Forestry	—	19.9	19.9
Kenya—Research and extension	—	24.9	24.9
Madagascar—Livestock	—	19.8	19.8
Malawi—Fisheries	—	8.8	8.8
Mali—Research and extension	—	24.4	24.4
Mauritius—Research and extension	10.0	—	10.0
Mexico—Agriculture sector loan	400.0	—	400.0
Mexico—Area development	350.0	—	350.0
Mozambique—Agriculture sector loan	—	15.4	15.4
Nigeria—Research and extension	—	78.0	78.0
Pakistan—Irrigation and drainage	36.3	47.3	83.6
Pakistan—Irrigation and drainage	—	20.0	20.0
Philippines—Agricultural credit	150.0	—	150.0
Philippines—Agriculture sector loan	158.0	66.0	224.0
Philippines—Irrigation and drainage	46.2	—	46.2
Poland—Agricultural credit	100.0	—	100.0
St. Kitts and Nevis—Agroindustry	1.5	1.5	3.0
Sri Lanka—Irrigation and drainage	—	29.6	29.6
Tanzania—Agriculture sector loan	—	16.1	16.1[b]
Thailand—Area development	30.0	—	30.0
Uganda—Agriculture sector loan	—	100.0	100.0
Uganda—Livestock	—	21.0	21.0
Yemen, Republic of—Fisheries	—	13.2	13.2
Total	1,913.1	1,794.2	3,707.3

(continued)

Table 7-2 (continued)

Sector[a]	IBRD	IDA	Total
Development Finance Companies			
Bangladesh	—	3.5	3.5[b]
Bolivia	—	14.5	14.5[b]
Brazil	300.0	—	300.0
Central African Republic	—	11.3	11.3
China	150.0	—	150.0
Colombia	200.0	—	200.0
Jamaica	30.0	—	30.0
Kenya	—	67.3	67.3[b]
Lesotho	—	21.0	21.0
Malawi	—	32.0	32.0
Malawi	—	7.2	7.2[b]
Mexico	300.0	—	300.0
Morocco	235.0	—	235.0
Poland	280.0	—	280.0
Poland	200.0	—	200.0
Total	1,695.0	156.8	1,851.8
Education			
Algeria	65.0	—	65.0
Brazil	245.0	—	245.0
Brazil	150.0	—	150.0
Burkina Faso	—	24.0	24.0
China	—	131.2	131.2
Dominican Republic	15.0	—	15.0
Ghana	—	14.7	14.7
Haiti	—	12.6	12.6
Hungary	150.0	—	150.0
India	—	307.1	307.1
Indonesia	150.0	—	150.0
Korea, Republic of	60.0	—	60.0
Korea, Republic of	30.0	—	30.0
Mexico	152.0	—	152.0
Morocco	145.0	—	145.0
Mozambique	—	53.7	53.7
Nigeria	—	120.0	120.0
Papua New Guinea	20.8	—	20.8
Philippines	200.0	—	200.0
Poland	100.0	—	100.0
Rwanda	—	23.3	23.3
Togo	—	9.2	9.2
Trinidad and Tobago	20.7	—	20.7
Tunisia	12.0	—	12.0
Yemen, Republic of	—	19.4	19.4
Zaire	—	21.0	21.0
Total	1,515.5	736.2	2,251.7
Energy			
Oil, gas, and coal			
Bangladesh	—	67.2	67.2
Brazil	260.0	—	260.0
Burundi	—	22.8	22.8

Sector[a]	IBRD	IDA	Total
Energy *(continued)*			
Chad...	—	11.0	11.0
Egypt	84.0	—	84.0
Guinea-Bissau	—	15.2	15.2
India..	450.0	—	450.0
Nigeria..	218.0	—	218.0
Pakistan...	130.0	—	130.0
Pakistan...	60.0	—	60.0[b]
Pakistan...	28.0	—	28.0[b]
Poland	340.0	—	340.0
Tanzania	—	44.0	44.0
Total..	1,570.0	160.2	1,730.2
Power			
Benin	—	15.0	15.0
India..	200.0	—	200.0
Indonesia..	275.0	—	275.0
Morocco	114.0	—	114.0
Togo..	—	15.0	15.0
Turkey..	300.0	—	300.0
Uganda	—	125.0	125.0
Yugoslavia	300.0	—	300.0
Total..	1,189.0	155.0	1,344.0
Industry			
Algeria—Industry sector loan.........................	350.0	—	350.0
China—Industry sector loan	50.0	64.3	114.3
Cyprus—Industry sector loan.........................	30.0	—	30.0
India—Fertilizer and other chemicals..................	245.0	—	245.0
India—Industry sector loan...........................	124.0	31.6	155.6
Indonesia—Fertilizer and other chemicals...............	221.7	—	221.7
Jordan—Fertilizer and other chemicals	15.0	—	15.0
Mexico—Mining, other extractive......................	200.0	—	200.0
Pakistan—Industry sector loan........................	56.4	—	56.4[b]
Philippines—Industry sector loan	175.0	—	175.0
Sri Lanka—Industry sector loan	—	120.0	120.0
Turkey—Industry sector loan.........................	200.0	—	200.0
Turkey—Industry sector loan.........................	100.0	—	100.0
Total..	1,767.1	215.9	1,983.0
Nonproject			
Benin	—	55.0	55.0
Burkina Faso	—	80.0	80.0
Comoros	—	8.0	8.0
Czechoslovakia	450.0	—	450.0
Egypt	300.0	—	300.0
El Salvador..	75.0	—	75.0
Ghana...	—	120.0	120.0
Ghana...	—	8.3	8.3[b]
Guyana	—	18.0	18.0[b]
Guyana	—	4.3	4.3[b]

(continued)

Table 7-2 (continued)

Sector[a]	IBRD	IDA	Total
Nonproject (continued)			
Honduras...	90.0	—	90.0
Honduras...	—	20.0	20.0[b]
Hungary...	250.0	—	250.0
Indonesia..	250.0	—	250.0
Jordan	10.0	—	10.0
Kenya	—	100.0	100.0
Mali	—	70.0	70.0
Poland	300.0	—	300.0
Rwanda	—	90.0	90.0
Senegal	—	7.1	7.1[b]
Sri Lanka	—	7.0	7.0[b]
Togo..	—	55.0	55.0
Uganda	—	2.0	2.0[b]
Uruguay...	65.0	—	65.0
Venezuela	150.0	—	150.0
Zambia..	—	210.0	210.0
Zambia..	—	27.2	27.2[b]
Total..	1,940.0	881.9	2,821.9
Population, Health, and Nutrition			
Algeria..	16.0	—	16.0
Bangladesh	—	180.0	180.0
Egypt	—	140.0	140.0
El Salvador..	26.0	—	26.0
Ghana...	—	27.0	27.0
Haiti..	—	11.3	11.3
Honduras..	—	20.0	20.0
India..	10.0	96.0	106.0
Indonesia..	104.0	—	104.0
Korea, Republic of	60.0	—	60.0
Madagascar..	—	31.0	31.0
Malawi..	—	55.5	55.5
Mali	—	26.6	26.6
Mexico..	180.0	—	180.0
Nigeria..	—	78.5	78.5
Nigeria..	70.0	—	70.0
Pakistan...	—	45.0	45.0
Rwanda	—	19.6	19.6
Senegal	—	35.0	35.0
Sri Lanka	—	57.5	57.5
Togo..	—	14.2	14.2
Tunisia..	30.0	—	30.0
Tunisia..	26.0	—	26.0
Venezuela	100.0	—	100.0
Yemen, Republic of	—	33.0	33.0
Zaire..	—	30.4	30.4
Zambia..	—	20.0	20.0
Zimbabwe	25.0	—	25.0
Total..	647.0	920.6	1,567.6

Sector[a]	IBRD	IDA	Total
Public-sector Management			
Argentina..	300.0	—	300.0
Colombia..	304.0	—	304.0
Madagascar..	—	1.7	1.7[b]
Mauritania..	—	4.0	4.0[b]
Thailand..	32.0	—	32.0
Total..	636.0	5.7	641.7
Small-scale Enterprises			
Indonesia...	125.0	—	125.0
Pakistan..	26.0	—	26.0
Philippines...	15.0	—	15.0
Sri Lanka	—	45.0	45.0
Total..	166.0	45.0	211.0
Technical Assistance			
Angola	—	23.0	23.0
Argentina...	23.0	—	23.0
Argentina...	23.0	—	23.0
Benin	—	5.4	5.4
Bolivia	—	11.3	11.3
Bulgaria	17.0	—	17.0
Central African Republic	—	6.5	6.5
Ghana..	—	15.0	15.0
Indonesia...	30.0	—	30.0
Jamaica	11.5	—	11.5
Romania	180.0	—	180.0
Zambia...	—	21.0	21.0
Total..	284.5	82.2	366.7
Telecommunications			
Hungary..	150.0	—	150.0
Poland	120.0	—	120.0
Rwanda	—	12.8	12.8
Sri Lanka	—	57.0	57.0
Total..	270.0	69.8	339.8
Transportation			
Bangladesh—Ports and waterways	—	45.0	45.0
Botswana—Highways.................................	14.9	—	14.9
China—Highways	100.0	53.6	153.6
Comoros—Highways	—	6.6	6.6
Dominican Republic—Highways	79.0	—	79.0
Ghana—Highways....................................	—	96.0	96.0
Jamaica—Highways..................................	35.0	—	35.0
Lao People's Democratic Republic—Highways	—	45.0	45.0
Morocco—Ports and waterways.......................	132.0	—	132.0
Pakistan—Ports and waterways	91.4	—	91.4
Philippines—Highways...............................	125.0	—	125.0
Senegal—Transportation sector loan....................	—	65.0	65.0
Sri Lanka—Highways................................	—	42.5	42.5
Tanzania—Railways	—	76.0	76.0
Turkey—Highways	300.0	—	300.0

(continued)

Table 7-2 (continued)

Sector[a]	IBRD	IDA	Total
Transportation (continued)			
Yemen, Republic of—Transportation sector loan..........	—	30.0	30.0
Zaire—Highways......................................	—	12.4	12.4
Zimbabwe—Railways..................................	38.6	—	38.6
Total...	915.9	472.1	1,388.0
Urban Development			
Argentina...	200.0	—	200.0
Burkina Faso	—	20.0	20.0
China	79.4	89.0	168.4
Colombia...	60.0	—	60.0
Djibouti	—	11.2	11.2
Ecuador..	104.0	—	104.0
Indonesia...	180.3	—	180.3
Indonesia...	61.0	—	61.0
Iran, Islamic Republic of.............................	250.0	—	250.0
Korea, Republic of	100.0	—	100.0
Mauritius...	12.4	—	12.4
Niger	—	20.0	20.0
Papua New Guinea	30.0	—	30.0
São Tomé and Principe	—	6.0	6.0
Uganda	—	28.7	28.7
Vanuatu..	—	3.4	3.4
Total...	1,077.1	178.3	1,255.4
Water Supply and Sewerage			
Argentina...	100.0	—	100.0
Bolivia...	—	35.0	35.0
Chile...	50.0	—	50.0
China	—	77.8	77.8
India...	—	109.9	109.9
Indonesia...	100.0	—	100.0
Mexico...	300.0	—	300.0
Nepal	—	60.0	60.0
Nigeria...	256.0	—	256.0
Pakistan..	—	136.7	136.7
Total...	806.0	419.4	1,225.4
Grand total	16,392.2	6,293.3	22,685.5

— Zero.

NOTE: For additional details, see Tables 7–3 and 7–4.

a. Many projects include activity in more than one sector or subsector.

b. Supplementary financing to a previous loan, not counted as a separate operation.

Table 7-3. Statement of IBRD Loans Approved during Fiscal Year 1991

Borrower or guarantor and purpose	Date of approval	Maturities	Principal amount (US$ millions)
Algeria			
Science and technology university development project	Nov. 6, 1990	1996/2008	65.0
Pilot public health management project	Mar. 5, 1991	1996/2008	16.0
Enterprise and financial sector adjustment loan............	June 21, 1991	1997/2008	350.0
Argentina			
Provincial development project	Dec. 18, 1990	1996/2007	200.0
Water supply and sewerage sector project	Dec. 18, 1990	1996/2007	100.0
Public enterprise reform adjustment loan	Feb. 12, 1991	1996/2008	300.0
Public enterprise reform execution loan..................	Feb. 12, 1991	1996/2008	23.0
Agricultural services and institutional development project .	Feb. 28, 1991	1996/2008	33.5
Public sector reform technical assistance loan	June 25, 1991	1997/2008	23.0
Botswana			
Tuli Block roads project	July 31, 1990	1996/2007	14.9
Brazil			
Science research and training project....................	Nov. 29, 1990	1996/2005	150.0
Brazil (Guarantor)			
Private sector finance project—Banco Nacional de Desenvolvimento Econômico e Social	Nov. 29, 1990	1996/2005	300.0
Hydrocarbon transport and processing project—Petróleo Brasileiro S.A.	June 26, 1991	1997/2006	260.0
Innovations in basic education project—State of São Paulo .	June 26, 1991	1996/2006	245.0
Bulgaria			
Technical assistance for economic reform project..........	June 27, 1991	1997/2008	17.0
Chile (Guarantor)			
Second Valparaiso water supply and sewerage project—Empresa de Obras Sanitarias de Valparaíso S.A.	May 28, 1991	1996/2008	50.0
China			
Fourth rural credit project	Oct. 30, 1990	1996/2010	75.0
Rural industrial technology project......................	Dec. 4, 1990	1996/2010	50.0
Medium-sized cities development project	Jan. 8, 1991	1996/2010	79.4
Shanghai industrial development project	Jan. 29, 1991	1996/2011	150.0
Jiangsu provincial transport project	Apr. 9, 1991	1996/2011	100.0
Irrigated agriculture intensification project	June 4, 1991	1997/2011	147.1
Colombia			
Rural development investment program..................	July 31, 1990	1996/2007	75.0
Public sector reform loan	Dec. 11, 1990	1996/2007	304.0
Municipal development project	May 30, 1991	1997/2008	60.0
Colombia (Guarantor)			
Industrial restructuring and development project—Banco de la República..	May 2, 1991	1996/2008	200.0
Congo			
National agricultural extension and adaptive research project...	Sept. 11, 1990	1996/2010	15.8
Côte d'Ivoire			
Women in development pilot support project..............	Aug. 2, 1990	1996/2010	2.2
Cyprus			
Industrial restructuring project.........................	Apr. 25, 1991	1997/2006	30.0
Czechoslovakia			
Structural adjustment loan	June 26, 1991	1997/2006	450.0

(continued)

Table 7-3 *(continued)*

Borrower or guarantor and purpose	Date of approval	Maturities	Principal amount (US$ millions)
Dominican Republic			
Fifth road rehabilitation and maintenance project	June 20, 1991	1997/2011	79.0
Primary education development project	June 20, 1991	1997/2011	15.0
Ecuador			
Lower Guayas flood control project	Dec. 6, 1990	1996/2007	59.0
Municipal development and urban infrastructure project....	Dec. 20, 1990	1996/2010	104.0
Egypt			
Structural adjustment loan	June 21, 1991	1996/2011	300.0
Egypt (Guarantor)			
Gas investment project—Egyptian General Petroleum Corporation	June 21, 1991	1996/2011	84.0
El Salvador			
Structural adjustment loan	Feb. 12, 1991	1996/2011	75.0
Social sector rehabilitation project	June 19, 1991	1997/2011	26.0
Honduras			
Second structural adjustment loan	Sept. 13, 1990	1996/2010	90.0
Hungary			
Human resources project	Mar. 28, 1991	1996/2006	150.0
Hungary (Guarantor)			
Second telecommunications project—Magyar Távközlési Vállalat	Oct. 9, 1990	1996/2005	150.0
Second structural adjustment loan—National Bank of Hungary	June 19, 1991	1997/2006	250.0
India			
Integrated child development services project	Sept. 4, 1990	1996/2010	10.0
Second petrochemicals development project	Sept. 13, 1990	1996/2010	12.0
Andhra Pradesh cyclone emergency reconstruction project .	Oct. 4, 1990	1996/2010	40.0
Agricultural development project—Tamil Nadu............	Mar. 12, 1991	1996/2011	20.0
Dam safety project	May 14, 1991	1997/2011	23.0
Industrial pollution control project	May 30, 1991	1997/2011	124.0
India (Guarantor)			
Second petrochemicals development project—Indian Petrochemical Corporation Ltd.	Sept. 13, 1990	1996/2010	233.0
Private power utilities project—Bombay Suburban Electric Supply Limited	June 13, 1991	1997/2011	200.0
Gas flaring reduction project—Oil and Natural Gas Commission	June 25, 1991	1997/2011	450.0
Indonesia			
Third Jabotabek urban development project...............	July 17, 1990	1996/2010	61.0
Second BRI/KUPEDES small credit project	July 31, 1990	1996/2010	125.0
Second private sector development loan	Nov. 13, 1990	1996/2010	250.0
Fertilizer restructuring project	Dec. 20, 1990	1996/2011	221.7
Fifth population project..................................	Mar. 5, 1991	1996/2011	104.0
Provincial irrigated agricultural development project	Mar. 14, 1991	1996/2011	125.0
East Java–Bali urban development project	Mar. 19, 1991	1996/2011	180.3
Yogyakarta upland area development project..............	Mar. 19, 1991	1996/2011	15.5
Second higher education development project	Mar. 26, 1991	1996/2011	150.0
Sulawesi–Irian Jaya urban development project............	June 6, 1991	1997/2011	100.0
Power transmission project..............................	June 19, 1991	1997/2011	275.0
Technical assistance project for public and private provision of infrastructure............................	June 27, 1991	1997/2011	30.0

Borrower or guarantor and purpose	Date of approval	Maturities	Principal amount (US$ millions)
Iran, Islamic Republic of (Guarantor)			
Earthquake recovery project—Central Bank of the Islamic Republic of Iran	Mar. 14, 1991	1996/2006	250.0
Jamaica			
Road infrastructure planning and maintenance project	Dec. 4, 1990	1996/2007	35.0
Second trade and financial sector adjustment loan	Mar. 21, 1991	1996/2008	30.0
Financial and program management improvement project	June 27, 1991	1997/2008	11.5
Jordan			
Emergency recovery project	Mar. 21, 1991	1996/2008	10.0
Jordan (Guarantor)			
Dead Sea industrial exports project—Arab Potash Company	June 21, 1991	1997/2008	15.0
Korea, Republic of			
Vocational education project	Mar. 28, 1991	1996/2006	30.0
Third technology advancement project	Apr. 2, 1991	1996/2006	60.0
Housing project	May 23, 1991	1996/2006	100.0
Health technology project	May 23, 1991	1996/2006	60.0
Mauritius			
Environmental monitoring and development project	Dec. 6, 1990	1996/2008	12.4
Agricultural management and services project	May 28, 1991	1997/2008	10.0
Mexico (Guarantor)			
Water supply and sanitation sector project—Banco Nacional de Obras y Servicios Públicos, S.N.C.	Nov. 29, 1990	1996/2008	300.0
Basic health care project—Nacional Financiera, S.N.C.	Nov. 29, 1990	1996/2007	180.0
Decentralization and regional development project for the disadvantaged states—Nacional Financiera, S.N.C.	Mar. 26, 1991	1996/2008	350.0
Export sector loan—Banco Nacional de Comercio Exterior, S.N.C.	Mar. 26, 1991	1996/2008	300.0
Agricultural sector adjustment loan II—Nacional Financiera, S.N.C.	June 25, 1991	1997/2008	400.0
Mining sector restructuring project—Nacional Financiera, S.N.C.	June 25, 1991	1997/2008	200.0
Third technical training project—Nacional Financiera, S.N.C.	June 25, 1991	1997/2008	152.0
Morocco			
Second rural electrification project	Oct. 4, 1990	1996/2010	114.0
Port sector project	Dec. 20, 1990	1996/2011	33.0
Rural basic education development project	Feb. 26, 1991	1996/2011	145.0
Financial sector development project	June 25, 1991	1997/2011	125.0
Morocco (Guarantor)			
Port sector project—Office d'exploitation des ports	Dec. 20, 1990	1996/2011	99.0
Financial sector development project—Banque nationale pour le développement économique	June 25, 1991	1997/2011	29.5
Financial sector development project—Banque marocaine du commerce extérieur	June 25, 1991	1997/2011	19.5
Financial sector development project—Banque commerciale du Maroc	June 25, 1991	1997/2011	13.5
Financial sector development project—Wafabank	June 25, 1991	1997/2011	8.5
Financial sector development project—Banque marocaine pour le commerce et l'industrie	June 25, 1991	1997/2011	9.5

(continued)

Table 7-3 (continued)

Borrower or guarantor and purpose	Date of approval	Maturities	Principal amount (US$ millions)
Morocco (Guarantor) *(continued)*			
Financial sector development project—Banque centrale populaire	June 25, 1991	1997/2011	9.5
Financial sector development project—Société générale marocaine de banque	June 25, 1991	1997/2011	11.5
Financial sector development project—Crédit du Maroc	June 25, 1991	1997/2011	8.5
Nigeria			
National water rehabilitation project	May 21, 1991	1996/2011	256.0
Health system fund project	May 21, 1991	1996/2011	70.0
Nigeria (Guarantor)			
Oso condensate field development project—Nigerian National Petroleum Corporation	Apr. 9, 1991	1996/2010	218.0
Pakistan			
Microenterprise project	Apr. 23, 1991	1996/2011	26.0
Third on-farm water management project	May 21, 1991	1996/2011	36.3
Karachi port modernization project	May 30, 1991	1996/2011	91.4
Cement industry modernization project (supplemental loan).	May 30, 1991	1993/2007	56.4
Second energy sector program (supplemental loan)	June 21, 1991	1995/2009	28.0
Pakistan (Guarantor)			
Corporate restructuring and system expansion project—Sui Northern Gas Pipelines Limited	Aug. 7, 1990	1996/2010	130.0
Corporate restructuring and system expansion project—Sui Northern Gas Pipelines Limited (supplemental loan)	June 21, 1991	1996/2010	60.0
Papua New Guinea			
Special interventions project	Jan. 29, 1991	1996/2011	30.0
Public sector training project	Jan. 29, 1991	1996/2011	20.8
Philippines			
Second elementary education project	July 3, 1990	1996/2010	200.0
Second communal irrigation development project	Oct. 4, 1990	1996/2010	46.2
Earthquake reconstruction project	Oct. 9, 1990	1996/2010	125.0
Environment and natural resources sector adjustment program	June 25, 1991	1997/2011	158.0
Philippines (Guarantor)			
Industrial restructuring project—Development Bank of the Philippines	Jan. 8, 1991	1996/2011	175.0
Cottage enterprise finance project—Development Bank of the Philippines	Mar. 26, 1991	1996/2011	15.0
Rural finance project—Land Bank of the Philippines	June 21, 1991	1997/2011	150.0
Poland			
Structural adjustment loan	July 31, 1990	1996/2007	300.0
Employment promotion and services project	June 4, 1991	1996/2008	100.0
Privatization and restructuring project	June 11, 1991	1996/2008	280.0
Financial institutions development loan	June 11, 1991	1996/2008	200.0
Agricultural development project	June 11, 1991	1996/2008	100.0
Heat supply restructuring and conservation project	June 26, 1991	1996/2008	75.0
Poland (Guarantor)			
First telecommunications project—Polish Post, Telephone and Telegraph Enterprise	Apr. 23, 1991	1996/2008	120.0
Heat supply restructuring and conservation project—District Heating Enterprise of Warsaw	June 26, 1991	1996/2008	100.0
Heat supply restructuring and conservation project—District Heating Enterprise of Katowice	June 26, 1991	1996/2008	55.0

Borrower or guarantor and purpose	Date of approval	Maturities	Principal amount (US$ millions)
Poland (Guarantor) *(continued)*			
Heat supply restructuring and conservation project—District Heating Enterprise of Gdansk.........	June 26, 1991	1996/2008	40.0
Heat supply restructuring and conservation project—District Heating Enterprise of Gdynia..........	June 26, 1991	1996/2008	25.0
Heat supply restructuring and conservation project—District Heating Enterprise of Krakow	June 26, 1991	1996/2008	25.0
Heat supply restructuring and conservation project—Bank of Poznan	June 26, 1991	1996/2008	20.0
Romania			
Technical assistance and critical imports project...........	June 25, 1991	1997/2006	180.0
St. Kitts and Nevis			
Agricultural development support project	May 28, 1991	1997/2008	1.5
Thailand			
Second land titling project	Sept. 4, 1990	1996/2010	30.0
Tax computerization project............................	Feb. 12, 1991	1996/2008	32.0
Trinidad and Tobago			
Education and training for youth employment project	May 21, 1991	1997/2006	20.7
Tunisia			
Employment and training fund project....................	Sept. 4, 1990	1996/2007	12.0
Hospital restructuring support project	Mar. 21, 1991	1996/2008	30.0
Population and family health project	Mar. 21, 1991	1996/2008	26.0
Turkey			
Technology development project.........................	Feb. 28, 1991	1996/2008	100.0
State and provincial roads project.......................	May 14, 1991	1997/2008	300.0
Private investment credit project........................	June 13, 1991	1996/2008	200.0
Turkey (Guarantor)			
TEK restructuring project—Turkish Electricity Authority ..	June 13, 1991	1996/2008	300.0
Uruguay			
Debt and debt service reduction program	May 14, 1991	1997/2006	65.0
Venezuela			
Social development project.............................	Nov. 29, 1990	1996/2006	100.0
Interest support loan	Dec. 13, 1990	1996/2005	150.0
Yugoslavia (Guarantor)			
Kolubara B thermal power and lignite mine project—Elektroprivreda of Serbia	June 25, 1991	1997/2006	300.0
Zimbabwe			
Second railways project................................	Dec. 4, 1990	1996/2011	38.6
Second family health project	June 4, 1991	1996/2011	25.0
Total			16,392.2
International Finance Corporation (total amount for fiscal 1991)...	—a	—b	200.0
Grand total...			16,592.2

NOTE: All loans approved in fiscal 1991 are at variable interest rates.

a. Various loans approved throughout the fiscal year.

b. Maturities vary for individual loans.

Table 7-4. Statement of IDA Credits Approved during Fiscal Year 1991

Country and purpose	Date of approval	Maturities	Principal amount (millions)	
			SDR	US$ equivalent
Angola				
Economic management capacity building project..............................	June 19, 1991	2001/2026	17.1	23.0
Bangladesh				
Financial sector adjustment credit (supplement)	Nov. 6, 1990	2000/2030	2.5	3.5
Third inland water transport project........	May 2, 1991	2001/2031	31.3	45.0
Agricultural support services project.......	May 2, 1991	2001/2031	24.4	35.0
National minor irrigation development project...............................	May 23, 1991	2001/2031	38.1	54.0
Shallow tubewell and low lift pump irrigation project.......................	May 30, 1991	2001/2031	52.2	75.0
Fourth population and health project.......	June 6, 1991	2001/2031	133.2	180.0
Liquefied petroleum gas transport and distribution project....................	June 11, 1991	2001/2031	49.8	67.2
Benin				
Second structural adjustment program......	June 27, 1991	2001/2031	41.3	55.0
Power rehabilitation and extension project..	June 27, 1991	2001/2031	11.3	15.0
Agricultural services restructuring project ..	June 27, 1991	2001/2031	9.3	12.3
Pre-investment project....................	June 27, 1991	2001/2031	4.1	5.4
Bolivia				
Financial sector adjustment credit (supplement)	Nov. 6, 1990	1998/2028	10.4	14.5
Major cities water and sewerage rehabilitation project	Dec. 4, 1990	2001/2030	25.2	35.0
Agricultural technology development project...............................	Mar. 14, 1991	2001/2031	15.0	21.0
Second public financial management operation	June 26, 1991	2001/2031	8.5	11.3
Burkina Faso				
Environmental management project........	April 25, 1991	2001/2031	11.5	16.5
Fourth education project..................	May 21, 1991	2001/2031	17.8	24.0
Structural adjustment program	June 27, 1991	2001/2031	60.0	80.0
Public works and employment project......	June 27, 1991	2001/2031	15.0	20.0
Burundi				
Energy sector rehabilitation project........	April 25, 1991	2001/2031	16.3	22.8
Central African Republic				
Enterprise rehabilitation and development project...............................	May 30, 1991	2001/2031	9.4	11.3
Social dimensions of adjustment and development project....................	June 20, 1991	2001/2031	5.6	6.5
Chad				
Petroleum and power engineering project ...	Nov. 20, 1990	2001/2030	7.9	11.0
China				
Mid-Yangtze agricultural development project...............................	Aug. 9, 1990	2000/2025	48.6	64.0
Fourth rural credit project	Oct. 30, 1990	2000/2025	143.7	200.0
Rural industrial technology project.........	Dec. 4, 1990	2001/2025	45.1	64.3
Medium-sized cities development project ...	Jan. 8, 1991	2001/2025	62.2	89.0
Key studies development project	Feb. 26, 1991	2001/2025	92.9	131.2

Country and purpose	Date of approval	Maturities	Principal amount (millions)	
			SDR	US$ equivalent
China (*continued*)				
Liaoning urban infrastructure project.......	Mar. 21, 1991	2001/2025	54.2	77.8
Jiangsu provincial transport project	April 9, 1991	2001/2025	38.5	53.6
Henan agricultural development project	May 14, 1991	2001/2026	81.4	110.0
Irrigated agriculture intensification project..	June 4, 1991	2001/2026	139.0	187.9
Comoros				
Highway maintenance project	Jan. 22, 1991	2001/2030	4.6	6.6
Macro-economic reform and capacity building credit	June 13, 1991	2001/2031	6.0	8.0
Djibouti				
Second urban development project.........	Jan. 15, 1991	2001/2030	7.8	11.2
Egypt				
Social fund project......................	June 21, 1991	2001/2026	105.0	140.0
Equatorial Guinea				
Crop diversification and agricultural services project........................	Oct. 30, 1990	2000/2030	4.7	6.3
Ghana				
Agricultural diversification project	Oct. 16, 1990	2000/2030	12.5	16.5
Second structural adjustment credit (supplement)	Nov. 6, 1990	1999/2029	6.0	8.3
Second transport rehabilitation project	Dec. 13, 1990	2001/2030	69.0	96.0
Second health and population project	Dec. 13, 1990	2001/2030	19.5	27.0
Economic management support project.....	Mar. 28, 1991	2001/2030	10.7	15.0
Program to promote private investment and sustained development	May 7, 1991	2001/2031	84.6	120.0
National agricultural research project	May 23, 1991	2001/2031	16.3	22.0
Community secondary schools construction project................................	June 25, 1991	2001/2031	11.1	14.7
Guinea-Bissau				
Energy project...........................	May 7, 1991	2001/2030	11.3	15.2
Guyana				
Second structural adjustment credit (supplement)	Nov. 6, 1990	2000/2030	3.1	4.3
Second structural adjustment credit (supplement)	June 11, 1991	2000/2030	13.2	18.0
Haiti				
Economic and social fund project..........	Jan. 17, 1991	2001/2030	7.9	11.3
Fifth education project	June 11, 1991	2001/2031	9.4	12.6
Honduras				
Structural adjustment credit (supplement)...	Jan. 29, 1991	2001/2025	14.3	20.0
Social investment fund project	Feb. 28, 1991	2001/2025	14.3	20.0
India				
Integrated child development services project...............................	Sept. 4, 1990	2000/2025	73.6	96.0
Andhra Pradesh cyclone emergency reconstruction project	Oct. 4, 1990	2000/2025	126.1	170.0
Agricultural development project—Tamil Nadu.................................	Mar. 12, 1991	2001/2025	64.1	92.8

(*continued*)

Table 7-4 *(continued)*

Country and purpose	Date of approval	Maturities	Principal amount (millions) SDR	Principal amount (millions) US$ equivalent
India *(continued)*				
Second technician education project	Mar. 28, 1991	2001/2025	213.5	307.1
Maharashtra rural water supply and environmental sanitation project.........	May 2, 1991	2001/2026	76.4	109.9
Dam safety project......................	May 14, 1991	2001/2026	96.2	130.0
Industrial pollution control project.........	May 30, 1991	2001/2026	23.4	31.6
Kenya				
Financial sector adjustment credit (supplement)	Nov. 6, 1990	1999/2024	48.2	67.3
Export development project..............	Dec. 20, 1990	2001/2030	69.5	100.0
Second national agricultural extension project...............................	Dec. 20, 1990	2001/2030	17.4	24.9
Forestry development project	Dec. 20, 1990	2001/2030	13.9	19.9
Second agricultural sector adjustment operation	Jan. 17, 1991	2001/2030	52.2	75.0
Lao People's Democratic Republic				
Highway improvement project............	Mar. 21, 1991	2001/2031	32.1	45.0
Lesotho				
Industrial and agroindustries development project...............................	Dec. 18, 1990	2001/2030	15.1	21.0
Madagascar				
Public sector adjustment (supplement)......	Nov. 6, 1990	1998/2028	1.2	1.7
Livestock sector project	May 16, 1991	2001/2031	14.0	19.8
Health sector improvement project	May 28, 1991	2001/2031	22.9	31.0
Malawi				
Industrial and trade policy adjustment credit (supplement)	Nov. 6, 1990	1998/2028	5.1	7.2
Population, health and nutrition sector credit................................	Mar. 26, 1991	2001/2031	38.6	55.5
Financial sector and enterprise development project...............................	Mar. 26, 1991	2001/2031	22.3	32.0
Fisheries development project............	April 2, 1991	2001/2031	6.2	8.8
Mali				
Structural adjustment program	Dec. 11, 1990	2001/2030	50.3	70.0
Second health, population and rural water supply project	Mar. 19, 1991	2001/2030	19.2	26.6
Agricultural services project	May 2, 1991	2001/2031	18.3	24.4
Mauritania				
Public enterprise sector adjustment (supplement)	Nov. 6, 1990	2000/2030	2.9	4.0
Mozambique				
Agricultural rehabilitation and development project...............................	Sept. 6, 1990	2000/2030	11.9	15.4
Second education project	Dec. 20, 1990	2001/2030	38.7	53.7
Nepal				
Urban water supply and sanitation rehabilitation project	May 7, 1991	2001/2031	45.5	60.0
Niger				
Public works and employment project......	Feb. 19, 1991	2001/2031	13.9	20.0

Country and purpose	Date of approval	Maturities	Principal amount (millions) SDR	Principal amount (millions) US$ equivalent

Nigeria

Country and purpose	Date of approval	Maturities	SDR	US$ equivalent
Primary education project.................	Dec. 13, 1990	2001/2025	90.6	120.0
National population project	May 7, 1991	2001/2026	54.2	78.5
National agricultural research project	June 11, 1991	2001/2026	58.5	78.0

Pakistan

Rural water supply and sanitation project...	April 23, 1991	2001/2026	96.4	136.7
Family health project.....................	May 7, 1991	2001/2026	31.8	45.0
Third on-farm water management project...	May 21, 1991	2001/2026	33.4	47.3
Second SCARP transition project..........	June 4, 1991	2001/2026	14.8	20.0

Philippines

Environment and natural resources sector adjustment program...................	June 25, 1991	2001/2026	50.0	66.0

Rwanda

Second communications project	Dec. 11, 1990	2001/2030	8.9	12.8
First education sector project	April 9, 1991	2001/2031	16.2	23.3
First structural adjustment program........	June 19, 1991	2001/2031	67.5	90.0
First population project...................	June 19, 1991	2001/2031	14.5	19.6

St. Kitts and Nevis

Agricultural development support project...	May 28, 1991	2001/2026	1.1	1.5

São Tomé and Principe

Second multi-sector project	June 27, 1991	2001/2031	4.5	6.0

Senegal

Fourth structural adjustment credit (supplement)	Nov. 6, 1990	2000/2029	5.1	7.1
Human resources development project	May 30, 1991	2001/2031	25.4	35.0
Transport sector adjustment/investment program	June 13, 1991	2001/2031	49.9	65.0

Sri Lanka

Third roads project......................	Nov. 6, 1990	2001/2030	30.6	42.5
Economic restructuring credit (supplement).	Nov. 6, 1990	2000/2030	5.0	7.0
Public manufacturing enterprises adjustment credit................................	Nov. 27, 1990	2001/2030	90.7	120.0
Poverty alleviation project	April 25, 1991	2001/2031	40.6	57.5
Second telecommunications project	May 28, 1991	2001/2031	39.7	57.0
Fourth small and medium industries project.	May 28, 1991	2001/2031	33.3	45.0
National irrigation rehabilitation project	June 6, 1991	2001/2031	21.9	29.6

Tanzania

Agricultural adjustment credit (supplement).	Dec. 13, 1990	2000/2029	11.5	16.1
Petroleum sector rehabilitation project	Jan. 15, 1991	2001/2030	33.7	44.0
Railways restructuring project.............	June 13, 1991	2001/2031	56.1	76.0

Togo

Power rehabilitation and extension project..	Aug. 2, 1990	2000/2030	11.4	15.0
Technical education and vocational training project...............................	Sept. 4, 1990	2001/2030	7.0	9.2
Fourth structural adjustment program......	Dec. 18, 1990	2001/2030	39.6	55.0
Population and health sector adjustment program	Feb. 28, 1991	2001/2030	10.2	14.2

(continued)

Table 7-4 *(continued)*

Country and purpose	Date of approval	Maturities	Principal amount (millions) SDR	US$ equivalent
Uganda				
Livestock services project	Sept. 11, 1990	2000/2030	16.1	21.0
Second economic recovery credit (supplement)	Nov. 6, 1990	2000/2029	1.5	2.0
Agricultural sector adjustment credit	Dec. 13, 1990	2001/2030	69.5	100.0
First urban project	Jan. 22, 1991	2001/2030	20.7	28.7
Third power project	June 13, 1991	2001/2031	86.9	125.0
Vanuatu				
Housing project.........................	June 11, 1991	2001/2031	2.5	3.4
Yemen, Republic of				
Multi-mode transport project	Sept. 11, 1990	2001/2030	22.7	30.0
Secondary teacher training project	Mar. 28, 1991	2001/2031	13.5	19.4
Emergency recovery project	June 6, 1991	2001/2031	24.8	33.0
Fourth fisheries development project.......	June 13, 1991	2001/2031	9.4	13.2
Zaire				
Pilot feeder roads project	Sept. 11, 1990	2000/2030	9.6	12.4
Social sector project	Dec. 18, 1990	2001/2030	21.9	30.4
Education sector rehabilitation project	Mar. 5, 1991	2001/2030	15.0	21.0
Zambia				
Economic recovery program	Mar. 5, 1991	2001/2030	149.6	210.0
Economic recovery program (supplement) ..	Mar. 5, 1991	2001/2030	19.4	27.2
Mining sector technical assistance project ..	June 13, 1991	2001/2031	15.6	21.0
Social recovery project	June 19, 1991	2001/2031	14.8	20.0
Total			4,554.4	6,293.3

NOTE: Starting with the sixth replenishment of IDA, credits are expressed in special drawing rights (SDRs). The US-dollar equivalent of the original principal amount of credits denominated in SDRs is shown at the rate approved by the executive board. All credits approved in fiscal 1991 have a service charge of 0.75 percent on the disbursed and outstanding balance.

Table 7-5. **Trends in Lending, IBRD and IDA, Fiscal Years 1989–91**

Sector	1989			1990			1991		
	IBRD	IDA	Total	IBRD	IDA	Total	IBRD	IDA	Total
	Millions of U.S. dollars								
Agriculture and Rural Development	2,066.1	1,423.9	3,490.0	1,994.5	1,661.6	3,656.1	1,913.1	1,794.2	3,707.3
Development Finance Companies	2,500.0	378.7	2,878.7	945.0	326.7	1,271.7	1,695.0	156.8	1,851.8
Education	514.6	449.1	963.7	530.1	956.5	1,486.6	1,515.5	736.2	2,251.7
Energy									
Oil, gas, and coal	799.5	31.2	830.7	86.0	—	86.0	1,570.0	160.2	1,730.2
Power	2,608.5	424.4	3,032.9	2,998.5	219.8	3,218.3	1,189.0	155.0	1,344.0
Industry	1,858.0	124.5	1,982.5	650.5	145.1	795.6	1,767.1	215.9	1,983.0
Nonproject	1,892.0	471.5	2,363.5	2,600.0	444.0	3,044.0	1,940.0	881.9	2,821.9
Population, Health, and Nutrition	326.5	223.5	550.0	524.6	408.8	933.4	647.0	920.6	1,567.6
Public-sector Management	500.0	—	500.0	480.0	45.6	525.6	636.0	5.7	641.7
Small-scale Enterprises	585.0	—	585.0	50.0	157.5	207.5	166.0	45.0	211.0
Technical Assistance	64.0	154.3	218.3	96.0	45.0	141.0	284.5	82.2	366.7
Telecommunications	53.1	107.9	161.0	592.2	24.5	616.7	270.0	69.8	339.8
Transportation	1,137.7	693.1	1,830.8	2,250.2	535.1	2,785.3	915.9	472.1	1,388.0
Urban Development	959.0	229.5	1,188.5	702.7	299.4	1,002.1	1,077.1	178.3	1,255.4
Water Supply and Sewerage	569.2	222.0	791.2	679.4	252.4	931.8	806.0	419.4	1,225.4
Total	16,433.2	4,933.6	21,366.8	15,179.7	5,522.0	20,701.7	16,392.2	6,293.3	22,685.5
	Percentage distribution by sector								
Agriculture and Rural Development	12.6	28.9	16.3	13.1	30.1	17.7	11.7	28.5	16.3
Development Finance Companies	15.2	7.7	13.5	6.2	5.9	6.1	10.3	2.5	8.2
Education	3.1	9.1	4.5	3.5	17.3	7.2	9.2	11.7	9.9
Energy									
Oil, gas, and coal	4.9	0.6	3.9	0.6	—	0.4	9.6	2.5	7.6
Power	15.9	8.6	14.2	19.8	4.0	15.5	7.3	2.5	5.9
Industry	11.3	2.5	9.3	4.3	2.6	3.8	10.8	3.4	8.7
Nonproject	11.5	9.6	11.1	17.1	8.0	14.7	11.8	14.0	12.4
Population, Health, and Nutrition	2.0	4.5	2.6	3.5	7.4	4.5	3.9	14.6	6.9
Public-sector Management	3.0	—	2.3	3.2	0.8	2.5	3.9	0.1	2.8
Small-scale Enterprises	3.6	—	2.7	0.3	2.9	1.0	1.0	0.7	0.9
Technical Assistance	0.4	3.1	1.0	0.6	0.8	0.7	1.7	1.3	1.6
Telecommunications	0.3	2.2	0.8	3.9	0.4	3.0	1.6	1.1	1.5
Transportation	6.9	14.0	8.6	14.8	9.7	13.5	5.6	7.5	6.1
Urban Development	5.8	4.7	5.6	4.6	5.4	4.8	6.6	2.8	5.5
Water Supply and Sewerage	3.5	4.5	3.7	4.5	4.6	4.5	4.9	6.7	5.4
Total	100.0	100.0	100.0	100.0	100.0	100.0	100.0	100.0	100.0

— Zero.

NOTE: Details may not add to totals because of rounding.

Table 7-6. **IBRD and IDA Cumulative Lending Operations, by Major Purpose and Region, June 30, 1991**
(millions of US dollars)

Purpose[b]	IBRD loans to borrowers, by region[a]				
	Africa	Asia	Europe, Middle East, and North Africa	Latin America and the Caribbean	Total
Agriculture and Rural Development					
Agricultural credit	319.8	1,568.4	2,898.8	2,660.9	7,447.9
Agriculture sector loan	16.8	585.3	1,332.0	2,507.1	4,441.2
Agroindustry	30.0	325.2	1,149.7	1,228.4	2,733.3
Area development	1,628.6	1,756.1	996.5	3,385.4	7,766.6
Fisheries......................	0.0	106.7	48.0	16.2	170.9
Forestry	349.5	78.0	317.5	116.0	861.0
Irrigation and drainage	110.2	4,110.8	2,713.1	2,274.5	9,208.6
Livestock	170.7	318.0	236.0	1,042.0	1,766.7
Perennial crops	634.5	1,410.8	108.0	123.0	2,276.3
Research and extension.........	111.7	448.4	207.4	585.0	1,352.5
Total	3,371.8	10,707.7	10,007.0	13,938.5	38,025.0
Development Finance Companies ...	1,059.0	5,377.8	6,843.7	7,311.1	20,591.6
Education	392.1	3,390.2	2,592.5	1,795.4	8,170.2
Energy					
Oil, gas, and coal	385.2	4,614.8	2,522.8	1,382.2	8,905.0
Power	1,782.1	14,747.7	6,707.2	11,239.7	34,476.7
Total	2,167.3	19,362.5	9,230.0	12,621.9	43,381.7
Industry					
Engineering	27.7	10.0	11.0	9.5	58.2
Fertilizer and other chemicals ...	0.0	2,167.8	791.4	848.5	3,807.7
Industry sector loan............	15.6	2,770.1	2,802.9	1,359.5	6,948.1
Iron and steel	20.0	189.0	512.8	1,067.0	1,788.8
Mining, other extractive	533.5	0.0	237.2	747.5	1,518.2
Paper and pulp	48.4	105.5	263.3	20.0	437.2
Textiles.......................	63.0	157.4	307.3	0.0	527.7
Tourism sector loan............	54.5	25.0	96.6	187.5	363.6
Total	762.7	5,424.8	5,022.5	4,239.5	15,449.5
Nonproject	1,943.6	3,829.3	6,085.9[c]	5,215.6	17,074.4
Population, Health, and Nutrition ..	289.4	618.8	335.2	1,105.8	2,349.2
Public-sector Management	0.0	32.0	130.0	1,454.0	1,616.0
Small-scale Enterprises............	440.7	1,431.5	834.0	1,985.6	4,691.8
Technical Assistance	138.8	53.0	254.8	286.8	733.4
Telecommunications	510.2	1,348.2	1,091.8	508.3	3,458.5
Transportation					
Airlines and airports	59.0	14.8	7.0	218.5	299.3
Highways	1,817.8	5,096.7	3,640.3	5,828.3	16,383.1
Pipelines	0.0	0.0	94.5	23.3	117.8
Ports and waterways	285.9	1,722.5	1,716.0	523.7	4,248.1
Railways......................	733.5	3,013.8	1,483.9	1,938.5	7,169.7
Transportation sector loan	61.6	377.2	556.0	188.6	1,183.4
Total	2,957.8	10,225.0	7,497.7	8,720.9	29,401.4
Urban Development	933.7	3,159.4	981.3	3,853.1	8,927.5
Water Supply and Sewerage	1,059.8	1,685.4	3,064.8	3,373.7	9,183.7
Grand total..................	16,026.9	66,645.6	53,971.2	66,410.2	203,053.9

a. Except for the total amount shown in footnote d, no account is taken of cancellations subsequent to original commitment. IBRD loans to the IFC are excluded.

b. Operations have been classified by the major purpose they finance. Many projects include activity in more than one sector or subsector.

IDA credits to borrowers, by region[a]					
Africa	Asia	Europe, Middle East, and North Africa	Latin America and the Caribbean	Total	Total IBRD and IDA
385.6	2,559.3	305.5	23.5	3,273.9	10,721.8
848.3	393.7	40.0	1.4	1,283.4	5,724.6
361.4	676.9	138.0	16.5	1,192.8	3,926.1
1,602.1	1,983.7	200.6	86.1	3,872.5	11,639.1
55.7	192.3	67.3	0.0	315.3	486.2
358.6	1,010.0	1.7	12.8	1,383.1	2,244.1
855.6	5,619.5	1,281.5	18.5	7,775.1	16,983.7
457.2	331.2	49.5	67.5	905.4	2,672.1
488.9	491.5	15.0	3.2	998.6	3,274.9
562.3	735.1	159.2	21.0	1,477.6	2,830.1
5,975.7	13,993.2	2,258.3	250.5	22,477.7	60,502.7
1,281.2	578.6	273.7	144.1	2,277.6	22,869.2
2,045.2	2,393.5	730.5	86.2	5,255.4	13,425.6
427.5	407.4	111.0	33.0	978.9	9,883.9
1,130.1	3,635.3	393.6	189.7	5,348.7	39,825.4
1,557.6	4,042.7	504.6	222.7	6,327.6	49,709.3
16.7	0.0	0.0	0.0	16.7	74.9
35.0	884.0	76.4	0.0	995.4	4,803.1
302.7	335.8	29.5	0.0	668.0	7,616.1
40.0	0.0	0.0	0.0	40.0	1,828.8
13.9	16.0	0.0	49.5	79.4	1,597.6
50.0	0.0	0.0	0.0	50.0	487.2
20.0	104.7	7.0	0.0	131.7	659.4
18.0	20.2	48.5	0.0	86.7	450.3
496.3	1,360.7	161.4	49.5	2,067.9	17,517.4
3,127.5	3,070.5	395.0	287.4	6,380.4	23,954.8
842.1	1,337.3	313.2	99.5	2,592.1	4,941.3
307.7	0.0	0.0	0.0	307.7	1,923.7
228.7	281.5	88.8	27.5	626.5	5,318.3
737.3	155.2	44.6	38.5	975.6	1,709.0
352.1	869.3	142.7	0.0	1,364.1	4,822.6
14.0	7.5	2.5	0.0	24.0	323.3
2,716.1	1,183.1	282.3	167.3	4,348.8	20,731.9
0.0	0.0	0.0	0.0	0.0	117.8
413.9	372.7	44.7	16.0	847.3	5,095.4
587.6	1,124.2	138.5	45.0	1,895.3	9,065.0
392.2	348.5	30.0	0.0	770.7	1,954.1
4,123.8	3,036.0	498.0	228.3	7,886.1	37,287.5
868.5	1,448.7	251.3	127.0	2,695.5	11,623.0
675.5	1,453.2	573.6	78.8	2,781.1	11,964.8
22,619.2	34,020.4	6,235.7	1,640.0	64,515.3	267,569.2[d]

c. Includes $497 million in European reconstruction loans made before 1952.

d. Cancellations amount to $14,080.12 million for the IBRD and $2,191.09 million for IDA, totaling $16,271.21 million.

Table 7-7. IBRD and IDA Cumulative Lending Operations, by Borrower or Guarantor, June 30, 1991
(amounts in millions of US dollars)

Borrower or guarantor	IBRD loans		IDA credits		Total	
	Number	Amount	Number	Amount	Number	Amount
Afghanistan	—	—	20	230.1	20	230.1
Algeria	46	3,965.5	—	—	46	3,965.5
Angola	—	—	1	23.0	1	23.0
Argentina	46	5,800.3	—	—	46	5,800.3
Australia	7	417.7	—	—	7	417.7
Austria	9	106.4	—	—	9	106.4
Bahamas, The	5	42.8	—	—	5	42.8
Bangladesh	1	46.1	132	5,708.3	133	5,754.4
Barbados	9	74.2	—	—	9	74.2
Belgium	4	76.0	—	—	4	76.0
Belize	4	26.2	—	—	4	26.2
Benin	—	—	33	450.8	33	450.8
Bhutan	—	—	5	22.8	5	22.8
Bolivia	14	299.3	33	637.2	47	936.5
Botswana	20	280.7	6	15.8	26	296.5
Brazil	189	18,936.6	—	—	189	18,936.6
Bulgaria	1	17.0	—	—	1	17.0
Burkina Faso	—	1.9	35	538.1	35	540.0
Burundi	1	4.8	39	564.9	40	569.7
Cameroon	43	1,271.4	15	253.0	58	1,524.4
Cape Verde	—	—	4	20.1	4	20.1
Caribbean Region	3	63.0	2	32.0	5	95.0
Central African Republic	—	—	22	361.1	22	361.1
Chad	—	—	24	331.9	24	331.9
Chile	45	2,718.7	—	19.0	45	2,737.7
China	56	5,881.7	37	4,905.1	93	10,786.8
Colombia	129	7,172.6	—	19.5	129	7,192.1
Comoros	—	—	10	55.1	10	55.1
Congo	10	216.7	8	74.6	18	291.3
Costa Rica	33	676.9	—	5.5	33	682.4
Côte d'Ivoire	59	2,537.9	1	7.5	60	2,545.4
Cyprus	29	386.8	—	—	29	386.8
Czechoslovakia	1	450.0	—	—	1	450.0
Denmark	3	85.0	—	—	3	85.0
Djibouti	—	—	8	51.6	8	51.6
Dominica	—	—	3	11.0	3	11.0
Dominican Republic	21	566.9	3	22.0	24	588.9
East African Community	10	244.8	—	—	10	244.8
Eastern and Southern Africa Region	—	—	1	45.0	1	45.0
Ecuador	47	1,530.9	5	36.9	52	1,567.8
Egypt	52	3,506.8	27	1,121.2	79	4,628.0
El Salvador	21	382.1	2	25.6	23	407.7
Equatorial Guinea	—	—	7	37.1	7	37.1
Ethiopia	12	108.6	47	1,264.8	59	1,373.4
Fiji	12	137.9	—	—	12	137.9

Borrower or guarantor	IBRD loans		IDA credits		Total	
	Number	Amount	Number	Amount	Number	Amount
Finland	18	316.8	—	—	18	316.8
France	1	250.0	—	—	1	250.0
Gabon	9	154.3	—	—	9	154.3
Gambia, The	—	—	20	134.3	20	134.3
Ghana	9	207.0	58	1,768.2	67	1,975.2
Greece	17	490.8	—	—	17	490.8
Grenada	—	—	1	5.0	1	5.0
Guatemala	21	585.1	—	—	21	585.1
Guinea	3	75.2	36	737.1	39	812.3
Guinea-Bissau	—	—	16	168.0	16	168.0
Guyana	12	80.0	7	157.6	19	237.6
Haiti	1	2.6	30	426.9	31	429.5
Honduras	33	717.3	7	123.2	40	840.5
Hungary	25	2,892.9	—	—	25	2,892.9
Iceland	10	47.1	—	—	10	47.1
India	142	19,431.2	180	17,893.1	322	37,324.3
Indonesia	159	16,466.9	46	931.8	205	17,398.7
Iran, Islamic Republic of	34	1,460.7	—	—	34	1,460.7
Iraq	6	156.2	—	—	6	156.2
Ireland	8	152.5	—	—	8	152.5
Israel	11	284.5	—	—	11	284.5
Italy	8	399.6	—	—	8	399.6
Jamaica	53	1,012.9	—	—	53	1,012.9
Japan	31	862.9	—	—	31	862.9
Jordan	33	1,043.4	15	85.3	48	1,128.7
Kenya	46	1,200.0	53	1,684.5	99	2,884.5
Korea, Republic of	96	7,404.0	6	110.8	102	7,514.8
Lao People's Democratic Republic	—	—	14	240.2	14	240.2
Lebanon	4	116.6	—	—	4	116.6
Lesotho	—	—	20	178.2	20	178.2
Liberia	21	156.0	14	114.5	35	270.5
Luxembourg	1	12.0	—	—	1	12.0
Madagascar	5	32.9	52	1,051.4	57	1,084.3
Malawi	9	124.1	49	962.0	58	1,086.1
Malaysia	77	2,784.6	—	—	77	2,784.6
Maldives	—	—	4	23.9	4	23.9
Mali	—	1.9	42	743.6	42	745.5
Malta	1	7.5	—	—	1	7.5
Mauritania	3	146.0	26	245.9	29	391.9
Mauritius	23	306.1	4	20.2	27	326.3
Mexico	130	19,245.6	—	—	130	19,245.6
Morocco	93	5,803.7	3	50.8	96	5,854.5
Mozambique	—	—	14	562.1	14	562.1
Myanmar	3	33.4	30	804.0	33	837.4
Nepal	—	—	57	1,118.3	57	1,118.3

(continued)

Table 7-7. (continued)

Borrower or guarantor	IBRD loans		IDA credits		Total	
	Number	Amount	Number	Amount	Number	Amount
Netherlands	8	244.0	—	—	8	244.0
New Zealand	6	126.8	—	—	6	126.8
Nicaragua	27	233.6	4	60.0	31	293.6
Niger	—	—	33	470.5	33	470.5
Nigeria	82	6,138.2	7	532.9	89	6,671.1
Norway	6	145.0	—	—	6	145.0
Oman	11	157.1	—	—	11	157.1
Pakistan	75	4,603.2	85	3,486.0	160	8,089.2
Panama	31	696.3	—	—	31	696.3
Papua New Guinea	23	462.1	9	113.2	32	575.3
Paraguay	27	458.1	6	45.5	33	503.6
Peru	60	1,711.9	—	—	60	1,711.9
Philippines	121	7,620.3	3	188.2	124	7,808.5
Poland	12	2,221.0	—	—	12	2,221.0
Portugal	32	1,338.8	—	—	32	1,338.8
Romania	34	2,364.3	—	—	34	2,364.3
Rwanda	—	—	40	572.3	40	572.3
St. Kitts and Nevis	1	1.5	—	1.5	1	3.0
St. Lucia	1	2.5	—	5.2	1	7.7
St. Vincent and the Grenadines	1	1.4	1	6.4	2	7.8
São Tomé and Principe	—	—	6	37.7	6	37.7
Senegal	19	164.9	51	939.8	70	1,104.7
Seychelles	1	6.2	—	—	1	6.2
Sierra Leone	4	18.7	12	116.1	16	134.8
Singapore	14	181.3	—	—	14	181.3
Solomon Islands	—	—	5	17.0	5	17.0
Somalia	—	—	39	492.1	39	492.1
South Africa	11	241.8	—	—	11	241.8
Spain	12	478.7	—	—	12	478.7
Sri Lanka	12	210.7	56	1,682.4	68	1,893.1
Sudan	8	166.0	47	1,336.9	55	1,502.9
Swaziland	11	75.8	2	7.8	13	83.6
Syrian Arab Republic	17	613.2	3	47.3	20	660.5
Tanzania	18	318.2	71	1,905.3	89	2,223.5
Thailand	95	4,248.6	6	125.1	101	4,373.7
Togo	1	20.0	34	509.5	35	529.5
Tonga	—	—	2	5.0	2	5.0
Trinidad and Tobago	16	189.5	—	—	16	189.5
Tunisia	85	2,598.2	5	74.6	90	2,672.8
Turkey	104	11,065.2	10	178.5	114	11,243.7
Uganda	1	8.4	41	1,367.3	42	1,375.7
Uruguay	34	1,113.1	—	—	34	1,113.1
Vanuatu	—	—	4	15.4	4	15.4
Venezuela	20	2,068.3	—	—	20	2,068.3
Viet Nam	—	—	1	60.0	1	60.0

Borrower or guarantor	IBRD loans		IDA credits		Total	
	Number	Amount	Number	Amount	Number	Amount
Western Africa Region	2	21.1	3	92.5	5	113.6
Western Samoa..........................	—	—	8	40.5	8	40.5
Yemen, Republic of.....................	—	—	94	961.9	94	961.9
Yugoslavia	90	6,114.7	—	—	90	6,114.7
Zaire	7	330.0	57	1,124.9	64	1,454.9
Zambia	28	679.1	22	595.3	50	1,274.4
Zimbabwe..............................	22	768.2	3	53.9	25	822.1
Other[a]	14	329.4	4	15.3	18	344.7
Total	3,302	203,053.9	2,108	64,515.3	5,410	267,569.2

— Zero.

NOTE: Joint IBRD/IDA operations are counted only once, as IBRD operations. When more than one loan is made for a single project, the operation is counted only once. Details may not add to totals because of rounding.

a. Represents IBRD loans and IDA credits made at a time when the authorities on Taiwan represented China in the World Bank (prior to May 15, 1980).

Financial Statements of the International Bank for Reconstruction and Development

Balance Sheets

June 30, 1991 and June 30, 1990
Expressed in thousands of US dollars

	1991	1990
Assets		
DUE FROM BANKS		
Unrestricted currencies	$ 127,512	$ 115,747
Currencies subject to restrictions—Note A	588,886	609,009
	716,398	724,756
INVESTMENTS—Note B		
Obligations of governments and other official entities	11,895,858	8,543,644
Time deposits and other obligations of banks and other financial institutions	8,472,355	8,302,080
	20,368,213	16,845,724
CASH COLLATERAL INVESTED—Note B	4,568,643	4,522,818
NONNEGOTIABLE, NONINTEREST-BEARING DEMAND OBLIGATIONS ON ACCOUNT OF SUBSCRIBED CAPITAL (subject to restrictions—Note A)	1,604,242	1,595,818
AMOUNTS REQUIRED TO MAINTAIN VALUE OF CURRENCY HOLDINGS—Note A		
Amounts receivable	787,058	704,546
Amounts deferred	342,846	268,781
	1,129,904	973,327
OTHER RECEIVABLES		
Net receivable from currency swaps—Note D	514,500	432,150
Receivable from investment securities sold	1,365,611	1,690,338
Accrued income on loans	2,138,623	2,155,651
Accrued interest on investments	172,563	186,373
	4,191,297	4,464,512
LOANS OUTSTANDING (see Summary Statement of Loans and Note C)		
Total loans	143,606,763	138,269,781
Less loans approved but not yet effective	12,789,900	10,202,300
Less undisbursed balance of effective loans	40,179,268	39,015,047
	90,637,595	89,052,434
OTHER ASSETS		
Unamortized issuance costs of borrowings	596,571	613,356
Miscellaneous	828,369	620,480
	1,424,940	1,233,836
Total assets	$124,641,232	$119,413,225

	1991	1990
Liabilities		
BORROWINGS (see Summary Statements of Borrowings and Note D)		
Short-term.	$ 5,388,081	$ 5,277,320
Medium- and long-term	84,797,428	81,218,793
	90,185,509	86,496,113
PAYABLE FOR CASH COLLATERAL RECEIVED	4,568,643	4,522,818
AMOUNTS REQUIRED TO MAINTAIN VALUE OF CURRENCY HOLDINGS—Note A		
Amounts payable.	42,836	75,050
Amounts deferred.	394,823	453,038
	437,659	528,088
OTHER LIABILITIES		
Accrued charges on borrowings	2,717,596	2,654,482
Net payable for currency swaps—Note D.	967,090	1,612,738
Payable for investment securities purchased.	1,847,269	1,407,224
Due to International Development Association and Debt Reduction Facility for IDA-Only Countries—Note G	870,059	946,502
Accounts payable and other liabilities	398,272	482,085
	6,800,286	7,103,031
ACCUMULATED PROVISION FOR LOAN LOSSES—Note C.	1,990,000	1,250,000
Total liabilities.	103,982,097	99,900,050
Equity		
CAPITAL STOCK (see Statement of Subscriptions to Capital Stock and Voting Power and Note A) Authorized capital (1,448,500 shares—June 30, 1991; 1,420,500 shares—June 30, 1990)		
Subscribed capital (1,153,231 shares—June 30, 1991; 1,038,357 shares—June 30, 1990)...	139,120,022	125,262,197
Less uncalled portion of subscriptions.	129,727,473	116,342,274
	9,392,549	8,919,923
PAYMENTS ON ACCOUNT OF PENDING SUBSCRIPTIONS (see Statement of Subscriptions to Capital Stock and Voting Power).	49,359	59,311
RETAINED EARNINGS (see Statements of Changes in Retained Earnings and Note E)	11,936,732	11,032,616
CUMULATIVE TRANSLATION ADJUSTMENT (see Statements of Changes in Cumulative Translation Adjustment).	(719,505)	(498,675)
Total equity.	20,659,135	19,513,175
Total liabilities and equity	$124,641,232	$119,413,225

See Notes to Financial Statements.

Statements of Income

For the fiscal years ended June 30, 1991 and June 30, 1990
Expressed in thousands of US dollars

	1991	1990
Income		
Income from loans—Note C		
Interest	$7,698,716	$6,627,871
Commitment charges	104,320	139,223
Income from investments—Note B	1,908,379	1,762,640
Other income	11,596	58,117
Total income	9,723,011	8,587,851
Expenses		
Borrowing expenses		
Interest on borrowings—Note D	6,778,487	6,077,627
Amortization of issuance costs and other borrowing costs	119,264	152,003
Interest on payable for cash collateral received	209,833	270,712
Administrative expenses—Notes F and H	573,870	507,892
Provision for loan losses—Note C	774,977	357,416
Other expenses	3,293	10,599
Total expenses	8,459,724	7,376,249
Operating Income	1,263,287	1,211,602
Contributions to special programs—Note F	63,311	60,242
Cumulative effect of change in accounting principle—Note I	—	105,500
Net Income	$1,199,976	$1,045,860

Statements of Changes in Retained Earnings

For the fiscal years ended June 30, 1991 and June 30, 1990
Expressed in thousands of US dollars

	1991	1990
Retained earnings at beginning of fiscal year	$11,032,616	$10,086,756
Transfer to International Development Association—Note G	(266,567)	—
Transfer to Global Environment Trust Fund—Note G	(29,293)	—
Transfer to Debt Reduction Facility for IDA-Only Countries—Note G	—	(100,000)
Net income for fiscal year	1,199,976	1,045,860
Retained earnings at end of fiscal year	$11,936,732	$11,032,616

Statements of Changes in Cumulative Translation Adjustment

For the fiscal years ended June 30, 1991 and June 30, 1990
Expressed in thousands of US dollars

	1991	1990
Cumulative translation adjustment at beginning of fiscal year	$(498,675)	$(1,124,689)
Translation adjustments for fiscal year	(220,830)	626,014
Cumulative translation adjustment at end of fiscal year	$(719,505)	$ (498,675)

See Notes to Financial Statements.

Statements of Cash Flows

For the fiscal years ended June 30, 1991 and June 30, 1990
Expressed in thousands of US dollars

	1991	1990
Cash flows from lending and development activities		
Loan disbursements.	$(11,581,191)	$(14,048,450)
Loan principal repayments	9,080,318	7,539,818
Loan principal prepayments	201,645	598,501
Transfer to International Development Association—Note G.	(322,495)	—
Transfer to Global Environment Trust Fund—Note G	(29,478)	—
Transfer to Debt Reduction Facility for IDA-Only Countries—Note G	(8,422)	—
Net cash used in lending and development activities	(2,659,623)	(5,910,131)
Cash flows from financing activities		
Medium- and long-term borrowings		
New issues.	10,841,411	12,596,193
Retirements.	(7,138,678)	(10,669,610)
Net cash flows from short-term borrowings	(80,128)	(104,899)
Net cash flows from currency swaps.	(404,370)	(436,549)
Net cash flows from capital transactions	330,768	216,361
Net cash provided by financing activities.	3,549,003	1,601,496
Cash flows from operating activities		
Net income	1,199,976	1,045,860
Adjustments to reconcile net income to net cash provided by operating activities		
Depreciation and amortization.	372,593	391,625
Provision for loan losses	774,977	357,416
Changes in assets and liabilities		
Increase in accrued income on loans and investments	(1,656)	(75,049)
(Increase) decrease in miscellaneous assets.	(230,151)	17,980
Increase in accrued charges on borrowings	119,795	115,586
Decrease in accounts payable and other liabilities	(94,457)	(176,184)
Net cash provided by operating activities.	2,141,077	1,677,234
Effect of exchange rate changes on unrestricted cash and liquid investments	(260,975)	515,209
Net increase (decrease) in unrestricted cash and liquid investments.	2,769,482	(2,116,192)
Unrestricted cash and liquid investments at beginning of fiscal year	17,244,585	19,360,777
Unrestricted cash and liquid investments at end of fiscal year.	$ 20,014,067	$ 17,244,585
Composed of		
Investments.	$ 20,368,213	$ 16,845,724
Unrestricted currencies.	127,512	115,747
Net (payable) receivable for investment securities purchased/sold	(481,658)	283,114
	$ 20,014,067	$ 17,244,585
Supplemental disclosure		
(Decrease) increase resulting from exchange rate fluctuations		
Loans outstanding.	$ (714,067)	$ 5,200,458
Borrowings	(280,013)	4,034,128
Net payable for currency swaps.	(323,593)	635,154

See Notes to Financial Statements.

Summary Statement of Loans

June 30, 1991
Expressed in thousands of US dollars

Borrower or guarantor[a]	Total loans	Loans approved but not yet effective[b]	Undisbursed loans[c]	Loans outstanding	Percentage of total loans outstanding
Algeria	$ 2,801,927	$ 191,600	$1,460,998	$1,149,329	1.27
Argentina[d]	3,855,168	356,500	1,028,433	2,470,235	2.73
Australia[a]	4,944	—	—	4,944	0.01
Bahamas, The	29,580	—	11,456	18,124	0.02
Bahamas, Barbados, Grenada, Guyana, Jamaica, Trinidad and Tobago, and United Kingdom[e]	47,235	—	20,000	27,235	0.03
Bangladesh	59,514	—	—	59,514	0.07
Barbados	40,100	—	8,668	31,432	0.03
Belize	25,918	—	8,963	16,955	0.02
Bolivia[d]	166,967	—	—	166,967	0.18
Botswana	176,989	—	39,013	137,976	0.15
Brazil	12,711,207	1,543,000	3,567,788	7,600,419	8.39
Bulgaria	17,000	17,000	—	—	—
Cameroon	1,020,524	—	373,106	647,418	0.71
Chile	2,221,659	50,000	408,575	1,763,084	1.95
China	5,507,612	397,100	2,211,129	2,899,383	3.20
Colombia	4,824,014	260,000	1,081,972	3,482,042	3.84
Congo	170,088	15,800	5,243	149,045	0.16
Costa Rica	491,769	60,000	80,516	351,253	0.39
Côte d'Ivoire[f]	2,048,266	—	239,731	1,808,535	2.00
Côte d'Ivoire, Ghana, and Togo[g]	304	—	—	304	*
Côte d'Ivoire and Senegal[h]	19,552	—	15,566	3,986	*
Cyprus	151,562	30,000	87,879	33,683	0.04
Czechoslovakia	450,000	450,000	—	—	—
Dominican Republic	409,060	94,000	88,064	226,996	0.25
Ecuador	1,097,721	163,000	176,711	758,010	0.84
Egypt	2,356,658	415,000	643,165	1,298,493	1.43
El Salvador	277,634	26,000	125,403	126,231	0.14
Ethiopia	22,520	—	—	22,520	0.02
Fiji	86,104	—	25,485	60,619	0.07
Gabon	91,571	—	23,068	68,503	0.08
Ghana	97,171	—	—	97,171	0.11
Greece	8,593	—	—	8,593	0.01
Guatemala	440,723	61,500	122,696	256,527	0.28
Guinea	18,430	—	—	18,430	0.02
Guyana	51,757	—	—	51,757	0.06
Honduras	564,650	—	70,729	493,921	0.54
Hungary	2,696,502	250,000	901,978	1,544,524	1.70
Iceland	5,347	—	—	5,347	0.01
India	15,589,466	915,000	7,084,548	7,589,918	8.37
Indonesia	14,086,827	405,000	4,255,165	9,426,662	10.40
Iran, Islamic Republic of	312,166	250,000	—	62,166	0.07
Iraq	42,170	—	—	42,170	0.05
Ireland	7,801	—	—	7,801	0.01
Jamaica	760,801	11,500	125,207	624,094	0.69
Jordan	757,716	15,000	275,635	467,081	0.52
Kenya[i]	748,856	—	4,218	744,638	0.82
Kenya, Tanzania, and Uganda[g]	1,463	—	—	1,463	*
Korea, Republic of	3,369,502	250,000	358,340	2,761,162	3.05
Lebanon	27,375	—	—	27,375	0.03
Liberia	129,317	—	—	129,317	0.14
Madagascar	22,310	—	—	22,310	0.02
Malawi	84,126	—	1,850	82,276	0.09
Malaysia	1,425,589	—	468,835	956,754	1.06

Borrower or guarantor[a]	Total loans	Loans approved but not yet effective[b]	Undisbursed loans[c]	Loans outstanding	Percentage of total loans outstanding
Mauritania	$ 44,281	$ —	$ —	$ 44,281	0.05
Mauritius	215,861	10,000	47,093	158,768	0.18
Mexico	14,389,480	1,282,000	2,581,064	$10,526,416	11.61
Morocco	4,500,760	626,000	960,374	2,914,386	3.22
Nicaragua	215,922	—	—	215,922	0.24
Nigeria	5,300,624	700,000	1,612,942	2,987,682	3.30
Oman	89,829	—	44,521	45,303	0.05
Pakistan	3,737,242	298,100	1,591,095	1,848,047	2.04
Panama	446,839	—	49,722	397,117	0.44
Papua New Guinea[a]	368,873	50,800	100,539	217,534	0.24
Paraguay	270,975	—	24,924	246,051	0.27
Peru	1,215,246	—	192,584	1,022,662	1.13
Philippines	5,752,603	323,000	1,791,275	3,638,328	4.01
Poland	2,209,014	1,140,000	918,633	150,381	0.17
Portugal	342,618	—	126,412	216,206	0.24
Romania	180,000	130,000	—	—	—
St. Kitts and Nevis	1,500	1,500	—	—	—
St. Lucia	2,500	—	2,500	—	—
St. Vincent and the Grenadines	1,400	—	1,400	—	—
Senegal	73,580	—	—	73,580	0.08
Seychelles	5,350	—	—	5,350	0.01
Sierra Leone	9,354	—	—	9,354	0.01
Singapore	4,249	—	—	4,249	*
Sri Lanka	72,363	—	—	72,363	0.08
Sudan	16,390	—	—	16,390	0.02
Swaziland	30,973	—	—	30,973	0.03
Syrian Arab Republic	423,248	—	—	423,248	0.47
Tanzania[i]	203,524	—	—	203,524	0.22
Thailand	2,441,467	32,000	278,306	2,131,161	2.35
Trinidad and Tobago	76,978	20,700	23,433	32,845	0.04
Tunisia	1,778,459	56,000	394,751	1,327,708	1.46
Turkey	8,821,133	900,000	2,195,588	5,725,545	6.32
Uganda	29,300	—	—	29,300	0.03
Uruguay	740,411	65,000	334,430	340,951	0.38
Venezuela	1,640,674	100,000	530,978	1,009,696	1.11
Yugoslavia	3,281,334	714,200	487,213	2,079,921	2.29
Zaire	91,265	—	34,882	56,383	0.06
Zambia	341,252	—	—	341,252	0.38
Zimbabwe	633,258	63,600	206,141	363,517	0.40
Subtotal members**	142,431,949	12,789,900	39,930,961	89,711,088	
International Finance Corporation	1,174,814	—	248,307	926,507	1.02
Total—June 30, 1991**	$143,606,763	$12,789,900	$40,179,268	$90,637,595	100.00
Total—June 30, 1990	$138,269,781	$10,202,300	$39,015,047	$89,052,434	

* Less than 0.005 percent.

** May differ from the sum of the individual figures shown because of rounding.

a. In some instances loans were made, with the guarantee of a member, in territories which at the time were included in that member's membership but which subsequently became independent and members of the IBRD. Liabilities for these loans are shown under the name of the original member (whose guarantee continues unaffected). Loans with outstanding balances equivalent to $4,944,000 ($7,405,000—June 30, 1990) are shown under Australia, the guarantor, but represent obligations of Papua New Guinea.

b. Loan agreements totaling $4,361,600,000 ($4,145,700,000—June 30, 1990) have been signed, but the loans do not become effective and disbursements thereunder do not start until the borrowers and guarantors, if any, take certain actions and furnish certain documents to the IBRD. Loans totaling $8,428,300,000 ($6,056,600,000—June 30, 1990) have been approved by the IBRD but the related agreements have not been signed.

(continued)

Summary Statement of Loans   *(continued)*

June 30, 1991
Expressed in thousands of US dollars

c. Of the undisbursed balance, the IBRD has entered into irrevocable commitments to disburse $1,456,262,000 ($1,054,214,000—June 30, 1990).

d. One loan with an outstanding balance equivalent to $654,000 ($1,939,000—June 30, 1990) is shown under Bolivia (Guarantor) but is also guaranteed by Argentina.

e. Loans made to the Caribbean Development Bank for the benefit of the territories of the members listed (in the case of the United Kingdom, the territories are those of its Associated States and Dependencies in the Caribbean region). The members will be severally liable as guarantors to the extent of subloans made in their territories.

f. One loan with an outstanding balance equivalent to $7,590,000 ($10,438,000—June 30, 1990) is shown under Côte d'Ivoire (Guarantor) but is also partially guaranteed by Burkina Faso.

g. Members are jointly and severally liable.

h. Loan made to the West African Development Bank for the benefit of the territories of the members listed. The members will be severally liable as guarantors to the extent of subloans made in their territories.

i. Includes portions of loans made to corporations of the East African Community.

Summary of Currencies Repayable on Loans Outstanding

Currency	1991	1990	Currency	1991	1990
Australian dollars	$ 93,587	$ 102,944	Malaysian ringgit	$ 35,498	$ 41,183
Austrian schillings	99,795	221,559	Mexican pesos	215	229
Belgian francs	212,229	320,759	Myanmar kyats	1,437	1,441
Canadian dollars	202,113	198,518	Netherlands guilders	4,107,986	5,474,004
Danish kroner	64,183	64,587	Norwegian kroner	64,497	66,848
Deutsche mark	19,059,906	19,832,796	Portuguese escudos	17,698	19,094
European currency units	44,094	534,209	Pounds sterling	280,575	306,034
Finnish markkaa	54,828	53,925	Rials Omani	638	638
French francs	433,450	394,181	Saudi Arabian riyals	92,479	93,050
Greek drachmas	597	743	Singapore dollars	4,522	4,339
Hungarian forint	1,797	—	South African rand	39,699	39,761
Icelandic krónur	1,112	1,169	Spanish pesetas	123,012	103,988
Indian rupees	27,167	24,581	Swedish kronor	89,114	92,838
Iranian rials	15,156	15,751	Swiss francs	13,926,195	15,490,459
Iraqi dinars	2,609	2,609	Tunisian dinars	116	128
Irish pounds	23,567	24,126	United Arab Emirates dirhams	667	666
Italian lire	176,393	255,796	United States dollars	25,415,032	21,723,059
Japanese yen	25,649,243	23,170,309	Venezuelan bolivares	9,384	11,048
Kuwaiti dinars	173,365	194,186	Other currencies	30	49
Libyan dinars	5,668	101,722			
Luxembourg francs	87,942	69,108	Loans outstanding	$90,637,595	$89,052,434

Maturity Structure of Loans*

Period	
July 1, 1991 through June 30, 1992	$ 9,043,180
July 1, 1992 through June 30, 1993	8,604,343
July 1, 1993 through June 30, 1994	9,252,109
July 1, 1994 through June 30, 1995	9,899,449
July 1, 1995 through June 30, 1996	10,611,004
July 1, 1996 through June 30, 2001	46,886,477
July 1, 2001 through June 30, 2006	27,541,894
July 1, 2006 through June 30, 2011	8,917,196
Undetermined**	61,211
Total	$130,816,863

* Total loans less loans approved but not yet effective.
** Represents cancellations and other adjustments that have not been allocated to specific maturities.
See Notes to Financial Statements.

Summary Statements of Borrowings

June 30, 1991 and June 30, 1990
Expressed in thousands of US dollars

Medium- and Long-term Borrowings and Currency Swaps

| | Medium- and long-term borrowings | | | Swap agreements[a] | | | Net currency obligations | |
| | Principal outstanding[b] | | Weighted average cost (%) | Currency swap payable (receivable) | | Weighted average cost (return) % | | |
	1991	1990	1991	1991	1990	1991	1991	1990
Australian dollars	$ 886,397	$ 839,069	13.79	$ (899,526)	$ (855,012)	(13.74)	$ (13,129)	$ (15,943)
Austrian schillings	348,212	375,908	7.85	(143,185)	(154,573)	(8.06)	205,027	221,335
Belgian francs	500,643	541,252	8.66	(445,081)	(481,184)	(8.87)	55,562	60,068
Canadian dollars	1,576,217	1,475,976	10.64	(1,305,979)	(1,198,870)	(10.73)[c]	270,238	277,106
Danish kroner	219,978	240,688	10.17	(217,727)	(238,257)	(10.16)	2,251	2,431
Deutsche mark	12,526,389	14,674,509	7.35	4,801,859	3,485,780	7.48[c]	17,281,843	18,111,299
				(46,405)	(48,990)	(5.90)[c]		
European currency units	1,709,727	1,927,920	8.63	(1,319,656)	(1,438,677)	(8.41)	390,071	489,243
Finnish markkaa	353,440	383,142	9.82	(349,605)	(378,985)	(9.80)	3,835	4,157
French francs	853,018	751,947	9.72	(356,964)	(211,801)	(10.11)	496,054	540,146
Hong Kong dollars	208,063	128,403	9.54	(208,018)	(128,372)	(9.54)	45	31
Italian lire	2,166,390[d]	1,423,173	11.48	(2,156,179)	(1,375,689)	(11.62)	10,211	47,484
Japanese yen	25,704,693	22,169,206	6.15	862,093	782,019	5.50[c]	25,105,948	22,014,434
				(1,460,838)	(936,791)	(6.99)[c]		
Kuwaiti dinars	111,203	120,947	7.63	—	—	—	111,203	120,947
Libyan dinars	—	102,936	—	—	—	—	—	102,936
Luxembourg francs	159,665	181,393	7.94	(80,096)	(86,593)	(8.22)	79,569	94,800
Netherlands guilders	3,504,745	4,369,474	7.82	712,261	777,229	6.71	3,577,700	4,617,897
				(639,306)	(528,806)	(7.63)		
New Zealand dollars	187,330	44,122	12.68	(187,835)	(44,102)	(12.68)	(505)	20
Norwegian kroner	71,521	78,101	10.33	—	—	—	71,521	78,101
Pounds sterling	2,337,615	2,284,247	10.69	(947,050)	(679,665)	(10.71)[c]	1,390,565	1,604,582
Spanish pesetas	939,175	791,812	12.14	(926,405)	(778,158)	(12.14)	12,770	13,654
Swedish kronor	267,981	222,637	10.82	(260,959)	(214,661)	(10.93)[c]	7,022	7,976
Swiss francs	7,032,799	8,050,638	6.25	4,813,523	5,627,317	5.32[c]	11,846,322	13,677,955
United States dollars	23,042,505[e]	19,954,757[e]	9.29	3,878,156	3,569,073	8.66[c]	24,256,173	20,242,186
				(2,664,488)	(3,281,644)	(9.46)[c]		
Principal at face value	84,707,706	81,132,257	7.93[f]					
Plus net unamortized discounts and premiums	89,722	86,536						
Total	$84,797,428	$81,218,793						

a. See Notes to Financial Statements—Note D.

b. Includes zero coupon borrowings which have been recorded at their discounted values. The aggregate face amounts and discounted values of these borrowings (in US-dollar equivalents) are:

| | Aggregate face amount | | Discounted value | |
Currency	1991	1990	1991	1990
Australian dollars	$ 115,050,000	$ 118,245,000	$104,057,000	$ 94,126,000
Canadian dollars	175,170,000	170,852,000	108,929,000	96,551,000
Deutsche mark	1,114,641,000	1,202,212,000	233,685,000	236,621,000
Swiss francs	836,820,000	924,938,000	185,097,000	193,757,000
United States dollars	3,169,998,000	2,412,730,000	553,306,000	482,957,000

c. Includes income and expense from interest rate swaps. The IBRD has entered into interest rate swap agreements with respect to notional principal amounts as follows (see Notes to Financial Statements—Note D):

| | Notional principal amounts | | | |
| | Currency amount | | US-dollar equivalent | |
Currency	1991	1990	1991	1990
Canadian dollars	149,363,000	—	$ 130,819,000	$ —
Deutsche mark	4,866,050,000	1,674,500,000	2,711,949,000	1,006,552,000
Japanese yen	35,000,000,000	5,000,000,000	252,708,000	32,415,000
Pounds sterling	100,285,000	—	163,364,000	—
Swedish kronor	300,000,000	300,000,000	46,204,000	49,751,000
Swiss francs	482,700,000	—	310,718,000	—
United States dollars	3,724,800,000	3,424,800,000	3,724,800,000	3,424,800,000

Ninety-two percent of these interest rate swap agreements are from floating rates into fixed rates.

(continued)

Summary Statements of Borrowings   *(continued)*

June 30, 1991 and June 30, 1990
Expressed in thousands of US dollars

d. Includes Italian lire 200,000,000,000 (US equivalent $149,423,000—June 30, 1991; $162,679,000—June 30, 1990) of variable interest rate borrowings.

e. Includes $98,800,000 ($288,720,000—June 30, 1990) of variable rate borrowings and $172,844,000 ($174,652,000—June 30, 1990) borrowed from the Interest Subsidy Fund. The Interest Subsidy Fund, which obtained its resources from voluntary contributions from member governments, was established to subsidize the interest payments to the IBRD on selected loans made to poorer developing countries.

f. The weighted average cost of medium- and long-term borrowings outstanding at June 30, 1991, after adjustment for swap activities, was 7.43 percent.

Maturity Structure of Medium- and Long-term Borrowings

Period	
July 1, 1991 through June 30, 1992	$ 8,239,740
July 1, 1992 through June 30, 1993	8,256,902
July 1, 1993 through June 30, 1994	7,173,995
July 1, 1994 through June 30, 1995	9,363,143
July 1, 1995 through June 30, 1996	9,994,209
July 1, 1996 through June 30, 2001	30,431,526
July 1, 2001 through June 30, 2006	3,900,169
July 1, 2006 through June 30, 2011	2,917,953
July 1, 2011 through June 30, 2016	2,394,243
Thereafter	2,035,826
Total	$84,707,706

Short-term Borrowings

	Principal outstanding 1991	Principal outstanding 1990	Weighted average cost (%) 1991
Short-term Notes (US-dollar obligations)			
Principal outstanding at face value	$2,749,750	$2,679,705	
Net unamortized premiums (discounts)	21,119	(29,427)	
Subtotal	2,770,869	2,650,278	5.96
Central Bank Facility (US-dollar obligations)	2,582,970	2,599,970	6.27
Continuously Offered Payment Rights (Swiss-franc obligations)	34,242	27,072	7.63
Total	$5,388,081	$5,277,320	6.12

See Notes to Financial Statements.

Statement of Subscriptions to Capital Stock and Voting Power

June 30, 1991
Expressed in thousands of US dollars

Member		Subscriptions				Voting power	
	Shares	Percentage of total	Total amounts	Amounts paid in (Note A)	Amounts subject to call (Note A)	Number of votes	Percentage of total
Afghanistan	300	0.03	$ 36,191	$ 3,619	$ 32,572	550	0.05
Algeria	5,192	0.45	626,337	52,390	573.947	5,442	0.46
Angola	2,676	0.23	322,819	17,464	305 355	2,926	0.25
Antigua and Barbuda[a]	292	0.03	35,225	445	34 780	542	0.05
Argentina	10,052	0.87	1,212,623	103,803	1,108 820	10,302	0.86
Australia	21,610	1.87	2,606,922	171,430	2,435,492	21,860	1.83
Austria	11,063	0.96	1,334,585	80,728	1,253,857	11,313	0.95
Bahamas, The	1,071	0.09	129,200	5,432	123,768	1,321	0.11
Bahrain	619	0.05	74,673	3,910	70,763	869	0.07
Bangladesh[a]	2,724	0.24	328,610	26,234	302,376	2,974	0.25
Barbados	948	0.08	114,362	4,496	109,866	1 198	0.10
Belgium	24,986	2.17	3,014,186	201,317	2,812,869	25 236	2.12
Belize	329	0.03	39,689	837	38,852	579	0.05
Benin	487	0.04	58,749	2,514	56,235	737	0.06
Bhutan	269	0.02	32,451	202	32,249	519	0.04
Bolivia	1,002	0.09	120,876	7,968	112,908	1,252	0.11
Botswana	615	0.05	74,191	1,987	72,204	865	0.07
Brazil	14,000	1.21	1,688,890	145,528	1,543,362	14,250	1.20
Bulgaria	2,927	0.25	353,099	28,257	324,842	3,177	0.27
Burkina Faso	487	0.04	58,749	2,514	56,235	737	0.06
Burundi	402	0.03	48,495	1,831	46,664	652	0.05
Cameroon[a]	857	0.07	103,384	6,575	96,809	1,107	0.09
Canada	35,892	3.11	4,329,831	302,713	4,027,118	36,142	3.03
Cape Verde	285	0.02	34,381	371	34,010	535	0.04
Central African Republic[a]	484	0.04	58,387	2,482	55,905	734	0.06
Chad	484	0.04	58,387	2,482	55,905	734	0.06
Chile	6,931	0.60	836,121	49,568	786,553	7,181	0.60
China[a]	34,971	3.03	4,218,727	299,479	3,919,248	35,221	2.95
Colombia	6,352	0.55	766,274	45,202	721,072	6,602	0.55
Comoros	282	0.02	34,019	339	33,680	532	0.04
Congo	520	0.05	62,730	2,868	59,862	770	0.06
Costa Rica[a]	233	0.02	28,108	1,949	26,159	483	0.04
Côte d'Ivoire	1,412	0.12	170,337	12,425	157,912	1,662	0.14
Cyprus	820	0.07	98,921	6,044	92,877	1,070	0.09
Czechoslovakia	5,345	0.46	644,794	53,781	591,013	5,595	0.47
Denmark	10,251	0.89	1,236,629	74,610	1,162,019	10 501	0.88
Djibouti[a]	314	0.03	37,879	679	37,200	564	0.05
Dominica	283	0.02	34,140	350	33,790	533	0.04
Dominican Republic	1,174	0.10	141,625	9,793	131,832	1,424	0.12
Ecuador	1,555	0.13	187,587	13,822	173,765	1,805	0.15
Egypt[a]	3,989	0.35	481,213	39,627	441,586	4,239	0.36
El Salvador	141	0.01	17,010	1,701	15,309	391	0.03
Equatorial Guinea	401	0.03	48,375	1,601	46,774	651	0.05
Ethiopia	978	0.08	117,981	4,722	113,259	1,223	0.10
Fiji	728	0.06	87,822	3,852	83,970	978	0.08

(continued)

Statement of Subscriptions to Capital Stock and Voting Power   *(continued)*

June 30, 1991
Expressed in thousands of US dollars

	Subscriptions					Voting power	
Member	Shares	Percentage of total	Total amounts	Amounts paid in (Note A)	Amounts subject to call (Note A)	Number of votes	Percentage of total
Finland	7,057	0.61	$ 851,321	$ 56,430	$ 794,891	7,307	0.61
France	69,397	6.02	8,371,707	520,364	7,851,343	69,647	5.84
Gabon	554	0.05	66,832	3,556	63,276	804	0.07
Gambia, The	305	0.03	36,794	660	36,134	555	0.05
Germany	72,399	6.28	8,733,853	542,921	8,190,932	72,649	6.09
Ghana[a]	856	0.07	103,264	10,326	92,938	1,106	0.09
Greece	945	0.08	114,000	11,400	102,600	1,195	0.10
Grenada	531	0.05	64,057	1,353	62,704	781	0.07
Guatemala	1,123	0.10	135,473	9,251	126,222	1,373	0.12
Guinea	725	0.06	87,460	5,037	82,423	975	0.08
Guinea-Bissau	303	0.03	36,552	562	35,990	553	0.05
Guyana	1,058	0.09	127,632	5,330	122,302	1,308	0.11
Haiti	599	0.05	72,260	3,697	68,563	849	0.07
Honduras	360	0.03	43,429	1,324	42,105	610	0.05
Hungary	8,050	0.70	971,112	58,031	913,081	8,300	0.70
Iceland	1,258	0.11	151,759	6,832	144,927	1,508	0.13
India	38,244	3.32	4,613,565	310,022	4,303,543	38,494	3.23
Indonesia	12,351	1.07	1,489,963	100,758	1,389,205	12,601	1.06
Iran, Islamic Republic of	13,293	1.15	1,603,601	138,221	1,465,380	13,543	1.14
Iraq	2,808	0.24	338,743	27,093	311,650	3,058	0.26
Ireland	5,271	0.46	635,867	37,077	598,790	5,521	0.46
Israel	2,666	0.23	321,613	25,664	295,949	2,916	0.24
Italy	44,795	3.88	5,403,845	334,838	5,069,007	45,045	3.78
Jamaica	1,824	0.16	220,038	14,057	205,981	2,074	0.17
Japan	93,770	8.13	11,311,944	703,452	10,608,492	94,020	7.89
Jordan	1,388	0.12	167,441	7,811	159,630	1,638	0.14
Kampuchea, Democratic	214	0.02	25,816	2,582	23,234	464	0.04
Kenya	2,461	0.21	296,883	15,900	280,983	2,711	0.23
Kiribati	261	0.02	31,486	133	31,353	511	0.04
Korea, Republic of	9,372	0.81	1,130,591	67,899	1,062,692	9,622	0.81
Kuwait	7,453	0.65	899,093	76,341	822,752	7,703	0.65
Lao People's Democratic Republic	100	0.01	12,064	1,206	10,858	350	0.03
Lebanon	340	0.03	41,016	1,086	39,930	590	0.05
Lesotho	372	0.03	44,876	1,294	43,582	622	0.05
Liberia	463	0.04	55,854	2,570	53,284	713	0.06
Libya	7,840	0.68	945,778	56,958	888,820	8,090	0.68
Luxembourg	1,362	0.12	164,305	8,749	155,556	1,612	0.14
Madagascar	798	0.07	96,267	5,812	90,455	1,048	0.09
Malawi	614	0.05	74,070	3,860	70,210	864	0.07
Malaysia	8,244	0.71	994,515	59,491	935,024	8,494	0.71
Maldives	263	0.02	31,727	137	31,590	513	0.04
Mali[a]	652	0.06	78,654	4,263	74,391	902	0.08
Malta	778	0.07	93,854	4,375	89,479	1,028	0.09
Mauritania[a]	505	0.04	60,921	2,704	58,217	755	0.06
Mauritius	697	0.06	84,083	4,739	79,344	947	0.08

Member	Subscriptions					Voting power	
	Shares	Percentage of total	Total amounts	Amounts paid in (Note A)	Amounts subject to call (Note A)	Number of votes	Percentage of total
Mexico	10,553	0.92	$1,273,061	S109,120	$1,163,941	10,803	0.91
Mongolia	466	0.04	56,216	2,280	53,936	716	0.06
Morocco	2,791	0.24	336,692	26,939	309,753	3,041	0.26
Mozambique	522	0.05	62,971	3,281	59,690	772	0.06
Myanmar	1,938	0.17	233,791	14,102	219,689	2,188	0.18
Namibia	855	0.07	103,143	6,386	96,757	1,105	0.09
Nepal	543	0.05	65,505	3,106	62,399	793	0.07
Netherlands	35,503	3.08	4,282,904	264,799	4,018,105	35,753	3.00
New Zealand	4,696	0.41	566,502	42,708	523,794	4,946	0.41
Nicaragua	341	0.03	41,137	1,098	40,039	591	0.05
Niger[a]	478	0.04	57,664	2,419	55,245	728	0.06
Nigeria[a]	7,102	0.62	856,750	72,610	784,140	7,352	0.62
Norway	9,982	0.87	1,204,179	72,577	1,131,602	10,232	0.86
Oman	876	0.08	105,676	6,626	99,050	1,126	0.09
Pakistan[a]	6,881	0.60	830,089	58,861	771,228	7,131	0.60
Panama	216	0.02	26,057	2,606	23,451	466	0.04
Papua New Guinea	726	0.06	87,581	5,049	82,532	976	0.08
Paraguay	690	0.06	83,238	4,661	78,577	940	0.08
Peru	2,992	0.26	360,940	29,050	331,890	3,242	0.27
Philippines	3,841	0.33	463,359	38,029	425,330	4,091	0.34
Poland	6,122	0.53	738,527	62,275	676,252	6,372	0.53
Portugal	5,460	0.47	658,667	38,503	620,164	5,710	0.48
Qatar	1,096	0.10	132,216	8,965	123,251	1,346	0.11
Romania	2,251	0.20	271,549	24,139	247,410	2,501	0.21
Rwanda	587	0.05	70,813	3,574	67,239	837	0.07
St. Kitts and Nevis	275	0.02	33,175	302	32,873	525	0.04
St. Lucia	552	0.05	66,591	1,512	65,079	802	0.07
St. Vincent and the Grenadines	278	0.02	33,537	297	33,240	528	0.04
São Tomé and Principe	278	0.02	33,537	297	33,240	528	0.04
Saudi Arabia	25,140	2.18	3,032,764	263,830	2,768,934	25,390	2.13
Senegal[a]	1,163	0.10	140,299	9,681	130,618	1,413	0.12
Seychelles	263	0.02	31,727	154	31,573	513	0.04
Sierra Leone	403	0.03	48,616	1,841	46,775	653	0.05
Singapore	320	0.03	38,603	3,860	34,743	570	0.05
Solomon Islands	288	0.02	34,743	403	34,340	538	0.05
Somalia	552	0.05	66,591	3,322	63,269	802	0.07
South Africa	13,462	1.17	1,623,983	98,821	1,525,167	13,712	1.15
Spain	20,222	1.75	2,439,481	163,080	2,276,401	20,472	1.72
Sri Lanka	3,147	0.27	379,638	23,702	355,936	3,397	0.28
Sudan	850	0.07	102,540	7,238	95,302	1,100	0.09
Suriname	412	0.04	49,702	1,954	47,748	662	0.06
Swaziland	440	0.04	53,079	2,015	51,064	690	0.06
Sweden	14,974	1.30	1,806,368	110,202	1,696,186	15,224	1.28
Syrian Arab Republic	1,236	0.11	149,105	10,458	138,647	1,486	0.12
Tanzania[a]	727	0.06	87,702	7,942	79,760	977	0.08

(continued)

Statement of Subscriptions to Capital Stock and Voting Power *(continued)*

June 30, 1991
Expressed in thousands of US dollars

| Member | Subscriptions | | | | | Voting power | |
	Shares	Percentage of total	Total amounts	Amounts paid in (Note A)	Amounts subject to call (Note A)	Number of votes	Percentage of total
Thailand	4,260	0.37	$ 513,905	$ 37,636	$ 476,269	4,510	0.38
Togo	620	0.05	74,794	3,924	70,870	870	0.07
Tonga	277	0.02	33,416	287	33,129	527	0.04
Trinidad and Tobago	1,495	0.13	180,349	13,406	166,943	1,745	0.15
Tunisia	719	0.06	86,737	5,658	81,079	969	0.08
Turkey	7,379	0.64	890,166	52,947	837,219	7,629	0.64
Uganda	617	0.05	74,432	4,376	70,056	867	0.07
United Arab Emirates	2,385	0.21	287,714	22,643	265,071	2,635	0.22
United Kingdom	69,397	6.02	8,371,707	539,526	7,832,181	69,647	5.84
United States	206,257	17.89	24,881,813	1,785,899	23,095,914	206,507	17.32
Uruguay	1,578	0.14	190,362	14,084	176,278	1,828	0.15
Vanuatu[a]	329	0.03	39,689	838	38,851	579	0.05
Venezuela	11,427	0.99	1,378,496	118,452	1,260,044	11,677	0.98
Viet Nam	543	0.05	65,505	6,550	58,955	793	0.07
Western Samoa	298	0.03	35,949	510	35,439	548	0.05
Yemen, Republic of	1,241	0.11	149,708	10,504	139,204	1,491	0.13
Yugoslavia[a]	4,381	0.38	528,502	46,463	482,039	4,631	0.39
Zaire[a]	2,643	0.23	318,838	25,379	293,459	2,893	0.24
Zambia[a]	1,577	0.14	190,241	15,556	174,685	1,827	0.15
Zimbabwe	1,866	0.16	225,105	17,136	207,969	2,116	0.18
Total—June 30, 1991*	1,153,231	100.00	$139,120,022	$9,392,549	$129,727,473	1,191,981	100.00
Total—June 30, 1990	1,038,357		$125,262,197	$8,919,923	$116,342,274	1,076,357	

*May differ from sum of individual figures shown because of rounding.

a. Amounts aggregating the equivalent of $49,359,400 have been received from members on account of increases in subscriptions which are in process of completion: Antigua and Barbuda $57,000, Bangladesh $308,000, Cameroon $2,000, Central African Republic $1,239,000, China $28,242,000, Costa Rica $163,000, Djibouti $4,000, Egypt $7,637,000, Ghana $47,000, Mali $400, Mauritania $31,000, Niger $181,000, Nigeria $936,000, Pakistan $5,850,000, Senegal $225,000, Tanzania $143,000, Vanuatu $93,000, Yugoslavia $3,174,000, Zaire $15,000, and Zambia $1,012,000.

See Notes to Financial Statements.

Notes to Financial Statements

Summary of Significant Accounting and Related Policies

The IBRD's principal financial statements are prepared in conformity with the accounting principles generally accepted in the United States and with International Accounting Standards.

Translation of Currencies

The IBRD's principal financial statements are expressed in terms of US dollars solely for the purpose of summarizing the IBRD's financial position and the results of its operations for the convenience of its members and other interested parties.

The IBRD is an international organization which conducts its operations in the currencies of all of its members and Switzerland. The IBRD's resources are derived from its capital, borrowings, and accumulated earnings in those various currencies. The IBRD has a number of general policies aimed at minimizing exchange-rate risk in a multicurrency environment. The IBRD matches its borrowing obligations in any one currency (after swap activities) with assets in the same currency, as prescribed by its Articles of Agreement, primarily by holding or lending the proceeds of its borrowings in the same currencies in which they are borrowed. In addition, the IBRD periodically undertakes currency conversions to more closely match the currencies underlying its reserves with those of the outstanding loans. With respect to its other resources, the IBRD does not convert one currency into another except for small amounts required to meet certain obligations and operational needs.

Assets and liabilities are translated at market rates of exchange at the end of the period. Income and expenses are translated at the market rate at the dates on which they are recognized or an average of the market rates of exchange in effect during each month. Translation adjustments, with the exception of those relating to capital subscriptions described in Note A, are charged or credited to Equity.

Valuation of Capital Stock

In the Articles of Agreement, the capital stock of the IBRD is expressed in terms of "US dollars of the weight and fineness in effect on July 1, 1944" (1944 dollars). Following the abolition of gold as a common denominator of the monetary system and the repeal of the provision of US law defining the par value of the US dollar in terms of gold, the pre-existing basis for translating 1944 dollars into current dollars or into any other currency disappeared. On October 14, 1986, the Executive Directors of the IBRD decided, effective June 30, 1987 until such time as the relevant provisions of the Articles of Agreement are amended, to interpret the words 'US dollars of the weight and fineness in effect on July 1, 1944" in Article II, Section 2(a) of the Articles of Agreement of the IBRD to mean the Special Drawing Right (SDR) introduced by the International Monetary Fund as the SDR was valued in terms of US dollars immediately before the introduction of the basket method of valuing the SDR on July 1, 1974, such value being $1.20635 for one SDR.

Retained Earnings

Retained Earnings consists of allocated amounts (Special Reserve, General Reserve, and Surplus) and Unallocated Net Income. The IBRD has not declared or paid any dividends to its members.

The Special Reserve consists of loan commissions set aside pursuant to Article IV, Section 6 of the Articles of Agreement which are to be held in liquid assets. These assets may be used only for the purpose of meeting liabilities of the IBRD on its borrowings and guarantees in the event of defaults on loans made, participated in, or guaranteed by the IBRD. The Special Reserve assets comprise obligations of the United States Government and its instrumentalities and are included under Investments. The

allocation of such commissions to the Special Reserve was discontinued in 1964 with respect to subsequent loans, and no further additions are being made to it.

The General Reserve consists of earnings from prior fiscal years which, in the judgment of the Executive Directors, should be retained in the IBRD's business.

Surplus consists of earnings from prior fiscal years which are retained by the IBRD until a further decision is made on their disposition.

Unallocated Net Income consists of earnings in the current fiscal year. Commencing in 1950, a portion or all of the Unallocated Net Income has been allocated to the General Reserve. From fiscal years 1964 to 1987, and in 1989, the IBRD's Board of Governors made transfers out of the Unallocated Net Income for those years to the International Development Association (or facilities administered by the International Development Association). The IBRD's Board of Governors made a transfer out of fiscal year 1990 Unallocated Net Income to Surplus, and subsequently to the International Development Association and the Global Environment Trust Fund.

Loans

All of the IBRD's loans are made to or guaranteed by members, with the except on of loans to the International Finance Corporation. The principal amounts of loans are repayable in the currencies lent. For loans negotiated since July 1980 (and for portions of certain earlier loans), the repayment obligations of borrowers in various currencies are determined on the basis of a currency pooling system, which is designed to equalize exchange-rate risks among borrowers. Interest on loans is accrued in the currencies lent.

Incremental direct costs associated with originating loans are expensed as incurred, as such amounts are considered immaterial.

The IBRD does not reschedule interest or principal payments on its loans or participate in debt rescheduling with respect to its loans. In exceptional cases, however, such as when implementation of a financed project has been delayed, the loan amortization schedule may be modified to avoid substantial repayments prior to project completion. It is the policy of the IBRD to place in nonaccrual status all loans made to or guaranteed by a member of the IBRD if principal, interest, or other charges with respect to any such loan are overdue by more than six months, unless IBRD management determines that the overdue amount will be collected in the immediate future. On the date a member's loans are placed in nonaccrual status, interest and other charges that had been accrued on loans outstanding to the member which remained unpaid are deducted from the income of the current period. Interest and other charges on nonaccruing loans are included in income only to the extent that payments have actually been received by the IBRD.

The IBRD determines the Accumulated Provision for Loan Losses based on an assessment of collectibility risk of the total loan portfolio, including loans in nonaccrual status. The Accumulated Provision is periodically adjusted based on a review of the prevailing circumstances and will be used to meet actual losses on loans. Should such losses occur in amounts in excess of the Accumulated Provision (and of the amount of the Special Reserve), the excess would be included in the determination of net income. Annual adjustments to the Accumulated Provision are recorded as a charge or credit to income.

Investments

In prior years, the IBRD recorded its investment securities at cost or amortized cost. As of July 1, 1990, the IBRD changed its policy and began carrying its investment securities at market value, since this was considered

(continued)

Notes to Financial Statements   *(continued)*

a more appropriate reflection of the value of the portfolio. The cumulative effect of this change of $17,380,000 was reflected as a reduction of investment income in the first quarter of fiscal year 1991. Both realized and unrealized gains and losses are included in income from investments. From time to time, the IBRD enters into forward contracts for the sale or purchase of investment securities; these transactions are recorded at the time of commitment.

Due to the nature of the investments held by the IBRD and its policies governing the level and use of such investments, the IBRD classifies the investment portfolio as an element of liquidity in the Statements of Cash Flows.

Reclassifications

Certain reclassifications of the prior year's information have been made to conform with the current year's presentation.

Note A—Capital Stock, Restricted Currencies, and Maintenance of Value

Capital Stock: At June 30, 1991, the IBRD's capital comprised 1,448,500 (1,420,500—June 30, 1990) authorized shares, of which 1,153,231 (1,038,357—June 30, 1990) shares had been subscribed. Each share has a par value of 100,000 1974 SDRs, valued at the rate of $1.20635 per 1974 SDR. Of the subscribed capital, $9,392,549,000 ($8,919,923,000—June 30, 1990) has been paid in, and the remaining $129,727,473,000 ($116,342,274,000—June 30, 1990) is subject to call only when required to meet the obligations of the IBRD created by borrowing or guaranteeing loans. As to $111,296,017,000 ($100,209,757,000—June 30, 1990), the restriction on calls is imposed by the Articles of Agreement, and as to $18,431,456,000 ($16,132,517,000—June 30, 1990), by resolutions of the Board of Governors.

Restricted Currencies: The portion of capital subscriptions paid in to the IBRD is divided into two parts: (1) $939,255,000 ($891,992,000—June 30, 1990) initially paid in gold or US dollars and (2) $8,453,294,000 ($8,027,931,000—June 30, 1990) paid in cash or noninterest-bearing demand obligations denominated either in the currencies of the respective members or in US dollars. The amounts mentioned in (1) above, $506,365,000 ($506,033,000—June 30, 1990) repurchased by members with US dollars, and $95,661,000 ($45,112,000—June 30, 1990), which were the proceeds from encashments of US-dollar-denominated notes, are freely usable by the IBRD in any of its operations. The portion of the amounts paid in US-dollar-denominated notes are encashed by the IBRD in accordance with the schedules agreed with the members and the IBRD. The remaining amounts paid in the currencies of the members, referred to as restricted currencies, are usable by the IBRD in its lending operations only with the consent of the respective members, and for administrative expenses. The equivalent of $4,875,690,000 ($4,759,714,000—June 30, 1990) has been used for lending purposes, with such consent.

Maintenance of Value: Article II, Section 9 of the Articles of Agreement provides for maintenance of value, as of the time of subscription, of such restricted currencies, requiring (1) the member to make additional payments to the IBRD in the event that the par value of its currency is reduced or the foreign exchange value of its currency has, in the opinion of the IBRD, depreciated to a significant extent in its territories and (2) the IBRD to reimburse the member in the event that the par value of its currency is increased.

Since currencies no longer have par values, maintenance-of-value amounts are determined by measuring the foreign exchange value of a member's currency against the standard of value of IBRD capital based on the 1974 SDR. Members are required to make payments to the IBRD if their currencies depreciate significantly relative to the standard of value. Furthermore, the

Executive Directors decided to adopt a policy of reimbursing members whose currencies appreciate significantly in terms of the standard of value.

With respect to restricted currencies out on loan, maintenance-of-value obligations become effective only as such currencies are recovered by the IBRD. The maintenance-of-value amounts relating to restricted currencies out on loan are included in Amounts Required to Maintain Value of Currency Holdings—Amounts Deferred.

Note B—Investments and Cash Collateral Invested

At June 30, 1991, the market value of investment securities and invested cash collateral received on loaned securities was $24,936,856,000 ($21,351,162,000—June 30, 1990), compared with a cost or amortized cost of $24,948,945,000 ($21,368,542,000—June 30, 1990). A summary of the currency composition of Investments and Cash Collateral Invested follows:

Currency	June 30, 1991
Deutsche mark	$ 1,630,575,000
Japanese yen	3,998,537,000
Pounds sterling	1,463,371,000
United States dollars.	15,554,292,000
Other currencies	2,290,081,000
Total	$24,936,856,000

As part of its overall portfolio management strategy, the IBRD is party to financial instruments with off-balance-sheet risk, including futures, forward contracts, covered forward contracts, options, and short sales. Futures and forward contracts are contracts for delayed delivery of securities or money market instruments in which the seller agrees to make delivery at a specified future date of a specified instrument, at a specified price or yield. At June 30, 1991, the total contract value of futures contracts was $8,445,147,000 ($3,403,220,000—June 30, 1990). The IBRD has minimal exposure to credit loss on futures contracts due to potential nonperformance of counterparties since changes in the market value of futures contracts on any given business day are settled in cash on the following business day. The total contract value of forward contracts at June 30, 1991 was $448,500,000 ($761,000,000—June 30, 1990) and the IBRD's exposure to credit loss in the event of nonperformance by counterparties was $333,000 ($405,000—June 30, 1990).

Covered forwards are agreements in which cash in one currency is converted into a different currency and, simultaneously, a forward exchange agreement is executed with either the same or a different counterparty providing for a future exchange of the two currencies in order to recover the currency converted. At June 30, 1991, the IBRD had gross receivables from covered forward agreements of $91,739,000 and gross payables from covered forward agreements of $86,374,000. The IBRD's exposure to credit loss in the event of nonperformance by counterparties was $5,365,000. There were no outstanding covered forward agreements at June 30, 1990.

Options are contracts that allow the holder of the option to purchase or sell a financial instrument at a specified price and within a specified period of time from the seller of the option. As a seller of options, the IBRD receives a premium at the outset and then bears the risk of an unfavorable change in the price of the financial instrument underlying the option. The total contract value of options sold at June 30, 1991 was $406,980,000. There were no outstanding options sold at June 30, 1990.

Short sales are sales of securities not held in the IBRD's portfolio at the time of the sale. The IBRD must purchase the security at a later date and bears the risk that the market value of the security will move adversely between the time of the sale and the time the security must be delivered. The total contract amount of short sales at June 30, 1991 was $210,200,000 ($146,592,000—June 30, 1990). This amount is included in Payable for Investment Securities Purchased.

For both on– and off–balance-sheet securities, the IBRD limits trading to a list of authorized dealers and counterparties. Strict credit limits have been established for each counterparty by type of instrument and maturity category.

As of July 1, 1990, the IBRD began carrying its investment portfolio at market value rather than cost or amortized cost. If the new policy had been applied retroactively, net income would have been $1,217,356,000 and $991,118,000 for the fiscal years 1991 and 1990, respectively.

The annualized rate of return on average investments, net of cash collateral received, held during the fiscal year ended June 30, 1991, including both realized and unrealized gains and losses, was 9.23 percent.

Note C—Loans, Cofinancing and Guarantees

Loans: At June 30, 1991, principal installments of $2,751,000 and interest and other charges of $2,525,000 payable to the IBRD on loans other than those referred to in the following paragraph were overdue by more than three months. The aggregate principal amount outstanding on these loans was $137,560,000. The aggregate principal amount outstanding on all loans to any borrowers, other than those referred to in the following paragraph, with any one loan overdue by more than three months was $149,045,000.

At June 30, 1991, the loans made to or guaranteed by certain member countries with an aggregate principal balance outstanding of $2,496,317,000 ($2,871,500,000—June 30, 1990), of which $949,749,000 ($932,165,000—June 30, 1990) was overdue, were in nonaccrual status. As of such date, overdue interest and other charges in respect of these loans totaled $832,915,000 ($824,835,000—June 30, 1990). If these loans had not been in nonaccrual status, income from loans for the fiscal year ended June 30, 1991 would have been higher by $148,758,000 ($248,405,000—June 30, 1990), which is net of interest received from such members during the fiscal year. A summary of borrowers in nonaccrual status follows:

Borrower	June 30, 1991		
	Principal outstanding	Principal and charges overdue	Nonaccrual since
Guatemala . . .	$ 256,527,000	$ 68,569,000	July 1990
Iraq	42,170,000	14,380,000	December 1990
Liberia	129,317,000	109,226,000	June 1987
Nicaragua . . .	215,922,000	220,108,000	December 1984
Panama.	397,117,000	201,426,000	May 1988
Peru.	1,022,652,000	855,969,000	August 1987
Sierra Leone. .	9,354,000	6,994,000	August 1987
Syrian Arab Republic . .	423,248,000	305,992,000	February 1987
Total	$2,496,317,000	$1,782,664,000	

In fiscal year 1991, Zambia paid off all of its arrears and therefore came out of nonaccrual status. As a result, income from loans for fiscal year 1991 was increased by $147,034,000 for income that would have been accrued in previous fiscal years.

An analysis of the changes to the accumulated provision for losses on loans follows:

	US$ thousands	
	June 30, 1991	June 30, 1990
Balance, beginning of fiscal year . .	$1,250,000	$ 800,000
Provision for loan losses	774,977	357,416
Translation adjustments	(34,977)	92,584
Balance, end of fiscal year	$1,990,000	$ 1,250,000

Cofinancing and Guarantees: The IBRD has entered into agreements for loans syndicated by other financial institutions either by a direct participation in, or a partial guarantee of, loans for the benefit of member countries or a partial guarantee of securities issued by an entity eligible for IBRD loans. The IBRD's direct participations in syndicated loans are included in reported loan balances.

Guarantees of $1,133,849,000 at June 30, 1991 ($934,741,000—June 30, 1990) were not included in reported loan balances. None of these guarantees were subject to call at June 30, 1991.

The IBRD has partially guaranteed the timely payment of interest amounts on certain loans that have been sold. At June 30, 1991, these guarantees, approximating $10,312,000 ($13,473,000—June 30, 1990), were subject to call.

Statutory Lending Limit: Under the Articles of Agreement, the total amount outstanding of guarantees, participations in loans, and direct loans made by the IBRD may not be increased to an amount exceeding 100 percent of the sum of subscribed capital, reserves, and surplus. On the IBRD's Balance Sheets, reserves and surplus correspond to items labeled Retained Earnings, Cumulative Translation Adjustment, and Accumulated Provision for Loan Losses. The IBRD's Executive Directors have issued guidelines pursuant to which all guarantees issued by the IBRD will be counted towards this limit at the time they first become callable, irrespective of the likelihood of an actual call. On March 26, 1991 the IBRD's Executive Directors decided that discussions on an additional capital increase would be initiated if the total amount outstanding of callable guarantees, participations in loans, and direct loans were to exceed 80 percent of the sum of subscribed capital, reserves, and surplus. As of June 30, 1991, such total amount was $90,647,907,000 or 60 percent (65 percent—June 30, 1990) of such sum.

Note D—Borrowings and Swaps

The IBRD has entered into currency swaps in which proceeds of a borrowing are converted into a different currency and, simultaneously, a forward exchange agreement is executed providing for a schedule of future exchanges of the two currencies in order to recover the currency converted. The combination of a borrowing and a currency swap produces the financial equivalent of substituting a borrowing in the currency obtained in the initial conversion for the original borrowing. The IBRD also undertakes interest rate swaps, which transform a fixed-rate payment obligation in a particular currency into a floating-rate obligation in that currency and vice-versa. The average cost of borrowings outstanding, including short-term borrowings, during the fiscal year ended June 30, 1991 was 7.41 percent (7.37 percent—June 30, 1990), reflecting a reduction in interest expense of $402,953,000 ($337,770,000—June 30, 1990) as a result of swaps.

At June 30, 1991, the IBRD had gross receivables from currency swaps at a book value of $14,615,302,000 ($13,060,831,000—June 30, 1990) and gross payables from currency swaps at a book value of $15,067,892,000 ($14,241,419,000—June 30, 1990). In addition, the IBRD had interest rate swap contracts covering a notional principal amount of $7,340,562,000 on June 30, 1991 ($4,513,513,000—June 30, 1990).

(continued)

Notes to Financial Statements   (continued)

The IBRD is exposed to credit loss in the event of nonperformance by its counterparties in an aggregate amount of $1,027,191,000 ($636,390,000—June 30, 1990) for outstanding currency swaps, and $25,818,000 ($28,445,000—June 30, 1990) for outstanding interest rate swaps, representing the estimated cost of replacing, at current market rates, all those outstanding swaps for which the IBRD would incur a loss in replacing the contracts.

The IBRD follows strict guidelines regarding the counterparties with whom it will enter into swap agreements and establishes strict credit limits for each of those counterparties. The IBRD does not anticipate nonperformance by any of its counterparties.

The IBRD also enters into deferred rate setting agreements in conjunction with some of its bond issues. These agreements allow the IBRD, through the use of a financial intermediary, to fix the effective interest cost on the issues in several tranches over a specified period of time after the issue date of the respective bond. The potential credit loss to the IBRD from nonperformance of the financial intermediary is limited to any accrued, but unsettled, profits. Periodic mark-to-market settlements on these agreements limit this risk, however. At June 30, 1991 (and June 30, 1990), the effective interest rate had been fixed on all tranches of the deferred rate setting agreements and the IBRD had no exposure to credit loss on the agreements.

Note E—Retained Earnings

Retained Earnings comprises the following elements as of June 30, 1991: Special Reserve $292,538,000 ($292,538,000—June 30, 1990), General Reserve $10,444,218,000 ($9,694,218,000—June 30, 1990), and Unallocated Net Income $1,199,976,000 ($1,045,860,000—June 30, 1990). There was no balance in Surplus at June 30, 1991 or 1990.

On May 13, 1991, the Board of Governors approved the transfer of the equivalent of SDR200,000,000 ($266,567,000) to the International Development Association and $29,293,000 to the Global Environment Trust Fund; such amounts had been held in Surplus.

Note F—Expenses

Administrative expenses are net of the management fee of $328,004,000 ($354,380,000—June 30, 1990) charged to the International Development Association and $65,198,000 ($48,340,000—June 30, 1990) charged to reimbursable programs. Service and support fees of $7,479,000 ($7,186,000—June 30, 1990) charged to the International Finance Corporation and $483,000 ($450,000—June 30, 1990) charged to the Multilateral Investment Guarantee Agency are included in reimbursable programs.

Contributions to special programs represent grants for agricultural research, the control of onchocerciasis, and other developmental activities.

Note G—Transfers to the International Development Association, the Debt Reduction Facility for IDA-Only Countries, and the Global Environment Trust Fund

The IBRD has authorized transfers by way of grants to the International Development Association totaling $3,045,056,000 from Unallocated Net Income for the fiscal years ended June 30, 1964 through June 30, 1987, and June 30, 1989 and 1990. Of these transfers, $778,481,000 remained payable at June 30, 1991 ($846,502,000—June 30, 1990). The 1990 amount was held in Surplus during fiscal year 1991.

In May 1991, the IBRD authorized a transfer by way of a grant to the Global Environment Trust Fund of $29,293,000 from Retained Earnings. This amount was held in Surplus during fiscal year 1991. These funds were paid to the Global Environment Trust Fund in the fiscal year ended June 30, 1991.

In September 1989, the IBRD authorized a transfer by way of a grant to the Debt Reduction Facility for IDA-Only Countries of $100,000,000 from net income for the fiscal year ended June 30, 1989. Of these funds, $91,578,000 remained payable at June 30, 1991.

Note H—Staff Retirement Plan

The IBRD has a defined benefit retirement plan covering substantially all of its staff. The Plan also covers the staff of the International Finance Corporation (IFC) and the Multilateral Investment Guarantee Agency (MIGA). Under the Plan, benefits are based on the years of contributory service and the highest three-year average of pensionable remuneration as defined in the Plan, with the staff contributing a fixed percentage of pensionable remuneration and the IBRD contributing the remainder of the actuarially determined cost of future Plan benefits. The IBRD uses the aggregate method for determining its contribution to the Plan. The amount of that contribution approximates the net periodic pension cost as detailed below. All contributions to the Plan and all other assets and income held for the purposes of the Plan are held by the IBRD separately from the other assets and income of the IBRD, IDA, the IFC, and MIGA and can be used only for the benefit of the participants in the Plan and their beneficiaries, until all liabilities to them have been paid or provided for. Plan assets consist primarily of equity and fixed income securities, with smaller holdings of cash, real estate, and other investments.

Net periodic pension cost for IBRD participants for the fiscal years ended June 30, 1991 and June 30, 1990 consisted of the following components:

	US$ thousands	
	1991	1990
Service cost—benefits earned during the period	$ 121,961	$ 141,285
Interest cost on projected benefit obligation	229,865	206,080
Actual return on plan assets . .	(193,521)	(254,966)
Net amortization and deferral . .	(91,269)	(34,463)
Net periodic pension cost.	$ 67,036	$ 57,936

The portion of this cost that relates to the IBRD and is included in Administrative Expenses for the fiscal year ended June 30, 1991 is $44,447,000 ($36,004,000—June 30, 1990). The balance has been charged to the International Development Association.

The following table sets forth the Plan's funded status at June 30, 1991 and June 30, 1990:

	US$ thousands	
	1991	1990
Actuarial present value of benefit obligations		
Accumulated benefit obligation		
Vested	$(2,411,214)	$(1,987,140)
Nonvested.	(42,021)	(183,605)
Subtotal	(2,453,235)	(2,170,745)
Effect of projected compensation levels	(1,125,947)	(1,130,664)
Projected benefit obligation	(3,579,182)	(3,301,409)
Plan assets at fair value	3,728,615	3,470,411
Plan assets in excess of projected benefit obligation	149,433	169,002
Remaining unrecognized net asset. . .	(155,864)	(168,853)
Unrecognized prior service cost	115,412	123,656
Unrecognized net gain	(108,981)	(123,805)
Prepaid pension cost	$ 0	$ 0

The weighted-average discount rate used in determining the actuarial present value of the projected benefit obligation was 8.25 percent (7.81 percent—June 30, 1990). The effect of projected compensation levels was calculated based on a scale that provides for a decreasing rate of salary increase depending on age, beginning with 13 percent at age 20 and decreasing to 7.6 percent at age 64. The expected long-term rate of return on assets was 9 percent (9 percent—June 30, 1990).

Note I—Non-Pension Retirement Benefits

The IBRD provides certain health care and life insurance benefits to retirees. All staff who are enrolled in the insurance programs while in active service and who meet certain requirements are eligible for benefits when they reach early or normal retirement age while working for the IBRD.

Prior to fiscal year 1990, the cost of retiree health care and life insurance benefits, net of retiree contributions, was recognized in expense on a cash basis. Effective June 30, 1990, the IBRD changed to an accrual method of accounting for these costs. The IBRD believes the accrual method is preferable to the method used previously since it is consistent with the accrual basis used in accounting for other liabilities.

Under the new method, the estimated cost for post-retirement health care and life insurance is accrued on an actuarially determined basis. Increases in costs resulting from plan amendments are deferred and amortized over 20 years; gains and losses due to the deviation of actual experience from actuarial assumptions are similarly deferred and amortized. Costs are funded as accrued through contributions to a Retired Staff Benefits Plan (RSBP), which also covers the staff of the IFC and MIGA. All contributions to the RSBP and all other assets and income held for the purposes of the RSBP are held by the IBRD separately from the other assets and income of the IBRD, IDA, the IFC, and MIGA and can be used only for the benefit of the participants in the RSBP and their beneficiaries until all liabilities to them have been paid or provided for.

The initial contribution to the RSBP on behalf of IBRD staff amounted to $158,880,000. Of this amount, $105,500,000 was charged to the IBRD and the remaining $53,380,000 was charged to IDA during fiscal year 1990. The expense allocated to the IBRD for the fiscal year ended June 30, 1991 was $9,130,000.

Report of Independent Accountants

Price Waterhouse	The Hague	Tokyo
(International Firm)	London	Washington
	New York	

Price Waterhouse

July 29, 1991

President and Board of Governors
    International Bank for Reconstruction
    and Development

In our opinion, the financial statements appearing on pages 188 through 205 of this Report present fairly, in all material respects, in terms of United States dollars, the financial position of the International Bank for Reconstruction and Development at June 30, 1991 and 1990, and the results of its operations and its cash flows for the years then ended in conformity with generally accepted accounting principles in the United States and with International Accounting Standards. These financial statements are the responsibility of management of the International Bank for Reconstruction and Development; our responsibility is to express an opinion on these financial statements based on our audits. We conducted our audits of these statements in accordance with generally accepted auditing standards, including International Auditing Guidelines, which require that we plan and perform the audit to obtain reasonable assurance about whether the financial statements are free of material misstatement. An audit includes examining, on a test basis, evidence supporting the amounts and disclosures in the financial statements, assessing the accounting principles used and significant estimates made by management, and evaluating the overall financial statement presentation. We believe that our audits provide a reasonable basis for the opinion expressed above.

Price Waterhouse
(International Firm)

Financial Statements of the International Development Association, the Special Fund Administered by IDA, and the Debt Reduction Facility for IDA-Only Countries Administered by IDA

Statements of Development Resources

June 30, 1991 and June 30, 1990
Expressed in thousands of US dollars

	IDA		Special Fund		Debt Reduction Facility	
	1991	1990	1991	1990	1991	1990
Development Resources						
NET ASSETS AVAILABLE FOR DEVELOPMENT ACTIVITIES						
Cash and investments immediately available for disbursement						
Due from banks	$ 53,774	$ 37,779	$ 1,130	$ 1,536		
Obligations of governments and other official entities—Note A	756,379	425,554	8,736	13,975		
Obligations of banks and other financial institutions—Note A	1,245,840	1,360,766	183,095	84,530		
Net payable on investment security transactions	(19,850)	(29,794)				
	2,036,143	1,794,305	192,961	100,041	—	—
Cash and investments not immediately available for disbursement—Note B						
Due from banks	6,810	7,867				
Obligations of governments and other official entities—Note A	102,485	145,869				
	109,295	153,736	—	—	—	—
Receivables on account of subscriptions and contributions						
Nonnegotiable, noninterest-bearing demand obligations	16,326,308	15,452,413	137,986	264,797		
Subscriptions and contributions—Note E						
Amounts due	387,784	42,289				
Amounts not yet due	8,848,780	829,393				
Restricted assets	280,006	270,840				
	25,842,878	16,594,935	137,986	264,797	—	—
Receivables from the International Bank for Reconstruction and Development—Note G	778,481	846,502			$ 91,578	$100,000
Other assets, net	105,729	89,194	(597)	56		
Grants payable—Note C					(11,578)	
Total net assets available for development activities	28,872,526	19,478,672	330,350	364,894	80,000	100,000
DEVELOPMENT CREDITS OUTSTANDING (see Summary Statement of Development Credits and Note D)						
Total development credits	66,096,491	60,723,122	92,293	149,973		
Less undisbursed balance	20,618,471	19,176,899	92,293	149,973		
Total development credits disbursed and outstanding	45,478,020	41,546,223	0	0		
Total development resources	$74,350,546	$61,024,895	$330,350	$364,894	$ 80,000	$100,000
Funding of Development Resources						
Member subscriptions and contributions (see Statement of Voting Power, and Subscriptions and Contributions and Note E)						
Unrestricted	$68,903,911	$55,666,155	$274,970	$315,906		
Restricted	280,006	270,840				
	69,183,917	55,936,995	274,970	315,906		
Other contributions—Notes F and G	3,016,325	2,761,850			$100,000	$100,000
Cumulative translation adjustment on development credits	1,607,240	1,947,674				
Accumulated surplus (see Statements of Changes in Accumulated Surplus and Grants)	543,064	378,376	55,380	48,988		
Accumulated grants (see Statements of Changes in Accumulated Surplus and Grants and Note C)					(20,000)	
Total funding of development resources	$74,350,546	$61,024,895	$330,350	$364,894	$ 80,000	$100,000

See Notes to Financial Statements.

Statements of Changes in Accumulated Surplus and Grants

For the fiscal years ended June 30, 1991 and June 30, 1990
Expressed in thousands of US dollars

	IDA		Special Fund		Debt Reduction Facility	
	1991	1990	1991	1990	1991	1990
Income from development credits—Notes D and H....	$ 346,881	$ 286,470				
Income from investments—Note H................	307,769	241,333	$ 20,719	$ 9,265		
Management fee charged by the International Bank for Reconstruction and Development—Note H........	(328,004)	(354,380)				
Amortization of discount on subscription advances	(6,453)	(5,567)				
Grants—Note C..............................					$(20,000)	
Changes from operations and grants	320,193	167,856	20,719	9,265	(20,000)	—
Effect of exchange rate changes on accumulated surplus	(155,505)	171,768	(14,327)	6,781		
Net changes	164,688	339,624	6,392	16,046	(20,000)	—
Balance at beginning of fiscal year...............	378,376	38,752	48,988	32,942		
Balance at end of fiscal year	$ 543,064	$ 378,376	$ 55,380	$48,988	$(20,000)	—

Statements of Cash Flows

For the fiscal years ended June 30, 1991 and June 30, 1990
Expressed in thousands of US dollars

	IDA		Special Fund		Debt Reduction Facility	
	1991	1990	1991	1990	1991	1990
Cash flows from development activities						
Development credit disbursements	$(4,511,430)	$(3,899,249)	$ (37,147)	$ (31,358)		
Development credit principal repayments	274,271	217,247				
Debt reduction grant disbursements					$ (8,422)	
Net cash used in development activities	(4,237,159)	(3,682,002)	(37,147)	(31,358)	(8,422)	—
Cash flows provided by member subscriptions and contributions	3,933,596	3,647,604	123,024	54,302	—	—
Cash flows provided by other contributions	322,495	63	—	—	8,422	
Cash flows from operating activities						
Changes from operations and grants	320,193	167,856	20,719	9,265	(20,000)	
Adjustments to reconcile changes from operations and grants to net cash provided by operating activities						
Amortization of discount on subscription advances	6,453	5,567				
Net changes in other assets and liabilities	(4,137)	(30,682)	668	267	11,578	
Decrease in receivables from the International Bank for Reconstruction and Development					8,422	
Net cash provided by operating activities	322,509	142,741	21,387	9,532	0	—
Effect of exchange rate changes on cash and investments immediately available for disbursement..	(99,603)	165,992	(14,344)	7,715		
Net increase in cash and investments immediately available for disbursement	241,838	274,398	92,920	40,191	0	—
Cash and investments immediately available for disbursement at beginning of fiscal year	1,794,305	1,519,907	100,041	59,850	0	
Cash and investments immediately available for disbursement at end of fiscal year	$ 2,036,143	$ 1,794,305	$192,961	$100,041	$ 0	—

See Notes to Financial Statements.

Summary Statement of Development Credits

June 30, 1991
Expressed in thousands of US dollars

	IDA		Special Fund[a]		Total		
Borrower or guarantor	Total development credits	Development credits outstanding	Total development credits	Development credits outstanding	Total development credits[b]	Development credits outstanding	Percentage of development credits outstanding
Afghanistan	$ 76,566	$ 76,566	$ —	$ —	$ 76,566	$ 76,566	0.17
Angola	22,531	—			22,531	—	*
Bangladesh	5,697,006	4,035,710	5,722	5,722	5,702,728	4,041,432	8.89
Benin	461,159	306,774	10,932	10,931	472,091	317,705	0.70
Bhutan	27,974	15,968	—	—	27,974	15,968	0.04
Bolivia	630,965	386,366	—	—	630,965	386,366	0.85
Botswana	13,432	13,432	—	—	13,432	13,432	0.03
Burkina Faso	523,489	275,441	—	—	523,489	275,441	0.61
Burundi	613,496	399,999	—	—	613,496	399,999	0.88
Cameroon	234,139	234,139	—	—	234,139	234,139	0.51
Cape Verde	20,545	13,871	—	—	20,545	13,871	0.03
Central African Republic	394,425	262,951	—	—	394,425	262,951	0.58
Chad	331,383	202,069	—	—	331,383	202,069	0.44
Chile	13,765	13,765	—	—	13,765	13,765	0.03
China	5,168,948	2,957,656	74,839	74,839	5,243,787	3,032,495	6.67
Colombia	14,127	14,127	—	—	14,127	14,127	0.03
Comoros	59,145	36,092	—	—	59,145	36,092	0.08
Congo	73,250	73,250	—	—	73,250	73,250	0.16
Costa Rica	3,296	3,296	—	—	3,296	3,296	0.01
Côte d'Ivoire	6,900	6,900	—	—	6,900	6,900	0.02
Djibouti	56,135	30,311	—	—	56,135	30,311	0.07
Dominica	11,964	10,047	—	—	11,964	10,047	0.02
Dominican Republic	19,932	19,932	—	—	19,932	19,932	0.04
Ecuador	31,298	31,298	—	—	31,298	31,298	0.07
Egypt	1,053,808	902,791	—	—	1,053,808	902,791	1.99
El Salvador	23,037	23,037	—	—	23,037	23,037	0.05
Equatorial Guinea	45,984	35,620	—	—	45,984	35,620	0.08
Ethiopia	1,316,631	824,148	—	—	1,316,631	824,148	1.81
Gambia, The	156,874	99,260	—	—	156,874	99,260	0.22
Ghana	1,982,824	1,264,663	44,650	44,650	2,027,474	1,309,313	2.88
Grenada	6,588	6,094	—	—	6,588	6,094	0.01
Guinea	776,111	417,827	—	—	776,111	417,827	0.92
Guinea-Bissau	188,744	139,804	5,139	5,135	193,883	144,939	0.32
Guyana	151,343	106,837	—	—	151,343	106,837	0.23
Haiti	420,085	307,662	15,811	11,387	435,896	319,049	0.70
Honduras	114,020	95,179	—	—	114,020	95,179	0.21
India	18,055,763	13,328,746	85,526	24,453	18,141,289	13,353,199	29.36
Indonesia	836,059	836,059	—	—	836,059	836,059	1.84
Jordan	76,617	76,617	—	—	76,617	76,617	0.17
Kenya	1,614,073	1,176,411	49,805	26,735	1,663,878	1,203,146	2.65
Korea, Republic of	96,621	96,621	—	—	96,621	96,621	0.21
Lao People's Democratic Republic	243,724	129,775	—	—	243,724	129,775	0.29
Lesotho	176,696	111,705	—	—	176,696	111,705	0.25
Liberia	103,577	100,714	—	—	103,577	100,714	0.22
Madagascar	1,162,102	786,091	36,761	36,727	1,198,863	822,818	1.81

| | IDA | | Special Fund[a] | | Total | | |
Borrower or guarantor	Total development credits	Development credits outstanding	Total development credits	Development credits outstanding	Total development credits[b]	Development credits outstanding	Percentage of development credits outstanding
Malawi	$ 1,030,522	$ 730,686	$ 17,254	$ 17,254	$ 1,047,776	$ 747,940	1.64
Maldives	24,435	11,678	—	—	24,435	11,678	0.03
Mali	780,419	487,672	14,004	12,744	794,423	500,416	1.10
Mauritania	286,364	204,984	—	—	286,364	204,984	0.45
Mauritius	18,677	18,677	—	—	18,677	18,677	0.04
Morocco	38,672	38,672	—	—	38,672	38,672	0.09
Mozambique	599,899	283,814	—	—	599,899	283,814	0.62
Myanmar	839,845	717,978	—	—	839,845	717,978	1.58
Nepal	1,153,539	653,241	—	—	1,153,539	653,241	1.44
Nicaragua	59,818	59,818	—	—	59,818	59,818	0.13
Niger	551,839	442,334	—	—	551,839	442,334	0.97
Nigeria	517,975	41,584	—	—	517,975	41,584	0.09
Pakistan	3,470,335	2,127,974	—	—	3,470,335	2,127,974	4.68
Papua New Guinea	111,232	111,232	—	—	111,232	111,232	0.24
Paraguay	40,726	40,726	—	—	40,726	40,726	0.09
Philippines	166,627	100,747	—	—	166,627	100,747	0.22
Rwanda	639,370	329,242	—	—	639,370	329,242	0.72
St. Kitts and Nevis	1,449	—	—	—	1,449	—	*
St. Lucia	5,270	577	—	—	5,270	577	*
St. Vincent and the Grenadines	2,372	1,412	5,270	5,246	7,642	6,658	0.01
São Tomé and Principe	43,085	23,649	—	—	43,085	23,649	0.05
Senegal	1,036,455	701,645	23,321	23,321	1,059,776	724,966	1.59
Sierra Leone	120,803	77,670	—	—	120,803	77,670	0.17
Solomon Islands	19,286	16,103	—	—	19,286	16,103	0.04
Somalia	517,259	398,449	—	—	517,259	398,449	0.88
Sri Lanka	1,601,955	917,469	—	—	1,601,955	917,469	2.02
Sudan	1,302,950	1,010,918	12,638	12,638	1,315,588	1,023,556	2.25
Swaziland	6,722	6,722	—	—	6,722	6,722	0.01
Syrian Arab Republic	43,908	43,908	—	—	43,908	43,908	0.10
Tanzania	1,953,229	1,276,784	—	—	1,953,229	1,276,784	2.81
Thailand	108,060	108,060	—	—	108,060	108,060	0.24
Togo	545,586	381,139	24,310	24,310	569,896	405,449	0.89
Tonga	5,243	2,477	—	—	5,243	2,477	0.01
Tunisia	58,529	58,529	—	—	58,529	58,529	0.13
Turkey	155,256	155,256	—	—	155,256	155,256	0.34
Uganda	1,467,163	957,054	—	—	1,467,163	957,054	2.10
Vanuatu	15,618	4,641	—	—	15,618	4,641	0.01
Viet Nam	58,205	58,205	—	—	58,205	58,205	0.13
Western Samoa	39,410	19,533	—	—	39,410	19,533	0.04
Yemen, Republic of	945,323	586,368	13,044	11,312	958,367	597,680	1.31
Zaire	1,414,578	1,083,238	—	—	1,414,578	1,083,238	2.38
Zambia	669,876	442,634	7,379	6,707	677,255	449,341	0.99
Zimbabwe	62,299	62,299	—	—	62,299	62,299	0.14
Subtotal members**	65,637,334	45,081,420	446,406	354,113	66,083,740	45,435,533	

(continued)

Summary Statement of Development Credits *(continued)*

June 30, 1991
Expressed in thousands of US dollars

	IDA		Special Fund[a]		Total		
Borrower or guarantor	Total development credits	Development credits outstanding	Total development credits	Development credits outstanding	Total development credits[b]	Development credits outstanding	Percentage of development credits outstanding
Regional development banks							
West African Development Bank[c]	$ 62,052	$ 16,495	$ —	$ —	$ 62,052	$ 16,495	0.04
Caribbean Development Bank[d]	33,262	16,262	—	—	33,262	16,262	0.04
Subtotal regional development banks	95,314	32,757	—	—	95,314	32,757	
Other[e]	9,730	9,730	—	—	9,730	9,730	0.02
Total—June 30, 1991**	$65,742,378	$45,123,907	$446,406	$354,113	$66,188,784	$45,478,020	100.00
Total—June 30, 1990	$60,402,870	$41,225,971	$470,225	$320,252	$60,873,095	$41,546,223	

*Less than 0.005 percent.

**May differ from the sum of the individual figures shown because of rounding.

a. At June 30, 1991, development credits outstanding of $354,113,000 ($320,252,000—June 30, 1990) which were originated under the Special Fund are shown under IDA in the Statements of Development Resources (see Notes to Financial Statements—Note D), since such amounts are repayable to IDA.

b. Of the undisbursed balance at June 30, 1991, IDA has entered into irrevocable commitments to disburse $249,327,000 ($296,095,000—June 30, 1990).

c. These development credits are for the benefit of Benin, Burkina Faso, Côte d'Ivoire, Niger, Senegal, and Togo.

d. These development credits are for the benefit of Grenada and territories of the United Kingdom (Associated States and Dependencies) in the Caribbean region.

e. Represents development credits made at a time when the authorities on Taiwan represented China in IDA (prior to May 15, 1980).

Maturity Structure of Development Credits*

Period	IDA	Special Fund[a]	Total
July 1, 1991 through June 30, 1992	$ 335,537	$ —	$ 335,537
July 1, 1992 through June 30, 1993	372,913	79	372,992
July 1, 1993 through June 30, 1994	438,403	1,734	440,137
July 1, 1994 through June 30, 1995	501,719	4,608	506,327
July 1, 1995 through June 30, 1996	580,972	4,608	585,580
July 1, 1996 through June 30, 2001	4,552,994	23,038	4,576,032
July 1, 2001 through June 30, 2006	7,738,307	43,909	7,782,216
July 1, 2006 through June 30, 2011	9,941,809	66,743	10,008,552
July 1, 2011 through June 30, 2016	11,434,416	66,743	11,501,159
July 1, 2016 through June 30, 2021	11,192,310	66,743	11,259,053
July 1, 2021 through June 30, 2026	9,880,898	66,744	9,947,642
July 1, 2026 through June 30, 2031	6,405,876	66,744	6,472,620
July 1, 2031 through June 30, 2036	2,267,926	34,713	2,302,639
July 1, 2036 through June 30, 2038	98,298	—	98,298
Total	$65,742,378	$446,406	$66,188,784

* Includes undisbursed balance.

a. At June 30, 1991, development credits outstanding of $354,113,000 ($320,252,000—June 30, 1990) which were originated under the Special Fund are shown under IDA in the Statements of Development Resources (see Notes to Financial Statements—Note D), since such amounts are repayable to IDA.

See Notes to Financial Statements.

Statement of Voting Power, and Subscriptions and Contributions

June 30, 1991
Expressed in thousands of US dollars

Member[a]	IDA			Special Fund contributions[b]
	Number of votes	Percentage of total	Subscriptions and contributions	
Part I Members				
Australia	106,645	1.40	$ 1,302,705	$ —
Austria	50,307	0.66	554,467	—
Belgium	81,027	1.06	867,960	48,091
Canada	241,554	3.16	3,376,165	163,474
Denmark	73,145	0.96	851,286	33,141
Finland	48,317	0.63	552,219	—
France	299,850	3.93	4,557,550	147,783
Germany	525,122	6.87	8,117,216	—
Iceland	19,538	0.26	12,086	—
Ireland	23,682	0.31	82,096	—
Italy	193,939	2.54	2,282,780	89,890
Japan	746,192	9.77	14,049,157	—
Kuwait	66,968	0.88	624,067	—
Luxembourg	20,528	0.27	35,753	—
Netherlands	146,491	1.92	2,095,785	—
New Zealand	23,657	0.31	76,922	—
Norway	72,613	0.95	831,929	40,011
South Africa	24,592	0.32	68,530	—
Sweden	156,897	2.05	1,911,329	75,592
United Arab Emirates	1,367	0.02	5,582	—
United Kingdom	420,870	5.51	5,607,344	—
United States	1,269,436	16.62	18,081,487	—
Subtotal	4,612,737	60.40	65,944,415	597,982
Part II Members				
Afghanistan	13,557	0.18	1,341	—
Algeria	18,481	0.24	5,099	—
Angola	45,662	0.60	8,245	—
Argentina	81,053	1.06	49,092	—
Bangladesh	47,175	0.62	7,153	—
Belize	1,788	0.02	243	—
Benin	4,800	0.06	623	—
Bhutan	3,559	0.05	61	—
Bolivia	13,748	0.18	1,328	—
Botswana	19,163	0.25	214	—
Brazil	129,916	1.70	76,598	—
Burkina Faso	9,720	0.13	647	—
Burundi	17,143	0.22	998	—
Cameroon	13,854	0.18	1,329	—
Cape Verde	516	0.01	97	—
Central African Republic	10,920	0.14	653	—
Chad	11,172	0.15	651	—
Chile	31,782	0.42	4,489	—
China	154,320	2.02	39,605	—
Colombia	34,350	0.45	22,479	—
Comoros	13,083	0.17	107	—
Congo	6,685	0.09	639	—
Costa Rica	7,844	0.10	254	—
Côte d'Ivoire	7,771	0.10	1,291	—
Cyprus	22,373	0.29	1,042	—
Czechoslovakia	41,462	0.54	7,317	—
Djibouti	532	0.01	193	—

(continued)

Statement of Voting Power, and Subscriptions and Contributions (continued)

June 30, 1991
Expressed in thousands of US dollars

	IDA			
Member[a]	Number of votes	Percentage of total	Subscriptions and contributions	Special Fund contributions[b]
Part II Members (continued)				
Dominica	10,468	0.14	$ 102	$ —
Dominican Republic	16,129	0.21	575	—
Ecuador	18,145	0.24	827	—
Egypt	34,710	0.45	6,541	—
El Salvador	6,244	0.08	403	—
Equatorial Guinea	6,284	0.08	410	—
Ethiopia	20,989	0.27	718	—
Fiji	2,130	0.03	701	—
Gabon	2,093	0.03	627	—
Gambia, The	10,644	0.14	338	—
Ghana	20,418	0.27	3,009	—
Greece	28,503	0.37	12,153	—
Grenada	14,496	0.19	123	—
Guatemala	12,713	0.17	508	—
Guinea	21,785	0.29	1,327	—
Guinea-Bissau	528	0.01	169	—
Guyana	18,160	0.24	1,017	—
Haiti	14,143	0.19	1,016	—
Honduras	16,598	0.22	389	—
Hungary	59,746	0.78	26,616	—
India	241,413	3.16	54,552	—
Indonesia	77,885	1.02	14,600	—
Iran, Islamic Republic of	15,455	0.20	5,853	—
Iraq	9,407	0.12	992	—
Israel	9,386	0.12	2,401	—
Jordan	19,893	0.26	398	—
Kampuchea, Democratic	7,826	0.10	1,284	—
Kenya	20,688	0.27	2,161	—
Kiribati	4,734	0.06	74	—
Korea, Republic of	29,233	0.38	69,140	—
Lao People's Democratic Republic	11,723	0.15	627	—
Lebanon	8,562	0.11	564	—
Lesotho	10,487	0.14	204	—
Liberia	13,867	0.18	1,016	—
Libya	7,771	0.10	1,303	—
Madagascar	702	0.01	1,218	—
Malawi	22,373	0.29	1,004	—
Malaysia	31,808	0.42	3,456	—
Maldives	18,459	0.24	40	—
Mali	22,638	0.30	1,207	—
Mauritania	11,067	0.14	649	—
Mauritius	22,942	0.30	1,181	—
Mexico	49,849	0.65	72,981	—
Mongolia	546	0.01	277	—
Morocco	37,266	0.49	4,741	—
Mozambique	774	0.01	1,653	—
Myanmar	29,166	0.38	2,802	—
Nepal	20,802	0.27	659	—
Nicaragua	19,893	0.26	405	—
Niger	16,541	0.22	672	—
Nigeria	9,477	0.12	4,263	—
Oman	19,896	0.26	438	—
Pakistan	71,936	0.94	13,590	—

| | IDA | | | |
Member[a]	Number of votes	Percentage of total	Subscriptions and contributions	Special Fund contributions[b]
Panama	5,657	0.07	$ 26	$ —
Papua New Guinea	13,050	0.17	1,125	—
Paraguay	11,419	0.15	382	—
Peru	5,699	0.07	2,135	—
Philippines	16,583	0.22	6,461	—
Poland	184,598	2.42	45,261	—
Rwanda	12,667	0.17	993	—
St. Kitts and Nevis	526	0.01	158	—
St. Lucia	17,847	0.23	207	—
St. Vincent and the Grenadines	514	0.01	84	—
São Tomé and Principe	4,739	0.06	86	—
Saudi Arabia	254,722	3.33	1,883,213	—
Senegal	22,640	0.30	2,262	—
Sierra Leone	12,667	0.17	953	—
Solomon Islands	518	0.01	109	—
Somalia	10,506	0.14	953	—
Spain	102,437	1.34	316,712	—
Sri Lanka	34,546	0.45	3,996	—
Sudan	13,884	0.18	1,283	—
Swaziland	11,073	0.14	407	—
Syrian Arab Republic	7,651	0.10	1,202	—
Tanzania	16,021	0.21	2,110	—
Thailand	34,546	0.45	4,157	—
Togo	17,143	0.22	1,023	—
Tonga	11,380	0.15	94	—
Trinidad and Tobago	770	0.01	1,629	—
Tunisia	2,793	0.04	1,893	—
Turkey	50,917	0.67	37,922	—
Uganda	16,021	0.21	2,106	—
Vanuatu	9,263	0.12	240	—
Viet Nam	8,889	0.12	1,893	—
Western Samoa	12,999	0.17	117	—
Yemen, Republic of	20,458	0.27	2,112	—
Yugoslavia	50,815	0.67	25,261	—
Zaire	12,164	0.16	3,785	—
Zambia	24,909	0.33	3,393	—
Zimbabwe	1,324	0.02	4,970	—
Subtotal	3,026,175	39.62	2,916,490	—
Total—June 30, 1991*	7,638,912	100.00	$68,860,905	$597,982
Total—June 30, 1990	6,905,454		$55,651,130	$601,771

* Total may differ from sum of individual figures shown because of rounding.

a. See Notes to Financial Statements—Note E for an explanation of the two categories of membership.

b. At June 30, 1991, Special Fund contributions of $323,012,000 ($285,865,000—June 30, 1990) are shown under IDA in the Statements of Development Resources (see Notes to Financial Statements—Note D), since the development credits that were funded using these resources are repayable to IDA.

See Notes to Financial Statements.

Notes to Financial Statements

Summary of Significant Accounting and Related Policies

Organization and Operations

IDA: IDA was established on September 24, 1960, to promote economic development, increase productivity, and raise the standard of living of its developing country members. Following a decision of the Executive Directors to terminate the Special Facility for Sub-Saharan Africa as of June 30, 1990, all assets and liabilities of the Special Facility for Sub-Saharan Africa have been transferred to IDA. IDA's financial position at June 30, 1990 was restated accordingly.

Special Fund: On October 26, 1982, IDA established the Special Fund, constituted by funds to be contributed by members of IDA and administered by IDA, to supplement the regular resources available for lending by IDA. The arrangements governing the Special Fund may be amended or terminated by IDA's Executive Directors subject to the agreement of a qualified majority of the contributors to the Special Fund. The resources of the Special Fund are kept separate from the resources of IDA.

Debt Reduction Facility: On September 28, 1989, IDA established the Debt Reduction Facility for IDA-Only Countries (the Debt Reduction Facility), constituted by contributions of the IBRD to facilitate commercial debt reduction for IDA-only countries. The Debt Reduction Facility is administered by IDA. The resources of the Debt Reduction Facility are kept separate from the resources of IDA.

Translation of Currencies

IDA's principal financial statements are expressed in terms of US dollars solely for the purpose of summarizing IDA's financial position and the results of its operations for the convenience of its members and other interested parties.

IDA: IDA is an international organization which conducts its operations in the currencies of all of its members and Switzerland. Assets and liabilities are translated at market rates of exchange at the end of the accounting period. Subscriptions and contributions are translated in the manner described below. Translation adjustments relating to the revaluation of development credits denominated in Special Drawing Rights (SDRs) are charged or credited to Cumulative Translation Adjustment on Development Credits. Other translation adjustments are charged or credited to the Accumulated Surplus.

Special Fund: Assets of the Special Fund are translated at market rates of exchange at the end of the period. Contributions are translated in the manner described below. Income is generally translated at market rates of exchange on dates of recognition of income.

Debt Reduction Facility: The resources and grants of the Debt Reduction Facility are denominated in US dollars.

Valuation of Subscriptions and Contributions

IDA: The subscriptions and contributions provided through the third replenishment are expressed in terms of "US dollars of the weight and fineness in effect on January 1, 1960" (1960 dollars). Following the abolition of gold as a common denominator of the monetary system and the repeal of the provision of the US law defining the par value of the US dollar in terms of gold, the pre-existing basis for translating 1960 dollars into current dollars or any other currency disappeared. On June 30, 1987, the Executive Directors of IDA decided, with effect on that date and until such time as the relevant provisions of the Articles of Agreement are amended, to interpret the words "US dollars of the weight and fineness in effect on January 1, 1960" in Article II, Section 2(b) of the Articles of Agreement of IDA to mean the Special Drawing Right (SDR) introduced by the Interna-

tional Monetary Fund as the SDR was valued in terms of US dollars immediately before the introduction of the basket method of valuing the SDR on July 1, 1974, such value being equal to $1.20635 for one SDR (the 1974 SDR), and also decided to apply the same standard of value to amounts expressed in 1960 dollars in the relevant resolutions of the Board of Governors.

The subscriptions and contributions provided through the third replenishment are expressed on the basis of the 1974 SDR. Prior to the decision of the Executive Directors, IDA had valued these subscriptions and contributions on the basis of the SDR at the current market value of the SDR.

The subscriptions and contributions provided under the fourth replenishment and thereafter are expressed in members' currencies or SDRs and are payable in members' currencies. Beginning July 1, 1986, subscriptions and contributions made available for disbursement in cash to IDA are translated at market rates of exchange on the dates they were made available. Prior to that date, subscriptions and contributions which had been disbursed or converted into other currencies were translated at market rates of exchange on dates of disbursement or conversion. Subscriptions and contributions not yet available for disbursements are translated at market rates of exchange at the end of the accounting period.

Special Fund: Beginning April 1, 1989, subscriptions and contributions received but not yet disbursed, as well as subscriptions and contributions disbursed or converted into other currencies, are translated at market rates of exchange on the dates they were made available for disbursement in cash to the Special Fund. Prior to that date, subscriptions and contributions which had been disbursed or converted into other currencies were translated at market rates of exchange on dates of disbursement or conversion. Subscriptions and contributions receivable are translated at market rates of exchange at the end of the accounting period.

Development Credits

All development credits are made to member governments or to the government of a territory of a member (except for development credits which have been made to regional development banks for the benefit of members or territories of members of IDA). It is IDA's policy to place in nonaccrual status all development credits made to a member government or to the government of a territory of a member if principal or charges with respect to any such credit are overdue by more than six months, unless IDA management determines that the overdue amount will be collected in the immediate future. On the date a member is placed in nonaccrual status, interest and other charges that had been accrued on loans outstanding to the member which remained unpaid are deducted from the income of the current period. In addition, if loans by the IBRD to a member government are placed in nonaccrual status, all credits to that member government will also be placed in nonaccrual status by IDA. Charges on nonaccruing credits are included in income only to the extent that payments have actually been received by IDA.

IDA has not suffered any losses on development credit receivables and has established no provision for credit losses because no losses are anticipated.

IDA: The repayment obligations of IDA's development credits funded from resources through the fifth replenishment are expressed in the development credit agreements in terms of 1960 dollars. On June 30, 1987, the Executive Directors decided to value those credits at the rate of $1.20635 per 1960 dollar on a permanent basis. Development credits funded from resources provided under the sixth replenishment and thereafter are denominated in SDRs; the principal amounts disbursed under such credits are to be repaid in currency amounts currently equivalent to the SDRs disbursed.

Special Fund: Special Fund credits are denominated in SDRs. The principal amounts disbursed under such credits are to be repaid in currency amounts currently equivalent to the SDRs disbursed.

Special Fund credits are made on the same terms as regular IDA credits except that the proceeds of Special Fund credits may be used only to finance expenditures for goods or services from (a) Part II members of IDA; (b) Part I members contributing to the Special Fund; and (c) Part I members contributing to the regular resources of IDA through IDA's FY84 Account who have notified IDA that such contributions are to be treated in the same manner as contributions to the Special Fund for purposes of any future adjustment of the voting rights of the members of IDA.

Debt Reduction Facility Grants

All Debt Reduction Facility grants are made to member governments for the purpose of assisting in clearly identified debt reduction operations. All IDA-only countries (countries below the operational threshold for which no IBRD lending is projected over the next few years) with a heavy debt burden are eligible to receive grants. Debt Reduction Facility grants are decided on a case-by-case basis, taking into account the existence of a medium-term adjustment program and a strategy for debt management acceptable to IDA. Debt Reduction Facility resources are available until September 28, 1992, unless this period is extended. Any funds not disbursed within that period will revert to IDA and be available for use in its general operations.

Investments

In prior years, IDA recorded its investment securities at cost or amortized cost. As of July 1, 1990, IDA changed its policy and began carrying its investment securities at market value, since this was considered a more appropriate reflection of the value of the portfolio. The cumulative effect of this change was not material to the financial statements. Both realized and unrealized gains and losses are included in income from investments.

Reclassifications

Certain reclassifications of the prior year's information have been made to conform with the current year's presentation.

Note A—Investments

Following is a summary of the currency composition of the investment portfolio at June 30, 1991:

| Currency | June 30, 1991 | |
	IDA	Special Fund
Australian dollars	$ 323,441,000	$ —
Canadian dollars	9,887,000	45,787,000
Danish kroner	10,819,000	2,030,000
Deutsche mark	326,805,000	—
French francs	116,909,000	66,402,000
Italian lire	125,610,000	53,042,000
Netherlands guilders	117,220,000	—
Pounds sterling	1,030,533,000	—
Swedish kronor	41,455,000	24,502,000
Other currencies	2,025,000	68,000
Total	$2,104,704,000	$191,831,000

As part of its overall portfolio management strategy, IDA enters into futures contracts, which are subject to some off-balance-sheet risk. Futures are contracts for delayed delivery of securities or money market instruments in which the seller agrees to make delivery at a specified future date of a specified instrument, at a specified price or yield. At June 30, 1991, the total contract value of futures contracts was $148,775,000. There were no outstanding futures contracts at June 30, 1990. IDA has minimal exposure

to credit loss on futures contracts due to potential nonperformance of counterparties since changes in the market value of futures contracts on any given business day are settled in cash on the following business day.

Covered forwards are agreements in which cash in one currency is converted into a different currency and, simultaneously, a forward exchange agreement is executed with either the same or a different counterparty providing for a future exchange of the two currencies in order to recover the currency converted. At June 30, 1991, IDA had gross receivables from covered forward agreements of $23,546,000 and gross payables from covered forward agreements of $23,787,000. IDA's exposure to credit loss in the event of nonperformance by counterparties was $359,000. There were no outstanding covered forward agreements at June 30, 1990.

Note B—Cash and Investments Not Immediately Available for Disbursement

Under the Articles of Agreement and the arrangements governing replenishments, IDA must take appropriate steps to ensure that, over a reasonable period of time, the resources provided by donors for lending by IDA are used on an approximately pro rata basis. Donors sometimes contribute resources substantially ahead of their pro rata share. Unless otherwise agreed, IDA does not disburse these funds ahead of donors' pro rata shares. Cash and Investments Not Immediately Available for Disbursement represents the difference between the amount contributed and the amount available for disbursements on a pro rata basis.

Note C—Debt Reduction Facility Grants

During the fiscal year ended June 30, 1991, the Executive Directors have approved debt reduction grants of $10,000,000 for Niger and $10,000,000 for Mozambique. As of June 30, 1991, $8,422,000 of these amounts has been disbursed for Niger. The remainder is reflected as Grants Payable.

Note D—Development Credits

Special Fund development credits disbursed and outstanding of $354,113,000 at June 30, 1991 ($320,252,000—June 30, 1990) are included in the Statements of Development Resources of IDA since principal repayments on these credits shall become part of the general resources of IDA, unless otherwise provided in a decision of IDA's Executive Directors to terminate administration of the Special Fund by IDA.

At June 30, 1991, principal installments of $177,000 and interest and other charges of $152,000 payable to IDA on development credits other than those referred to in the following paragraph were overdue by more than three months. The aggregate principal amount outstanding on these credits was $40,450,000. The aggregate principal amount outstanding on all credits to any borrowers, other than those referred to in the following paragraph, with any one credit overdue by more than three months was $73,250,000.

At June 30, 1991, the development credits made to or guaranteed by certain member countries with an aggregate principal balance outstanding of $282,110,000 ($539,416,000—June 30, 1990), of which $7,556,000 ($7,435,000—June 30, 1990) was overdue, were in nonaccrual status. As of such date, overdue charges in respect of these credits totaled $10,652,000 ($16,606,000—June 30, 1990). If these credits had not been in nonaccrual status, income from credits for the fiscal year ended June 30, 1991 would have been higher by $1,515,000 ($5,747,000—June 30, 1990), which is net of charges received from such members during the fiscal year. A summary of borrowers in nonaccrual status follows:

(continued)

Notes to Financial Statements   (continued)

Borrower	Principal outstanding	June 30, 1991 Principal and charges overdue	Nonaccrual since
Liberia	$100,714,000	$ 5,117,000	April 1988
Nicaragua	59,818,000	5,634,000	April 1988
Sierra Leone	77,670,000	4,434,000	April 1988
Syrian Arab Republic	43,908,000	3,023,000	April 1988
Total	$282,110,000	$18,208,000	

In fiscal year 1991, Zambia paid off all of its arrears and therefore came out of nonaccrual status. As a result, income from credits for the year was increased by $7,965,000 for income that would have been accrued in previous fiscal years.

On July 2, 1991, development credits made to or guaranteed by Somalia were placed in nonaccrual status. The aggregate principal balance outstanding on the development credits made to or guaranteed by Somalia was $398,449,000, of which $920,000 was overdue. As of June 30, 1991, overdue interest and other charges in respect of these credits totaled $1,491,000. Income previously accrued but not yet received as of June 30, 1991, amounting to $2,163,000, was excluded from income from loans for the fiscal year ended June 30, 1991.

Note E—Member Subscriptions and Contributions

Restricted Assets and Subscriptions: For the purposes of its financial resources, the membership of IDA is divided into two categories: (1) Part I members, which make payments of subscriptions and contributions provided to IDA in convertible currencies which may be freely used or exchanged by IDA in its operations; (2) Part II members, which make payments of 10 percent of their initial subscriptions in freely convertible currencies, and the remaining 90 percent of their initial subscriptions and all additional subscriptions and contributions in their own currencies or in freely convertible currencies. IDA's Articles of Agreement and subsequent replenishment agreements provide that the currency of any Part II member paid in by it may not be used by IDA for projects financed by IDA and located outside the territories of the member except by agreement between the member and IDA.

Maintenance of Value: Article IV, Sections 2(a) and (b) of IDA's Articles of Agreement provides for maintenance-of-value payments on account of the local currency portion of the initial subscription whenever the par value of the member's currency or its foreign exchange value has, in the opinion of IDA, depreciated or appreciated to a significant extent within the members' territories, so long as and to the extent that such currency shall not have been initially disbursed or exchanged for the currency of another member. The provisions of Article IV, Sections 2(a) and (b) have by agreement been extended to cover additional subscriptions and contributions of IDA through the third replenishment but are not applicable to those of the fourth and subsequent replenishments.

The Executive Directors decided on June 30, 1987 that settlements of maintenance-of-value obligations, which would result from the resolution of the valuation issue on the basis of the 1974 SDR, would be deferred until the Executive Directors decide to resume such settlements.

Ninth Replenishment: On May 8, 1990, the Board of Governors of IDA adopted a resolution authorizing the ninth replenishment of IDA resources. The ninth replenishment provides IDA with resources to fund credits committed during the period July 1, 1990 to June 30, 1993. The amount of the replenishment, including supplementary contributions provided by certain members and resources from Switzerland, is equivalent to SDR11,679,000,000 (at the exchange rates determined pursuant to a formula agreed by IDA and contributing donors) equivalent to $15,388,000,000 at June 30, 1991 exchange rates. The ninth replenishment became effective on January 23, 1991.

Subscriptions and Contributions Not Yet Due: At June 30, 1991, unrestricted subscriptions and contributions not yet due will become due as follows:

Fiscal year	June 30, 1991
1992	$4,450,952,000
1993	4,356,820,000
1994	5,117,000
1995	16,338,000
Undetermined	19,553,000
Total	$8,848,780,000

Contributions to the Special Fund: Member contributions to the Special Fund totaling $597,982,000 as of June 30, 1991 are reflected as Member Subscriptions and Contributions in the Statements of Development Resources. As of June 30, 1991, the Special Fund total is reflected net of $323,012,000 ($285,865,000—June 30, 1990), which represents development credit disbursements that are repayable to and included in Member Subscriptions and Contributions of IDA.

Note F—Contribution by Switzerland

IDA has received cumulative contributions in the amount of Swiss francs 181,480,000 (historical US-dollar equivalent of $51,173,000) from the Swiss Confederation, which is not a member of IDA. The agreements between the Swiss Confederation and IDA provide for converting these grant contributions into subscriptions or contributions if Switzerland should become a member of IDA.

Note G—Transfers from the International Bank for Reconstruction and Development (IBRD)

IDA: The IBRD has authorized transfers by way of grants to IDA totaling $3,045,056,000 from net income of the IBRD for the fiscal years ended June 30, 1964 through June 30, 1987, and June 30, 1989 and 1990. Of the total amount, $79,905,000 has been disbursed for grants for agricultural research, the control of onchocerciasis, and other developmental activities. Of the balance of $2,965,151,000 available for general purposes, $2,186,670,000 has been received and $778,481,000 is reflected as a receivable from the IBRD, as of June 30, 1991.

Debt Reduction Facility: The IBRD authorized a transfer to the Debt Reduction Facility of $100,000,000 from net income for the fiscal year ended June 30, 1989. Of this amount, $8,422,000 has been received and $91,578,000 is reflected as a receivable from the IBRD, as of June 30, 1991.

Note H—Income and Expenses

IDA: IDA pays a management fee to the IBRD representing its share of the administrative expenses incurred by the IBRD.

Special Fund: The service and commitment charges payable by borrowers under Special Fund development credits are paid directly to IDA to compensate it for services as administrator of the Special Fund. Income from investments of the Special Fund becomes part of the resources of the Special Fund.

Report of Independent Accountants

Price Waterhouse	The Hague	Tokyo
(International Firm)	London	Washington
	New York	

Price Waterhouse

July 29, 1991

President and Board of Governors
  International Development Association, the
  Special Fund Administered by the International
  Development Association, and the Debt Reduction
  Facility for IDA-Only Countries Administered
  by the International Development Association

In our opinion, the financial statements appearing on pages 208 through 218 of this Report present fairly, in all material respects, in terms of United States dollars, the financial position of the International Development Association, the Special Fund Administered by the International Development Association, and the Debt Reduction Facility for IDA-Only Countries Administered by the International Development Association at June 30, 1991 and 1990, and the changes in their accumulated surplus and grants and their cash flows for the years then ended in conformity with generally accepted accounting principles in the United States and with International Accounting Standards. These financial statements are the responsibility of management; our responsibility is to express an opinion on these financial statements based on our audits. We conducted our audits of these statements in accordance with generally accepted auditing standards, including International Auditing Guidelines, which require that we plan and perform the audit to obtain reasonable assurance about whether the financial statements are free of material misstatement. An audit includes examining, on a test basis, evidence supporting the amounts and disclosures in the financial statements, assessing the accounting principles used and significant estimates made by management, and evaluating the overall financial statement presentation. We believe that our audits provide a reasonable basis for the opinion expressed above.

Price Waterhouse
(International Firm)

IBRD/IDA Appendices

Governors and Alternates of the World Bank

Appendix 1

June 30, 1991

Member	Governor	Alternate
Afghanistan	Mohammad Hakim	Mohammad Ehsan
Algeria	Ghazi Hidouci	Kacim Brachemi
Angola	Fernando van Dunem	Fernando A. G. Teixeira
Antigua and Barbuda[a]	John E. St. Luce	Ludolph Brown
Argentina	Domingo Cavallo	Roque Fernández
Australia	John Kerin	Bob Dun
Austria	Ferdinand Lacina	Othmar Haushofer
Bahamas, The[a]	Paul L. Adderley	Warren Rolle
Bahrain[a]	Ibrahim Abdul Karim	Isa Abdulla Borshaid
Bangladesh	M. Saifur Rahman	Enam Ahmed Chaudhury
Barbados[a]	L. Erskine Sandiford	Winston A. Cox
Belgium	Philippe Maystadt	Alfons Verplaetse
Belize	Said W. Musa	Joseph D. Waight
Benin	Paul Dossou	Fatiou Adekounte
Bhutan	Dawa Tsering	Karma Dorjee
Bolivia	Enrique García	Raúl Boada
Botswana	Festus G. Mogae	Baledzi Gaolathe
Brazil	Marcilio Marques Moreira	Francisco Gros
Bulgaria[a]	Ivan Kostov	Atanas Paparisov
Burkina Faso	Frederic A. Korsaga	Henri Bruno Bessin
Burundi	Gérard Niyibigira	Salvator Nkeshimana
Cameroon	Tchouta Moussa	Esther Dang
Canada	Donald Mazankowski	Marcel Masse
Cape Verde	Jose Tomas Veiga	Antônio Hilario Da Cruz
Central African Republic	Thierry Bingaba	Gregoire Zowaye
Chad	Hassan Fadoul Kittir	Gali Gatta Ngothe
Chile	Alejandro Foxley	José Pablo Arellano
China	Wang Bingqian	Chi Haibin
Colombia	Rudolf Hommes	Francisco J. Ortega
Comoros	Mohamed Ali	Said Mohamed Mshangama
Congo	Pierre Moussa	Dieudonné Diabatantou
Costa Rica	Thelmo Vargas Madrigal	Jorge Guardia Quirós
Côte d'Ivoire	Kablan D. Duncan	N'Golo Coulibaly
Cyprus	George Syrimis	Michael Erotokritos
Czechoslovakia	Vaclav Klaus	Josef Tosovsky
Denmark	Uffe Ellemann-Jensen	Ole Loensmann Poulsen
Djibouti	Moussa Bouraleh Robleh	Ibrahim Kassim Chehem
Dominica	Mary Eugenia Charles	Gilbert Williams
Dominican Republic	Luis Toral Córdova	Manuel E. Gómez Pieterz
Ecuador	Pablo Better	Mauricio Valencia
Egypt	Kamal El-Ganzoury	Maurice Makram-Allah
El Salvador	Mirna Liévano de Márques	José Roberto Orellana Milla
Equatorial Guinea	Marcelino Nguema Onguene	Miguel Edjang Angue
Ethiopia	Bekele Tamirat	Seyoum Alemayehu
Fiji	J. N. Kamikamica	Rigamoto Taito
Finland	Iiro Viinanen	Toimi Kankaanniemi
France	Jacques de Larosière	Jean-Claude Trichet
Gabon	Marcel Doupamby-Matoka	Richard Onouviet
Gambia, The	Saihou S. Sabally	Alieu M. Ngum
Germany	Carl-Dieter Spranger	Horst Koehler
Ghana	Kwesi Botchwey	Kwesi Bekoe Amissah-Arthur
Greece	Efthimios Christodoulou	George Vlachos
Grenada	George Ignatius Brizan	Lauriston F. Wilson, Jr.

Member	Governor	Alternate
Guatemala	Richard Aitkenhead Castillo	Juan Luis Mirón Aguilar
Guinea	Ibrahima Sylla	Kerfalla Yansane
Guinea-Bissau	Pedro A. Godinho Gomes	José Lima Barber
Guyana	Carl Greenidge	Winston Murray
Haiti	Marie Michele Rey	Renaud Bernardin
Honduras	Benjamín Villanueva	Ricardo Maduro Joest
Hungary	Mihaly Kupa	Imre Tarafas
Iceland	Jon Sigurdsson	Fridrik Sophusson
India	Manmohan Singh	S. P. Shukla
Indonesia	J. B. Sumarlin	Hasudungan Tampubolon
Iran, Islamic Republic of	Mohsen Noorbakhsh	Mehdi Navab
Iraq	Subhi Frankool	Hashim Ali Obaid
Ireland	Albert Reynolds	Sean P. Cromien
Israel	Michael Bruno	Shalom Singer
Italy	Carlo Azeglio Ciampi	Mario Draghi
Jamaica[a]	P. J. Patterson	Omar Davies
Japan	Ryutaro Hashimoto	Yasushi Mieno
Jordan	Khalid Amin Abdullah	Ibrahim Badren
Kampuchea, Democratic	(vacant)	(vacant)
Kenya	George Saitoti	Charles S. Moindyo
Kiribati	Teatao Teannaki	Baraniko Baaro
Korea, Republic of	Yong-Man Rhee	Kun Kim
Kuwait	Nasser Abdullah Al-Roudhan	Bader Meshari Al-Humaidhi
Lao People's Democratic Republic	Sisavath Sisane	Soulingong Nhouyvanisvong
Lebanon	Ali El-Khalil	Habib Abu-Sakr
Lesotho	A. L. Thoahlane	T. N. Thokoa
Liberia	Elijah E. Taylor	Mary B. Dennis
Libya	Mohamed El Madni Al-Bukhari	Bashir Ali Khallat
Luxembourg	Jean-Claude Juncker	Yves Mersch
Madagascar	Jean Robiarivony	Nirina Andriamanerasoa
Malawi	L. Chimango	Graham Chipande
Malaysia	Anwar Ibrahim	Zain Azraai
Maldives	Fathulla Jameel	(vacant)
Mali	Bakary Mariko	Souleymane Dembele
Malta[a]	George Bonello Du Puis	Edgar Wadge
Mauritania	Mohamedou Ould Michel	M'Rabih Rabou Ould Cheikh Bounena
Mauritius	Beergoonath Ghurburrun	Dharam Dev Manraj
Mexico	Pedro Aspe Armella	José Angel Gurría
Mongolia	Gochoogiin Khuderchuluun	Dalrain Davaasambuu
Morocco	Mohamed Berrada	Mohammed Dairi
Mozambique	Abdul Magid Osman	Eneas da Conceição Comiche
Myanmar	D. O. Abel	Min Aung
Namibia[a]	Zedekia Ngavirue	Godfrey Gaoseb
Nepal	Devendra Raj Panday	Sash Narayan Shah
Netherlands	W. Kok	J. P. Pronk
New Zealand	Graham C. Scott	Chris N. Pinfield
Nicaragua	Emilio Pereira	Silvio De Franco
Niger	Almoustapha Soumaila	Nassirou Sabo
Nigeria	Abubakar Alhaji	Ahmadu Abubakar
Norway	Sigbjoern Johnsen	Grete Faremo
Oman	Qais Abdul-Munim Al-Zawawi	Mohammed Bin Musa Al Yousef
Pakistan	Sartaj Aziz	R. A. Akhund

(continued)

Governors and Alternates of the World Bank *(continued)*

Appendix 1

June 30, 1991

Member	Governor	Alternate
Panama	Guillermo Ford B.	Luis H. Moreno, Jr.
Papua New Guinea	Paul Pora.	Morea Vele
Paraguay	Juan J. Díaz Pérez	(vacant)
Peru	Carlos Boloña Behr.	Alfredo Jalilie Awapara
Philippines	Jesús P. Estanislao	José Cuisia, Jr.
Poland	Grzegorz Wojtowicz	Wladyslaw Golebiowski
Portugal[a]	Luis Miguel Beleza	Carlos Manuel Tavares da Silva
Qatar[a]	Abdul Aziz Khalifa Al-Thani	Abdullah Khalid Al-Atiyyah
Romania[a]	Theodor Dumitru Stolojan	Marian Crisan
Rwanda	Benoit Ntigulirwa	Felicien Ntahondi
St. Kitts and Nevis	Kennedy A. Simmonds	William V. Herbert
St. Lucia	John G. M. Compton	Bernard Lacorbiniere
St. Vincent and the Grenadines	James F. Mitchell	Dwight Venner
São Tomé and Principe	Noberto Costa Alegre	Manuel de Nazareh Mendes
Saudi Arabia	Mohammad Abalkhail	Hamad Al-Sayari
Senegal	Famara Ibrahima Sagna	Awa Thiongane
Seychelles[a]	Danielle de St. Jorre	Bertrand Rassool
Sierra Leone	Thomas Taylor Morgan	Y. T. Sesay
Singapore[a]	Richard Hu Tsu Tau	Ngiam Tong Dow
Solomon Islands	Christopher C. Abe	Snyder Rini
Somalia	Abdurahman Jama Barre	Said Ahmed Yusuf
South Africa	C. L. Stals	Simon Streicher Brand
Spain	Carlos Solchaga	Mariano Rubio Jiménez
Sri Lanka	D. B. Wijetunga	R. Paskaralingam
Sudan	Abdul Rahim Mahmood Hamdi	Mohamed Khair El Zubair
Suriname[a]	Jules Wijdenbosch	R. W. Braam
Swaziland	Elliot Bhembe	Noreen N. Maphalala
Sweden	Allan Larsson	Lena Hjelm-Wallen
Syrian Arab Republic	Mohammed Khaled Mahayni	Adnan Al-Saty
Tanzania	K. A. Malima	Simon Mbilinyi
Thailand	Suthee Singhasaneh	Panas Simasathien
Togo	Barry Moussa Barque	Kwassi Klutse
Tonga	James Cecil Cocker	Selwyn Percy Jones
Trinidad and Tobago	Selby Wilson	William G. Demas
Tunisia	Mustapha Kamel Nabli	Abdellatif Saddem
Turkey	Namik Kemal Kilic	Mahfi Egilmez
Uganda	Joshua Mayanja Nkangi	James Kahoza
United Arab Emirates	Hamdan bin Rashid Al Maktoum	Ahmed Humaid Al-Tayer
United Kingdom	Robin Leigh-Pemberton	Timothy Lankester
United States	Nicholas F. Brady	Richard T. McCormack
Uruguay[a]	Enrique Braga	Conrado Hughes
Vanuatu	S. J. Regenvanu	George Pakoa
Venezuela[a]	Miguel Rodríguez	Carlos Stark Rausseo
Viet Nam	Cao Si Kiem	Le Van Chau
Western Samoa	Tuilaepa S. Malielegaoi	Epa Tuioti
Yemen, Republic of	Farag Bin Ghanem	(vacant)
Yugoslavia	Branimir Zekan	Slavoljub Stanic
Zaire	Ilunga Ilunkamba	Mbonga Magalu Engwanda
Zambia	M. N. Masheke	Leonard Nkhata
Zimbabwe	B. T. G. Chidzero	K. J. Moyana

a. Member of the IBRD only.

Executive Directors and Alternates of the World Bank and Their Voting Power

Appendix 2

June 30, 1991

Executive director	Alternate	Casting votes of	IBRD Total votes	IBRD % of total	IDA Total votes	IDA % of total
Appointed						
E. Patrick Coady	Mark T. Cox, IV	United States	206,507	17.59	1,269,436	16.71
Masaki Shiratori	(vacant)[a]	Japan	94,020	8.01	746,192	9.82
Gerhard Boehmer[b]	Harald Rehm	Germany	72,649	6.19	525,122	6.91
Jean-Pierre Landau	Philippe de Fontaine Vive	France	69,647	5.93	299,850	3.95
David Peretz	Robert Graham-Harrison	United Kingdom	69,647	5.93	420,870	5.54
Elected						
Jacques de Groote (Belgium)	Walter Rill (Austria)	Austria, Belgium, Czechoslovakia, Hungary, Luxembourg, Turkey	59,685	5.08	303,987	4.00
Rosario Bonavoglia (Italy)	Fernando S. Carneiro (Portugal)	Greece, Italy, Malta,* Poland, Portugal*	59,350	5.06	407,040	5.36
Frank Potter (Canada)	Clarence Ellis (Guyana)	Antigua and Barbuda,* The Bahamas,* Barbados,* Belize, Canada, Dominica, Grenada, Guyana, Ireland, Jamaica,* St. Kitts and Nevis, St. Lucia, St. Vincent and the Grenadines	51,854	4.42	329,035	4.33
Eveline Herfkens (Netherlands)	Boris Skapin (Yugoslavia)	Bulgaria,* Cyprus, Israel, Netherlands, Romania,* Yugoslavia	50,048	4.26	229,065	3.02
Moisés Naim (Venezuela)	Silvia Charpentier[c] (Costa Rica)	Costa Rica, El Salvador, Guatemala, Honduras, Mexico, Nicaragua, Panama, Spain, Venezuela*	46,866	3.99	221,235	2.91
J. S. Baijal (India)	M. A. Syed (Bangladesh)	Bangladesh, Bhutan, India, Sri Lanka	45,384	3.87	326,693	4.30
Jonas H. Haralz[d] (Iceland)	Jorunn Maehlum (Norway)	Denmark, Finland, Iceland, Norway, Sweden	44,772	3.81	370,510	4.88
John H. Cosgrove (Australia)	A. John Wilson (New Zealand)	Australia, Kiribati, Korea (Republic of), New Zealand, Papua New Guinea, Solomon Islands, Vanuatu, Western Samoa	39,580	3.37	200,099	2.63
Wang Liansheng (China)	Jin Liqun (China)	China	35,221	3.00	154,320	2.03
Mohamed Benhocine (Algeria)	Salem Mohamed Omeish (Libya)	Afghanistan, Algeria, Ghana, Iran (Islamic Republic of), Libya, Morocco, Tunisia	32,741	2.79	115,741	1.52
Vibul Aunsnunta (Thailand)	Aung Pe (Myanmar)	Fiji, Indonesia, Lao People's Democratic Republic, Malaysia, Myanmar, Nepal, Singapore,* Thailand, Tonga, Viet Nam	31,804	2.71	228,329	3.01
Ernest Leung (Philippines)	Paulo C. Ximenes-Ferreira (Brazil)	Brazil, Colombia, Dominican Republic, Ecuador, Haiti, Philippines, Suriname,* Trinidad and Tobago	31,428	2.68	230,036	3.03
Fawzi Hamad Al-Sultan (Kuwait)	Mohamed W. Hosny (Arab Republic of Egypt)	Bahrain,* Egypt (Arab Republic of), Jordan, Kuwait, Lebanon, Maldives, Oman, Pakistan, Qatar,* Syrian Arab Republic, United Arab Emirates, Yemen (Republic of)	30,767	2.62	269,900	3.55

(continued)

Executive Directors and Alternates of the World Bank and Their Voting Power *(continued)*

Appendix 2

June 30, 1991

Executive director	Alternate	Casting votes of	IBRD Total votes	IBRD % of total	IDA Total votes	IDA % of total
J. Ayo Langley (The Gambia)	O. K. Matambo (Botswana)	Angola, Botswana, Burundi, Ethiopia, The Gambia, Guinea, Kenya, Lesotho, Liberia, Malawi, Mozambique, Namibia,* Nigeria, Seychelles,* Sierra Leone, Sudan, Swaziland, Tanzania, Uganda, Zambia, Zimbabwe	30,083	2.56	308,951	4.07
Ibrahim A. Al-Assaf (Saudi Arabia)	Ahmed M. Al-Ghannam (Saudi Arabia)	Saudi Arabia	25,390	2.16	254,722	3.35
Félix Alberto Camarasa (Argentina)	Nicolás Flaño (Chile)	Argentina, Bolivia, Chile, Paraguay, Peru, Uruguay*	24,745	2.11	143,701	1.89
Jean-Pierre Le Bouder (Central African Republic)	Ali Bourhane (Comoros)	Benin, Burkina Faso, Cameroon, Cape Verde. Central African Republic, Chad, Comoros, Congo (People's Republic of the), Côte d'Ivoire, Djibouti, Equatorial Guinea, Gabon, Guinea-Bissau, Madagascar, Mali, Mauritania, Mauritius, Niger, Rwanda, São Tomé and Principe, Senegal, Somalia, Togo, Zaire	21,843	1.86	241,707	3.18

In addition to the executive directors and alternates shown in the foregoing list, the following also served after October 31, 1990:

Executive director	End of period of service	Alternate director	End of period of service
Cesare Caranza (Italy)	February 11, 1991	Abdulaziz Al-Sehail (Saudi Arabia)	December 21, 1990
Chang-Yuel Lim (Republic of Korea)	May 31, 1991	Robert G. Carling (Australia)	February 28, 1991
		Bernd Esdar (Germany)	January 31, 1991
		M. Mustafizur Rahman (Bangladesh)	April 30, 1991
		Yukio Yoshimura (Japan)	June 7, 1991

NOTE: Iraq (3,058 votes in the IBRD and 9,407 votes in IDA), Democratic Kampuchea (464 votes in the IBRD and 7,826 votes in IDA), Mongolia (716 votes in the IBRD and 546 votes in IDA), and South Africa (13,712 votes in the IBRD and 24,592 votes in IDA) did not participate in the 1990 regular election of executive directors.

* Member of the IBRD only.

a. Kiyoshi Kodera (Japan) was appointed effective July 8, 1991.

b. To be succeeded by Fritz Fischer (Germany) as of July 1, 1991.

c. To be succeeded by Gabriel Castellanos (Guatemala) as of July 1, 1991.

d. To be succeeded by Einar Magnussen (Norway) as of August 1, 1991.

Officers and Department Directors of the World Bank

Appendix 3

June 30, 1991

President	Barber B. Conable*
Senior Vice President, Operations	Moeen A. Qureshi**
Senior Vice President, Finance	Ernest Stern**
Senior Vice President, Policy, Research, and External Affairs	Wilfried P. Thalwitz**

Finance

Vice President and Controller	Stephen D. Eccles
Vice President and Treasurer	Donald Roth
Vice President, Financial Policy and Risk Management	D. Joseph Wood

Operations

Vice President, Latin America and the Caribbean Regional Office	S. Shahid Husain
Vice President, Africa Regional Office	Edward V. K. Jaycox
Vice President, Asia Regional Office	Attila Karaosmanoglu
Vice President, Cofinancing and Financial Advisory Services	Koji Kashiwaya
Vice President, Europe, Middle East, and North Africa Regional Office	Willi A. Wapenhans

Policy, Research, and External Affairs

Vice President, Development Economics and Chief Economist	Lawrence H. Summers
Vice President, Sector Policy and Research	Visvanathan Rajagopalan

Operations Evaluation

Director-General	Yves Rovani

Corporate Planning and Budgeting

Vice President	Robert Picciotto

Legal

Vice President and General Counsel	Ibrahim F. I. Shihata**

Secretary's

Vice President and Secretary	Timothy T. Thahane**

Personnel and Administration

Vice President	Bilsel Alisbah

Office of the President

Director	Sven Sandstrom

Finance

Director, Financial Operations Department	Jessica P. Einhorn
Director, Resource Mobilization Department	Basil G. Kavalsky
Director, Tokyo Office	Nobuaki Kemmochi
Deputy Treasurer and Director, Treasury Operations	Caio K. Koch-Weser
Director, Cash Management Department	Walter Peyerl
Director, Loan Department	V. S. Raghavan
Director, Investment Department	Jean-François Rischard
Director, Accounting Department	Michael E. Ruddy
Director, Risk Management and Financial Policy Department	Everardus J. Stoutjesdijk

Operations

Director, Operations Staff	David R. Bock
Director, Economic Advisory Staff	Enzo R. Grilli
Director, Cofinancing and Financial Advisory Services Department	John M. Niehuss
Director, Central Operations Department	Hans Wyss

Africa Regional Office

Director, Country Department: Angola, Burundi, Comoros, Djibouti, Madagascar, Rwanda, Seychelles, Zaire	Francisco Aguirre-Sacasa
Director, Country Department: Botswana, Lesotho, Malawi, Mozambique, Namibia, South Africa, Swaziland, Tanzania, Zambia, Zimbabwe	Stephen M. Denning
Director, Country Department: Benin, Cameroon, Central African Republic, the Congo, Côte d'Ivoire, Equatorial Guinea, Gabon, Guinea, Togo	Michael J. Gillette

(continued)

Officers and Department Directors of the World Bank *(continued)*

Appendix 3

June 30, 1991

Director, Country Department: Ghana, Guinea-Bissau, Liberia, Nigeria, São Tomé and Principe,
Sierra Leone .... Edwin R. Lim
Director, Country Department: Ethiopia, Kenya, Mauritius, Somalia, Sudan, Uganda .... Callisto E. Madavo
Director, Country Department: Burkina Faso, Cape Verde, Chad, The Gambia, Mali, Mauritania,
Niger, Senegal .... Katherine Marshall
Director, Technical Department .... Ismail Serageldin

Asia Regional Office
Director, Country Department: Bangladesh, Bhutan, Nepal, Sri Lanka .... Shinji Asanuma[a]
Director, Country Department: China, Mongolia .... Shahid Javed Burki
Director, Country Department: Fiji, Indonesia, Kiribati, Maldives, Papua New Guinea, Solomon
Islands, Tonga, Vanuatu, Western Samoa .... Marianne Haug
Director, Country Department: Democratic Kampuchea, Republic of Korea, Lao People's Democratic
Republic, Malaysia, Myanmar, Philippines, Thailand, Viet Nam .... Gautam S. Kaji
Director, Country Department: India .... Heinz Vergin
Director, Technical Department .... Daniel Ritchie

Europe, Middle East, and North Africa Regional Office
Director, Country Department: Bahrain, Egypt, Islamic Republic of Iran, Iraq, Jordan, Kuwait,
Lebanon, Qatar, Oman, Saudi Arabia, Syria, United Arab Emirates, Republic of Yemen .... Ram Kumar Chopra
Director, Country Department: Algeria, Libya, Malta, Morocco, Portugal, Tunisia .... Kemal Dervis[b]
Director, Country Department: Bulgaria, Cyprus, Czechoslovakia, Hungary, Poland, Romania,
Yugoslavia .... Eugenio F. Lari[c]
Director, Country Department: Afghanistan, Pakistan, Turkey .... Michael H. Wiehen
Director, Technical Department .... Harinder S. Kohli

Latin America and the Caribbean Regional Office
Director, Country Department: Antigua and Barbuda, the Bahamas, Barbados, Belize, Bolivia,
Colombia, Dominica, Dominican Republic, Grenada, Guyana, Haiti, Jamaica, St. Kitts and Nevis,
St. Lucia, St. Vincent and the Grenadines, Suriname, Trinidad and Tobago .... Yoshiaki Abe
Director, Country Department: Argentina, Chile, Ecuador, Paraguay, Uruguay .... Pieter P. Bottelier[d]
Director, Country Department: Brazil, Peru, Venezuela .... Armeane M. Choksi
Director, Country Department: Costa Rica, El Salvador, Guatemala, Honduras, Mexico, Nicaragua,
Panama .... Rainer B. Steckhan
Director, Technical Department .... Edilberto L. Segura

Policy, Research, and External Affairs
Director, Geneva Office .... Jean Baneth
Director, Industry and Energy Department .... Anthony A. Churchill
Director, Environment Department .... Mohamed T. El-Ashry
Director, Publications .... James K. Feather
Director, Economic Development Institute .... Amnon Golan
Director, Population and Human Resources Department .... Ann O. Hamilton
Director, Policy and Review Department .... Paul Isenman
Director, European Office .... Olivier Lafourcade
Director, Country Economics Department .... Johannes F. Linn
Director, Agriculture and Rural Development Department .... Michel J. Petit
Director, Infrastructure and Urban Development Department .... Louis Y. Pouliquen
Director, International Economics Department .... D. C. Rao
Director, External Affairs Department .... Alexander Shakow
Head, Research Advisory Staff .... Gregory K. Ingram
Executive Secretary, Consultative Group on International Agricultural Research .... Alexander von der Osten-Sacken

Operations Evaluation
Director, Operations Evaluation Department .... Hans-Eberhard Köpp

Corporate Planning and Budgeting
Auditor-General, Internal Auditing Department .... Allan D. Legg
Director, Planning and Budgeting Department .... Richard B. Lynn
Head, Organization Planning Staff .... Ian A. Scott

Legal
Associate General Counsel, Legal Department .... Hugh N. Scott
Assistant General Counsel, Legal Department .... David M. Goldberg
Assistant General Counsel, Legal Department .... Eva L. Meicher
Assistant General Counsel, Legal Department .... Stephen A. Silard

Personnel and Administration
Director, Personnel Operations Department .... Alberto de Capitani
Director, Information, Technology, and Facilities Department .... Hywel M. Davies
Director, General Services Department .... Harold W. Messenger
Director, Health Services Department .... Dr. Bernard H. Liese
Director, Personnel Policy Department .... Everardo C. Wessels

* Chairman, President's Council.

** Member, President's Council.

a. To be succeeded by Jochen Kraske as of July 1, 1991.

b. To be succeeded by Pieter P. Bottelier as of July 15, 1991.

c. As of July 1, 1991, Bulgaria, Cyprus, Romania, and Yugoslavia will be split off into a new country department, with Russell J. Cheetham as director, and Kemal Dervis will serve as director of the country department comprising Czechoslovakia, Hungary, and Poland.

d. To be succeeded by Ping-Cheung Loh as of July 15, 1991.

Offices of the World Bank

June 30, 1991

Headquarters: 1818 H Street, N.W., Washington, D.C. 20433, U.S.A.

New York Office	G. David Loos Special Representative to the United Nations	The World Bank Mission to the United Nations/New York Office 747 Third Avenue (26th Floor) New York, N.Y. 10017, U.S.A.
European Office	Olivier Lafourcade Director	The World Bank 66, avenue d'Iéna 75116 Paris, France
Geneva Office	Jean Baneth Director	The World Bank ITC Building 54, rue de Montbrillant Geneva, Switzerland (mailing address: P.O. Box 104, 1211 Geneva 20 CIC, Switzerland)
Tokyo Office	Nobuaki Kemmochi Director	The World Bank Kokusai Building (Room 916) 1-1, Marunouchi 3-chome Chiyoda-ku, Tokyo 100, Japan
Regional Mission in Eastern Africa	Peter Eigen[a] Director	The World Bank View Park Towers Monrovia Street Nairobi, Kenya (mailing address: P.O. Box 30577)
Regional Mission in Western Africa	Elkyn A. Chaparro Chief	The World Bank Corner of Booker Washington & Jacques AKA Streets Cocody, Abidjan 01 Côte d'Ivoire (mailing address: B.P. 1850)
Regional Mission in Thailand	Philippe E. Annez Chief	The World Bank Udom Vidhya Building (5th Floor) 956 Rama IV Road, Sala Daeng Bangkok 10500, Thailand
Argentina	Myrna L. Alexander Resident Representative	Banco Mundial Bartolome Mitre 797—Piso 8 Buenos Aires, Argentina
Bangladesh	Christopher Willoughby Chief, Resident Mission	The World Bank 3A Paribagh Dhaka 1000, Bangladesh (mailing address: G.P.O. 97)
Benin	Eduardo Locatelli Resident Representative	The World Bank Zone Résidentielle de la Radio Cotonou, Benin (mailing address: B.P. 03-2112)
Bolivia	Constance A. Bernard Resident Representative	Banco Mundial Edifício BISA, Piso 9 16 de Julio 1628 La Paz, Bolivia (mailing address: Casilla 8692)

Brazil	George P. Papadopoulos Resident Representative	Banco Mundial Setor Comercial Sul, Quadra 1, Bloco H Edifício Morro Vermelho—8 Andar Brasília, DF 70.302, Brazil
Brazil	George P. Papadopoulos Representative	Banco Mundial c/o Furnas Centrais Elétricas, S.A. Rua Real Grandeza, 219, Botafogo Edifício A, Piso 901 22283 Rio de Janeiro, RJ, Brazil
Brazil	Christoph Diewald Head of Field Office	Banco Mundial, S/127 Edifício SUDENE Cidade Universitária 50,000 Recife PE. Brazil
Burkina Faso	Claude R. Delapierre Resident Representative	The World Bank Immeuble BICIA (3ème étage) Ouagadougou, Burkina Faso (mailing address: B.P. 622)
Burundi	Maurice H. Gervais Resident Representative	The World Bank 45, avenue de la Poste Bujumbura, Burundi (mailing address: B.P. 2637)
Cameroon	Raymond Rabeharisoa Resident Representative	The World Bank Immeuble Kennedy Avenue Kennedy Yaoundé, Cameroon (mailing address B.P. 1128)
Central African Republic	Jean-Paul Dailly Resident Representative	Banque mondiale Rue des missions Bangui, C.A.R. (mailing address: B.P. 819)
Chad	Horst M. Scheffold[b] Resident Representative	The World Bank P.O. Box 146 N'djamena, Chad
China	Attila Sonmez Chief, Resident Mission	The World Bank No. 2 Fu Cheng Lu Diaoyutai, Building No. 5 Beijing 100830, China (mailing address: P.O. Box 802)
Colombia	Padmanabha Hari Prasad Resident Representative	Banco Mundial Carrera 10. No. 86-21, Piso 3 Apartado Aéreo 10229 Bogotá, D.E., Colombia (mailing address: Apartado Aéreo 10229)
Congo	Manga Kuoh-Moukouri Resident Representative	Banque mondiale Immeuble Arc (5ème étage) Avenue Amilcar Cabral Brazzaville Congo (mailing address: B.P 14536)

(continued)

Offices of the World Bank   *(continued)*   Appendix 4

June 30, 1991

Ethiopia	Theodore J. Goering
	Resident Representative
		The World Bank
		I.B.T.E. New Telecommunications
		    Building (1st Floor)
		Churchill Road
		Addis Ababa, Ethiopia
		    (mailing address: P.O. Box 5515)

Ghana	Silvio Capoluongo Resident Representative	The World Bank 69 Eighth Avenue Extension Northridge Residential Area Accra, Ghana (mailing address: P.O. Box M27)
Guinea	Michael J. Wilson Resident Representative	Banque mondiale Immeuble de l'Archevêché Face Baie des Anges Conakry, Guinea (mailing address: B.P. 1420)
Guinea-Bissau	Yves J. Tencalla Resident Representative	Banco Mundial Apartado 78 1041, Guinea-Bissau

India	Jochen Kraske
	Chief, Resident Mission
		The World Bank
		55 Lodi Estate
		New Delhi 110003, India
		    (mailing address: P.O. Box 416,
		    New Delhi 110001)

Indonesia	Nicholas C. Hope Director	The World Bank Jalan Rasuna Said, Kav. B-10 (Suite 301) Kuningan, Jakarta 12940, Indonesia (mailing address: P.O. Box 324/JKT)
Madagascar	Jose A. Bronfman Resident Representative	Banque mondiale 1, rue Patrice Lumumba Antananarivo 101, Madagascar (mailing address: B.P. 4140)
Malawi	John M. Malone Resident Representative	Banque mondiale Development House Capital City Lilongwe 3, Malawi (mailing address: P.O. Box 30557)
Mali	Monique P. Garrity Resident Representative	The World Bank Immeuble SOGEFIH Quartier du Fleuve Avenue Moussa Travele Bamako, Mali (mailing address: B.P. 1864)
Mauritania	Sunil Mathrani Resident Representative	The World Bank Villa No. 30, Ilot A Quartier Socofim Nouakchott, Mauritania (mailing address: B.P. 667)
Mexico	Eugene D. McCarthy Resident Representative	Banco Mundial Plaza Nafin Insurgentes Sur 1971 Nivel Paseo, Locales 71 y 72 Col. Guadalupe Inn 01020 México, D.F. México

Mozambique	Nils O. Tcheyan Resident Representative	The World Bank Av. 25 de Setembro, 1218 2-Andar Maputo, Mozambique
Nepal	Nigel Roberts Resident Representative	The World Bank Jyoti Bhawan, Kantipath Kathmandu, Nepal (mailing address: P.O. Box 798)
Niger	Whitney P. Foster Resident Representative	Banque mondiale Rue des Dallois Niamey, Niger (mailing address: B.P. 12402)
Nigeria	Tariq Husain Resident Representative	The World Bank 1st Floor Plot PC-10 Engineering Close, off Idowu Taylor Street Victoria Island Lagos, Nigeria (mailing address: P.O. Box 127)
Pakistan	Abdallah El Maaroufi Chief, Resident Mission	The World Bank 20 A Shahrah-e-Jamhuriat Islamabad, Pakistan (mailing address: P.C. Box 1025)
Philippines	Thomas W. Allen Resident Representative	The World Bank Central Bank of the Philippines Multi-Storey Building, Room 200 Roxas Boulevard Manila, Philippines
Poland	Ian M. Hume Resident Representative	The World Bank Intraco I Building 17th Floor 2 Stawki Street 00-193 Warsaw, Poland
Rwanda	Emmanuel Akpa Resident Representative	The World Bank Blvd. de la Révolution BRD Building Kigali, Rwanda (mailing address: P.O. Box 609)
Saudi Arabia	John R. Bowlin Director	The World Bank Riyadh, Saudi Arabia 11432 (mailing address: P.O. Box 5900)
Senegal	François-Marie Patorni Resident Representative	Banque mondiale Immeuble S.D.I.H. 3, place de l'Indépendance Dakar, Sénegal (mailing address: B.F. 3296)
Somalia	Luciano Borin Resident Representative	The World Bank Savoy Centre (2nd Floor) Mogadishu, Somalia (mailing address: P.O. Box 1825)

(continued)

Offices of the World Bank   *(continued)*   Appendix 4

June 30, 1991

Sri Lanka	Hari C. Aggarwal
	Resident Representative
		The World Bank
		Development Finance Corporation of Ceylon
		  (DFCC) Building (1st Floor)
		73/5 Galle Road
		Colombo 3, Sri Lanka
		  (mailing address: P.O. Box 1761)

Sudan	Abhay Deshpande Resident Representative	The World Bank AAAID Building Block 9 East Khartoum, Sudan (mailing address: P.O. Box 2211)
Tanzania	Ian C. Porter Resident Representative	The World Bank N.I.C. Building (7th Floor, B) Dar es Salaam, Tanzania (mailing address: P.O. Box 2054)
Togo	Jacques Daniel Resident Representative	Banque mondiale 169, boulevard du 13 janvier Immeuble BTCI (8ème étage) Lomé, Togo (mailing address: B.P. 3915)
Turkey	Luis de Azcárate Resident Representative	The World Bank Ataturk Bulvari, No. 211 Gama-Guris Building Kat 6 06683 Kavaklidere, Ankara, Turkey
Uganda	Seung Hong Choi Resident Representative	The World Bank P.O. Box 4463 Kampala, Uganda
Zaire	William J. Grau (acting) Resident Representative	The World Bank Immeuble de la Communauté Hellénique Boulevard du 30 Juin Kinshasa 1, Zaire (mailing address: P.O. Box 14816)
Zambia	John A. Innes Resident Representative	The World Bank CMAZ Building Ben Bella Road Lusaka, Zambia 10101 (mailing address: P.O. Box 35410)
Zimbabwe	Christiaan J. Poortman Resident Representative	The World Bank CABS Centre (11th Floor) Jason Moyo Avenue Harare, Zimbabwe (mailing address: P.O. Box 2960)

a. To be succeeded by F. Stephen O'Brien as of July 1, 1991.
b. To be succeeded by Noel M. Carrere as of July 1, 1991.

Index